Prestwick House
Pre-AP: Readings
and Exercises

BY DOUGLAS GRUDZINA

PRESTWICK HOUSE, INC.

"Everything for the English Classroom!"

Writer
Douglas Grudzina

Senior Editor
Paul Moliken

Cover and Text Design
Larry Knox

Layout and Production
Jeremy Clark

PRESTWICK HOUSE, INC.
"Everything for the English Classroom!"

ISBN: 978-1-935468-57-8

* AP is a registered trademark of The College Board,
which neither sponsors nor endorses this product.

Prestwick House
Pre-AP:* Readings
and Exercises

BY DOUGLAS GRUDZINA

PRESTWICK HOUSE, INC.

"Everything for the English Classroom!"

Prestwick House Pre-AP: Readings and Exercises

Table of Contents

Appendices:

**Prestwick House
Pre-AP: Readings
and Exercises**

Acknowledgments

"I Stand Here Ironing," copyright © 1961 Tillie Olsen from TELL ME A RIDDLE, reprinted by permission of the Frances Goldin Literary Agency.

"The Standard of Living," copyright 1941 by Dorothy Parker, renewed © 1969 by Lillian Hellman, from THE PORTABLE DOROTHY PARKER by Dorothy Parker, edited by Marion Meade. Used by permission of Viking Penguin, a division of Penguin Group (USA) Inc.

"Cars in Parking Lot," property of the Farm Security Administration—Office of War Information Photograph Collection in the Library of Congress. Photograph by John Collier.

"Flag Burners" by John Trever, www.politicalcartoons.com.

Westward Expansion, from The Social Studies Help Center, found at http://www.socialstudieshelp.com/Images/Westward_Exp.gif.

Introduction: What *is* Pre-AP?

AP (ADVANCED PLACEMENT) IS A PROGRAM of the College Board, the group that brings you the SAT, PSAT, and a number of other infamous exams. While the College Board does not offer an Advanced Placement *course* or *curriculum*, there are currently no fewer than thirty-four Advanced Placement exams offered to high school students each year. Based on a student's overall score on a particular exam and the college he or she chooses to attend, an AP student may receive college credit in that subject.

(Exam scores are usually reported on a range from 1 to 5 with 1 being low, 5 high, and 3 and 4 being the typical target scores.)

Indeed, that's where the name, *Advanced Placement*, comes from. A student's high school work (and AP exam score) might net him or her advanced placement or standing when he or she arrives in college. Some students manage to take so many AP exams and score high enough on them that they enter college with a full semester's worth of credit or more.

Students typically take their AP English exams in either the eleventh or twelfth grade. The College Board offers *two* AP English exams: *Language and Composition* and *Literature and Composition*. Typically, students take their *Language* and Composition exams in the eleventh grade and their *Literature* and Composition exams in the twelfth. The courses they take during those school years may actually be designated as Advanced Placement Courses, and preparing to take the exam is a significant component of the course.

Central to the idea of a designated AP course, the material on an AP exam, and the possibility of receiving college credit is the assumption that the AP student has taken a college-level course in high school.

An "AP course," then is more than a challenging or accelerated course; it is intended to be *a college-level course*.

Pre-AP is based on the idea that a student, even a good student, is probably not going to master the full depth of understanding and the mental habits he or she will need to succeed on the AP exam in only one year. Instruction and assignments in the ninth and tenth grades (and sometimes in the seventh and eighth grades as well) should introduce students to the depth of knowledge and the levels of skill they will need in their junior and senior years.

The seventh-, eighth-, ninth-, and tenth-grade classes that help to prepare a student for his or her eleventh- and twelfth-grade AP exams are … *pre-AP classes*.

This book, being a pre-AP English text, is designed to serve two purposes.

First, because the College Board assumes that the AP student has completed a college-level *English* course, this text is an *English* textbook, a source of challenging, high-quality literature—both fiction and nonfiction—with questions and writing assignments that begin to approach college-level knowledge and skills.

Individual chapters do not focus on the stuff of traditional English texts— questions that ask you to review the plots or basic facts, prompts that require nothing more of you than an emotional reaction to the material. Each chapter in this book focuses on an deeper aspect of literature and language—interpretation, analysis, evaluation, and synthesis.

These *deeper aspects*, however, are all introductory. There are models to illustrate for you how to apply each new insight and skill to a reading passage. They will set you on the path that will lead to confidence and success on both your AP Language and AP Literature exams.

Second, and because pre-AP material assumes that you will be sitting and taking an AP exam in two or three years, this book is an AP-prep-style book. The writing assignments and multiple-choice questions look and sound like the ones you'll face on the Language and Literature exams. Mini-chapters explore in greater depth the components of the exam so that not only will you have the content knowledge and skills you need, you will experience less anxiety because you have a clear understanding of how the test works.

Using this book as your introduction, by the time you complete this year in school and a year of AP English whatever, you'll be familiar with the content and purpose of the exam, and well-educated in the content material that you would learn in a rigorous college-level course. And, even if you don't plan to take an AP course or exam, you may change your mind, and you'll still probably find the passages and exercises in this book stimulating, challenging, and well worth your effort.

AP is a registered trademark of The College Board, which neither sponsors nor endorses this product.

Dealing with Meaning (not theme)

CHAPTER 1

IF YOU'RE READING THIS SENTENCE, you're probably planning to take an Advanced Placement English exam (Advanced Placement in English Language and Composition or Advanced Placement in English Literature and Composition) in a year or two. Since an Advanced Placement course is, theoretically, a college-level course, preparing for an AP exam requires you to build a pretty extensive body of knowledge and develop some new mental skills, habits, and attitudes.

The first of those mental attitudes is the realization that reading is as much about—probably more about—determining what the author intended than it is about expressing what the reader finds. Consider the following sentences, from Abraham Lincoln's Gettysburg Address:

> It is altogether fitting and proper that we should do this. But in a larger sense, we cannot dedicate, we cannot consecrate, we cannot hallow this ground. The brave men, living and dead who struggled here have consecrated it far above our poor power to add or detract.

The *this* is the dedication of part of the Gettysburg battlefield as a national cemetery for fallen Civil War soldiers. What Lincoln is saying (using two rhetorical devices, *anaphora* and *climax*) is that (1) it is right for them to dedicate this land as a cemetery, (2) but the persons gathered at this occasion are not really able to make the ground any more holy than (3) the soldiers who fought there already did.

When Lincoln first delivered this speech, it was criticized for being too brief and too "ineloquent." Critics thought its language was too simple. If there were any Southern sympathizers in Lincoln's audience, they would most likely have listened, bitterly recalling the devastating Confederate defeat that occurred at this battlefield. Those who had lost loved ones in the battle might have felt Lincoln's words did not even come close to expressing their grief. Every single listener would have brought his or her own feelings and thoughts to the speech.

But whether they agreed or disagreed with Lincoln; whether they were inspired, angered, or bored; whether they fought in the battle, knew someone who did, or had never even heard of the battle until that morning, is all irrelevant. Not one listener's or reader's attitude changes what the sentence means, what Lincoln intended.

When you sit down to take your Advanced Placement exam, you will not be asked for your *reaction* to any text you've read or they give you to read. You will be asked to deal with *what* the text means and *how* the author conveys that meaning to his or her readers.

Your first new habit, then, is to read to figure out *what the text means*.

The first step in figuring out what the text means is to examine each individual word, to know what the author is saying by knowing what the words he or she is using really mean.

Issues of Comprehension: Denotation

Consider the following from the opening of O. Henry's famous short story, "The Gift of the Magi":

> Pennies saved one and two at a time by bulldozing the grocer and the vegetable man and the butcher until one's cheeks burned with the silent <u>imputation</u> of <u>parsimony</u> that such <u>close</u> dealing implied.

O. Henry (his real name was William Sydney Porter) was a late-nineteenth- and early-twentieth-century writer, and modern readers are often put off by his frequent use of words and phrases that aren't used all that much anymore. Part of the problem is, of course, that readers simply do not know what these unfamiliar words mean. They may be able to infer their meaning from the context, but their guess—while close—is not likely to perfectly match the actual, literal dictionary definition—the denotation—of the word. The result is a less-than-perfect understanding of the sentence, the paragraph, the story in which the unfamiliar word is used.

This less-than-perfect understanding might be fine for a recreational reader, someone who just wants to enjoy the story. If you want to construct a valid interpretation, perform an analysis, maybe even offer an evaluation of the story, you need a better than less-than-perfect understanding. You need as close-to-perfect an understanding as you can achieve.

And sometimes, that means you have to look up unfamiliar words in the dictionary to learn what they *really* mean, not simply what you *think* they mean.

When we consult a dictionary (in this case I'm looking at the *Webster's New Explorer College Dictionary* 2003), we find that

- *to impute* can mean both *"to accuse or blame"* and *"to give credit for"*;
- *parsimony* means *"stinginess"* (if you guessed, perhaps, poverty, you would actually have been wrong);
- *close* (probably the easy one you thought you didn't have to look up!) means *"reluctant to give up money or possessions"* (not "near" or "precise" or anything like that).

So, a quick glance at a dictionary to make sure we know what the words in the story *really mean* tells us that the person in the above quoted "sentence" is embarrassed (her cheeks are burning) because the grocer, butcher, and vegetable man are silently *accusing* her of being *stingy* because she is so obviously *unwilling to part with her money*.

She's not embarrassed that she's poor.

If you were writing an essay for an AP exam, that would be an important distinction to be able to make. Let's look at the entire story and see how an appreciation of a word's *denotation* is often an essential first step toward really understanding the story.

After the story, you'll find some sample multiple-choice and free-response questions similar to the ones that could be on an AP exam. Because we're focusing on word meanings at this point, that will also be the focus of the questions—but, on the actual exam, questions will not be grouped thematically or topically like that.

(Just so you know.)

The Gift of the Magi

O. Henry (1862 – 1910)

1 ONE DOLLAR AND EIGHTY-SEVEN CENTS. That was all. And sixty cents of it was in pennies. Pennies saved one and two at a time by bulldozing the grocer and the vegetable man and the butcher until one's cheeks burned with the silent <u>imputation</u> of <u>parsimony</u> that such <u>close</u> dealing implied.[1] Three times Della counted it. One dollar and eighty-seven cents. And the next day would be Christmas.

There was clearly nothing to do but flop down on the shabby little couch and howl. So **2** Della did it. Which <u>instigates</u>[2] the moral <u>reflection</u>[3] that life is made up of sobs, sniffles, and smiles, with sniffles predominating.

3 While the mistress of the home is gradually <u>subsiding</u>[4] from the first stage to the second, take a look at the home. A furnished flat at $8 per week. It did not exactly

---

Sample Student Commentary

[1] You already know that Della is embarrassed by her perceived stinginess, not her perceived poverty.

[2] To instigate is to "goad or urge." Its negative association, to instigate trouble, is a connotation.

[3] Since "instigate" is not denotatively a negative word, it can be used to "goad or urge" something positive like deep, moral consideration.

[4] Dictionary entries for "subside" include "to settle oneself." Notice that it is Della who is "subsiding," not her sorrow.

beggar[5] description, but it certainly had that word on the lookout for the <u>mendicancy squad</u>.[6]

4   In the <u>vestibule</u>[7] below was a letter-box into which no letter would go, and an electric button from which no mortal finger could coax a ring. Also <u>appertaining</u>[8] thereunto was a card bearing the name "Mr. James Dillingham Young."

5   The "Dillingham" had been flung to the breeze during a former period of prosperity when its possessor was being paid $30 per week. Now, when the income was shrunk to $20, though, they were thinking seriously of contracting to a modest and unassuming D. But whenever Mr. James Dillingham Young came home and reached his flat above he was called "Jim" and greatly hugged by Mrs. James Dillingham Young, already introduced to you as Della. Which is all very good.

6   Della finished her cry and attended to her cheeks with the powder rag. She stood by the window and looked out dully at a gray cat walking a gray fence in a gray backyard. Tomorrow would be Christmas Day, and she had only $1.87 with which to buy Jim a present. She had been saving every penny she could for months, with this result. Twenty dollars a week doesn't go far. Expenses had been greater than she had calculated. They always are. Only $1.87 to buy a present for Jim. Her Jim. Many a happy hour she had spent planning for something nice for him. Something fine and rare and <u>sterling</u>[9]— something just a little bit near to being worthy of the honor of being owned by Jim.

7   There was a <u>pier-glass</u>[10] between the windows of the room. Perhaps you have seen a pier-glass in an $8 flat. A very thin and very agile person may, by observing his reflection in a rapid sequence of <u>longitudinal</u>[11] strips, obtain a fairly accurate conception of his looks. Della, being slender, had mastered the art.

8   Suddenly she whirled from the window and stood before the glass. Her eyes were shining brilliantly, but her face had lost its color within twenty seconds. Rapidly she pulled down her hair and let it fall to its full length.

9   Now, there were two possessions of the James Dillingham Youngs in which they both took a mighty pride. One was Jim's gold watch that had been his father's and his

---

Sample Student Commentary

[5] You may feel you know what a beggar (noun) is, but in this sentence, "beggar" is used as a verb. As a verb, it can mean "to be beyond one's ability or capacity." O. Henry is saying that the apartment is not exactly beyond his ability to describe, but its appearance is beggarly. His use of the word here is a sort of pun.

[6] A mendicant is a beggar; the mendicancy squad would be the authorities charged with arresting unlicensed beggars. So, while O. Henry's use of the word *beggar* had nothing to do with poverty, he fully establishes his pun by saying the apartment looked like the home of beggars.

[7] The vestibule is the lobby.

[8] To belong or be connected to.

[9] While it is not one of the top entries, one of the definitions of "sterling" is "conforming to the highest standard, of the highest quality." The denotation that best applies to the word's use in something you are reading will often come late in the definition. Resist the temptation to look at the first or second definition and assume you've "got it."

[10] A tall and thin mirror, usually placed on the wall between two windows.

[11] "Placed or running lengthwise." The word's association with length (versus width) came long before its association with maps.

grandfather's. The other was Della's hair. Had the queen of Sheba lived in the flat across the <u>airshaft</u>,[12] Della would have let her hair hang out the window some day to dry just to <u>depreciate</u>[13] Her Majesty's jewels and gifts. Had King Solomon been the janitor, with all his treasures piled up in the basement, Jim would have pulled out his watch every time he passed, just to see him pluck at his beard from envy.

10   So now Della's beautiful hair fell about her rippling and shining like a <u>cascade</u>[14] of brown waters. It reached below her knee and made itself almost a garment for her. And then she did it up again nervously and quickly. Once she faltered for a minute and stood still while a tear or two splashed on the worn red carpet.

11   On went her old brown jacket; on went her old brown hat. With a whirl of skirts and with the brilliant sparkle still in her eyes, she fluttered out the door and down the stairs to the street.

12   Where she stopped the sign read: "Mne. Sofronie. Hair Goods of All Kinds." One flight up Della ran, and collected herself, panting. Madame, large, too white, chilly, hardly looked the "Sofronie."

13   "Will you buy my hair?" asked Della.

14   "I buy hair," said Madame. "Take yer hat off and let's have a sight at the looks of it."

15   Down rippled the brown cascade.

16   "Twenty dollars," said Madame, lifting the mass with a practised hand.

17   "Give it to me quick," said Della.

18   Oh, and the next two hours tripped by on rosy wings. Forget the <u>hashed</u>[15] metaphor. She was ransacking the stores for Jim's present.

19   She found it at last. It surely had been made for Jim and no one else. There was no other like it in any of the stores, and she had turned all of them inside out. It was a platinum fob chain simple and <u>chaste</u>[16] in design, properly proclaiming its value by substance alone and not by <u>meretricious ornamentation</u>[17]—as all good things should do. It was even worthy of The Watch. As soon as she saw it she knew that it must be Jim's. It was like him. Quietness and value—the description applied to both. Twenty-one dollars they took from her for it, and she hurried home with the 87 cents. With that chain on his watch Jim might be properly anxious about the time in any company. Grand as the watch was, he sometimes looked at it on the sly on account of the old leather strap that he used in place of a chain.

Sample Student Commentary

[12] Not a sheet metal duct, as a modern reader might expect, but a narrow space, almost like a courtyard in the center of the building, that allowed interior apartments to have windows.

[13] To lower the price or value of something.

[14] A steep and usually small waterfall; also anything that falls or rushes forward in a vast quantity.

[15] To try and picture a chopped-up metaphor does not make much sense. The denotations of "hash," however, include "to confuse or muddle" and "to restate what is already known [rehash]."

[16] While the most common denotations of "chaste" involve sexual purity, there are dictionary entries that denote "simple, modest, and pure in design."

[17] If you were trying word attack skills to infer the meaning of "meretricious," you might decide the words meant something worthy, of merit. Its denotation, however, is actually the opposite—"falsely or misleadingly attractive." Ornamentation, of course, is rooted in "ornament"—an item or detail for decoration.

20   When Della reached home her intoxication[18] gave way a little to prudence[19] and reason. She got out her curling irons and lighted the gas and went to work repairing the ravages[20] made by generosity added to love. Which is always a tremendous task, dear friends—a mammoth task.

21   Within forty minutes her head was covered with tiny, close-lying curls that made her look wonderfully like a truant[21] schoolboy. She looked at her reflection in the mirror long, carefully, and critically.

22   "If Jim doesn't kill me," she said to herself, "before he takes a second look at me, he'll say I look like a Coney Island chorus girl. But what could I do—oh! what could I do with a dollar and eighty-seven cents?"

23   At 7 o'clock the coffee was made and the frying-pan was on the back of the stove hot and ready to cook the chops.

24   Jim was never late. Della doubled the fob chain in her hand and sat on the corner of the table near the door that he always entered. Then she heard his step on the stair away down on the first flight, and she turned white for just a moment. She had a habit of saying a little silent prayer about the simplest everyday things, and now she whispered: "Please God, make him think I am still pretty."

25   The door opened and Jim stepped in and closed it. He looked thin and very serious. Poor fellow, he was only twenty-two—and to be burdened with a family! He needed a new overcoat and he was without gloves.

26   Jim stopped inside the door, as immovable as a setter at the scent of quail.[22] His eyes were fixed upon Della, and there was an expression in them that she could not read, and it terrified her. It was not anger, nor surprise, nor disapproval, nor horror, nor any of the sentiments[23] that she had been prepared for. He simply stared at her fixedly[24] with that peculiar expression on his face.

27   Della wriggled off the table and went for him.

28   "Jim, darling," she cried, "don't look at me that way. I had my hair cut off and sold because I couldn't have lived through Christmas without giving you a present. It'll grow out again—you won't mind, will you? I just had to do it. My hair grows awfully fast. Say 'Merry Christmas!' Jim, and let's be happy. You don't know what a nice—what a beautiful, nice gift I've got for you."

Sample Student Commentary

[18] As we've seen a few times already, we have to look beyond the first one or two denotations, which have to do with alcohol. The final notation for "intoxicate" in our Webster's *New Explorer* reads, "to excite or elate to the point of enthusiasm or frenzy." The is probably what O. Henry means; not that Della is drunk.

[19] The ability to govern and control one's actions and thoughts by the use of reason.

[20] "To ravage" means "to destroy or ruin." As a noun, "ravage" means the "damage or destruction."

[21] Some who shirks his or her duty, especially a student who misses school without permission.

[22] A "setter" is a type of hunting dog. Its chief characteristic is that it sniffs out game and then assumes a posture or "set," standing absolutely still to help the hunter locate the animal. A quail is a small game bird.

[23] The understanding of "sentiment" as an excessive or overly sweet emotion is a connotation. Most of the dictionary entries for "sentiment" have to do with ideas, sensibilities, or opinions prompted or motivated by feelings.

[24] "To fix" is not only to repair, but also "to set or make stationary."

29 "You've cut off your hair?" asked Jim, <u>laboriously</u>,[25] as if he had not arrived at that <u>patent</u>[26] fact yet even after the hardest mental labor.

30 "Cut it off and sold it," said Della. "Don't you like me just as well, anyhow? I'm me without my hair, ain't I?"

31 Jim looked about the room curiously.

32 "You say your hair is gone?" he said, with an air almost of idiocy.

33 "You needn't look for it," said Della. "It's sold, I tell you—sold and gone, too. It's Christmas Eve, boy. Be good to me, for it went for you. Maybe the hairs of my head were numbered," she went on with sudden serious sweetness, "but nobody could ever count my love for you. Shall I put the chops on, Jim?"

34 Out of his trance Jim seemed quickly to wake. He enfolded his Della. For ten seconds let us regard with discreet <u>scrutiny</u>[27] some <u>inconsequential</u>[28] object in the other direction. Eight dollars a week or a million a year—what is the difference? A mathematician or a wit would give you the wrong answer. The <u>magi</u>[29] brought valuable gifts, but that was not among them. This dark assertion will be illuminated later on.

35 Jim drew a package from his overcoat pocket and threw it upon the table.

36 "Don't make any mistake, Dell," he said, "about me. I don't think there's anything in the way of a haircut or a shave or a shampoo that could make me like my girl any less. But if you'll unwrap that package you may see why you had me going a while at first."

37 White fingers and nimble tore at the string and paper. And then an <u>ecstatic</u>[30] scream of joy; and then, alas! a quick feminine change to hysterical tears and wails, necessitating the immediate employment of all the comforting powers of the lord of the flat.

38 For there lay The Combs—the set of combs, side and back, that Della had worshipped long in a Broadway window. Beautiful combs, pure tortoise shell, with jeweled rims— just the shade to wear in the beautiful vanished hair. They were expensive combs, she knew, and her heart had simply craved and yearned over them without the least hope of possession. And now, they were hers, but the tresses that should have adorned the <u>coveted</u>[31] adornments were gone.

39 But she hugged them to her bosom, and at length she was able to look up with dim eyes and a smile and say: "My hair grows so fast, Jim!"

40 And then Della leaped up like a little singed cat and cried, "Oh, oh!"

Sample Student Commentary

[25] The second dictionary definition denotes "laborious" as meaning "requiring or characterized by hard or toilsome effort."

[26] "Patent" has numerous independent entries in the dictionary, each with many definitions. Deep within one of the earlier entries is "evident or obvious." Remember that the first one or two printed definitions will not necessarily be the most helpful to you.

[27] Discreet (eet) mean subtle, not obvious. A "scrutiny" is a thorough examination or study.

[28] Unimportant.

[29] "Magi" is plural for "magus," a Latin word for a wise man from Persia, a magician.

[30] You may immediately associate *ecstatic* with "happy or joyful," but the denotation of *ecstasy* is actually, "a state of being beyond reason and self-control; a state of overwhelming emotion." If O. Henry had meant *joyful*, Della would be uttering a "joyful scream of joy."

[31] Because of the Judeo-Christian Tenth Commandment, you might believe that *covet* means to envy. Its denotation is actually "to desire or wish for."

41   Jim had not yet seen his beautiful present. She held it out to him eagerly upon her open palm. The dull precious metal seemed to flash with a reflection of her bright and ardent spirit.

42   "Isn't it a dandy, Jim? I hunted all over town to find it. You'll have to look at the time a hundred times a day now. Give me your watch. I want to see how it looks on it."

43   Instead of obeying, Jim tumbled down on the couch and put his hands under the back of his head and smiled.

44   "Dell," said he, "let's put our Christmas presents away and keep 'em a while. They're too nice to use just at present. I sold the watch to get the money to buy your combs. And now suppose you put the chops on."

45   The magi, as you know, were <u>wise</u>[32] men—wonderfully wise men—who brought gifts to the Babe in the manger. They invented the art of giving Christmas presents. Being wise, their gifts were no doubt wise ones, possibly bearing the privilege of exchange in case of duplication. And here I have lamely related to you the uneventful chronicle of two foolish children in a flat who most unwisely sacrificed for each other the greatest treasures of their house. But in a last word to the wise of these days let it be said that of all who give gifts these two were the wisest. Of all who give and receive gifts, such as they are wisest. Everywhere they are wisest. They are the magi.

Sample Student Commentary

[32] Having or showing good judgment. Sensible. If you read "wise" as "smart" or "knowing a lot," you would actually miss the irony.

Sample Multiple-Choice Questions

1. The primary source of irony in this story is the incongruous use of the word
    A. ecstatic.
    B. fixedly.
    C. sentiments.
    D. beggar.
    E. wise.

2. If you were to ignore, or be unaware of, certain key words' denotations, you might misinterpret Della as
    A. unpredictably emotional.
    B. argumentative and envious.
    C. thrifty.
    D. vain.
    E. reasonable.

3. O. Henry's frequent use of absolute, often unfamiliar, denotations contributes to an overall tone of
    A. comic familiarity.
    B. thoughtful seriousness.
    C. bitter sarcasm.
    D. ironic formality.
    E. mocking wit.

4. All of the following are valid inferences from paragraph 38 EXCEPT that Della
    A. never intended to own the combs.
    B. would have envied the woman who bought the combs.
    C. appreciated the value of the combs.
    D. knew at once the irony of receiving that gift on that day.
    E. regretted having sold her hair.

5. Overall, O. Henry's word choice in this story can best be defined as
    A. archaic.
    B. poetic.
    C. precise.
    D. cavalier.
    E. stilted.

Answers and Explanations:

1. While an accurate understanding of O. Henry's point requires the reader to discern the connotations or most familiar denotations of *ecstatic* (A), *fix* (B), and *sentiment* (C) with their less-known denotations, none of these words is used oddly or inexplicably. O. Henry does make a pun employing two denotations of *beggar* (D), but neither use of the word is incongruous; nor can this pun be considered the *primary* source of irony. The entire point of the story, however, hinges on O. Henry's insistence that both the "wonderfully *wise*" men of the Christmas story brought "wise," or sensible gifts and that the foolish sacrifices of Della and Jim were likewise wise or sensible. **Thus, (E) is the best answer**.

2. Strictly speaking, (A) and (C) are not misinterpretations of Della's character, and the denotations of the words used to describe Della's emotions clearly support these interpretations. While Della is not vain (D), her use of the *pier-glass* (paragraph 7) and her repair of the *ravages* to her beauty (paragraph 20) would not inevitably lead a reader to this conclusion. Likewise, while the overall depiction of Della does not show her to be reasonable (E), it is only in an ironic use of the word *wise* that O. Henry insists that we see her in this light. While O. Henry describes Della's behavior and attitudes with words like *instigates* (paragraph 2) and *coveted* (paragraph 38), these words do not denote the argumentative and envious associations that modern readers attach to them. **Thus (B) is the best answer**.

3. (A) is certainly tempting because there are times when O. Henry addresses his reader directly and intrudes into the narrative with personal observations and comments, but this familiar tone is not strong enough to be considered "comic," and it is achieved more by word choice and narrative structure than by subtleties of word meaning. (B) is also tempting, but can be eliminated by the fact that there are puns and some other word play, and even when the narrator sounds serious, there is a tongue-in-cheek attitude to his asides and observations. (C) is the least tempting of the choices, as none of the words O. Henry uses denotes bitterness, and his irony is not strong enough to be considered sarcasm. (E) might also tempt a few students as O. Henry does employ wit, and there are times when he seems to mock his characters, calling them "foolish children" (paragraph 45) and describing Della's emotional outbursts as characteristic and inevitable (paragraph 27), but neither criticism reaches the severity of true mocking, and this wit is not the overall tone of the piece. The use of phrases like *instigates the moral reflection* (paragraph 2) instead of less formal alternatives like *causes one to think; appertaining thereunto* rather than *attached to which*, and so on, creates a formal, almost academic and detached, tone. This formality is made ironic, however, by the context, which includes the wit, the gentle mockery, and the familiar asides and observations. **Thus, (D) is the best answer**.

4. (A) might tempt some students, but as much as Della "coveted," "craved," and "yearned over" the combs, the reader is told that her desire was "without the least hope of possession." (C) is probably the least tempting because the paragraph clearly states that the combs were expensive and that Della knew it. (D) is eliminated by the two references in the paragraph to her "vanished hair." (E) is possibly tempting, but it is not unreasonable to infer that, in her two realizations that her hair is gone, Della does, at least for a second, regret the hair's loss. Only (B) is not a possible reference. If one believes that *covet* means "to envy," then this choice might tempt. However, knowing that the "coveted combs" are merely the "strongly desired combs" (a reiteration of the fact that Della had "worshipped," "craved," and "yearned over" the combs) eliminates a supposition of envy. **Thus, (B) is the best answer**.

5. Modern readers may be tempted by (A), but it must be remembered that O. Henry was writing over a century ago, and many words that are now archaic were in common use then. (B) is largely eliminated by the reliance on specific denotations. (D) is likewise eliminated by O. Henry's reliance on the literal dictionary definitions of key words rather than slang or colloquial understandings. (E) might tempt some who simply do not like the writing of an earlier style, but as O. Henry does achieve some wit, humor, and irony, his writing can hardly be dismissed as "stilted." **(C), however, is the best answer**. O. Henry's choice of words with denotations that often contradict connotative or colloquial understandings and the irony that he creates with these words suggest that he was most careful, almost painstaking in his word choice.

On an actual AP exam, you would never write two essays about the same passage, or even the same piece of literature. We offer these two essays for an example only.

Sample free-response item one (text-based):

Carefully read O. Henry's famous short story, "The Gift of the Magi." Then write an essay in which you analyze how O. Henry uses careful and specific word choice to communicate his narrator's attitude toward the characters.

 Do not be misled. This prompt is not inviting you to discuss O. Henry's condescension or sense of amusement at Della and Jim's behavior and attitudes. The scorers of this essay will be looking for an essay about how O. Henry uses language. Let's see how a reasonably good student would answer this question. (Remember that the response is supposed to be an essay.)

Sample Student Essay

In addition to its surprise ending, O. Henry's story "The Gift of the Magi" is famous for the warm-hearted and amused tone that he uses to describe his two characters, James (Jim) and Della Dillingham Young. It is clear that the narrator likes this young couple and that he approves of the sacrifices they make for each other (even though he claims not to and calls them "foolish").[1] O. Henry communicates this friendly approval to his reader by the specific words and phrases he uses.[2] He creates irony by using overly formal words when simpler ones might be expected, and he uses vivid images and precise shades of meaning to specify exactly what he wants his reader to notice and to feel.[3] "The Gift of the Magi" is an excellent story to study for the importance of careful and purposeful word choice.

From the first paragraph, O. Henry uses highly formal words and expressions to explain simple ideas.[4] Della is not thrifty, cheap, or stingy, she is parsimonious. The name card is not simply attached to their mailbox, it is described as "appertaining" to the mailbox.[5] Such formal words to describe plain, poor, and simple Jim and Della is ironic. This irony is not criticism, however. It is almost humorous. O. Henry is

---

Scorer Commentary

[1] While the prompt does not invite you to describe or analyze O. Henry's attitude, it would be difficult to analyze how he communicates that attitude without mentioning what that attitude was.

[2] Here's where the student begins to address the assigned topic.

[3] After a general repetition of the topic in the prompt, the student provides a more specific introduction to what he is going to discuss in his essay.

[4] First sub-point as promised in the introduction.

[5] Specific, textual evidence. You simply cannot expect a top score on your essay without it.

not laughing at Jim and Della's poverty, he is laughing <u>with</u> them.[6] Similarly, when O. Henry says that the couple's furnished flat "beggar[s] description," he is not calling them beggars, but his use of the word emphasizes how poor they are and makes the reader look back to the bargaining and haggling Della must have done with the shop keepers in order to save her $1.87. Yet, he is careful to note that Della is more embarrassed by the "imputation" of stinginess than of her need to negotiate as she does. "Imputation" instead of <u>accusation</u> or <u>insinuation</u> is another use of a formal word for a simple idea. It makes the charge of stinginess against Della more legal and, therefore, less a judgment on her character.

O. Henry also uses important-sounding phrases[7] to suggest how he feels about his characters. After we already know that Della and Jim are poor and that Della has scrimped and saved and risked being called <u>stingy</u> in order to amass the grand total of $1.87 for Jim's Christmas present, O. Henry calls her the "mistress of the home," clearly elevating her status from <u>housewife</u> or even <u>homemaker</u>. One can almost picture the "mistress of the home" lounging on the sofa, eating chocolates, and being pampered by a host of servants. It is important, also, that O. Henry uses the word "home" instead of the more common <u>house</u>. First, this is more accurate, since Jim and Della live in an apartment, a "flat," and not a house. It is also more accurate, however, because poor as they are, and shabby as their apartment must be, it is indeed a <u>home</u>, with everything that that word suggests in terms of love and happiness.[8]

Along those same lines, Jim and Della's use of "Dillingham" on the name card on their mailbox is described as "flung to the breeze," and their reaction to Jim's reduced income is to think "seriously of contracting to a modest and unassuming D." Again, the word choice and phrasing, which sounds more appropriate for talking about wealthy people, is ironic. At first glance, Jim and Della might sound pretentious, but "flung to the breeze" suggests a carefree act, not a pompous one, and O. Henry dismisses any sense of pretension when he refers to the period when Jim made $30 a week as "a former period of prosperity." There is definitely more glibness than criticism in O. Henry's choice of phrases.

After Della gets the idea to sell her hair, her actions are described in dazzling, almost magical terms. She "flutters" out the door, with a "whirl of skirts" and a "brilliant sparkle" in her eyes. These strong and vivid words reflect the quality of her heart, not her outward appearance. They also contrast with the "gray cat walking a gray fence in a gray backyard" that describe Della's surroundings, but not Della.

The final significant word choice that reveals O. Henry's affection for these characters actually appears in the title. The "Magi" referred to are the Wise Men

---

Scorer Commentary

[6] After the quotations, however, is discussion and explanation of why those quotations are relevant. Both textual evidence and discussion are necessary for a top score.

[7] The introduction does promise a discussion of both words and phrases.

[8] This discussion of home versus house fulfills the promise in the introduction to deal with "precise shades of meaning."

of the Christmas story, who traveled to Bethlehem and gave the baby Jesus gifts of gold, frankincense, and myrrh. O. Henry relies on our understanding of these men as "wise" when he compares them to Jim and Della. The irony, of course, is that Jim and Della are "foolish" for each sacrificing his or her most prized possession for the other's Christmas gift. Still, O. Henry repeats the word <u>wise</u> five times and <u>wisest</u> three times. He calls Jim and Della "the wisest" of "all who give and receive gifts." There is no irony here, no criticism, not even any humor; but there is an intentional use of a word open to more than one interpretation. In what way are Della and Jim "wise"? What does <u>wisdom</u> mean?[9]

That is, finally, the question raised by the story.

O. Henry calls Jim and Della "two foolish children in a flat who most unwisely sacrificed for each other," but he has also been careful to make sure the reader knows the "flat" is a "home," and the "children" are a happy, loving couple.

O. Henry follows his observation about Jim and Della's foolishness with a contradiction and a clarification of what he means by <u>wise</u>, but he does it in "a last word to the wise of these days." The "wisdom" of "the wise of these days" is the same wisdom that would call Jim's and Della's sacrifices "foolish." However, O. Henry now praises Jim and Della as "the wisest," wise in the same sense that the Magi of the Christmas story were wise. So, at the very end, O. Henry states his approval of Jim and Della, and all of his previous ironic comments and questionable word choices, which could have been read as either critical or humorous, turn out to be intended to be read as amused and approving.[10]

Scorer Commentary

[9] The "wise" – "wisdom" discussion also helps to fulfill the "shades of meaning" promise in the introduction.

[10] The strong conclusion wraps up the discussion and reasserts the original point about O. Henry's careful and deliberate word choice.

Sample free-response item two (independent:

 You will find that this prompt is not terribly different from Sample one. On the actual exam, you will never be asked to write two essays on such similar topics, nor will there be two Free-Response Questions on the same piece of literature. These are offered simply as examples of the two types of question you will face.

The difference between the right word and the almost right word is the difference between lightning and the lightning bug.

In addition to these large rules, there are some little ones. These require that the author shall:
- *Say* what he is proposing to say, not merely come near it.
- Use the right word, not its second cousin.

—Mark Twain

Consider the above reflections about the writer's obligation to choose his words carefully. Then select a novel, story, or play in which tone, mood, and meaning are created by the writer's careful and intentional word choice and write an essay analyzing how the author's "using the right word [and] not its second cousin" creates the tone and contributes to the piece's overall meaning.

 Again, be careful. If you are tempted to mention O. Henry's tongue-in-cheek humor or mild mockery, do not devote more than a sentence to tone. The prompt is inviting you to write about word choice—how the author creates tone.

You may choose a work from the list that follows or another novel or play of comparable literary merit.

 Most of the independent Free-Response questions will provide a list of "suggestions" on which you might choose to write. You are not obligated to write about any of the "suggestions." They are merely provided to help you think of an appropriate story to write about. Our model student has chosen to write about "The Gift of the Magi."

Sample Student Essay

Many people assume that synonyms are different words that "mean the same thing." They consider synonyms to be interchangeable, when in fact, they are not. To use the wrong synonym in a sentence is, I believe, what Mark Twain means when he criticizes using the right word's "second cousin" instead of the right word. The fine distinction between synonyms like fragile and frail might seem unimportant, but paying attention to the exact meaning of each word can make the difference between proper and incorrect, clear and vague, or interesting and dull.[1] The great American short story writer, O. Henry, was a master at conveying very precise meanings and creating vivid moods through careful word choice. The lighthearted tone in which he tells "The Gift of the Magi" is a perfect example.[2] By using strict dictionary definitions of words and letting different meanings play against each other, he makes a story that could be depressing almost humorous. One can almost hear a glint in his eye and see a smile on his face as he tells the story. This is the result of careful word choice.[3]

Although the story starts out on a sad note—the main character is upset about how little money she has, and she throws herself on the sofa to cry—O. Henry manages to dispel the unhappy mood by describing the couch as "shabby" and Della's crying as "howl[ing]." Considering some of the synonyms O. Henry could have used (threadbare, tattered, or decrepit for "shabby" and wail or sob for "howl"), this word choice creates an image that is almost cute.[4] Della's crying also makes O. Henry pause and offer a brief statement about life, what he describes in inflated language, especially when compared to the trivial language of Della's crying, as "a moral reflection." This "reflection," however dismisses life's sorrows—including Della's extreme disappointment—as "sobs [and] sniffles...with sniffles predominating." "Sobs and sniffles" are not nearly as horrible as the hardships or tragedies O. Henry could have mentioned. Even though "sobs" indicates a more serious type of crying than "howl," it is still not as clear or horrible as a disaster or catastrophe.[5] Clearly the author does not want the reader to be overly moved by Della's sadness. In fact, he almost makes a joke of it.[6]

This tone or attitude is all the result of O. Henry's choice of one word over another with a similar—but significantly different—meaning.[7]

Another word choice technique O. Henry uses is to play with a word that has more than one meaning. After telling the story of Jim and Della's sacrifices for each other, O. Henry calls them both "wise" and "foolish." These are not synonyms; in

Scorer Commentary

[1] Restating a part of the prompt is a basic, but often effective, way to focus an exam essay.

[2] As the student was instructed to choose a piece of literature to write about, it is important that she identifies her choice as early as possible in the essay.

[3] The thesis statement must address the topic assigned in the prompt.

[4] Very early on, this student has found a pair of synonyms in order to make sure she really does discuss what was assigned.

fact, they are almost antonyms, but people understand "wise" in so many different ways that what seems "wise" to some may indeed seem "foolish" to others. This is exactly what O. Henry is doing in this story.

He first uses "wise" in relation to Jim and Della when, after identifying the Magi as the Wise Men of the Christmas story, he calls his characters "two foolish children in a flat who most unwisely sacrificed for each other the greatest treasures of their house." Here he clearly describes them as "foolish" and "unwise." However, his next sentence introduces a contradiction, "but in a last word," and this last word of contradiction is directed toward "the wise of these days." The context of the paragraph makes it clear that these "wise" are the ones who would consider Jim and Della "foolish." And this "last word" is "of all who give gifts these two [Jim and Della] were the wisest."[8]

He has just called them "foolish," and now says they were "the wisest." This is a paradox, and it means that, to O. Henry, what the world might consider foolishness is the real wisdom. So he uses "wise" and "foolish" in the same paragraph just as if they were synonyms.[9] And the mood he creates with this play on words is to make the reader feel happy at the end of a story that could have been very, very sad.[10]

Scorer Commentary

[5] Plenty of direct textual support. Remember, you cannot hope to receive a high score without supporting everything you say with the text.

[6] And this student also shares her conclusions. This is also necessary for a top score.

[7] This sentence restates the assigned topic and begins to deliver on one of the promised subpoints from the introduction.

[8] This discussion is not too different from the earlier essay, but this point is essential in a discussion about words and word meanings in this story.

[9] This student has earned very high points for organization by bringing her discussion back to the point on which she began.

[10] The prompt did ask to consider the story's overall meaning, and this essay does not do that, so this is probably not at the absolute top of the grading scale; but it is a thorough, focused, and supported analysis of word choice in the story, so it will receive a high score.

Exercise One:

Questions 1–5. Read the following passage carefully before you choose your answers.

Miss Brill

KATHERINE MANSFIELD (1888–1923)

1   ALTHOUGH IT WAS SO BRILLIANTLY FINE—the blue sky powdered with gold and great spots of light like white wine splashed over the *Jardins Publiques*[1]—Miss Brill was glad that she had decided on her fur. The air was motionless, but when you opened your mouth there was just a faint chill, like a chill from a glass of iced water before you sip, and now and again a leaf came drifting—from nowhere, from the sky. Miss Brill put up her hand and touched her fur. Dear little thing! It was nice to feel it again. She had taken it out of its box that afternoon, shaken out the moth-powder, given it a good brush, and rubbed the life back into the dim little eyes. "What has been happening to me?" said the sad little eyes. Oh, how sweet it was to see them snap at her again from the red eiderdown!... But the nose, which was of some black composition, wasn't at all firm. It must have had a knock, somehow. Never mind—a little dab of black sealing-wax when the time came— when it was absolutely necessary... Little rogue! Yes, she really felt like that about it. Little rogue biting its tail just by her left ear. She could have taken it off and laid it on her lap and stroked it. She felt a tingling in her hands and arms, but that came from walking, she supposed. And when she breathed, something light and sad—no, not sad, exactly— something gentle seemed to move in her bosom.

2   There were a number of people out this afternoon, far more than last Sunday. And the band sounded louder and gayer. That was because the Season had begun. For although the band played all the year round on Sundays, out of season it was never the same. It was like some one playing with only the family to listen; it didn't care how it played if there weren't any strangers present. Wasn't the conductor wearing a new coat, too? She was sure it was new. He scraped with his foot and flapped his arms like a rooster about to crow, and the bandsmen sitting in the green rotunda blew out their cheeks and glared at the music. Now there came a little "flutey" bit—very pretty!—a little chain of bright drops. She was sure it would be repeated. It was; she lifted her head and smiled.

3   Only two people shared her "special" seat: a fine old man in a velvet coat, his hands clasped over a huge carved walking-stick, and a big old woman, sitting upright, with a roll of knitting on her embroidered apron. They did not speak. This was disappointing, for Miss Brill always looked forward to the conversation. She had become really quite expert, she thought, at listening as though she didn't listen, at sitting in other people's lives just for a minute while they talked round her.

4   She glanced, sideways, at the old couple. Perhaps they would go soon. Last Sunday, too, hadn't been as interesting as usual. An Englishman and his wife, he wearing a dreadful Panama hat and she button boots. And she'd gone on the whole time about how she ought to wear spectacles; she knew she needed them; but that it was no good getting

---

[1] Public gardens. The story is set in a unnamed town in France on a Sunday afternoon in early autumn.

any; they'd be sure to break and they'd never keep on. And he'd been so patient. He'd suggested everything—gold rims, the kind that curved round your ears, little pads inside the bridge. No, nothing would please her. "They'll always be sliding down my nose!" Miss Brill had wanted to shake her.

5 The old people sat on the bench, still as statues. Never mind, there was always the crowd to watch. To and fro, in front of the flower-beds and the band rotunda, the couples and groups paraded, stopped to talk, to greet, to buy a handful of flowers from the old beggar who had his tray fixed to the railings. Little children ran among them, swooping and laughing; little boys with big white silk bows under their chins, little girls, little French dolls, dressed up in velvet and lace. And sometimes a tiny staggerer came suddenly rocking into the open from under the trees, stopped, stared, as suddenly sat down "flop," until its small high-stepping mother, like a young hen, rushed scolding to its rescue. Other people sat on the benches and green chairs, but they were nearly always the same, Sunday after Sunday, and—Miss Brill had often noticed—there was something funny about nearly all of them. They were odd, silent, nearly all old, and from the way they stared they looked as though they'd just come from dark little rooms or even—even cupboards!

6 Behind the rotunda the slender trees with yellow leaves down drooping, and through them just a line of sea, and beyond the blue sky with gold-veined clouds.

7 Tum-tum-tum tiddle-um! tiddle-um! tum tiddley-um tum ta! blew the band.

8 Two young girls in red came by and two young soldiers in blue met them, and they laughed and paired and went off arm-in-arm. Two peasant women with funny straw hats passed, gravely, leading beautiful smoke-coloured donkeys. A cold, pale nun hurried by. A beautiful woman came along and dropped her bunch of violets, and a little boy ran after to hand them to her, and she took them and threw them away as if they'd been poisoned. Dear me! Miss Brill didn't know whether to admire that or not! And now an ermine toque[1] and a gentleman in grey met just in front of her. He was tall, stiff, dignified, and she was wearing the ermine toque she'd bought when her hair was yellow. Now everything, her hair, her face, even her eyes, was the same colour as the shabby ermine, and her hand, in its cleaned glove, lifted to dab her lips, was a tiny yellowish paw. Oh, she was so pleased to see him—delighted! She rather thought they were going to meet that afternoon. She described where she'd been—everywhere, here, there, along by the sea. The day was so charming—didn't he agree? And wouldn't he, perhaps?... But he shook his head, lighted a cigarette, slowly breathed a great deep puff into her face, and even while she was still talking and laughing, flicked the match away and walked on. The ermine toque was alone; she smiled more brightly than ever. But even the band seemed to know what she was feeling and played more softly, played tenderly, and the drum beat, "The Brute! The Brute!" over and over. What would she do? What was going to happen now? But as Miss Brill wondered, the ermine toque turned, raised her hand as though she'd seen someone else, much nicer, just over there, and pattered away. And the band changed again and played more quickly, more gaily than ever, and the old couple on Miss Brill's seat got up and marched away, and such a funny old man with long whiskers hobbled along in time to the music and was nearly knocked over by four girls walking abreast.

---

[1] A type of hat.

9   Oh, how fascinating it was! How she enjoyed it! How she loved sitting here, watching it all! It was like a play. It was exactly like a play. Who could believe the sky at the back wasn't painted? But it wasn't till a little brown dog trotted on solemn and then slowly trotted off, like a little "theatre" dog, a little dog that had been drugged, that Miss Brill discovered what it was that made it so exciting. They were all on the stage. They weren't only the audience, not only looking on; they were acting. Even she had a part and came every Sunday. No doubt somebody would have noticed if she hadn't been there; she was part of the performance after all. How strange she'd never thought of it like that before! And yet it explained why she made such a point of starting from home at just the same time each week—so as not to be late for the performance—and it also explained why she had quite a queer, shy feeling at telling her English pupils how she spent her Sunday afternoons. No wonder! Miss Brill nearly laughed out loud. She was on the stage. She thought of the old invalid gentleman to whom she read the newspaper four afternoons a week while he slept in the garden. She had got quite used to the frail head on the cotton pillow, the hollowed eyes, the open mouth and the high pinched nose. If he'd been dead she mightn't have noticed for weeks; she wouldn't have minded. But suddenly he knew he was having the paper read to him by an actress! "An actress!" The old head lifted; two points of light quivered in the old eyes. "An actress—are ye?" And Miss Brill smoothed the newspaper as though it were the manuscript of her part and said gently; "Yes, I have been an actress for a long time."

10   The band had been having a rest. Now they started again. And what they played was warm, sunny, yet there was just a faint chill—a something, what was it?—not sadness—no, not sadness—a something that made you want to sing. The tune lifted, lifted, the light shone; and it seemed to Miss Brill that in another moment all of them, all the whole company, would begin singing. The young ones, the laughing ones who were moving together, they would begin, and the men's voices, very resolute and brave, would join them. And then she too, she too, and the others on the benches—they would come in with a kind of accompaniment—something low, that scarcely rose or fell, something so beautiful—moving... And Miss Brill's eyes filled with tears and she looked smiling at all the other members of the company. Yes, we understand, we understand, she thought—though what they understood she didn't know.

11   Just at that moment a boy and girl came and sat down where the old couple had been. They were beautifully dressed; they were in love. The hero and heroine, of course, just arrived from his father's yacht. And still soundlessly singing, still with that trembling smile, Miss Brill prepared to listen.

12   "No, not now," said the girl. "Not here, I can't."

13   "But why? Because of that stupid old thing at the end there?" asked the boy. "Why does she come here at all—who wants her? Why doesn't she keep her silly old mug at home?"

14   "It's her fu-ur which is so funny," giggled the girl. "It's exactly like a fried whiting.[1]"

15   "Ah, be off with you!" said the boy in an angry whisper. Then: "Tell me, *ma petite chere*[2]—"

16   "No, not here," said the girl. "Not yet."

---

[1] a fish that is usually eaten either smoked or fried
[2] French: "my darling"

*****

17   On her way home she usually bought a slice of honey-cake at the baker's. It was her Sunday treat. Sometimes there was an almond in her slice, sometimes not. It made a great difference. If there was an almond it was like carrying home a tiny present—a surprise— something that might very well not have been there. She hurried on the almond Sundays and struck the match for the kettle in quite a dashing way.

18   But to-day she passed the baker's by, climbed the stairs, went into the little dark room—her room like a cupboard—and sat down on the red eiderdown. She sat there for a long time. The box that the fur came out of was on the bed. She unclasped the necklet quickly; quickly, without looking, laid it inside. But when she put the lid on she thought she heard something crying.

Multiple-Choice Questions

1. The capitalized word Season in the second paragraph most likely refers to

A. early autumn.

B. the arrival of socialites on vacation.

C. a period of increased social activity.

D. a change in the weather.

E. the time during which the band plays.

2. All of the following help to communicate Miss Brill's attitude toward people EXCEPT

A. ermine.

B. velvet.

C. silk.

D. toque.

E. cupboards.

3. The most prominent effect created by Mansfield's use of color is

A. vivid description.

B. a realistic setting.

C. contrasting imagery.

D. character development.

E. an intimate atmosphere.

4. Based on its use in paragraph five, the word staggerer most like refers to a/n

A. toddler.

B. latecomer.

C. automated toy.

D. intoxicated musician.

E. unsteady senior.

5. Which of the following best accounts for the overall mood of this story?
   A. narrative intrusion
   B. indirect dialogue
   C. first-person narration
   D. limited omniscience
   E. stream-of-consciousness

Free-Response Question One (text-based):

Carefully read Katherine Mansfield's short story "Miss Brill." Then, write an essay in which you analyze the various ways Mansfield uses language to communicate her view of the title character to the reader.

Before you write your essay:

1. **Make sure you understand exactly what you're being asked to write about.** A typical Advanced Placement prompt will contain two or three direct verbs, one of which will almost always be to "read" the selection provided.

   In this prompt, you are directed to

   - read "Miss Brill,"
   - write an essay,
   - analyze...uses of language.

   Be especially aware of **the verb that describes the essay** you are to write (e.g., *Write an essay in which you analyze...* or *Write an essay that analyzes...*). There is a very important difference between *analyze, describe, argue, evaluate,* and so on. Make certain you do what the prompt tells you to do.

   Also be aware of **the direct object of that verb** (e.g., *analyze the author's choice of words, evaluate the effectiveness, argue whether the character can be considered...,* and so on).

   Most of the time, even if your test booklet is collected, it will never be used again, so underline any key words or write any margin notes that will help you understand the topic and what exactly you are asked to do with it.

2. **Make sure you have something valid to write about.** Consider the directives in the prompt and write a single sentence (two at the most) that makes a positive and focused statement about the topic.

For example, the writer of the first essay about "The Gift of the Magi" might have written these preliminary sentences:

> *The narrator likes Jim and Della, and he approves of the sacrifices they make for each other. He communicates this approval by using overly formal words when simpler ones might be expected, and he uses vivid images and precise shades of meaning to specify exactly what he wants his reader to notice and to feel.*

Make sure these sentences address all of the issues and subpoints specified in the prompt.

3. **Keeping these sentences in mind, review the selection and find your textual support.** Again, the text booklet is probably never going to be used again, so go ahead and underline or bracket the words or phrases that will illustrate and support your points—that will give substance to what you've identified as the main idea of your essay.

Find as much support as you can from throughout the selection. If you end up with more support than you can use in your essay, you can always leave some out. But you don't want to be caught with an essay that is too short and underdeveloped.

If you cannot *find* textual support, or enough textual support, take that as a clue that whatever you're saying in your sentences is simply not going to work and write new sentences.

Consider this: suppose the writer of the "Gift of the Magi" essay thought that the narrator seemed indifferent or apathetic to the characters. He'd have had a very hard time finding much textual support. And if he couldn't find the words and phrases to support his claim, he'd be foolish to continue to try to base his essay on that thesis.

4. **Write your essay.** Keep referring to the prompt and whatever you underlined or highlighted in the selection to make sure you're on track and addressing everything the prompt wants you to address. ⏻

Free-Response Question Two (independent):

One of the chief goals of the modernist movement of the early twentieth century was to shatter the norms and conventions of previous literary movements. This challenge included developing new techniques for communicating characters' inner lives. Choose a modernist short story and write a carefully reasoned and well-supported essay in which you evaluate the extent to which it achieves the goals of the modernist movement.

Before you write your essay:

1. **Make sure you understand exactly what you're being asked to write about.** A typical Advanced Placement independent prompt will usually mention some aspect or element of literature or a literary topic about which you presumably have some knowledge.

   - In the "Gift of the Magi" independent prompt, this topic is the power of words and the distinction between words that might have similar meanings but very different uses.

   - In the above "Miss Brill" prompt, the topic is Modernist literature.

   It is important that you understand this topic because your essay will receive a fairly low score if you simply ramble on about literature in general or the piece you've chosen.

   These prompts will also contain direct verbs to tell you what you are to do with the literature you've chosen.

   In this prompt, you are directed to
   1. choose a modernist short story,
   2. write an essay,
   3. evaluate the extent to which it achieves modernist goals.

   As with the text-based prompt, be especially aware of **the verb that describes the essay** you are to write (e.g., *Write an essay in which you analyze... or Write an essay that analyzes...*).

Make certain you do what the prompt tells you to do. In this prompt, you are being directed to *evaluate* to pass judgment on the success of a story to challenge traditional literary norms.

You also need to be aware of **the direct object of that verb**. Again, in this prompt, you are being asked to evaluate *the extent to which* the story you have chosen *achieves the goals of the modernist movement* [to challenge literary norms and find ways of exploring the characters' inner lives].

As with the earlier prompt, if this were an actual test and you were not using a textbook, you'd be able to underline any key words or write any margin notes that would help you understand the topic and what exactly you are asked to do with it.

2. **Choose an appropriate selection.** And there are a few different understandings for "appropriate" in this sense.

First of all, the literature you choose *must* be in the assigned genre. If you are told to choose a short story, you cannot write about a poem. If told to write about a novel, you cannot write about a play. Usually, the instructions will give you some leeway: "choose a novel or play..."

Second, the literature you choose must lend itself to the assigned discussion. If you're told to choose a play with a narrator, then you *must* choose a play (not a novel or poem) that has an actual narrator (e.g., the Stage Manager in *Our Town*, Tom in *The Glass Menagerie*). You would not choose, for example *The Great Gatsby* (narrated by Nick) because *The Great Gatsby* is a novel. Nor would you choose *Hamlet* (a play) because *Hamlet* has no narrator.

Finally, the literature you choose must be worth writing about on an Advanced Placement Exam. Sometimes the prompt will stipulate a work of "literary quality." What this means is open to interpretation and will be discussed later, but you need to think more along the lines of what you would study in a college-level English class than what you may have read in elementary or middle school. This is one reason that your AP and pre-AP courses have had such extensive reading lists— probably even summer reading lists. You want to have read a *lot* of *good* stories, poems, books, and play so that you will have a large body of work to choose from when faced with this question.

3. **Make sure you have something to say about both the topic and your selected literature.** Jot down what you remember about the literature you've chosen. List key plot events, but also think in terms of plot structure: rising action, climax, falling action, and so on. List characters, but also think in terms of function or role—protagonist or antagonist—and in terms of type—hero, anti-hero, foil, clown, etc. Always remember what the prompt is directing you to write about, and make sure you jot down notes that pertain to the assigned topic.

Jot down quotations or at least close paraphrases. *If you cannot remember this level of detail in the literature you've chosen, choose another piece of literature.*

Also jot down everything you know and remember about the assigned topic. What does the prompt mean by "the characters' inner lives"? What would constitute the "norms and conventions of previous literary movements"? These are the specific points you are going to need to address in your essay.

4. **Make sure you are clear about what you are going to say.** As you did for your text-based essay, consider the directives in the prompt and write a single sentence (two at the most) that makes a positive and focused statement about the assigned topic.

The writer of the second essay about "The Gift of the Magi" might have written something like this:

> In "The Gift of the Magi," O. Henry uses strict dictionary definitions of words and lets different meanings play against each other in order to create a lighthearted tone and make a story that could be depressing almost humorous.

Make sure these sentences address all of the issues and subpoints specified in the prompt.

5. **Write your essay.** Keep referring to the prompt and your notes to make sure you're on track and addressing everything the prompt wants you to address. ⏻

Connotations, ambiguities, and other meanings

Even as you develop a respect for the literal, dictionary definitions of the words used by an author, you must also be aware that just about every word an author might choose to use has, in addition to its denotation, any number of *connotations*—meanings that are commonly accepted by speakers, readers, and writers. The challenge that being aware of possible connotative meanings is that these connotations can change over time and place. Depending on time and place, for example, *to redeem* can mean to save a soul from eternal torment, pay a ransom for a prisoner taken in battle, or turn in a coupon for a fifty-cent discount.

Even after you look up the word in a dictionary, you cannot hope to fully understand the words—or the text they build—without also taking into consideration what the words may have meant at the time and in the place the author wrote them.

This issue of connotation is one of the factors that make different interpretations possible. It *is* true that a single text may have several possible meanings. It is also possible, however, for a reader's interpretation to be inaccurate or invalid if it is not grounded in what the words really mean—whether denotatively or connotatively.

Another factor that can complicate your effort to understand the text's meaning is the fact that even the denotations of many words can be vague, abstract, open to interpretation. Some words are simply vague. When does the weather pass from *cool* to *cold*? (By the same token, at what temperature does something that was *warm* become *hot*?)

Some words are ambiguous. They have two or more denotations that might often seem incompatible or contradictory. Consider the simple word *cut*. One can *cut* a class without *cutting* it from his or her schedule. If you are not *cut*, then you have made the *cut*. A *cut* on your arm is probably a bad thing, but a *cut* of meat can be a good thing.

While an author's use of *cut* might be absolutely clear, there might also be subtle implications in the author's choice of a word like *cut* as opposed to a clearer, less ambiguous alternative like *skip* or *miss*, *excise*, or *reduce*. Just as it is important to consider what the word *literally* means according to a reliable dictionary, it is important to consider what *else* the writer may have meant by choosing a particular word.

The following story, Jack London's "To Build a Fire," seems to present no challenges to a reader looking for comprehension, but some of the clearest words have multiple meanings and a variety of connotations that create several levels of tone, mood, and meaning. The text has been annotated to point out to you how a full understanding of the words' meanings will contribute to a reader's understanding of the text as a whole.

To Build a Fire

JACK LONDON (1876 – 1916)

1 DAY HAD BROKEN COLD AND GREY, exceedingly cold and grey, when the man turned aside from the main Yukon trail and climbed the high earth-bank, where a dim and little-travelled trail led eastward through the fat spruce timberland. It was a steep bank, and he paused for breath at the top, excusing the act to himself by looking at his watch. It was nine o'clock. There was no sun nor hint of sun, though there was not a cloud in the sky. It was a clear day, and yet there seemed an intangible <u>pall</u>[1] over the face of things, a subtle gloom that made the day dark, and that was due to the absence of sun. This fact did not worry the man. He was used to the lack of sun. It had been days since he had seen the sun, and he knew that a few more days must pass before that <u>cheerful orb</u>,[2] due south, would just peep above the sky-line and dip immediately from view.

2 The man flung a look back along the way he had come. The Yukon lay a mile wide and hidden under three feet of ice. On top of this ice were as many feet of snow. It was all pure white, rolling in gentle undulations where the ice-jams of the freeze-up had formed. North and south, as far as his eye could see, it was unbroken white, save for a dark hair-line that curved and twisted from around the spruce-covered island to the south, and that curved and twisted away into the north, where it disappeared behind another spruce-covered island. This dark hair-line was the trail—the main trail—that led south five hundred miles to the Chilcoot Pass, Dyea, and salt water; and that led north seventy miles to Dawson, and still on to the north a thousand miles to Nulato, and finally to St. Michael on Bering Sea, a thousand miles and half a thousand more.

3 But all this—the mysterious, far-reaching hairline trail, the absence of sun from the sky, the <u>tremendous cold</u>,[3] and the strangeness and weirdness of it all—made no impression on the man. It was not because he was long used to it. He was a new-comer in the land, a *chechaquo*, and this was his first winter. The trouble with him was that he was without imagination. He was quick and alert in the things of life, but only in the things, and not in the significances. Fifty degrees below zero meant eighty odd degrees of frost. Such fact impressed him as being cold and <u>uncomfortable</u>,[4] and that was all. It did not lead him to meditate upon his frailty as a creature of temperature, and upon man's frailty in general, able only to live within certain <u>narrow limits</u>[5] of heat and cold;

Sample Student Commentary

[1] Literally, a pall is a shroud, a sheet used to cover a corpse. It has also come to mean any dismal or somber covering, even a permeating feeling of gloom.

[2] An orb is a sphere, so this is a literal reference to the sun. To ascribe the attribute of cheerfulness to the sun is personification. It projects the cheer of a person seeing the sun after a long period of darkness onto the sun and contrasts the cheer of the sun's appearance with the gloom of the long, northern night.

[3] Denotations of *tremendous* include "inspiring awe or wonder," and "extremely large." Both denotations are broadened to communicate just how cold it is.

[4] A literal use of the word but probably an understatement.

[5] Literally, London means "narrow range." but his unconventional choice of limits emphasizes the narrowness.

and from there on it did not lead him to the conjectural field of immortality and man's place in the universe. Fifty degrees below zero stood for a <u>bite of frost</u>[6] that hurt and that must be guarded against by the use of mittens, ear-flaps, warm moccasins, and thick socks. Fifty degrees below zero was to him just precisely fifty degrees below zero. That there should be anything more to it than that was a thought that never entered his head.

4   As he turned to go on, he spat speculatively. <u>There was a sharp, explosive[7] crackle</u> that startled him. He spat again. And again, in the air, before it could fall to the snow, the spittle crackled. He knew that at fifty below spittle crackled on the snow, but this spittle had crackled in the air. Undoubtedly it was colder than fifty below—how much colder he did not know. But the temperature did not matter. He was bound for the old claim on the left fork of Henderson Creek, where the boys were already. They had come over across the divide from the Indian Creek country, while he had come the roundabout way to take a look at the possibilities of getting out logs in the spring from the islands in the Yukon. He would be in to camp by six o'clock; a bit after dark, it was true, but the boys would be there, a fire would be going, and a hot supper would be ready. As for lunch, he pressed his hand against the protruding bundle under his jacket. It was also under his shirt, wrapped up in a handkerchief and lying against the naked skin. It was the only way to keep the biscuits from freezing. He smiled agreeably to himself as he thought of those biscuits, each cut open and sopped in bacon grease, and each enclosing a generous slice of fried bacon.

5   He <u>plunged</u>[8] in among the big spruce trees. The trail was faint. A foot of snow had fallen since the last sled had passed over, and he was glad he was without a sled, travelling light. In fact, he carried nothing but the lunch wrapped in the handkerchief. He was surprised, however, at the cold. It certainly was cold, he concluded, as he rubbed his numbed nose and cheek-bones with his mittened hand. He was a <u>warm-whiskered[9] man</u>, but the hair on his face did not protect the high cheek-bones and the <u>eager nose</u>[10] that thrust itself aggressively into the frosty air.

6   At the man's heels trotted a dog, a big native husky, the proper wolf-dog, grey-coated and without any visible or temperamental difference from its brother, the wild wolf. The animal was depressed by the tremendous cold. It knew that it was no time for travelling. Its instinct told it a truer tale than was told to the man by the man's judgment. In reality, it was not merely colder than fifty below zero; it was colder than sixty below, than seventy below. It was seventy-five below zero. Since the freezing-point is thirty-two above zero, it meant that one hundred and seven degrees of frost <u>obtained</u>.[11] The dog did not know

---

Sample Student Commentary

[6] Frostbite is, indeed, the literal term for the damage done to the body by severe cold. The word itself, however, is both personification and metaphor. Frost cannot literally "bite."

[7] Another stretch of a literal definition into hyperbole.

[8] Actually a literal use of the word, and it does create a graphic image of the man's movement.

[9] A colloquialism among men in the Yukon at that time. It certainly presents a vivid image of the man's beard.

[10] The nose, of course, cannot literally be "eager," but because of its position and shape, it does tend to travel an inch or so ahead of the rest of the man's body, as if it were eager to arrive first.

[11] An archaic definition of *obtain* is to succeed in the sense of "to follow" or "come after."

anything about thermometers. Possibly in its brain there was no sharp consciousness of a condition of very cold such as was in the man's brain. But the brute[12] had its instinct. It experienced a vague but menacing apprehension that subdued it and made it slink along at the man's heels, and that made it question eagerly every unwonted movement of the man as if expecting him to go into camp or to seek shelter somewhere and build a fire. The dog had learned fire, and it wanted fire, or else to burrow under the snow and cuddle its warmth away from the air.

7 The frozen moisture of its breathing had settled on its fur in a fine powder of frost, and especially were its jowls, muzzle, and eyelashes whitened by its crystalled breath[13]. The man's red beard and moustache were likewise frosted, but more solidly, the deposit taking the form of ice and increasing with every warm, moist breath he exhaled. Also, the man was chewing tobacco, and the muzzle of ice[14] held his lips so rigidly that he was unable to clear his chin when he expelled the juice. The result was that a crystal beard of the color and solidity of amber was increasing its length on his chin. If he fell down it would shatter itself, like glass, into brittle fragments. But he did not mind the appendage. It was the penalty all tobacco-chewers paid in that country, and he had been out before in two cold snaps. They had not been so cold as this, he knew, but by the spirit thermometer[1] at Sixty Mile he knew they had been registered at fifty below and at fifty-five.

8 He held on through the level stretch of woods for several miles, crossed a wide flat of nigger-heads[2], and dropped down a bank to the frozen bed of a small stream. This was Henderson Creek, and he knew he was ten miles from the forks. He looked at his watch. It was ten o'clock. He was making four miles an hour, and he calculated that he would arrive at the forks at half-past twelve. He decided to celebrate that event by eating his lunch there.

9 The dog dropped in again at his heels, with a tail drooping discouragement, as the man swung along the creek-bed. The furrow of the old sled-trail was plainly visible, but a dozen inches of snow covered the marks of the last runners. In a month no man had come up or down that silent creek. The man held steadily on. He was not much given to thinking, and just then particularly he had nothing to think about save that he would eat lunch at the forks and that at six o'clock he would be in camp with the boys. There was nobody to talk to and, had there been, speech would have been impossible because of the ice-muzzle on his mouth. So he continued monotonously to chew tobacco and to increase the length of his amber beard.

10 Once in a while the thought reiterated itself that it was very cold and that he had never experienced such cold. As he walked along he rubbed his cheek-bones and nose with the

---

[1] A thermometer made with alcohol (distilled spirit) instead of mercury.

[2] An archaic, colloquial term for any of a number of grasses that grow in bunches or tufts.

Sample Student Commentary

[12] Denotatively, brute does have to do with animals and animal nature. Connotatively, it carries a sense of savagery not necessarily included in the denotation.

[13] Literally, to crystallize includes any substance's taking on a crystalline form. The connotative image of glittering, diamond-like crystals is what gives this description its power as an image.

[14] Another image based largely on the denotation of muzzle as a covering for the mouth of an animal to prevent biting.

back of his mittened hand. He did this automatically, now and again changing hands. But rub as he would, the instant he stopped his cheek-bones went numb, and the following instant the end of his nose went numb. He was sure to frost his cheeks; he knew that, and experienced a pang of regret that he had not devised a nose-strap of the sort Bud wore in cold snaps. Such a strap passed across the cheeks, as well, and saved them. But it didn't matter much, after all. What were frosted cheeks? A bit painful, that was all; they were never serious.

11   Empty as the man's mind was of thoughts, he was keenly observant, and he noticed the changes in the creek, the curves and bends and timber-jams, and always he sharply noted where he placed his feet. Once, coming around a bend, he shied abruptly, like a startled horse, curved away from the place where he had been walking, and retreated several paces back along the trail. The creek he knew was frozen clear to the bottom—no creek could contain water in that arctic winter—but he knew also that there were springs that bubbled out from the hillsides and ran along under the snow and on top the ice of the creek. He knew that the coldest snaps never froze these springs, and he knew likewise their danger. They were traps. They hid pools of water under the snow that might be three inches deep, or three feet. Sometimes a skin[15] of ice half an inch thick covered them, and in turn was covered by the snow. Sometimes there were alternate layers of water and ice-skin, so that when one broke through he kept on breaking through for a while, sometimes wetting himself to the waist.

12   That was why he had shied in such panic. He had felt the give under his feet and heard the crackle of a snow-hidden ice-skin. And to get his feet wet in such a temperature meant trouble and danger. At the very least it meant delay, for he would be forced to stop and build a fire, and under its protection to bare his feet while he dried his socks and moccasins. He stood and studied the creek-bed and its banks, and decided that the flow of water came from the right. He reflected awhile, rubbing his nose and cheeks, then skirted to the left, stepping gingerly and testing the footing for each step. Once clear of the danger, he took a fresh chew of tobacco and swung along at his four-mile gait.

13   In the course of the next two hours he came upon several similar traps. Usually the snow above the hidden pools had a sunken, candied appearance that advertised the danger. Once again, however, he had a close call; and once, suspecting danger, he compelled the dog to go on in front. The dog did not want to go. It hung back until the man shoved it forward, and then it went quickly across the white, unbroken surface. Suddenly it broke through, floundered to one side, and got away to firmer footing. It had wet its forefeet and legs, and almost immediately the water that clung to it turned to ice. It made quick efforts to lick the ice off its legs, then dropped down in the snow and began to bite out the ice that had formed between the toes. This was a matter of instinct. To permit the ice to remain would mean sore feet. It did not know this. It merely obeyed the mysterious prompting that arose from the deep crypts[16] of its being. But the

---

Sample Student Commentary

[15] Another connotative use based closely on the word's primary denotation.

[16] Here is an excellent metaphoric use based on an unconventional use of the word's connotation. Literally, a crypt is an underground chamber. Connotatively, it is associated with deep secrets and often death. By using this word to name the origins of the animal's instinct, London is emphasizing the sense of mysterious, hidden knowledge that is instinct. Crypt's association with death also contributes to the story's mood of gloom and foreboding.

man knew, having achieved a judgment on the subject, and he removed the mitten from his right hand and helped tear out the ice-particles. He did not expose his fingers more than a minute, and was astonished at the swift numbness that <u>smote</u>[17] them. It certainly was cold. He pulled on the mitten hastily, and beat the hand <u>savagely</u>[18] across his chest.

14   At twelve o'clock the day was at its brightest. Yet the sun was too far south on its winter journey to clear the horizon. The bulge of the earth intervened between it and Henderson Creek, where the man walked under a clear sky at noon and cast no shadow. At half-past twelve, to the minute, he arrived at the forks of the creek. He was pleased at the speed he had made. If he kept it up, he would certainly be with the boys by six. He unbuttoned his jacket and shirt and drew forth his lunch. The action consumed no more than a quarter of a minute, yet in that brief moment the numbness laid hold of the exposed fingers. He did not put the mitten on, but, instead, struck the fingers a dozen sharp smashes against his leg. Then he sat down on a snow-covered log to eat. The sting that followed upon the striking of his fingers against his leg ceased so quickly that he was startled, he had had no chance to take a bite of biscuit. He struck the fingers repeatedly and returned them to the mitten, baring the other hand for the purpose of eating. He tried to take a mouthful, but the ice-muzzle prevented. He had forgotten to build a fire and thaw out. He chuckled at his foolishness, and as he chuckled he noted the numbness creeping into the exposed fingers. Also, he noted that the stinging which had first come to his toes when he sat down was already passing away. He wondered whether the toes were warm or numbed. He moved them inside the moccasins and decided that they were numbed.

15   He pulled the mitten on hurriedly and stood up. He was a bit frightened. He stamped up and down until the stinging returned into the feet. It certainly was cold, was his thought. That man from Sulphur Creek had spoken the truth when telling how cold it sometimes got in the country. And he had laughed at him at the time! That showed one must not be too sure of things. There was no mistake about it, it was cold. He strode up and down, stamping his feet and threshing his arms, until reassured by the returning warmth. Then he got out matches and proceeded to make a fire. From the undergrowth, where high water of the previous spring had lodged a supply of seasoned twigs, he got his firewood. Working carefully from a small beginning, he soon had a roaring fire, over which he thawed the ice from his face and in the protection of which he ate his biscuits. For the moment the cold of space was outwitted. The dog took satisfaction in the fire, stretching out close enough for warmth and far enough away to escape being singed.

16   When the man had finished, he filled his pipe and took his comfortable time over a smoke. Then he pulled on his mittens, settled the ear-flaps of his cap firmly about his ears, and took the creek trail up the left fork. The dog was disappointed and yearned back toward the fire. This man did not know cold. Possibly all the generations of his

---

Sample Student Commentary

[17] Literally, to strike with a weapon. Its connotative association with medieval fighting and the romantic slaying of dragons adds a sense that the cold is an armed and skilled warrior, a formidable foe.

[18] Literally, the word establishes the image of the man's pounding his chest. Connotatively, savagely joins emphasizes the implied comparison and contrast between the man and the wolf.

ancestry had been ignorant of cold, of real cold, of cold one hundred and seven degrees below freezing-point. But the dog knew; all its ancestry knew, and it had inherited the knowledge. And it knew that it was not good to walk abroad in such fearful cold. It was the time to lie snug in a hole in the snow and wait for a curtain of cloud to be drawn across the face of outer space whence this cold came. On the other hand, there was keen intimacy between the dog and the man. The one was the toil-slave of the other, and the only caresses it had ever received were the caresses of the whip-lash and of harsh and menacing throat-sounds that threatened the whip-lash. So the dog made no effort to communicate its apprehension to the man. It was not concerned in the welfare of the man; it was for its own sake that it yearned back toward the fire. But the man whistled, and spoke to it with the sound of whip-lashes, and the dog swung in at the man's heels and followed after.

17   The man took a chew of tobacco and proceeded to start a new amber beard. Also, his moist breath quickly powdered with white his moustache, eyebrows, and lashes. There did not seem to be so many springs on the left fork of the Henderson, and for half an hour the man saw no signs of any. And then it happened. At a place where there were no signs, where the soft, unbroken snow seemed to advertise solidity beneath, the man broke through. It was not deep. He wetted himself half-way to the knees before he floundered out to the firm crust.

18   He was angry, and cursed his luck aloud. He had hoped to get into camp with the boys at six o'clock, and this would delay him an hour, for he would have to build a fire and dry out his foot-gear. This was imperative at that low temperature—he knew that much; and he turned aside to the bank, which he climbed. On top, tangled in the underbrush about the trunks of several small spruce trees, was a high-water deposit of dry firewood—sticks and twigs principally, but also larger portions of seasoned branches and fine, dry, last-year's grasses. He threw down several large pieces on top of the snow. This served for a foundation and prevented the young flame from drowning itself in the snow it otherwise would melt. The flame he got by touching a match to a small shred of birch-bark that he took from his pocket. This burned even more readily than paper. Placing it on the foundation, he fed the young flame with wisps of dry grass and with the tiniest dry twigs.

19   He worked slowly and carefully, keenly aware of his danger. Gradually, as the flame grew stronger, he increased the size of the twigs with which he fed it. He squatted in the snow, pulling the twigs out from their entanglement in the brush and feeding directly to the flame. He knew there must be no failure. When it is seventy- five below zero, a man must not fail in his first attempt to build a fire—that is, if his feet are wet. If his feet are dry, and he fails, he can run along the trail for half a mile and restore his circulation. But the circulation of wet and freezing feet cannot be restored by running when it is seventy-five below. No matter how fast he runs, the wet feet will freeze the harder.

20   All this the man knew. The old-timer on Sulphur Creek had told him about it the previous fall, and now he was appreciating the advice. Already all sensation had gone out of his feet. To build the fire he had been forced to remove his mittens, and the fingers had quickly gone numb. His pace of four miles an hour had kept his heart pumping blood to the surface of his body and to all the extremities. But the instant he stopped, the action of the pump eased down. The cold of space <u>smote</u>[19] the unprotected tip of the planet, and he, being on that unprotected tip, received the full force of the <u>blow</u>.[20] The blood of his body recoiled before it. The blood was alive, like the dog, and like the dog it wanted to hide away and cover itself up from the <u>fearful</u>[21] cold. So long as he walked four miles an hour, he pumped that blood, willy-nilly, to the surface; but now it ebbed away and sank down into the recesses of his body. The extremities were the first to feel its absence. His wet feet froze the faster, and his exposed fingers numbed the faster, though they had not yet begun to freeze. Nose and cheeks were already freezing, while the skin of all his body chilled as it lost its blood.

21   But he was safe. Toes and nose and cheeks would be only touched by the frost, for the fire was beginning to burn with strength. He was feeding it with twigs the size of his finger. In another minute he would be able to feed it with branches the size of his wrist, and then he could remove his wet foot-gear, and, while it dried, he could keep his naked feet warm by the fire, rubbing them at first, of course, with snow. The fire was a success. He was safe. He remembered the advice of the old-timer on Sulphur Creek, and smiled. The old-timer had been very serious in laying down the law that no man must travel alone in the Klondike after fifty below. Well, here he was; he had had the accident; he was alone; and he had saved himself. Those old-timers were rather <u>womanish</u>,[22] some of them, he thought. All a man had to do was to keep his head, and he was all right. Any man who was a man could travel alone. But it was surprising, the rapidity with which his cheeks and nose were freezing. And he had not thought his fingers could go lifeless in so short a time. Lifeless they were, for he could scarcely make them move together to grip a twig, and they seemed remote from his body and from him. When he touched a twig, he had to look and see whether or not he had hold of it. The wires were pretty well down between him and his finger-ends.

22   All of which counted for little. There was the fire, snapping and crackling and promising life with every dancing flame. He started to untie his moccasins. They were coated with ice; the thick German socks were like sheaths of iron half-way to the knees; and the moccasin strings were like rods of steel all twisted and knotted as by some <u>conflagration</u>[23]. For a moment he tugged with his numbed fingers, then, realizing the folly of it, he drew his sheath-knife.

Sample Student Commentary

[19] London has used this word before to the same effect. This time, however, the foe is the Universe itself.

[20] Blow continues the sense of combat.

[21] Nicely ambiguous. Literally, the cold is "fearful," having instilled a sense of fear in the man. In the context of this paragraph, it also advances the combat motif—the sense that Nature is an armed and menacing foe.

[22] Literally, this would be an anatomical or physiological assessment. Connotatively, it brings to mind whatever traits are stereotypically attributed to women. The precise intent of the adjective is, of course, determined by the time and place of its use. London's dismissal of the Old-Timers' fears is based on turn-of-the-twentieth-century notions of "womanhood"; quite different from our twenty-first-century ideas.

[23] A conflagration is a large, damaging fire. In this sentence, it is part of a simile to describe the hard and twisted condition of the moccasin strings. It's use, here, is doubly ironic. First, the damage to the moccasin strings has been caused by a cold so severe it is nearly the opposite of a conflagration; and the point of the story is the man's attempt to build a fire.

23 But before he could cut the strings, it happened. It was his own fault or, rather, his mistake. He should not have built the fire under the spruce tree. He should have built it in the open. But it had been easier to pull the twigs from the brush and drop them directly on the fire. Now the tree under which he had done this carried a weight of snow on its boughs. No wind had blown for weeks, and each bough was fully <u>freighted</u>.[24] Each time he had pulled a twig he had communicated a <u>slight agitation</u>[25] to the tree— an <u>imperceptible agitation</u>[26], so far as he was concerned, but an <u>agitation</u>[27] <u>sufficient</u> to bring about the disaster. High up in the tree one bough <u>capsized</u>[28] its load of snow. This fell on the boughs beneath, capsizing them. This process continued, spreading out and involving the whole tree. It grew like an avalanche, and it descended without warning upon the man and the fire, and the fire was <u>blotted</u>[29] out! Where it had burned was a mantle of fresh and disordered snow.

24 The man was shocked. It was as though he had just heard his own sentence of death. For a moment he sat and stared at the spot where the fire had been. Then he grew very calm. Perhaps the old-timer on Sulphur Creek was right. If he had only had a trail-mate he would have been in no danger now. The trail-mate could have built the fire. Well, it was up to him to build the fire over again, and this second time there must be no failure. Even if he succeeded, he would most likely lose some toes. His feet must be badly frozen by now, and there would be some time before the second fire was ready.

25 Such were his thoughts, but he did not sit and think them. He was busy all the time they were passing through his mind, he made a new foundation for a fire, this time in the open; where no <u>treacherous</u>[30] <u>tree</u> could blot it out. Next, he gathered dry grasses and tiny twigs from the <u>high-water flotsam</u>.[31] He could not bring his fingers together to pull them out, but he was able to gather them by the handful. In this way he got many rotten twigs and bits of green moss that were undesirable, but it was the best he could do. He

---

Sample Student Commentary

[24] A pun, a play on the fact that freight and weight rhyme. Freight, however, connotes a load or a burden that is not necessarily suggested by weight.

[25] One of the denotations of communicate is to cause to pass from one to another, like a communicable disease.

[26] An obsolete denotation of agitate is to cause motion. Remember when London lived and wrote; this definition is quite possibly what he intended. That agitate also connotes unease or distress contributes to London's overall mood of impending calamity.

[27] This is the third repetition of agitation at the end of three successive clauses. This is a rhetorical device called epistrophe. Repeating this word emphasizes both the fact that the slight motion is moving from one bough to another and the sense of foreboding.

[28] This word's association with boats is purely connotative, but this connotation contributes to the sense of drenching that will result from this accident.

[29] Ironically, to blot means literally to make dry by soaking up excess fluid (like blotting up a spill with a paper towel). London's unconventional use of this word emphasizes the way the fire is drenched by the falling snow.

[30] The use of this one word serves London several purposes. It is a strong example of the pathetic fallacy, ascribing human attributes to things in nature. It also provides London with an opportunity to exhibit his Naturalist's disavowal of Romantic philosophy. While the Romantics argued that Nature was benevolent, the Naturalists believed in a neutral or amoral Nature.

[31] This is a literal use of the word, and it emphasizes the motif of water and wetness.

worked methodically, even collecting an armful of the larger branches to be used later when the fire gathered strength. And all the while the dog sat and watched him, a certain yearning wistfulness in its eyes, for it looked upon him as the fire-provider, and the fire was slow in coming.

26 When all was ready, the man reached in his pocket for a second piece of birch-bark. He knew the bark was there, and, though he could not feel it with his fingers, he could hear its crisp rustling as he fumbled for it. Try as he would, he could not clutch hold of it. And all the time, in his consciousness, was the knowledge that each instant his feet were freezing. This thought tended to put him in a panic, but he fought against it and kept calm. He pulled on his mittens with his teeth, and threshed his arms back and forth, beating his hands with all his might against his sides. He did this sitting down, and he stood up to do it; and all the while the dog sat in the snow, its wolf-brush of a tail curled around warmly over its forefeet, its sharp wolf-ears pricked forward intently as it watched the man. And the man as he beat and threshed with his arms and hands, felt a great surge of envy as he regarded the creature that was warm and secure in its natural covering.

27 After a time he was aware of the first far-away signals of sensation in his beaten fingers. The faint tingling grew stronger till it evolved into a stinging ache that was excruciating, but which the man hailed with satisfaction. He stripped the mitten from his right hand and fetched forth the birch-bark. The exposed fingers were quickly going numb again. Next he brought out his bunch of sulphur matches. But the tremendous cold had already driven the life out of his fingers. In his effort to separate one match from the others, the whole bunch fell in the snow. He tried to pick it out of the snow, but failed. The dead[32] fingers could neither touch nor clutch. He was very careful. He drove the thought of his freezing feet; and nose, and cheeks, out of his mind, devoting his whole soul[33] to the matches. He watched, using the sense of vision in place of that of touch, and when he saw his fingers on each side the bunch, he closed them—that is, he willed to close them, for the wires were drawn, and the fingers did not obey. He pulled the mitten on the right hand, and beat it fiercely against his knee. Then, with both mittened hands, he scooped the bunch of matches, along with much snow, into his lap. Yet he was no better off.

28 After some manipulation he managed to get the bunch between the heels of his mittened hands. In this fashion he carried it to his mouth. The ice crackled and snapped when by a violent effort he opened his mouth. He drew the lower jaw in, curled the upper lip out of the way, and scraped the bunch with his upper teeth in order to separate a match. He succeeded in getting one, which he dropped on his lap. He was no better off. He could not pick it up. Then he devised a way. He picked it up in his teeth and scratched it on his leg. Twenty times he scratched before he succeeded in lighting it. As it flamed he held it with his teeth to the birch-bark. But the burning brimstone went up

---

Sample Student Commentary

[32] The fingers, of course, are not literally dead, but London uses this word to advance the foreboding sense of impending death that he started in the opening passage of the story.

[33] For a Naturalist to refer to the human soul is ironic. However, since the man's life depends on his lighting the matches, this simple act could be interpreted as having religious significance.

his nostrils and into his lungs, causing him to cough spasmodically. The match fell into the snow and went out.

29   The old-timer on Sulphur Creek was right, he thought in the moment of controlled despair that ensued: after fifty below, a man should travel with a partner. He beat his hands, but failed in exciting any sensation. Suddenly he bared both hands, removing the mittens with his teeth. He caught the whole bunch between the heels of his hands. His arm-muscles not being frozen enabled him to press the hand-heels tightly against the matches. Then he scratched the bunch along his leg. It flared into flame, seventy sulphur matches at once! There was no wind to blow them out. He kept his head to one side to escape the strangling fumes,[34] and held the blazing bunch to the birch-bark. As he so held it, he became aware of sensation in his hand. His flesh was burning. He could smell it. Deep down below the surface he could feel it. The sensation developed into pain that grew acute. And still he endured it, holding the flame of the matches clumsily to the bark that would not light readily because his own burning hands were in the way, absorbing most of the flame.

30   At last, when he could endure no more, he jerked his hands apart. The blazing matches fell sizzling into the snow, but the birch-bark was alight. He began laying dry grasses and the tiniest twigs on the flame. He could not pick and choose, for he had to lift the fuel between the heels of his hands. Small pieces of rotten wood and green moss clung to the twigs, and he bit them off as well as he could with his teeth. He cherished the flame[35] carefully and awkwardly. It meant life, and it must not perish. The withdrawal of blood from the surface of his body now made him begin to shiver, and he grew more awkward. A large piece of green moss fell squarely on the little fire. He tried to poke it out with his fingers, but his shivering frame made him poke too far, and he disrupted the nucleus of the little fire, the burning grasses and tiny twigs separating and scattering. He tried to poke them together again, but in spite of the tenseness[36] of the effort, his shivering got away with him, and the twigs were hopelessly scattered. Each twig gushed a puff of smoke[37] and went out. The fire-provider had failed. As he looked apathetically about him, his eyes chanced on the dog, sitting across the ruins of the fire from him, in the snow, making restless, hunching movements, slightly lifting one forefoot and then the other, shifting its weight back and forth on them with wistful eagerness.

31   The sight of the dog put a wild idea into his head. He remembered the tale of the man, caught in a blizzard, who killed a steer and crawled inside the carcass, and so was saved.

Sample Student Commentary

[34] Literally, fumes cannot strangle, but this word provides a much more vivid image than other words London could have chosen.

[35] A lesser-known dictionary entry for cherish is to keep or cultivate with care and affection. Clearly, London is using the word literally in this case, but as with several of London's other word choices, cherish presents the reader with a vivid image of the man's tending his tiny fire as well as an emotional appreciation for the value of that fire.

[36] Anyone who has ever concentrated over a difficult task can appreciate London's unconventional use of the word tense.

[37] Gush is generally associated with fluids, not vapors. It does, however, provide another vivid image of the smoke from the extinguished fire and continues the water/drenching motif.

He would kill the dog and bury his hands in the warm body until the numbness went out of them. Then he could build another fire. He spoke to the dog, calling it to him; but in his voice was a strange note of fear that frightened the animal, who had never known the man to speak in such way before. Something was the matter, and its suspicious nature sensed danger,—it knew not what danger but somewhere, somehow, in its brain arose an apprehension of the man. It flattened its ears down at the sound of the man's voice, and its restless, hunching movements and the liftings and shiftings of its forefeet became more pronounced but it would not come to the man. He got on his hands and knees and crawled toward the dog. This unusual posture again excited suspicion, and the animal sidled mincingly away.

32   The man sat up in the snow for a moment and struggled for calmness. Then he pulled on his mittens, by means of his teeth, and got upon his feet. He glanced down at first in order to assure himself that he was really standing up, for the absence of sensation in his feet left him <u>unrelated to the earth</u>[38]. His erect position in itself started to drive the webs of suspicion from the dog's mind; and when he spoke peremptorily, with the sound of whip-lashes in his voice, the dog rendered its customary allegiance and came to him. As it came within reaching distance, the man lost his control. His arms flashed out to the dog, and he experienced genuine surprise when he discovered that his hands could not clutch, that there was neither bend nor feeling in the fingers. He had forgotten for the moment that they were frozen and that they were freezing more and more. All this happened quickly, and before the animal could get away, he encircled its body with his arms. He sat down in the snow, and in this fashion held the dog, while it snarled and whined and struggled.

33   But it was all he could do, hold its body encircled in his arms and sit there. He realized that he could not kill the dog. There was no way to do it. With his helpless hands he could neither draw nor hold his sheath-knife nor throttle the animal. He released it, and it <u>plunged</u>[39] wildly away, with tail between its legs, and still snarling. It halted forty feet away and surveyed him curiously, with ears sharply pricked forward. The man looked down at his hands in order to locate them, and found them hanging on the ends of his arms. It struck him as curious that one should have to use his eyes in order to find out where his hands were. He began threshing his arms back and forth, beating the mittened hands against his sides. He did this for five minutes, violently, and his heart pumped enough blood up to the surface to put a stop to his shivering. But no sensation was aroused in the hands. He had an impression that they hung like weights on the ends of his arms, but when he tried to run the impression down, he could not find it.

34   A certain fear of death, dull and oppressive, came to him. This fear quickly became poignant as he realized that it was no longer a mere matter of freezing his fingers and toes, or of losing his hands and feet, but that it was a matter of life and death with the

Sample Student Commentary

[38] Unrelated is another ambiguous word, suggesting that the man is not only disoriented, but also no longer a part of earth's family—estranged from earth.

[39] This is London's second use of this word in this story. The first use described the man's movement; this one describes the dog's.

chances against him. This threw him into a panic, and he turned and ran up the creek-bed along the old, dim trail. The dog joined in behind and kept up with him. He ran blindly, without intention, in fear such as he had never known in his life. Slowly, as he <u>ploughed and floundered</u>[40] through the snow, he began to see things again—the banks of the creek, the old timber-jams, the leafless aspens, and the sky. The running made him feel better. He did not shiver. Maybe, if he ran on, his feet would thaw out; and, anyway, if he ran far enough, he would reach camp and the boys. Without doubt he would lose some fingers and toes and some of his face; but the boys would take care of him, and save the rest of him when he got there. And at the same time there was another thought in his mind that said he would never get to the camp and the boys; that it was too many miles away, that the freezing had too great a start on him, and that he would soon be stiff and dead. This thought he kept in the background and refused to consider. Sometimes it pushed itself forward and demanded to be heard, but he thrust it back and strove to think of other things.

35   It struck him as <u>curious</u>[41] that he could run at all on feet so frozen that he could not feel them when they struck the earth and took the weight of his body. He seemed to himself to skim along above the surface and to have no connection with the earth. Somewhere he had once seen a winged Mercury, and he wondered if Mercury felt as he felt when skimming over the earth.

36   His theory of running until he reached camp and the boys had one flaw in it: he lacked the endurance. Several times he stumbled, and finally he tottered, crumpled up, and fell. When he tried to rise, he failed. He must sit and rest, he decided, and next time he would merely walk and keep on going. As he sat and regained his breath, he noted that he was feeling quite warm and comfortable. He was not shivering, and it even seemed that a warm glow had come to his chest and trunk. And yet, when he touched his nose or cheeks, there was no sensation. Running would not thaw them out. Nor would it thaw out his hands and feet. Then the thought came to him that the frozen portions of his body must be extending. He tried to keep this thought down, to forget it, to think of something else; he was aware of the panicky feeling that it caused, and he was afraid of the panic. But the thought asserted itself, and persisted, until it produced a vision of his body totally frozen. This was too much, and he made another wild run along the trail. Once he slowed down to a walk, but the thought of the freezing extending itself made him run again.

37   And all the time the dog ran with him, at his heels. When he fell down a second time, it curled its tail over its forefeet and sat in front of him facing him curiously eager and intent. The warmth and security of the animal angered him, and he cursed it till it flattened down its ears appeasingly. This time the shivering came more quickly upon the man. He was losing in his battle with the frost. It was creeping into his body from all

---

Sample Student Commentary

[40] Compare the image of the active, energetic, and intentional plunging with the type of motion suggested by these verbs.

[41] Another literal but lesser-known use. This use suggests both the oddness of the man's being able to run and his sense of wonder at the ability.

sides. The thought of it drove him on, but he ran no more than a hundred feet, when he staggered and pitched headlong. It was his last panic. When he had recovered his breath and control, he sat up and entertained in his mind the conception of meeting death with dignity. However, the conception did not come to him in such terms. His idea of it was that he had been making a fool of himself, running around like a chicken with its head cut off—such was the simile that occurred to him. Well, he was bound to freeze anyway, and he might as well take it decently. With this new-found peace of mind came the first glimmerings of drowsiness. A good idea, he thought, to sleep off to death. It was like taking an anaesthetic. Freezing was not so bad as people thought. There were lots worse ways to die.

38   He pictured the boys finding his body next day. Suddenly he found himself with them, coming along the trail and looking for himself. And, still with them, he came around a turn in the trail and found himself lying in the snow. He did not belong with himself any more, for even then he was out of himself, standing with the boys and looking at himself in the snow. It certainly was cold, was his thought. When he got back to the States he could tell the folks what real cold was. He drifted on from this to a vision of the old-timer on Sulphur Creek. He could see him quite clearly, warm and comfortable, and smoking a pipe.

39   "You were right, old hoss; you were right," the man mumbled to the old-timer of Sulphur Creek.

40   Then the man drowsed off into what seemed to him the most comfortable and satisfying sleep he had ever known. The dog sat facing him and waiting. The brief day drew to a close in a long, slow twilight. There were no signs of a fire to be made, and, besides, never in the dog's experience had it known a man to sit like that in the snow and make no fire. As the twilight drew on, its eager yearning for the fire mastered it, and with a great lifting and shifting of forefeet, it whined softly, then flattened its ears down in anticipation of being chidden by the man. But the man remained silent. Later, the dog whined loudly. And still later it crept close to the man and caught the scent of death. This made the animal bristle and back away. A little longer it delayed, howling under the stars that leaped and danced and shone brightly in the cold sky. Then it turned and trotted up the trail in the direction of the camp it knew, where were the other food-providers and fire-providers.

Sample Multiple-Choice Questions

1. **Yet the sun was too far south on its winter journey to clear the horizon. The bulge of the earth intervened between it and Henderson Creek, where the man walked under a clear sky at noon and cast no shadow.**

   The cold of space smote the unprotected tip of the planet, and he, being on that unprotected tip, received the full force of the blow.

   Sentences like the above help to establish London as a writer of what movement?
   A. *Naturalism*
   B. Realism
   C. Romanticism
   D. Modernism
   E. Transcendentalism

2. **London's word choice can best be described as**
   A. precise and scientific.
   B. poetic.
   C. *equivocal.*
   D. unclear.
   E. simple and direct.

3. **Which of the following contributes most to the vividness of the image in which it is used?**
   A. intangible pall (paragraph 1)
   B. dead fingers (paragraph 27)
   C. crypts (paragraph 13)
   D. *cherish (paragraph 30)*
   E. gushed a puff (paragraph 30)

4. **What does the passage suggest is the most important distinction between the man and the dog?**
   A. *The man has lost touch with natural law that still governs the dog's behavior.*
   B. The man has reason and knowledge while the dog has instinct.
   C. The man is foolish while the dog is wise.
   D. The man is better able to provide for their needs than the dog is.
   E. The man is a creature of civilization while the dog is a creature of nature.

5. **All of the following contribute to a motif of water, drenching, or drowning EXCEPT**
   A. plunged. (paragraphs 5 and 33)
   B. capsized. (paragraph 23)
   C. flotsam. (paragraph 25)
   D. gushed. (paragraph 30)
   E. *crystalled. (paragraph 7)*

Answers and Explanations:

1. Since this question specifies the sentences on which students are to base their answers, it does not require outside knowledge of London as much as it does knowledge of the definitions and characteristics of the various literary movements. The two sentences provided both suggest the individual man's placement in a natural universe and the impact of that universe on his condition. (B) might tempt some students, but Realism tends to focus more on social forces than natural ones. (C) is eliminated by the realization that, in both sentences, Nature is neither benevolent nor malevolent; it just *is*. (D) is also eliminated because, aside from some unconventional word use, there is no evidence that London is challenging any of the traditional devices of storytelling. (E), like (C) can be eliminated by the realization that the sentences depict neither a benevolent nature nor a perfectible man. The sentences do, however, present scientific facts about the position of the sun relative to the earth and the impact of that astronomic relationship on the life of this individual man on earth. **Thus, (A) is the correct answer.**

2. (A) might tempt some because of the conventions of Naturalism in which the writer clearly places his character in an environment governed by natural laws that are neither good nor bad but neutral. (B) is fairly easily eliminated because, although London uses a good deal of vivid imagery, and his word choice is careful and sometimes unconventional, it is not as unconventional as might be considered "poetic." (D) is tempting if that is how one understands *ambiguous*, but the words London uses that have double meanings often contribute to his most vivid images and suggest levels of meaning. They do not tend to create a lack of clarity. (E) might also tempt some, but it does not address London's many unconventional and ambiguous word choices. Equivocal, however, denotes the fact of a message's being interpreted in more than one way. Its association with deception is a connotation. **Thus, in this case, (C) is the best answer.**

3. While (A) is a noun phrase, and London is employing a somewhat non-literal sense of *pall*, this phrase is not an image. Similarly, (B) describes the fingers' sensation of numbness, not their appearance. (C) is also a non-literal use but not an image. (E) is indeed an image of the movement of the smoke, but it is not the most vivid of the choices. (D), however, in that it is a verb with multiple meanings—literally, tending the fire carefully *and* deeply loving the life-saving fire. The single word, *cherish*, conveys a clear image of *how* the man is handling the fuel and blowing on the flames. **Thus, (D) is the best answer.**

4. (B) is not incorrect, but the simple *fact* of reason versus knowledge is not sufficient. London does much in the story to evaluate the distinction between human reason and animal instinct. (C) is probably the most tempting of the incorrect answers because the man is indeed foolish and, on the surface, the dog appears wise. Part of London's Naturalist theme, however, is that animals are not driven by human attributes like reason or wisdom; they are driven by natural instinct. (D) is clearly incorrect, as the man fails to provide the second fire. (E) might also tempt some because a large part of the man's failure is the result of his relying on reason and understanding, but London was a Naturalist, and there are several times in the story when he illustrates that humans, too, are part of Nature and subject to Nature's laws. (A), however, is almost a close modification of (E). As London suggests when he writes "the absence of sensation in his feet left him unrelated to the earth," and he seemed "to have no connection with the earth," it is not the case that the man is not a part of Nature but that he has lost contact with the Nature of which he is a part. **Thus, (A) is the best answer.**

5. The most familiar denotation of *plunge* (A) is to run or dive into water. Likewise, to *capsize* (B) connotes the turning over of a boat. *Flotsam* (C) is the debris that floats on top of water and is left behind after a flood recedes or the tide goes out. To *gush* is a verb usually connoted with a heavy or rapid jet of fluid. Only (E) is not necessarily associated with water. While, in this story, the crystals are indeed frozen water vapor, the word more readily connotes gems or sugar crystals in confections. **Thus, (E) is the best answer.**

Remember, we will provide you with an example of each type of writing prompt—text-based and independent—but the actual AP exam will never contain two essays about the same piece of literature.

Sample free-response item one (text-based):

Carefully read Jack London's "To Build a Fire." Then write a well-reasoned and well-supported essay in which you analyze London's word choice and show how his diction contributes to his imagery and helps to establish the overall mood of the story.

The mood of Jack's London's story, "To Build a Fire," is somber.[1] It is, after all, a story of death, and from the beginning, London foreshadows the man's death. This foreshadowing is very subtle, however. On the surface, while the man faces harder and harder challenges, he never considers that he won't survive. It is through images of death and words related with death that London creates his mood.[2]

The first fact we learn is that the day is "cold and gray."[3] While this phrase does not refer only to death, it is bleak and makes one think of the dead, maybe a dead body.[4] Literally, this grayness is caused by the fact that the story takes place north of the Arctic Circle, and the sun will not rise above the horizon for several weeks. London goes on to describe the day. Even though it is clear and cloudless, it feels as if there is an "intangible pall"[5] over the day. A "pall," of course, is a shroud, a sheet used to cover a dead body.[6] London makes sure the reader gets the impression by saying that it was a "subtle gloom," and not the lack of sun, that made the day dark.[7]

London uses another death-related word when he describes the dog's instinct, a "mysterious prompting that arose from the deep crypts of its being." A "crypt" is a dark, underground chamber, especially one that holds corpses.

Suggestions of death appear also in the two times the man builds a fire. London has made it very clear that it is cold—very cold. When the man tries to eat his lunch, he first forgets to build a fire, and his "exposed" hands grow "numb" with a speed that frightens him. After his accident, however, the "numb" fingers become "lifeless,"[8] and the suggestion that this man—now considerably behind schedule and

---

Scorer Commentary

[1] It is appropriate to tell your reader what the mood is, but remember that the prompt does not ask you to analyze the mood.

[2] Here is the student's thesis, the statement that specifies the exact argument of this essay.

[3] As with the previous essays in this book, you cannot hope to receive a top score without textual support.

[4] You need the quotation, but you also must have discussion of the quotation.

[5] Quotation.

[6] Discussion of the quotation.

[7] Further discussion...explain the relevance of the quotation to your thesis.

[8] This student has done a good job identifying the key to this essay—the precise use of words that conveys the mood, not the mood itself.

wet half-way up to his knees—is in danger, grave danger, and he might die.

Using the scientific language of a Naturalist, London explains why it is so cold. He tells the reader that the "lifeless" fingers are the result the man's blood, which is "alive," "recoil[ing]" from the severe cold. Still, the man believes he is safe because he has succeeded in building a fire.

What happens next, London calls a "disaster." This is a strong word, both denotatively and connotatively. It is not open to too much interpretation. While an emergency or a crisis might be survived, "disaster" connotes death. London even tells us that the man "had heard his own death sentence."[9] The "disaster," of course, is that the fire has been built under a snow-covered tree, which has dumped all of its snow and doused the fire. Again, London's word choice, even more than the events themselves, foreshadow the man's death. The tree does not merely dump the snow, each bough "capsize[s]" its snow. Literally, to "capsize" means to turn over, like a boat. To "capsize" means to completely disable the boat, and it carries with it a suggestion of panic and drowning. In the story, it is literally the fire that is drowned, but the suggestion that this "disaster" is going to result in the man's death is clear.

While the man attempts to build his second fire, London remarks, not only on the fingers' numbness, but he tells us, "the tremendous cold had already driven the life out of his fingers." In the next sentence, he describes the fingers as "dead." In a touch of irony, as London lists the parts of the body that are freezing, he steps up the tension by saying, he "devot[ed] his whole soul to the matches." On the one hand, London is simply stressing the fact that the man is focusing his entire being on the task of building a fire. After all, it is now a simple scientific fact that, without this fire, the man will die. On the other hand, however, the use the word "soul" at this point has to have some religious or spiritual importance. Religion teaches that death is when the soul leaves the body. Mention of the soul, then, especially in the context of listing the parts of the body that are dying, makes the fact of the man's approaching death almost obvious.

Once the fact that the man is probably going to die is made clear, London relies less on careful word choice and allows death to be apparent on the surface.[10] The man thinks that, if he kills the dog, he can warm his hands inside the dog's carcass. But the fact is that he does not have the means to kill the dog. This is the point at which real panic takes over, and the man begins to act desperately and without thought.

In the final paragraph, however, London again returns to subtle and careful word choice. He never tells us that the man is dead. Instead, he tells us that the man falls into "the most comfortable and satisfying sleep he had ever known." While the man is clearly dying, London observes the progress of the sun just beneath the horizon: "The brief day drew to a close in a long, slow twilight."

Scorer Commentary

[9] Here is an excellent discussion of a quotation.

[10] Always this student remains true to the prompt—not what is the mood, but how is the mood conveyed?

The man is dead, and the dog runs away. The image of the twilight sky returns us back to the beginning of the story, where London described the bleak sky as a covering for the dead. All along, the mood of the story has been bleak like the sky. London has been hinting that the man was going to die. Death has been present in the story, almost like another character. But London never comes right out and says the man is going to die. His hints come in subtle and precise word choice. It is this word choice that makes this otherwise simple story so exciting.[11]

Scorer Commentary

[11] The conclusion reminds us of the original issue assigned in the prompt. This is a very strong essay, focused, organized, and supported.

Sample free-response item two (independent):

The concrete is better than the abstract. The detail is better than the commonplace. The sensual is better than the intellectual. The visual is better than the mental.

—Ellen Hunnicutt

Consider the above quotation specifying some of the concerns that should govern a writer's word choice. Choose a novel, story, or play in which the author's choice of the "concrete," the "detail," the "sensual," and the "visual" is notable and makes a strong contribution to the piece's impact and meaning. Then write a well-organized essay in which you analyze the impact of the author's word choice.

You may choose a work from the list below or another novel, story, or play of comparable literary merit.

As Ellen Hunnicutt observed, in creative writing, concrete details are better than abstract commonplaces. Words that evoke sensory images are better than those that give us ideas, and what we can see is better than what we imagine[1]. Jack London's Naturalist[2] short story "To Build a Fire" is a perfect example of how a writer's effective choice of concrete, sensory, and visual words helps to create a foreboding sense of the inevitable, while also maintaining the distant or objective tone typical of a Naturalist writer. Specifically, London's concrete and sensory word choice helps him describe the overall gloominess of the day, the

---

Scorer Commentary

[1] Again, restating the issue of the prompt in your own words can help you to start out with the right focus.

[2] The writers of the AP exam will assume you have some knowledge of genre, literary movement, and so on. So, even if it is not specifically demanded by the prompt, if this kind of literary knowledge is relevant to your essay, by all means, use it.

intense cold, and the process of death.[3]

An important factor in this story is the gloom of the day.[4] The first sentence tells the reader—twice—that the day was "grey." While this is indeed a specific and visual word, it is still open to interpretation since a reader might assume that it is cloudy. To make certain his reader has a full and accurate understanding of the quality of the day, London gets even more detailed and concrete:

There was no sun nor hint of sun, though there was <u>not a cloud in the sky</u>. It was a clear day, and yet there seemed an intangible pall over the face of things, a subtle gloom that made the day dark, and that was due <u>to the absence of sun</u>.

"Not a cloud in the sky" is absolutely specific. While it doesn't explain why the day is grey, it does remove the inaccurate image the reader first got. "The absence of the sun" explains the gloom. We don't yet know why there is no sun, but an accurate reading can give the reader only a picture of a clear, cloudless, but sunless sky. Beyond the literal image, however, London also provides the evaluation of the image's impact. The greyness creates a "subtle gloom." While neither "subtle" nor "gloom" is concrete or very visual, the "pall" that the darkness casts on the day is. A "pall" is a shroud, the cloth in which dead bodies are wrapped for burial. It gives a specific name to the gloom, makes it the gloom of death.[5]

Once London establishes the physical darkness and the psychological gloom of the day, he goes on to tell his story. At noon of the day in the story, however, he pauses again to remind the reader that this is a dark, sunless day:

At twelve o'clock the day was at its brightest. Yet the sun was too far south on its winter journey to clear the horizon. The bulge of the earth intervened between it and Henderson Creek, where the man walked under a clear sky at noon and cast no shadow.

The sun's being "too far south...to clear the horizon" is probably an example of the <u>intellectual</u> language that is not as desirable as <u>sensual</u> language. "The bulge of the earth" is more visual and allows the reader to visualize the sun south of the equator so that it does not appear above the Arctic Circle. The phrase makes it absolutely clear how it can be a cloudless day and still there is no sun.

The final mention of the darkness comes at the end of the story, when the man dies. Rather than tell us explicitly that the man is dying, London says, "The brief day drew to a close in a long, slow twilight." So, the day broke "cold and grey" and ended "in a long, slow twilight." It had been a cloudless day, but it had been a short and dark day because the sun was south of the equator and the story takes place in the Arctic. These are concrete, detailed, visual facts that London provides to communicate to the reader the overall gloom of the story.

Scorer Commentary

[3] After she has stated her essential argument, this student specifies the precise aspects of the story she is going to examine.

[4] This is the first of the three aspects promised in the introduction.

[5] Again, the absolutely essential quotation and explanation/discussion. Notice that the student has formatted this relatively long quotation as a block separated from the main body of the essay.

The first sentence of the story also communicates, not only that the day was grey, but that it was "cold...exceedingly cold."[6] "Cold" is subject to interpretation, and "exceedingly cold" is not really any clearer. It is intellectual, not sensory, mental rather than visual. To make his reader's understanding of the cold more concrete, London provides the temperature, "Fifty degrees below zero," and even compares it to freezing temperature, which a reader should be able to understand, "eighty odd degrees of frost."

Even naming the temperature, however, might be considered too _mental_ or _intellectual_,[7] so London provides a few even clearer images of just how cold it is. First there is the man's beard. The moisture in his breath freezes and gives him a "muzzle of ice." This is definitely a concrete and visual image.

There is also the spittle from the man's chewing tobacco. Twice the man spits, and the spittle freezes before it even hits the ground. London writes:

[the man] spat speculatively. There was a sharp, explosive crackle that startled him. He spat again. And again, in the air, before it could fall to the snow, the spittle crackled. He knew that at fifty below spittle crackled on the snow, but this spittle had crackled in the air. Undoubtedly it was colder than fifty below—how much colder he did not know.

The "colder than fifty below" might not communicate anything meaningful to the reader, but the spittle freezing in mid-air gives us something to visualize. We know how cold it is, even if we have never experienced such cold.[8]

The cold, of course, is the cause of the man's death, which is foreshadowed by the grey gloom of the day. The process of the man's dying is another theme that London establishes using concrete, detailed, and visual language.[9] The man does not begin his slow march to death until more than halfway through the story, when he falls through some ice and wets himself and then his life-saving fire is drenched by snow from a tree. The language London uses to explain the severe cold might sound mental, but it is really extremely visual: "The cold of space smote the unprotected tip of the planet, and he, being on that unprotected tip, received the full force of the blow." "Unprotected tip" is visual and calls to mind the man's exposed nose that was freezing earlier in the story. And the verb "to smite" raises images of knights fighting dragons. This story is no longer simply about a man in the cold, it is about a man being engaged in fierce combat by the cold. It is important that it is the "cold of space" that is smiting the earth. This makes the cold the victorious knight and the man the dragon to be defeated.[10]

Scorer Commentary

[6] The coldness of the day is the second sub-topic promised in the introduction. Notice that this essay is organized by sub-topics and not by the chronology of the plot. The first discussion took the reader through the entire story, and this discussion now brings us back to the beginning.

[7] This student is very careful not to stray too far from the prompt.

[8] This is an effective combination of quotation, summary, and paraphrase, as well as original discussion.

[9] This is the third sub-topic promised in the introduction.

[10] The student carried her discussion to a full conclusion, drawing the conclusion for the reader, not leaving it up to speculation.

London continues the combat imagery. The next paragraph again might sound too scientific or mental to please Ellen Hunnicutt, but London's words are much more visual than scientifically accurate. When the body is exposed to extreme cold, the blood does indeed withdraw into the body's core. The body can live without toes or fingers, even without feet and hands, or legs and arms; but if the heart or the lungs or any other vital organ freezes, the body dies.[11] But the blood cannot "recoil" as London says it does. "Recoil" is a vivid verb that calls to mind the image of the wounded dragon shrinking away from the smiting knight. This recoiling blood is "alive," and it finds the cold "fearful." This is personification and more concrete and visual than a simple statement that the man was freezing.

When the first fire is doused, and the man struggles to build a second one, London makes the struggle absolutely concrete when he describes, not only the numbness of the man's hands, but the fact that the fingers cannot grasp the twigs and kindling, and his shivering prevents him from laying the wood for the fire.[12]

The man is dying. He is cold, and his body is freezing. In the final paragraph, when there is no doubt that this story is about the man's death, London returns to pure imagery to describe rather than narrate the death. As is true of hypothermia, the man "drows[es] off into what seem[s] to him the most comfortable and satisfying sleep he ha[s] ever known." Then the focus shifts from the man altogether, and his death is clearly implied when London writes, "The brief day drew to a close in a long, slow twilight."[13]

The "brief day," the imagery of the overall gloom of the sunless, cloudless day has foreshadowed this death from the very beginning of the story. Now, the sun that has never really risen, is setting, and the cold, dark night is falling. And the man is dying.

As a Naturalist, London does rely on "mental" or scientific language to convey his theme, but he also effectively uses vivid, visual, and other sensory words to give that theme an emotional and psychological impact. "To Build a Fire" is a suspenseful and moving piece for all of London's supposedly neutral and scientific attitude. [14]

Scorer Commentary

[11] The student is drawing on her own prior knowledge, but she is safe as long as she stays on this general, factual level. If she were to stray into interpretation of scientific fact or evaluation of London's scientific knowledge, then she might risk losing her focus.

[12] Especially given the limited time and space for an on-demand exam essay, it would be pointless for the student to quote the lines in which this situation is described. This is a literal, factual summary and is sufficient for this purpose.

[13] These are both metaphors rather than images, but the point is valid, and this has been a very strong essay up to now.

[14] Again, the well-crafted conclusion reminds us of the student's original argument and establishes that she has not lost her focus.

Exercise Two:

Multiple-choice Questions 6–10. Read the following passage and then choose the best answer to the multiple-choice questions that follow.

"A Mad Tea Party"
from *Alice's Adventures in Wonderland*

LEWIS CARROLL (1834–1898)

THERE WAS A TABLE SET OUT under a tree in front of the house, and the March Hare[1] and the Hatter[2] were having tea at it: a Dormouse[3] was sitting between them, fast asleep, and the other two were using it as a cushion, resting their elbows on it, and talking over its head. "Very uncomfortable for the Dormouse," thought Alice; "only, as it's asleep, I suppose it doesn't mind."

The table was a large one, but the three were all crowded together at one corner of it: "No room! No room!" they cried out when they saw Alice coming. "There's *plenty* of room!" said Alice indignantly, and she sat down in a large arm-chair at one end of the table.

"Have some wine," the March Hare said in an encouraging tone.

Alice looked all round the table, but there was nothing on it but tea. "I don't see any wine," she remarked.

"There isn't any," said the March Hare.

"Then it wasn't very civil of you to offer it," said Alice angrily.

"It wasn't very civil of you to sit down without being invited," said the March Hare.

"I didn't know it was *your* table," said Alice; "it's laid for a great many more than three."

"Your hair wants cutting," said the Hatter. He had been looking at Alice for some time with great curiosity, and this was his first speech.

"You should learn not to make personal remarks," Alice said with some severity; "it's very rude."

The Hatter opened his eyes very wide on hearing this; but all he *said* was, "Why is a raven like a writing-desk?"

"Come, we shall have some fun now!" thought Alice. "I'm glad they've begun asking riddles.—I believe I can guess that," she added aloud.

"Do you mean that you think you can find out the answer to it?" said the March Hare.

"Exactly so," said Alice.

---

[1] A hare is a rabbit-like rodent. To be "mad as a March hare," was a common English expression presumably derived from the hare's apparently strange behavior during the March breeding season.

[2] Notice that Carroll does *not* call this character "the Mad Hatter." "Mad as a hatter" was another common expression in England. The exact origin of the expression is not known, but two possible explanations are that the mercury often used in making men's hats occasionally resulted in madness and early death for men who followed the hatter's trade and that the verb *hatter*, meaning "to harass or to make weary," may have come to be used as a noun, a process known as "nominalization." In an earlier chapter, the Cheshire Cat told Alice that the Hatter and the March Hare were both mad.

[3] a very small rodent, mostly found in Europe, and known for its long periods of hibernation

"Then you should say what you mean," the March Hare went on.

"I do," Alice hastily replied; "at least—at least I mean what I say—that's the same thing, you know."

"Not the same thing a bit!" said the Hatter. "You might just as well say that 'I see what I eat' is the same thing as 'I eat what I see'!"

"You might just as well say," added the March Hare, "that 'I like what I get' is the same thing as 'I get what I like'!"

"You might just as well say," added the Dormouse, who seemed to be talking in his sleep, "that 'I breathe when I sleep' is the same thing as 'I sleep when I breathe'!"

"It *is* the same thing with you," said the Hatter, and here the conversation dropped, and the party sat silent for a minute, while Alice thought over all she could remember about ravens and writing-desks, which wasn't much.

The Hatter was the first to break the silence. "What day of the month is it?" he said, turning to Alice: he had taken his watch out of his pocket, and was looking at it uneasily, shaking it every now and then, and holding it to his ear.

Alice considered a little, and then said "The fourth."

"Two days wrong!" sighed the Hatter. "I told you butter wouldn't suit the works!" he added looking angrily at the March Hare.

"It was the *best* butter," the March Hare meekly replied.

"Yes, but some crumbs must have got in as well," the Hatter grumbled: "you shouldn't have put it in with the bread-knife."

The March Hare took the watch and looked at it gloomily: then he dipped it into his cup of tea, and looked at it again: but he could think of nothing better to say than his first remark, "It was the *best* butter, you know."

Alice had been looking over his shoulder with some curiosity. "What a funny watch!" she remarked. "It tells the day of the month, and doesn't tell what o'clock it is!"

"Why should it?" muttered the Hatter. "Does *your* watch tell you what year it is?"

"Of course not," Alice replied very readily: "but that's because it stays the same year for such a long time together."

"Which is just the case with *mine*," said the Hatter.

Alice felt dreadfully puzzled. The Hatter's remark seemed to have no sort of meaning in it, and yet it was certainly English. "I don't quite understand you," she said, as politely as she could.

"The Dormouse is asleep again," said the Hatter, and he poured a little hot tea upon its nose.

The Dormouse shook its head impatiently, and said, without opening its eyes, "Of course, of course; just what I was going to remark myself."

"Have you guessed the riddle yet?" the Hatter said, turning to Alice again.

"No, I give it up," Alice replied: "what's the answer?"

"I haven't the slightest idea," said the Hatter.

"Nor I," said the March Hare.

Alice sighed wearily. "I think you might do something better with the time," she said, "than waste it in asking riddles that have no answers."[1]

---

[1] The fact is, Lewis Carroll intended this riddle to have no answer. When pressed by readers for the solution, he created a few but always insisted that he never intended this riddle to have an answer.

"If you knew Time as well as I do," said the Hatter, "you wouldn't talk about wasting it. It's *him*."

"I don't know what you mean," said Alice.

"Of course you don't!" the Hatter said, tossing his head contemptuously. "I dare say you never even spoke to Time!"

"Perhaps not," Alice cautiously replied: "but I know I have to beat time when I learn music."

"Ah! that accounts for it," said the Hatter. "He won't stand beating. Now, if you only kept on good terms with him, he'd do almost anything you liked with the clock. For instance, suppose it were nine o'clock in the morning, just time to begin lessons: you'd only have to whisper a hint to Time, and round goes the clock in a twinkling! Half-past one, time for dinner!"

("I only wish it was," the March Hare said to itself in a whisper.)

"That would be grand, certainly," said Alice thoughtfully: "but then—I shouldn't be hungry for it, you know."

"Not at first, perhaps," said the Hatter: "but you could keep it to half-past one as long as you liked."

"Is that the way *you* manage?" Alice asked.

The Hatter shook his head mournfully. "Not I!" he replied. "We quarrelled last March—just before *he* went mad, you know—" (pointing with his tea spoon at the March Hare,) "—it was at the great concert given by the Queen of Hearts, and I had to sing

"Twinkle, twinkle, little bat!

How I wonder what you're at!"

You know the song, perhaps?"

"I've heard something like it," said Alice.

"It goes on, you know," the Hatter continued, "in this way:—

"Up above the world you fly,

Like a tea-tray in the sky.

Twinkle, twinkle—"

Here the Dormouse shook itself, and began singing in its sleep "Twinkle, twinkle, twinkle, twinkle—" and went on so long that they had to pinch it to make it stop.

"Well, I'd hardly finished the first verse," said the Hatter, "when the Queen jumped up and bawled out, 'He's murdering the time! Off with his head!'"

"How dreadfully savage!" exclaimed Alice.

"And ever since that," the Hatter went on in a mournful tone, "he won't do a thing I ask! It's always six o'clock now."

A bright idea came into Alice's head. "Is that the reason so many tea-things are put out here?" she asked.

"Yes, that's it," said the Hatter with a sigh: "it's always tea-time, and we've no time to wash the things between whiles."

"Then you keep moving round, I suppose?" said Alice.

"Exactly so," said the Hatter: "as the things get used up."

"But what happens when you come to the beginning again?" Alice ventured to ask.

"Suppose we change the subject," the March Hare interrupted, yawning. "I'm getting tired of this. I vote the young lady tells us a story."

"I'm afraid I don't know one," said Alice, rather alarmed at the proposal.

"Then the Dormouse shall!" they both cried. "Wake up, Dormouse!" And they pinched it on both sides at once.

The Dormouse slowly opened his eyes. "I wasn't asleep," he said in a hoarse, feeble voice: "I heard every word you fellows were saying."

"Tell us a story!" said the March Hare.

"Yes, please do!" pleaded Alice.

"And be quick about it," added the Hatter, "or you'll be asleep again before it's done."

"Once upon a time there were three little sisters," the Dormouse began in a great hurry; "and their names were Elsie, Lacie, and Tillie; and they lived at the bottom of a well—"

"What did they live on?" said Alice, who always took a great interest in questions of eating and drinking.

"They lived on treacle," said the Dormouse, after thinking a minute or two.

"They couldn't have done that, you know," Alice gently remarked; "they'd have been ill."

"So they were," said the Dormouse; "*very* ill."

Alice tried to fancy to herself what such an extraordinary ways of living would be like, but it puzzled her too much, so she went on: "But why did they live at the bottom of a well?"

"Take some more tea," the March Hare said to Alice, very earnestly.

"I've had nothing yet," Alice replied in an offended tone, "so I can't take more."

"You mean you can't take *less*," said the Hatter: "it's very easy to take *more* than nothing."

"Nobody asked *your* opinion," said Alice.

"Who's making personal remarks now?" the Hatter asked triumphantly.

Alice did not quite know what to say to this: so she helped herself to some tea and bread-and-butter, and then turned to the Dormouse, and repeated her question. "Why did they live at the bottom of a well?"

The Dormouse again took a minute or two to think about it, and then said, "It was a treacle-well."

"There's no such thing!" Alice was beginning very angrily, but the Hatter and the March Hare went "Sh! sh!" and the Dormouse sulkily remarked, "If you can't be civil, you'd better finish the story for yourself."

"No, please go on!" Alice said very humbly; "I won't interrupt again. I dare say there may be *one*."

"One, indeed!" said the Dormouse indignantly. However, he consented to go on. "And so these three little sisters—they were learning to draw, you know—"

"What did they draw?" said Alice, quite forgetting her promise.

"Treacle," said the Dormouse, without considering at all this time.

"I want a clean cup," interrupted the Hatter: "let's all move one place on."

He moved on as he spoke, and the Dormouse followed him: the March Hare moved into the Dormouse's place, and Alice rather unwillingly took the place of the March Hare. The

Hatter was the only one who got any advantage from the change: and Alice was a good deal worse off than before, as the March Hare had just upset the milk-jug into his plate.

Alice did not wish to offend the Dormouse again, so she began very cautiously: "But I don't understand. Where did they draw the treacle from?"

"You can draw water out of a water-well," said the Hatter; "so I should think you could draw treacle out of a treacle-well—eh, stupid?"

"But they were *in* the well," Alice said to the Dormouse, not choosing to notice this last remark.

"Of course they were," said the Dormouse; "—well in."

This answer so confused poor Alice, that she let the Dormouse go on for some time without interrupting it.

"They were learning to draw," the Dormouse went on, yawning and rubbing its eyes, for it was getting very sleepy; "and they drew all manner of things—everything that begins with an M—"

"Why with an M?" said Alice.

"Why not?" said the March Hare.

Alice was silent.

The Dormouse had closed its eyes by this time, and was going off into a doze; but, on being pinched by the Hatter, it woke up again with a little shriek, and went on: "—that begins with an M, such as mouse-traps, and the moon, and memory, and muchness— you know you say things are 'much of a muchness'[1]—did you ever see such a thing as a drawing of a muchness?"

"Really, now you ask me," said Alice, very much confused, "I don't think—"

"Then you shouldn't talk," said the Hatter.

This piece of rudeness was more than Alice could bear: she got up in great disgust, and walked off; the Dormouse fell asleep instantly, and neither of the others took the least notice of her going, though she looked back once or twice, half hoping that they would call after her: the last time she saw them, they were trying to put the Dormouse into the teapot.

"At any rate I'll never go *there* again!" said Alice as she picked her way through the wood. "It's the stupidest tea-party I ever was at in all my life!"

---

[1] a common phrase in Great Britain that means two things are so similar as to be virtually indistinguishable

Multiple-Choice Questions 6-10:

6. In this passage, the March Hare's and the Hatter's "madness" is primarily the result of a/n

    A. lack of commonly-accepted social manners.

    B. inattention to dialectical differences.

    C. application of cultural stereotypes and archetypes.

    D. strict adherence to literal meanings.

    E. total disregard for denotation and accepted convention.

7. In this passage, Lewis Carroll uses language primarily to

    A. clarify and defend.

    B. instruct and enlighten.

    C. challenge and dispute.

    D. confuse and perplex.

    E. amuse and delight.

8. On a thematic level, this passage most likely illustrates the

    A. basic incivility of people.

    B. insufficiency of language.

    C. willfulness of young girls.

    D. comic possibilities of caricature.

    E. complexities of human emotion.

9. The play on the word *draw* in the Dormouse's story is based on the words' being

    A. homonyms.

    B. homophones.

    C. homographs.

    D. synonyms.

    E. antonyms.

10. All of the following contribute to the comedy of this passage EXCEPT

    A. stereotype.

    B. misperception.

    C. slapstick.

    D. non sequitur.

    E. word play.

Free-response item 3 (text-based)

Carefully read "A Mad Tea Party" from Lewis Carroll's *Alice's Adventures in Wonderland* and then write a thoughtful, well-supported essay in which you analyze the ways in which Carroll uses wordplay, ambiguity, and other quirks of language to create an illusion of madness and illogic. Do not merely summarize the plot of the selection.

Before you write your essay:

1. **Make sure you understand exactly what you're being asked to write about.**

   - List all of the verbs in the prompt.

   - Underline the verb that describes the essay.

   - Write the direct object of that verb.

2. **Make sure you have something valid to write about.**

   - Write a sentence or two that make a positive and focused statement about the topic.

   - Make sure these sentences address all of the issues and subpoints specified in the prompt.

3. **Review the selection and find your textual support.**

4. **Write your essay.**

   - Keep referring to the prompt and whatever you underlined or highlighted in the selection to make sure you're on track and addressing everything the prompt wants you to address.

Free-response item 4 (independent)

Sigmund Freud (1856–1939) wrote, "Neurosis is the inability to tolerate ambiguity." This notion of madness—a rational individual's inability to understand or adapt to the apparently irrational—is a common theme in Western literature. Think of a novel or play in which the theme or conflict is based on something like Freud's definition of neurosis. Then, write a well-organized and reasoned essay in which you analyze the role of madness in the overall meaning of the work. Do not merely summarize the plot of the novel or play.

Before you write your essay:

1. **Make sure you understand exactly what you're being asked to write about.**

   - List all of the verbs in the prompt.
   - Underline the verb that describes the essay.
   - Write the direct object of that verb.

2. **Choose an appropriate selection.**

   Actually, because you're using this book, your teacher probably wants you to write your essay on whatever story, article, or poem, etc., the writing prompt follows.

3. **Make sure you have something to say about both the topic and your selected literature.**

   - Jot down key plot events
   - Think in terms of plot structure: rising action, climax, falling action, and so on.
   - List characters
   - Think in terms of function or role—protagonist or antagonist
   - Think in terms of type—hero, anti-hero, foil, clown, etc.

4. **Make sure you jot down notes that pertain to the assigned topic.**

   - Jot down quotations or at least close paraphrases.

   - Jot down everything you know and remember about the assigned topic.

5. **Make sure you are clear about what you are going to say.**

   - Write a sentence or two that make a positive and focused statement about the topic.

   - Make sure these sentences address all of the issues and subpoints specified in the prompt.

6. **Write your essay.** ⏻

Issues of Interpretation and Inference

There is a common misperception about topics that are open to multiple interpretations. Many people—many intelligent and educated people—mistakenly believe that if something is open to a number of interpretations, *none* of those interpretations can be wrong. A similar misperception is that all possible interpretations are equally valid.

You may even accept those two misperceptions and are right now planning the letter you are going to write to argue with us—so let's examine a few examples.

Consider the first stanza of a famous poem by Scottish poet Robert Burns:

> O, my love is like a red, red rose,
> That is newly sprung in June.
> O, my love is like the melody,
> That is sweetly played in tune.

Certainly, the similes are open to interpretation. In what way(s) is Burns's love like a rose, specifically a red rose? Is she like a rose because she, too, is red? Burns goes on to say that this rose was "newly sprung in June," so perhaps his love is young, like a new June rose. Roses are generally regarded as beautiful, so perhaps Burns simply means that his love is beautiful.

Perhaps he means some combination of these—or all of these, plus a few we have not mentioned yet.

Some might say that roses in the florist shop are expensive, so maybe he is criticizing his love for being extravagant, for costing him too much money. Anyone who has tended a rose garden knows that roses are not the lowest-maintenance plants available. They are subject to insects, molds, wilt, and a whole host of other maladies. Perhaps, then, Burns is criticizing his love for being spoiled, high maintenance, demanding.

Chances are, though, he's not. Chances are the person who is eager to focus on the negative traits of the rose and transfer them to the subject of the poem is missing the point and offering an unsupportable or invalid interpretation. Anyone who would offer a valid and supportable interpretation must keep in mind that Burns's "rose" is "newly sprung in June." We must also take into account that the love is also "melody / That is sweetly played in tune."

Chances are the positive connotations of this sweet and in-tune melody would cancel out any negative interpretations we would want to attach to the rose. Burns is clearly not criticizing or complaining about his love.

Just because there *are* many possible interpretations does not mean that they are all equally valid.

The same is true of an inference. Almost certainly you have had someone at some time take something you have said "the wrong way," getting angry or hurt or insulted and causing you to protest, "That's not what I meant," or "I didn't mean it that way."

Not every reader's or listener's inference reflects a complete or careful or accurate understanding of what the writer or speaker has actually said.

The key—as always when dealing with language and literature—is the text.

The Difference between Interpretation and Inference

Inference is the thought process by which a person must think beyond whatever information is immediately before him or her to arrive at a conclusion. Katherine Mansfield never explicitly states that Miss Brill (see page 30) is saddened by the young couple's reaction to her fur stole, but the reader infers her sorrow from her actions in the closing paragraphs of the story:

> On her way home she usually bought a slice of honey-cake at the baker's. It was her Sunday treat. Sometimes there was an almond in her slice, sometimes not. It made a great difference. If there was an almond it was like carrying home a tiny present—a surprise—something that might very well not have been there. She hurried on the almond Sundays and struck the match for the kettle in quite a dashing way.
>
> But to-day she passed the baker's by, climbed the stairs, went into the little dark room—her room like a cupboard—and sat down on the red eiderdown. She sat there for a long time. The box that the fur came out of was on the bed. She unclasped the necklet quickly; quickly, without looking, laid it inside. But when she put the lid on she thought she heard something crying.

The ability to examine a text and infer meaning is an important skill for the Advanced Placement student. It is a skill that can be learned, but like all skills, it must be practiced. Also like most skills, there are more effective and less effective ways to arrive at a conclusion.

Contrary to what you might believe, while there most certainly is a wide range of appropriate inferences to be drawn from most texts, there is also a fairly wide range of *inappropriate inferences* that can be drawn from a text.

When one is understanding on an inferential level, one might indeed be wrong.

The processes of drawing an inference mirror the thought process of **inductive** and **deductive** reasoning.

Inductive reasoning is the process of drawing a conclusion (an inference) from a variety of independent facts, details, etc. When a pollster surveys 10,000 people about their opinions on school safety and then reports that Americans feel their schools are safe, the pollster has arrived at that conclusion by **inductive reasoning**.

When a soap company chooses a certain number of urban neighborhoods, towns, and suburban communities to test-market a new soap product and then decides not to put the soap on the market, the company has arrived at that decision by **inductive reasoning**.

In order for the inference or conclusion arrived at through inductive reasoning to be valid, certain conditions must be met. If any of them are not, the reasoning is flawed, and the conclusion will be faulty, if not downright invalid.

1. All of the facts, details, etc., that contributed to the conclusion must be true and verifiable or mutually agreed upon by all parties. There must also be a large enough number of examples on which to base a valid conclusion.

   - e.g., Memorial Day always falls on a Monday. Presidents Day always falls on a Monday. Christmas and Easter fall on Mondays. Monday must be the day for big holidays.

     It is not factually true that Christmas and Easter fall on Mondays (in fact, Easter never falls on Monday), so the conclusion cannot be valid. Also, four examples is not nearly enough to support such a broad conclusion. All one would have to do is provide one or two non-Monday holidays to refute this conclusion.

     On June 17, the sun rises a minute earlier and sets a minute later than on June 16. Likewise, on June 18, the sun rises a minute earlier and sets a minute later than on June 17. The same phenomenon occurs on June 19 and June 20. Eventually, the sun will rise so early and set so late that there will be no night.

Clearly, this is an invalid conclusion, even though it seems based on accurate observation and reporting of a valid phenomenon. The problem is that, had the observer made a few more observations, he would have seen the phenomenon reverse itself to produce shorter days and longer nights.

2. The conclusion must follow logically from the facts, details, etc., that contributed to the conclusion. A conclusion that does not is called a *non sequitur.*

   - e.g., All of the boys and girls in Mr. Kaplan's homeroom wore red polo shirts yesterday. Red polo shirts must have been on sale at the department store.

   Of all the reasons for all of the students to wear identical shirts on the same day, a sale in a particular store is probably one of the least *likely.*

   Julius Caesar took a day from February and added it to the month that bore his name, July. Caesar Augustus also took a day from February and added it to "his" month, August. They must have enjoyed the warm weather and wanted to make the summer longer.

   The logic of this conclusion is flawed on at least two levels. Clearly the name or number of a particular day has nothing to do with that day's weather, but to conclude that Caesar's primary reason for adding a day to a month named in his honor was related to the climate —and not his egotism —is certainly a non sequitur.

Deductive reasoning is the process of examining one or more fairly specific ideas or *premises*, that are already known and using them to arrive at a **conclusion (inference)** about something that is not yet known. If that soap company knows that environmentally friendly products appeal to upper-middle-class professionals, and that these upper-middle-class professionals usually live either in the suburbs or in certain "gentrified" neighborhoods in the city, their decision to market their environmentally friendly soap in those areas is the result of **deductive reasoning**.

Pollsters love to infer future events based on past outcomes. If they know that Independent male voters aged 30 and over tend to vote for any non-mainstream candidate, and they see that Candidate X is basing his campaign on the fact that he is the offspring of an illegal immigrant and a cancer-surviving woman, their conclusion that this candidate will appeal to this demographic is based on **deductive reasoning**.

Again, however, certain conditions must be met in order for an inference based on deductive reasoning to be valid. If any of them are not, the reasoning is flawed, and the conclusion will be faulty if not downright invalid.

1. Both premises must be agreed upon as true by all parties. *To base an argument on a premise that not everyone accepts as true it called* **begging the question.**

   - e.g., Since *Huckleberry Finn* is such an offensive, racist book, it should be dropped from the curriculum and removed from the school library.

     In order for the decision to drop the book from the curriculum to be at all valid, we must first make sure that everyone involved agrees with the premise that it is "an offensive, racist book."

     Everyone knows that multiple-choice questions serve no purpose, so our mid-term and final exams should contain only essay questions.

     Does "everyone know" that multiple-choice questions "serve no purpose"?

2. The conclusion must follow logically from the premises. A conclusion that does not follow logically from the premises is another form of *non sequitur.*

   - e.g., Listening to music is enjoyable, but the hearing impaired cannot listen to music. They must be very unhappy.

     Let's assume for the sake of argument that we all generally agree with the first premise, that listening to music is enjoyable—if we didn't, we would be **begging the question.** *Even then, however, the conclusion that the hearing impaired are unhappy does not* **necessarily** *follow from the fact that they cannot hear music. Thus, even with valid premises, we have an invalid conclusion or inference.*

     One of the stated purposes for sports programs in high school is to teach sportsmanship, so students who do not participate in sports never get to learn this important attitude.

     Unless it's true that participation in sports is the only *way to learn sportsmanship, the conclusion does not follow the premise—even though the premise is true.*

3. To prove the validity of a conclusion (or inference), the arguer should be absolutely clear about all of the steps between the initial premises and the final conclusion. To arrive at even a valid conclusion without revealing all of the points that led there is to make a type of *non sequitur* often called a **quantum leap.**

   - e.g., If all humans breathe air, and all politicians are humans, they should see the need to pass this anti-pollution legislation.

     Both of the premises are true, and the conclusion might actually be something worth considering, but there are quite a few ideas that need to be considered on the way from politicians being human to the passage of clean air legislation—the health benefits of clean air, something about the legislation's being in their own best interests, etc.

- e.g., So much marine life is threatened by commercial overfishing, they should just ban seafood altogether.

*To dismiss another's argument on the basis of a quantum leap is to fall into the logical fallacy of the **slippery slope**.*

- e.g., If we relax the dress code to allow jeans on Friday, soon kids will be coming to school in their pajamas.

First, regardless of how many amendments are made to the dress code, it is highly unlikely that pajamas will ever really be allowed. Second, the progression from jeans on Friday to pajamas involves many more than the single step suggested here.

- e.g., Giving women the right to vote will be the destruction of the American family!

Inference, then, takes available information and looks outward to a prediction or conclusion. An inference can be inappropriate or invalid if it is not based on facts, an accurate understanding of the facts, or leaves out important steps in the reasoning process.

Interpretation, on the other hand, examines the available information and strives to understand it on more than only a literal level. There are two significant clues to the condition of Miss Brill's fur piece. First is the description of the fur essentially from Miss Brill's perception:

> She had taken it out of its box that afternoon, shaken out the moth-powder, given it a good brush, and rubbed the life back into the dim little eyes. "What has been happening to me?" said the sad little eyes. Oh, how sweet it was to see them snap at her again from the red eiderdown!... But the nose, which was of some black composition, wasn't at all firm. It must have had a knock, somehow. Never mind—a little dab of black sealing-wax when the time came—when it was absolutely necessary...

Apparently, the fur is old—dulled with "moth powder," its "dim little" and "sad little" eyes lifeless, and the artificial nose soft and in need of sealing wax. Nevertheless, at least in Miss Brill's eyes, the beloved fur piece is fully presentable, and she is pleased to be wearing it again.

Then, toward the end of the story, Katherine Mansfield provides the girl's perception of the same fur:

> "It's her fu-ur which is so funny," giggled the girl. "It's exactly like a fried whiting."

This assessment is not a complete contradiction of the earlier one, but it does cast a different light on how the reader views what Miss Brill was so fond of. The fur is old and shabby.

This understanding of Miss Brill's fur is not an inference because it does not rely on any prior knowledge or outside information on the part of the reader. By simply reading the text and comparing the information provided in two different sections, the reader arrives at the conclusion that Miss Brill's fur is shabby.

This is **interpretation**.

Like inference, there is usually going to be a range of acceptable interpretations to a particular passage. Also, like inference, however, there are going to be a number of inappropriate or invalid interpretations. The validity of an interpretation depends largely on the interpreter's ability to understand the meanings (both denotative and connotative) of the words, phrases, and sentences in the text.

Let's look at a few passages that rely heavily on reader inference and interpretation to establish their point. Then we'll look at how an Advanced Placement student might deal with questions about these passages on an exam.

Letter to President Thomas Jefferson and Jefferson's Reply

Beginning in the sixteenth century, English Protestants who believed the religious reforms that had established the official Church of England were superficial and ineffective formed a series of "dissenter" or "separatist" groups. Each of these groups developed its own system of beliefs and practices, one of which was the baptism of adults instead of infants and baptism by full immersion into water. These "Baptists," as they came to be known, like every other minority religion in England, were allowed to practice their own faith, but were also required to attend Anglican worship services as least once a year and to pay a tax to the Anglican Church.

When England began to colonize America, the colonists brought with them the tension between the official Church of England and the several minority faiths that desired full religious freedom. Even after the Revolutionary War, the issue of whether any one faith or denomination could hold sway over any others was debated. The original Constitution did not provide any protections for minority religions and their adherents, so these protections were included in the First Amendment.

Many state Constitutions, however, still did not specify an individual's protection against being forced to participate in, or financially support, a church not of his or her choosing. In October 1801, the Danbury Baptist Association of Danbury, Connecticut sent the following letter to newly elected President Thomas Jefferson. In this famous letter, they express their concern about the lack in the Connecticut State Constitution of explicit protection of religious liberty. Their fear, as stated in their letter to Jefferson, was that, since the practice of their religion was seen as a privilege extended by the legislature and not as a right, laws could be enacted either prohibiting the practice of their religion or severely curtailing their rights as citizens because of such practice.

Here is their letter:

1   The address of the Danbury Baptists Association in the state of Connecticut, assembled October 7, 1801. To Thomas Jefferson, Esq., President of the United States of America.

Sir,

2   Among the many million in America and Europe who rejoice in your election to office; we embrace the first opportunity which we have enjoyed in our collective capacity, since your inauguration, to express our great satisfaction, in your appointment to the <u>chief magistracy in the United States:</u>[1] And though our mode of expression may be less courtly and pompous than what many others clothe their addresses with, we beg you, sir, to believe that <u>none are more sincere.</u>[2]

3   Our sentiments are uniformly on the side of <u>religious liberty</u>—[3] <u>that religion is at all times and places a matter between God and individuals</u>—[4] <u>that no man ought to suffer in name, person, or effects on account of his religious</u> opinions—[5] <u>that the legitimate power of civil government extends no further than to punish the man who works ill to his neighbors;</u>[6] But, sir, our constitution of government is not specific.[7] Our ancient charter together with the law made coincident therewith, were adopted as the basis of our government, <u>at the time of our revolution;</u>[8] and such had been our laws and usages, and such still are; that religion is considered as the first object of legislation; and therefore what religious privileges we enjoy <u>(as a minor part of the state)</u>[9] we enjoy as favors granted, and not as <u>inalienable rights;</u>[10] and these favors we receive at the expense of such

---

Sample Student Commentary

[1] This opening is potentially confusing, as it might sound to a modern reader as if the writer were confusing the president and chief justice. In the eighteenth and early nineteenth centuries, however, the phrase Chief Magistrate was used to describe the presidency. In his second inaugural address in 1793, George Washington himself referred to the president as the nation's "Chief Magistrate." Thus, the writer of this letter is using accepted terminology of the day.

[2] Are the writers, perhaps, sounding defensive that their letter might be ignored because of the simplicity of their language? Are they, perhaps, less educated and afraid that they will not be taken seriously? Or are they, perhaps, simply being polite in their greeting?

[3] A modern reader might wonder about the use of the dash, but before the early twentieth century, the dash was used as a substitute for several punctuation marks, including the comma and the colon. What follows each dash is essentially an appositive, additional information on what the writers mean by "religious liberty."

[4] First appositive.

[5] Second appositive.

[6] Third appositive.

[7] As the First Amendment to the Constitution of the United States has been law for ten years, the writers must be referring to the Constitution of the State of Connecticut.

[8] Since the U.S. Constitution was not adopted as law until 1788, this sentence further suggests that the writers are talking about their state constitution.

[9] "Minor parts of the state" = "minorities."

[10] "The word choice and sentence structure are difficult here, but they are decipherable. Essentially, the writers are noting that their "privilege" to practice their minority religion exists—under their state law—as a "favor granted" by the government rather than an "inalienable right."

degrading acknowledgements as are inconsistent with the rights of freemen.[11] It is not to be wondered at therefore; if those who seek after power and gain under the pretense of government and religion should reproach their fellow men—should reproach their Chief magistrate, as an enemy of religion, law, and good order,[12] because he will not, dare not, assume the prerogatives of Jehovah and make laws to govern the kingdom of Christ.[13]

4 Sir, we are sensible that the president of the United States is not the national legislator, and also sensible that the national government cannot destroy the laws of each state;[14] but our hopes are strong that the sentiments of our beloved president, which have had such genial effect already,[15] like the radiant beams of the sun, will shine and prevail through all these states and all the world, till hierarchy and tyranny be destroyed from the earth. Sir, when we reflect on your past services, and see a glow of philanthropy and good will shining forth in a course of more than thirty years we have reason to believe that America's God has raised you up to fill the chair of state out of that goodwill which he bears to the millions which you preside over.[16] May God strengthen you for your arduous task which providence and the voice of the people have called you to sustain and support you enjoy administration[17] against all the predetermined opposition of those who wish to raise to wealth and importance on the poverty and subjection of the people.[18]

5 And may the Lord preserve you safe from every evil and bring you at last to his heavenly kingdom through Jesus Christ our Glorious Mediator.

Signed in behalf of the association,
Nehemiah Dodge
Ephraim Robbins
Stephen S. Nelson

Sample Student Commentary

[11] The writers do not specify what the "degrading acknowledgments" are, but remember that in England, members of any minority denomination were required to attend an Anglican service at least once a year and pay a tax to the Anglican church.

[12] Jefferson had indeed been called an "enemy of religion" for his refusal to support any state or national "official religion" or to support any law requiring religious practice of individual citizens. At this point, however, it might not be clear whether the writers of this letter, by saying, "It is not to be wondered at…" are also criticizing Jefferson.

[13] Here it seems clear that they are not criticizing Jefferson. Surely, an association of clergypersons would not support the president's assuming the prerogatives of God.

[14] Both are facts according to the Constitution of the United States.

[15] The writers do not specify which of Jefferson's "sentiments" have had this "genial effect" or what this "genial effect" is, but the context of the earlier paragraph supports a conclusion that the writers are still talking about the rights of citizens to practice minority religions without penalty.

[16] The "you" referred to in this sentence must be Jefferson, the man to whom this letter is addressed. The "he" must be "America's God."

[17] According to the Oxford English Dictionary, one denotation of enjoy is to put into a joyous condition, to make happy. Therefore, this sentence might literally be read: May God strengthen you…sustain and support you… [and] give joy to [your] administration.

[18] This final complaint might seem out of context unless we consider that the "expense of…degrading acknowledgements" complained of in the second paragraph might very well include mandatory attendance in a church not of the writers' choosing and mandatory tax payments to a church not of their choosing.

This is President Jefferson's response. While copies of the original draft of the letter still exist, the following reflects the letter as Jefferson edited and sent it:

Mr. President[19]

6   To messers Nehemiah Dodge, Ephraim Robbins, & Stephen S. Nelson, a committee of the Danbury Baptist association in the state of Connecticut.

Gentlemen

7   The affectionate sentiments of esteem and approbation which you are so good as to express towards me, on behalf of the Danbury Baptist association, give me the highest satisfaction. <u>My duties dictate a faithful and zealous pursuit of the interests of my constituents,</u>[20] <u>& in proportion as they</u>[21] are persuaded of my fidelity to those duties, the discharge of them becomes more and more pleasing.

8   Believing with you[22] <u>that religion is a matter which lies solely between Man & his God,</u>[23] <u>that he owes account to none other for his faith or his worship,</u>[24] <u>that the legitimate powers of government reach actions only, & not opinions, I</u>[25] contemplate with sovereign reverence that act of the whole American people which declared that their legislature should "<u>make no law respecting an establishment of religion, or prohibiting the free exercise thereof,</u>"[26] <u>thus building a wall of separation between Church & State.</u>[27] Adhering to this expression of the supreme will of the nation[28] in behalf of the rights of conscience, I shall see with sincere satisfaction the progress of those sentiments which tend to restore to man all his <u>natural rights,</u>[29] convinced he has <u>no natural right in opposition to his social duties.</u>[30]

9   I reciprocate your kind prayers for the protection & blessing of the common father and creator of man, and tender you for yourselves & your religious association assurances of my high respect & esteem.

(signed) Thomas Jefferson
Jan.1.1802.

Sample Student Commentary

[19] Of the Danbury Baptist Association.

[20] As the writers of the Danbury letter expressed hope that their complaint would be heard, Jefferson is assuring them that he does listen to the citizenry of the United States.

[21] Grammatically, "they" must refer to Jefferson's "constituents."

[22] There will be a total of three relative clauses that specify on what points Jefferson agrees with the Danbury Association. This is the first.

[23] The second.

[24] And this is the third.

[25] Grammatically, we have ended the dependent clause that began "Believing with you." "I" is subject of the main clause of this sentence.

[26] This is a direct quotation from the First Amendment.

[27] This is a famous and often debated phrase that has been subject to countless interpretations.

[28] Why would Jefferson emphasize not merely "the will" of the people, but "the supreme will of the nation"?

[29] To infer what Jefferson might mean by "all his natural rights," we must refer to the Danbury letter in which the writers complained that whatever "religious privileges [they] enjoy[ed] (as a minor part of the state) [they] enjoy as favors granted, and not as inalienable rights."

[30] In order to interpret this closing statement accurately and justly, you'd have to find what Jefferson may have meant by social duties. He did, in fact, write quite a bit about what an individual owed to his or her society, and these included support of "private charities" and "public purposes," as well as "contributing to the necessities of society." In this closing sentence of the body of the letter, Jefferson is saying that no individual has a "natural right" to ignore his "social duties."

Sample Multiple-Choice Questions

1. **When the writers of the Danbury letter call themselves "a minor part of the state" (paragraph 3), they most likely mean that they are**
   A. underage.
   B. *small in number.*
   C. unimportant.
   D. lacking influence.
   E. a fledgling group.

2. **President Jefferson does all of the following in his reply EXCEPT**
   A. agree in principle.
   B. offer assurance.
   C. express gratitude.
   D. voice optimism.
   E. *promise assistance.*

3. **One can reasonably infer from the Danbury writers' assertion, "It is not to be wondered at therefore; if those who seek after power and gain under the pretense of government and religion should reproach their fellow men—should reproach their Chief magistrate, as an enemy of religion, law, and good order..." (paragraph 3), that**
   A. Jefferson stood opposed to religion.
   B. the Danbury writers joined in criticism of Jefferson.
   C. *Jefferson had been criticized as "an enemy of religion."*
   D. the Jefferson administration had become a "pretense of government."
   E. the Danbury writers were criticizing the courts.

4. **The most likely interpretation of "degrading acknowledgements" (paragraph 3) is**
   A. *loss of status and property.*
   B. fines and imprisonment.
   C. public renunciation of doctrine.
   D. infringement on worship.
   E. denial of natural rights.

5. **Which of the following phrases, as used in the passage, can be interpreted as synonymous with *religious faith*?**
   A. religious privileges.
   B. *religious opinion.*
   C. faith and worship.
   D. sovereign reverence.
   E. rights of conscience.

Answers and Explanations:

1. While (A) is certainly one denotation of "minor," the writers of the letter are all, presumably, licensed preachers, members of an association, and probably adults. Certainly, nothing in the letter alludes to their age. (C) and (D) might be tempting, as the writers clearly feel as if they have been relegated to a secondary, powerless status, but they allude to themselves as "minor" in fact, not in attitude—and *they* acknowledge this "minor" status. Nothing suggests (E), and (E) is not a primary understanding of the term. **(B) is the most likely answer.** The writers are recognizing their status as a numerical minority in their society and are questioning the fact that their lack of numbers has resulted in their being dealt with unjustly by the laws of their state.

2. (A) is eliminated by the opening of the second paragraph of Jefferson's letter: "Believing with you…" (B) is eliminated in the same paragraph by his quoting the portion of the First Amendment that addresses the Danbury Association's concerns. (C) occurs in the opening of the letter. Jefferson's assertion, "I shall see with sincere satisfaction the progress of those sentiments…" eliminates D. Nowhere in the letter, however, does Jefferson actually offer to take any kind of action or to help them in any way. His letter assures them of his agreement, reminds them of the "establishment clause" in the First Amendment, and expresses the hope that popular sentiment will evolve into a state of complete religious tolerance. **Thus, (E) is the correct answer.**

3. The idiom "it is not to be wondered at" is clearly the equivalent of today's "no wonder." The surface meaning of the sentence, then, can be paraphrased, "It is no wonder that those who use the pretext of government and religion to increase their own wealth and power criticize their President as anti-religion." The point is that Jefferson has been thus criticized, not that he is opposed to religion. Thus, (A) is eliminated. (B) can be eliminated by the writers' identifying Jefferson's critics as "those who seek after power and gain under the pretense of government and religion," a condemnation they would not levy on themselves when later they complain that they have been reduced to "poverty and subjection." (D) is easily eliminated as, grammatically and syntactically, the phrase "pretense of government" refers to "those who seek after power and gain" and not the President or his administration. (E) would tempt only those students who misread the identification of the president at the "Chief magistrate." **(C) is the only reasonable inference.** The explanation of why Jefferson has been criticized in this way follows the quoted clause ("because he will not, dare not, assume the prerogatives of Jehovah and make laws to govern the kingdom of Christ"). The Danbury writers are claiming that, because of Jefferson's admitted stance on freedom of religion, it is no wonder those who hoped to use religion and government as a means of increasing their own wealth and power would criticize Jefferson as an "enemy of religion."

4. What exactly the Danbury writers mean by this phrase is never made explicit. Historical precedent, of course, suggests that members of minority religions may have been required to attend worship and financially support the majority or "official" church. That they complain of being reduced to "poverty" might suggest they are fined, to infer "imprisonment" from "subjection" is a stretch, so (B) is eliminated. (C) and (D) are clearly unsupportable as the Danbury writers have been granted "religious privileges." The issue is that these privileges have come at a price. (E) might tempt some, but again, the Danbury writers have not really been denied the right. The right has been granted them, however, in the guise of a privilege or a "favor granted." Historically, we know that practitioners of a minority religion were granted a lower status as citizens, required to attend a church they did not choose and to pay a tax to that official church. **Thus, (A) is the best answer**.

5. (A) refers to the *right* to one's religious convictions, not to the *nature* of those convictions. (C) alludes to both content and practice, but a term cannot be a synonym of itself, so this is an unlikely choice. (D) refers to Jefferson's attitude toward the First Amendment. (E) is tempting, but it clearly refers to the right to one's own faith rather than to the faith itself. **(B) is the best answer**. The Danbury writers argue that one's "religious opinions" should not be the cause of pain, or loss of life or property. These "opinions" are clearly the substance of the religion, the faith.

Sample free-response item one (text-based):

"Separation of Church and State" is an oft-quoted phrase and a hotly debated issue in the United States. Carefully read *Letter to President Thomas Jefferson and Jefferson's Reply*, in which the expression is first used. Then write a thoughtful, well-organized, and well-supported essay in which you analyze the Danbury writers' concerns and Jefferson's response and argue what Thomas Jefferson most likely meant when he coined the now-controversial phrase.

A close reading of the two documents that first raised the issue of "the separation of Church and State" should give us strong clues to what Thomas Jefferson might have meant when he first used the phrase.[1] Writing in response to a letter from the Danbury Baptists Association, Jefferson wanted to assure them that it was, ultimately, against the law for them to be treated as second-class citizens because of their religious beliefs. The exact nature of the Baptist Association's complaint and the exact words of Jefferson's reply strongly suggest that Jefferson's idea of a "wall of separation of Church and State" meant a complete exclusion of the government from matters of religion.[2]

In October of 1801, members of the "Danbury Baptists Association in the State of Connecticut" wrote to then-President Thomas Jefferson, congratulating him on his recent election and inauguration as president and informing him that their "sentiments are uniformly on the side of religious liberty." What they mean by "uniformly" is open to interpretation. Perhaps they mean that they are unanimous in their support of religious liberty, or they might mean that they support the "uniform" granting of this religious liberty. Both interpretations can be supported.[3]

It is clear what the Baptists Association meant by "religious liberty," however, because they continue the same sentence[4] by saying, "religion is at all times and places a matter between God and individuals" and "that the legitimate power of civil government extends no further than to punish the man who works ill to his neighbors." This makes it pretty clear what the Danbury Association believes is the government's role in enforcing religious practice: none.[5]

Scorer Commentary

[1] This student is not focused or specific in her opening, but she does mention the phrase that is the basis of the prompt.

[2] The prompt does assign the student to "argue what Thomas Jefferson most likely meant," and this thesis statement does that quite strongly.

[3] Grammatically and syntactically, this is a debatable interpretation, but the student says she can support it, so we'll wait to see.

[4] This student bases much of her interpretation not only on the words and phrases themselves, but on their context, their placement in the sentence and paragraph. Context is a perfectly legitimate basis for interpretation.

[5] "Pretty clear" is probably not the best word choice, but it is effective that this student pauses in her examination of the letter to remind her reader of her thesis.

They later make it even clearer. Apparently, Thomas Jefferson had been called "an enemy of religion, law, and good order." In this same sentence,[6] they say these charges are because Jefferson has refused to "assume the prerogatives of Jehovah and make laws to govern the kingdom of Christ." The words the Danbury Baptists Association use in their letter clearly show that they see the laws of the United States having the power to punish criminals, but that civil government had no right to meddle with religious law, the "laws that govern the kingdom of Christ."[7]

Jefferson's response is that he also believed that "religion is a matter which lies solely between Man and his God," that "he owes account to none other for his faith or his worship," and that "the legitimate powers of government reach actions only, and not opinions."

If we compare the two letters,[8] we find that both the Danbury Baptist Association and Thomas Jefferson define the "legitimate powers" of government." The Danbury Baptists Association restrict this legitimate power to "punish[ing] the man who works ill to his neighbors." We can infer from this that they mean thieves, murderers, slanderers, even stalkers who frighten and harass their victims. To infer from these words that they believed the government had the "legitimate power" to require church attendance or prayer in school is impossible to support. The person who chooses to pray in private or who chooses not to pray at all is not someone who "works ill to his neighbors."

And does anyone really believe that compulsory prayer would be an effective punishment for "the man who works ill to his neighbors"?[9]

Jefferson's words are very similar. He limits the legitimate powers of government to "actions only, and not opinions." If we're tempted to infer, then, that Jefferson would allow the government to require prayer and church attendance,[10] we must look earlier in this same sentence where Jefferson says that he believes "religion is a matter which lies solely between Man and his God" and that "he [man][11] owes account to none other [than God][12] for his faith or his worship." If a man owes an account of his worship to no one but God, then Jefferson is pretty clearly saying

---

Scorer Commentary

[6] Here again she points out the context as a means of supporting her interpretation.

[7] And again, she very carefully pauses to remind the reader of the significance of the passages she is quoting.

[8] So far, it has seemed as if the student were going to address one letter and then the next. Here she suggests that there is also going to be a more focused point-to-point comparison between the two.

[9] While rhetorical questions can be effective in public speaking, they are generally not advisable in persuasive writing. The student is relying on the readers' answering the question the way she wants them to.

[10] This is another rhetorical device, procatalepsis. Here, the student anticipates a potential objection to her point and addresses it.

[11] The use of brackets in a quotation is legitimate as long as the material within the brackets fairly and accurately maintains the meaning of the quotation. In this case, the student is merely taking the antecedent (man) from the previous clause to clarify the pronoun (he) in this clause.

[12] Here, the student is merely reminding the reader that "God" appeared in an earlier clause in this same sentence. Pointing out probable meanings based on context is a valid part of analysis and interpretation.

that it is not in the government's power to require compulsory attendance at worship or compulsory prayer.[13]

So, when Jefferson quotes from the First Amendment, "[Congress shall] make no law respecting an establishment of religion, or prohibiting the free exercise thereof," and he says that this amendment builds "a wall of separation between Church and State," it is clear that he is separating the laws of the United States from the laws of God, just as the Danbury Baptists Association were doing in their letter.

The situation that motivated the Danbury Baptists Association letter is also a clue to what they meant by "religious liberty" and what Jefferson meant by his "wall of separation." Apparently,[14] the Connecticut State Constitution did not guarantee religious freedom. The Danbury Baptist Association complains "our constitution of government is not specific." They tell Jefferson, "what religious privileges we enjoy (as a minor part of the state) we enjoy as favors granted, and not as inalienable rights." Apparently, these Baptists are in the minority in Connecticut. Apparently, they are allowed to believe what they choose and worship as they choose, but these liberties (they call them "privileges") are held to be favors granted by the state, not their basic, fundamental right.

There also seems to be some penalty inflicted on the Baptists Association for their participation in a minority religion.[15] In their letter, they mention "such degrading acknowledgements as are inconsistent with the rights of freemen." They never specify what these "acknowledgements" are, but we know that, historically, persons who did not choose to be members of the official Church of England were allowed to practice their own religion, but were also required to attend Anglican worship several times a year and were also required to pay taxes to support the Anglican Church.[16] In fact, toward the end of their letter, the Danbury Baptists Association calls the supporters of an official, or majority, church "those who wish to raise to wealth and importance on the poverty and subjection of the people"—the same people the Danbury Baptists Association earlier referred to as "[those] who seek after power and gain under the pretense of government and religion." We can conclude that the Danbury Baptist Association may have indeed been required to pay a tax to the majority church of Connecticut or serve that church in some way.[17]

As members of a minority religion, the Danbury Baptists Association desire a complete withdrawal of government from religion.[18] They not only want to be able to practice their religion, they do not want to be required to "acknowledge"

Scorer Commentary

[13] And, again, here the student restates the point in her own words to keep her readers focused on her thesis.

[14] "Apparently" introduces an inference. The quotations that follow provide the support for that inference.

[15] This is another inference, and the student does follow it with support.

[16] It is, of course, legitimate to bring in outside knowledge or information gained through research in support of a thesis, as long as that outside information is accurate and presented accurately and fairly.

[17] This conclusion is another inference, but the student has been careful always to provide the actual text on which she is basing her inferences.

[18] This reminds the reader of the original thesis.

the majority or official religion. Jefferson agrees. He answers them that the First Amendment builds a "wall of separation" between civil matters and religious matters. Therefore, the famous and now-controversial phrase "separation of Church and State" can only mean that the government cannot "dare [to] assume the prerogatives of Jehovah and make laws to govern the kingdom of Christ."[19]

Scorer Commentary

[19] This essay would receive a high score on an AP exam. Whether you agree or disagree with the student's thesis, she makes that thesis clear in the first paragraph, continues to remind the reader of that thesis, provides adequate textual support, and is careful to explain the significance of that support in her own words.

Sample free-response item two (independent):

"Historical Revisionism" is often criticized as a dishonest technique by which some try to slant others' understanding of the past. Others argue that, as new information becomes available, and scholars reexamine already-familiar documents, our understanding of the past changes and becomes clearer and more accurate. Still others believe that no one can ever fully understand the thoughts, feelings, and intentions of people long dead; all knowledge of history is, therefore, incomplete and biased. Consider these three views on historical knowledge and then write a thoughtful and well-supported essay in which you argue for the validity of one of them. Draw on whatever knowledge you have of primary source documents in order to support your stance.

Whether you believe that "historical revisionism" is a valid process that allows each generation to reexamine and reevaluate its traditions and beliefs or that this reevaluation is nothing more than propaganda to advance a political or social agenda, it is clear that no one can ever claim to fully understand the past.[1] Even the most honest attempts are incomplete, subjective, and biased.[2] Two or three people involved in the same event cannot all agree on what happened a day or two after the event, let alone expecting anyone who was not a participant to really know anything about something that happened hundreds of years ago. It is even more impossible to really know what historical persons were thinking when they did the things or write the things that made them historical.

Modern interpretations of the 1801 letter written by the Danbury Baptist Association to President Thomas Jefferson and his 1802 reply are[3] a perfect

Scorer Commentary

[1] This student has also chosen to begin her essay by repeating a part of the prompt.

[2] The prompt asked the student to choose one of the three views to support. Here this student identifies her choice.

[3] Here she identifies the primary source documents on which she is going to base her essay.

example. Interpretations range from the argument that Jefferson intended only to suggest that no one denomination of Christianity would be held as more official than any other to the thesis that Jefferson meant that the government of the United States should be religion-neutral or religion-free. While proponents of both arguments, and all of the positions in between, claim to be "right," neither can really know what Jefferson really meant.[4] All we can do is look at the words he wrote and the circumstances he wrote them under.

Even then, what we claim to know is really nothing more than interpretation and inference, and those are almost certainly going to be shaped by the beliefs, prejudices, and biases of the people who make them.[5]

The issue of the original letter, from the Danbury Baptist Association, written in October of 1801, is clearly that members of the Baptist denomination in Connecticut are being discriminated against, that the Connecticut Constitution does not protect religious liberty as a right. We know that they are discriminated against by the fact that, in their letter, they complain that they receive the "favor" of "religious liberty" at the price of "such degrading acknowledgements as are inconsistent with the rights of freemen." It is clear in their letter that the cause of the discrimination is their religion (Baptist), which makes them "a minor part of the state."[6] Their complaint to President Jefferson is that they want their right to be Baptists to be recognized by law, not considered a favor granted by the state. Jefferson's assurance, then, that the First Amendment to the Constitution, that Congress will "make no law respecting an establishment of religion, or prohibiting the free exercise thereof," might be interpreted by some to mean only that one denomination would not be allowed to be supreme over any other denomination. After all, the Baptists are Christians, and it is only the differences in their Christian beliefs and practices that make them a minority.

The Baptists themselves refer to Jefferson's unwillingness to allow the government to legislate religion as his refusal to "assume the prerogatives of Jehovah and make laws to govern the kingdom of Christ." It almost makes sense for people to infer that the Baptists are limiting their idea of religious liberty to freedom of Christians to decide for themselves which denomination to join.

On the other hand, in assuring the Baptist Association that their right to worship as they chose is protected by United States law, Jefferson writes that there is a "wall of separation between Church and State." This is a very strong statement that can rightly be interpreted to mean all religions, not only Christianity. The Baptists do write that they are "uniformly on the side of religious liberty." Again, they are not saying that they support "Christian" liberty but religious liberty. The only way someone could infer from this that they meant only "Christian" liberty

---

Scorer Commentary

[4] It seems for a sentence or two that this student has lost her focus and is going to discuss all three views, but she tightens her focus again, reestablishing that she is going to discuss the third view.

[5] Here is where she brings in the notion of bias, as requested in the prompt.

[6] As is the case with other essays, there must be direct textual support of all interpretations and inferences.

would be to assume that there were no other religions in the United States in 1801 and 1802.

Historically, however, we know that there were Jews in America as early as 1654. The second oldest synagogue in the United States is in Philadelphia and was founded in 1740.[7] Certainly, Thomas Jefferson and the other Founding Fathers intended to include Jews' right to their "religious opinions." While the Baptists refer specifically to "the kingdom of Christ," Jefferson writes of "the common father and creator of man." This is a much broader reference and could include a Jewish notion of God, while the Baptists are not necessarily including Jews in their understanding of "religious liberty."[8]

Who can say with any certainty whether or not the Danbury Baptist Association intentionally excluded Jews from their idea or simply forgot that there were other "minor part(s) of the state" besides them? They were, after all Christians writing from a Christian perspective. It might not even ever have occurred to them that the persecution they were experiencing might have also been inflicted on others as well.[9]

And no one can claim to absolutely know that Jefferson meant to suggest that Jews as well as Christians of every denomination enjoyed inalienable "rights of conscience."

All we have are the documents they left behind,[10] and the best we can do is read them carefully and completely. We must also be very careful of placing too much trust in anyone—no matter what the interpretation—who claims to absolutely know what Jefferson or the Danbury Baptists meant in this early exchange of letters about the "separation of Church and State."

Scorer Commentary

[7] The prompt does not require it, but there is no harm bringing in the student's knowledge of history—as long as it is accurate, and the entire thesis does not rely on it.

[8] The sentence beginning "certainly" commits the same error this student's chosen view criticizes, but she redeems herself by returning to the text and an interpretation of Jefferson's words.

[9] While it is brief, this is the student's discussion of the role of bias suggested in the third view.

[10] The prompt requires and this student's introduction promises an examination of primary source documents.

Exercise Three:

Questions 11–15. Read the following passage carefully before you choose your answers.

In September 1897, eight-year-old Virginia O'Hanlon asked her father whether there really was a Santa Claus. As is typical of children of that age, Virginia had begun doubting the existence of the Jolly Old Elf and had been told by some of her friends that Santa did not really exist. For reasons we will never know, Dr. Philip O'Hanlon did not answer his daughter's question, but advised her to write to the then-prominent New York Sun. "If you see it in the Sun," O'Hanlon told his daughter, "it's so." On September 21, 1897, Virginia's letter and an unsigned response appeared on the editorial page of the Sun. It was later learned that the famous response was the work of Francis Pharcellus Church, a veteran newsman who had been a war correspondent during the Civil War. The New York Sun was owned by Church's brother, William Church. Francis Church died in 1906. He had no children, but his famous answer to young Virginia's letter has touched the lives of children for over a century.

1   DEAR EDITOR: I am 8 years old. Some of my little friends say there is no Santa Claus. Papa says, "If you see it in *The Sun* it's so." Please tell me the truth; is there a Santa Claus?

VIRGINIA O'HANLON
115 WEST NINETY-FIFTH STREET.

2   Virginia, your little friends are wrong. They have been affected by the skepticism of a skeptical age. They do not believe except [what] they see. They think that nothing can be which is not comprehensible by their little minds. All minds, Virginia, whether they be men's or children's, are little. In this great universe of ours man is a mere insect, an ant, in his intellect, as compared with the boundless world about him, as measured by the intelligence capable of grasping the whole of truth and knowledge.

3   Yes, Virginia, there is a Santa Claus. He exists as certainly as love and generosity and devotion exist, and you know that they abound and give to your life its highest beauty and joy. Alas! how dreary would be the world if there were no Santa Claus. It would be as dreary as if there were no Virginias. There would be no childlike faith then, no poetry, no romance to make tolerable this existence. We should have no enjoyment, except in sense and sight. The eternal light with which childhood fills the world would be extinguished.

4   Not believe in Santa Claus! You might as well not believe in fairies! You might get your papa to hire men to watch in all the chimneys on Christmas Eve to catch Santa Claus, but even if they did not see Santa Claus coming down, what would that prove? Nobody sees Santa Claus, but that is no sign that there is no Santa Claus. The most real things in the world are those that neither children nor men can see. Did you ever see fairies dancing on the lawn? Of course not, but that's no proof that they are not there. Nobody can conceive or imagine all the wonders there are unseen and unseeable in the world.

5   You may tear apart the baby's rattle and see what makes the noise inside, but there is a veil covering the unseen world which not the strongest man, nor even the united strength of all the strongest men that ever lived, could tear apart. Only faith, fancy, poetry, love, romance, can push aside that curtain and view and picture the supernal beauty and glory beyond. Is it all real? Ah, Virginia, in all this world there is nothing else real and abiding.

6   No Santa Claus! Thank God! he lives, and he lives forever. A thousand years from now, Virginia, nay, ten times ten thousand years from now, he will continue to make glad the heart of childhood.

Multiple-Choice Questions 11 - 15:

11. Francis Church's use of the phrase "little minds" can best be described as
A. sincere.
B. ironic.
C. literal.
D. caustic.
E. ambiguous.

12. As it is used in paragraph 5 (*Only faith, fancy, poetry, love, romance, can push aside that curtain...*), the word *fancy* most nearly means
A. ornate.
B. dreamlike.
C. desire.
D. fantasy.
E. ideal.

13. According to the editorial, the "truth" of Santa Claus's existence can best be described as
A. idealistic.
B. absolute.
C. fictitious.
D. figurative.
E. relative.

14. A reader can infer all of the following from Church's editorial EXCEPT

A. Francis Church was an idealist.

B. scientific knowledge was burgeoning in the late nineteenth century.

C. Francis Church disliked humanity.

D. late nineteenth-century Americans were experiencing a loss of idealism.

E. Francis Church had a strong affection for children.

15. The logical fallacy at the base of paragraphs 3 and 4 can best be described as

A. proof based on what is not disproved.

B. reliance on unproven hypotheses.

C. begging the question.

D. untrue or unproven premises.

E. faulty analogy.

Free-Response Question 5 (text-based):

Carefully read Virginia O'Hanlon's 1897 letter to the *New York Sun* and Francis Church's famous response. Then write a thoughtful, well-supported essay in which you argue the extent to which Church tells Virginia "the truth." Explain what Church means when he tells the child that there is a Santa Claus.

Do not merely summarize or paraphrase the letter.

Free-Response Question 6 (independent):

Abstract terms like *love*, *truth*, and *justice* are often considered indefinable or completely open to interpretation. When writers use such abstract terms, they must define precisely what they mean, or they run the risk of being misunderstood and doubted. Choose an essay, article, or story in which the writer's point depends on his or her use of an abstract term and then write a well-reasoned essay in which you evaluate the writer's effectiveness in communicating an understanding of the abstract term and establishing his or her point.

Do not merely summarize the passage you choose or summarize the writer's point.

Prestwick House Pre-AP: Readings and Exercises

Some tips for succeeding with multiple-choice questions

MINI-CHAPTER 1.5:

EVEN WHILE USING A BOOK LIKE THIS to help you prepare for you AP English exams, you should be aware of the resources available to you on the College Board/ Advanced Placement website.

According to this site's "test formats" page,* the 2010 and 2011 AP Language and Composition exams each included 54 multiple-choice questions, which accounted for 45% of students' score. Students were given 60 minutes on the multiple-choice section. This is a timed test, so when the test administrator says to "put your pencils down," you will have to stop work.

The 2011 AP Literature and Composition exams each included 55 multiple-choice questions, again comprising 45% of your score. Again, students were allowed 60 minutes for this section.

> Sixty minutes for 54 or 55 questions amounts to less than one minute per question when you factor in reading the passage, so you do need to know in advance what you're going to be facing. Test day is not the time to figure out how to work these questions.

Clearly, with so much (45% of your score) riding on so little time (60 minutes), you'll want to be prepared to breeze through this section painlessly and profitably.

Luckily, there are a few generalities about these questions that make them somewhat predictable, so you *can* prepare yourself:

1. All of the multiple-choice questions will be based on a passage that will be provided in the test.

2. Usually, there are between 5 and 10 questions for each passage.

3. Passages on the Language exam will be almost exclusively nonfiction, while passages on the Literature exam might be novel excerpts, short stories or story excerpts, poems, or nonfiction selections.

4. None of the questions will require you to know anything about the text or the author that you cannot learn from what is actually given to you on the test.

---

* (http://apcentral.collegeboard.com/apc/members/exam/exam_information/2001.html)

5. Some of the questions might be based on whatever introductory material is provided before the passage, so it is in your best interest to read it.

6. Any question that requires "outside knowledge" will ask about **language** (grammar, rhetorical or figurative device, etc.) or **literature** (plot structure, character development, tone or mood, etc.).

7. Very few questions will ask you merely to define or identify a term (*this is a metaphor*; *this is an example of irony*).

8. When the instructions ask you to identify the "best" choice, *they mean it.*

   • Every choice will be tempting for one reason or another.

   • Often the best way to identify this best choice is to eliminate the others.

   • The best choice will *always* be fully supportable by the text.

9. Most of the questions will focus on analysis rather than comprehension or even interpretation—how the text works, not only what it means.

Anatomy of a Multiple-Choice Question:

Multiple-choice questions comprise two parts, the *stem* and the *distracters*. The *stem* is the question or the beginning of the sentence that you are asked to complete.

The *distracters* are the answers to the stem or the possible completions of the stem sentence.

On the AP Language and Literature exams, there are always five distracters (A – E).

Most *stems* are worded so that you can answer them (or complete the sentence) before you look at the distracters, and you should do this. Then, the "best answer" will most likely be the one that comes closest to your answer.

Consider the following examples:

   • In the second and third paragraphs of the passage, the author uses an extended metaphor comparing what two ideas?

   • In the final paragraph, "uncommon valor" refers to

   • In context, the word "playful" (line 12) is best interpreted to mean

Of course, we don't have the passages, so we can't read the second and third paragraphs, the final paragraph, or line 12, but if these had been questions about Jefferson's metaphor, "a wall of separation"; Francis Church's use of the phrase, "heart of childhood"; or the meaning of "skepticism" in Church's "Dear Virginia" letter, you probably wouldn't need the distracters to suggest the correct answer to you.

A few of the questions will require you to read and consider the distracters, but these will be the exceptions rather than the rule. And even these stems will provide enough information to anticipate the correct answer, so you don't need to spend precious time pondering each distracter:

- Which of the following words is synonymous with "humor" (paragraph 3)?
- The speaker mentions Ebenezer Scrooge and *King Lear* (paragraph 6) as examples of which of the following?
- Which of the following best describes the rhetorical function of the second paragraph?
- The poem is an example of which of the following verse forms?

A closer look at these stems reveals that they are not really all that different from the examples presented earlier. You know that you are going to have to select your answer from "one of the following" choices, and even before you look at the distracters, you should know the passage's verse form (sonnet, villanelle) or the key word's connotative meaning.

Answering the question from the stem and then choosing the distracter that best matches your answer will save you precious seconds on this portion of your test. After all, if (A) matches your answer, you don't need to look at (B) – (E), do you? Just color in the bubble and go on to the next question.

If, however, you need the distracters to help you "find" the right answer, *even if you really have only a vague notion of what the correct answer might be*, knowing some of the strategies that went into writing the distracters might help you eliminate one, two, or three and allow you to choose from among the rest.

 According to the College Board's Fall 2010 AP English Language and Literature Course Description, there is no penalty for an incorrect answer on the multiple-choice section. Therefore, you have nothing to lose by answering every question. Any time you can eliminate one or more distracters as incorrect, you stand a good chance of raising your overall score.

Consider the following question:

The closing lines of "Over the Rainbow" are an example of which of the following?

A. conditional construction

B. metaphor

C. paradox

D. rhetorical question

E. logical fallacy

Since this is a multiple-choice question, you'll have the passage—in this case, the lyrics to "Over the Rainbow"—so you'll know that the lines in question are: *If happy little bluebirds fly / Beyond the rainbow / Why, oh why can't I?* So, the question itself requires no prior knowledge of the song. Of course, you need to know not only what each of the distracters means, why each might tempt you to select it, but also why one is ultimately the "best" out of all of them.

So, let's look at each one:

(A) conditional construction

> TEMPTING BECAUSE: *If ... then ... statements* are *often conditional—If it rains, then I will get wet. If she does not come in five more minutes, [then] I will leave without her.*

> ELIMINATED BECAUSE: *In these lines, the birds' flying is not a condition under which the singer will fly. In these lines, if is used to mean since.*

(B) metaphor

> TEMPTING BECAUSE: *The entire song develops an extended metaphor—over the rainbow = a place where there are no troubles or sorrow or disappointment.*

> ELIMINATED BECAUSE: *These final lines are not a metaphor in and of themselves.*

(C) paradox

> TEMPTING BECAUSE: *This is probably the least tempting distracter to students who understand that a paradox is essentially a self-contradictory statement.*

> ELIMINATED BECAUSE: *While these lines are (1) untrue and (2) implausible, they are not paradoxical.*

(D) rhetorical question

> TEMPTING BECAUSE: *In this particular item, the question mark at the end of the song might be a clue to a student who honestly has no idea. Dorothy is indeed asking why she can't fly [since] the birds do. As she is "alone" on screen, the device is that she is asking no one in particular and does not expect an answer.*

> ELIMINATED BECAUSE: **This is the best answer**, *not only because the others can be eliminated but because of the fact that the lines are a question and the context suggests it more strongly than any of the others.*

(E) logical fallacy

> TEMPTING BECAUSE: *Dorothy's "flying" above the rainbow (i.e., discovering a place where there is no trouble or sorrow) is implausible. Some students might suspect an error in logic because of the "if ... then ..." construction. Others might protest Dorothy's [fallacious] premise that bluebirds do, in fact, "fly beyond the rainbow." This could, in fact, be the fallacy known as* Begging the Question.

> ELIMINATED BECAUSE: *Each of the other choices names the specific use, device, or grammatical mood. This choice cites only a category. It might be true that these lines are an example of a logical fallacy, but given the specificity of choice (D), this is not the best answer.*

It may seem like a painfully long and tedious process to have to weigh the pros and cons of each distracter, but there are a few guiding principles behind *how* the incorrect distracters are wrong. If you can anticipate the kinds of distracters you might encounter, you might be able to recognize them and eliminate them faster.

- **Parallel or similar but not *this*.** As in **(A)** above, this is a distracter that presents one legitimate use of the term or understanding of the concept in question *but not the specific one applied in the passage.* In our example, an *if … then* statement *can* be conditional, but the use in this passage is not. Variations of this type of wrong distracter include synonyms or connotations that do not apply to the passage or interpretations based on information not available in the passage.

- **True of the passage but not of the specific portion cited in the question.** This is **(B)**. You might think "metaphor" is the right answer because the song is indeed a metaphor. You need to be careful to note, however, that the question is not asking about the song but about the closing lines. This type of wrong distracter can appear as a genre or form question or a question about tone and mood of a passage (e.g., a scene of comic relief in a tragedy).

- **Vaguely familiar but based on a misunderstanding of either the term or the passage.** You know you've heard of paradox. You can maybe even recite the definition. But you never quite *understood* what it meant, and the examples you've seen didn't really clarify the issue for you. So, you know there's something "not right" about the assumption that bluebirds fly over the rainbow and little girls can, too, so you opt for **(C)**. Variations include any formal name of a rhetorical or literary device—especially in cases in which the names or definitions are similar—subjunctives (if … contrary to fact) that are taken for conditional, or actual misreads so that what is figurative is taken literally or what is literal is taken figuratively.

- **Right category, wrong specific.** This is related to the "vaguely familiar" type above, but it presents itself in a few different forms. If the stem establishes something like *The author uses all of the following rhetorical devices* except …, you know that the four incorrect distracters are going to be the names of rhetorical devices; they'll just be the wrong devices. Other cases won't be so obvious, but if you know the category of answer you're looking for, you can eliminate the distracters that do not fit clearly into that category. Then, you apply your knowledge (or your luck) to guess from among the remaining ones.

- **Not incorrect but too little.** This explains why (E), though not incorrect, is the wrong answer. The closing lines of the song are indeed an example of a logical fallacy—begging the question—but, since all of the other choices are more specific, this lack of specificity eliminates (E) as a potential answer. Variations of this principle include the moderate adjective when something stronger is required (*angry* as opposed to *furious*), the imprecise word or phrase, or the approximation rather than the certain.

- **Not incorrect but too much.** This is the opposite phenomenon. These are the distracters that exceed the correct answer—*furious* when the best answer is *angry*, *always* when the best answer is *often* or *usually*, and so on.

Of course, nothing beats a good, solid knowledge of language and literature—you know a sonnet when you see one, and you understand how the subjunctive mood works—but when you're pressed for time, under pressure to score as highly as you can, and facing texts that you probably have never read before, understanding the test as well as the subject matter might help you increase your speed and accuracy.

Identification and Beyond— What to Do with Literary and Rhetorical Devices

CHAPTER 2

To ILLUSTRATE THE POINT OF THIS CHAPTER (and boost your future AP exam score from a 2 to at least a 3), we'd like you to take the following brief multiple-choice quiz. There is no penalty for a wrong answer, so feel free to guess if you think you don't know the right answer.

1. A simile is best defined as
   A. a comparison using the words "like" or "as."
   B. a comparison without the words "like" or "as."
   C. a word that sounds out its meaning, like *knock* or *buzz.*
   D. the repetition of the beginning sounds of words.
   E. the repetition of the same words at the beginning of subsequent sentences.

2. A metaphor is best defined as
   A. a comparison using the words "like" or "as."
   B. a comparison without the words "like" or "as."
   C. a word that sounds out its meaning, like *knock* or *buzz.*
   D. the repetition of the beginning sounds of words.
   E. the repetition of the same words at the beginning of subsequent sentences.

3. Onomatopoeia is best defined as
   A. a comparison using the words "like" or "as."
   B. a comparison without the words "like" or "as."
   C. a word that sounds out its meaning, like *knock* or *buzz.*
   D. the repetition of the beginning sounds of words.
   E. the repetition of the same words at the beginning of subsequent sentences.

4. Alliteration is best defined as

    A. a comparison using the words "like" or "as."

    B. a comparison without the words "like" or "as."

    C. a word that sounds out its meaning, like *knock* or *buzz*.

    D. the repetition of the beginning sounds of words.

    E. the repetition of the same words at the beginning of subsequent sentences.

5. Anaphora is best defined as

    A. a comparison using the words "like" or "as."

    B. a comparison without the words "like" or "as."

    C. a word that sounds out its meaning, like *knock* or *buzz*.

    D. the repetition of the beginning sounds of words.

    E. the repetition of the same words at the beginning of subsequent sentences.

Chances are, the terms in questions 1 – 4 were already familiar to you. You've probably had them defined for you, and you've identified them in stories. *Anaphora* may have been new to you, but now you know its definition, too.

Being able to merely recognize the correct definition of a term, however, is not a very useful skill. It would be like being able to define a term like "measuring cup" without ever actually seeing one. But perhaps you've also taken quizzes like this one.

1. To describe radio as "like television but without a picture" uses which of the following literary devices?

    A. simile

    B. metaphor

    C. onomatopoeia

    D. alliteration

    E. anaphora

2. When a teacher talks about education as a "gateway to a world of opportunity," he or she is using which of the following literary devices?

    A. simile

    B. metaphor

    C. onomatopoeia

    D. alliteration

    E. anaphora

3. *From the jingling and the tinkling of the bells.*
...
In the clamor and the clangor of the bells!

The above lines from Edgar Allen Poe's poem "The Bells" illustrate which of the following literary devices?

A. simile

B. metaphor

C. onomatopoeia

D. alliteration

E. anaphora

4. *The siege and assault having ceased at Troy*
as its blazing battlements blackened to ash,
the man who had planned and plotted that treason
had trial enough for the truest traitor!

Which of the following literary devices is most prominent in the above lines, from the opening of *Sir Gawain and the Green Knight*?

A. simile

B. metaphor

C. onomatopoeia

D. alliteration

E. anaphora

5. *We will not falter; we will not stumble; we will not retreat; we will advance and conquer.*

The above line is an example of

A. simile.

B. metaphor.

C. onomatopoeia.

D. alliteration.

E. anaphora.

This test is a little more challenging, and perhaps a little more effective in helping you learn the various tools writers use to establish their points and achieve their intended effects on their readers. The ability to recognize a device in action does require a deeper level of knowledge than merely reciting words you copied into your notebook and memorized ... but not much deeper.

After all, there is not likely to be a question on your AP exam that will ask you to list all of the hyperboles or allusions in a given passage. It won't really do you any good to know that such-and-so asked fifteen rhetorical questions. Knowing the names and definitions of literary and rhetorical devices and being able to recognize and name them when you encounter them in something you're reading, however, is important because you cannot analyze the text—talk about what it means or how the author is communicating that meaning—without using the right words to describe how the piece is constructed.

What Are Literary and Rhetorical Devices?

As you probably already know (or at least suspect from the preceding multiple-choice questions above), *Literary Devices* are those language tools that allow writers to use words in non-literal or figurative ways. A *metaphor*, for example, is a non-literal comparison—*Clarise's voice was musical, and her laugh was crystal.* Clearly Clarise's laugh was *not* identical to the "ping" made when one taps expensive glassware, but the metaphor clearly suggests the pitch and clarity of the young woman's laugh.

Literary devices, then, are tools like that.

Rhetorical devices are not too terribly different. They are language tools that allow the writer to create various effects. Strictly speaking, *rhetoric* has to do with persuasion, so rhetorical devices are generally regarded as the tools of a nonfiction writer while literary devices are seen as the tools of the fiction writer. Still, the two terms are so nearly synonymous that many people make no distinction between whether they are discussing a literary or a rhetorical device.

This book is *not* going to present a list of rhetorical and figurative devices and their definitions—it's not that kind of book, and there are all sorts of resources available for that basic knowledge. We have defined all of the devices and literary terms actually used in the book in the glossary in Appendix 2 at the back of the book.

Our primary purpose, however, is for you to know *what to do with* the terms once you've learned them. Why and how do you talk about them?

The following passages are especially notable for how their authors use rhetorical and literary devices both to communicate their ideas and achieve some emotional effect on their readers. The first one, President Franklin Delano Roosevelt's first inaugural address, has been annotated to reflect how a student taking an Advanced Placement exam in English might consider the writer's use of those devices. The student's answers to the multiple-choice and free-response questions reflects this thinking.

The second passage, Brutus's and Antony's funeral speeches from Act III, scene ii of William Shakespeare's *The Tragedy of Julius Caesar*, is for you to read and work out.

First Inaugural Address
President Franklin Delano Roosevelt
MARCH 4, 1933

The 1932 presidential race between Franklin D. Roosevelt and incumbent Herbert Hoover was largely defined by the ever-worsening Great Depression. While not revealing details of his precise plan to raise the United States from its economic difficulties, Roosevelt campaigned on a platform of hope through activism.

Roosevelt was elected the thirty-second president of the United States on November 8, 1932, and delivered the following address at his inauguration on March 4, 1933.

Note the President's use of figurative and rhetorical devices to maintain a tone of hope and to convey an almost spiritual sense of mission.

1 I AM CERTAIN THAT MY FELLOW AMERICANS expect that on my induction into the Presidency I will address them with a candor and a decision which the present situation of our people impel. This is preeminently the time to speak the truth, the whole truth,[1] frankly and boldly. Nor need we shrink from honestly facing conditions in our country today. This great Nation will endure as it has endured, will revive and will prosper.[2] So, first of all, let me assert my firm belief that the only thing we have to fear is fear itself[3]— nameless, unreasoning, unjustified terror[4] which paralyzes needed efforts to convert retreat into advance. In every dark hour of our national life a leadership of frankness and vigor has met with that understanding and support of the people themselves which is essential to victory. I am convinced that you will again give that support to leadership in these critical days.

2 In such a spirit on my part and on yours we face our common difficulties. They concern, thank God, only material things. Values have shrunken to fantastic levels; taxes have risen; our ability to pay has fallen;[5] government of all kinds is faced by serious

---

Sample Student Commentary

[1] The repetition of truth with an additional detail added is a rhetorical device called AMPLIFICATION. It helps to both emphasize and clarify the term being repeated.

[2] This underlined portion is masterfully filled with rhetoric. The ANAPHORA, the repetition of will suggests a strong certainty. The progression of the three verbs, from endure to prosper, is called CLIMAX and strengthens amplifies the hope.

[3] This sentence is an APHORISM. The idea is original to Roosevelt, and he is expressing it in a concise, witty, and memorable manner. This is the statement of Roosevelt's main point, and he uses the APHORISM to increase the likelihood of his audience's noting it and remembering it. Indeed, this will survive as the most memorable phrase in the entire speech.

[4] Although Roosevelt uses a synonym rather than a blatant repetition of fear, this phrase is still an example of AMPLIFICATION. The fear that is the only thing the audience must fear is now clarified as "nameless, unreasoning," and "unjustified." So, it is not only abstract; it is pointless as well The ASYNDETON quickens the pace to give the AMPLIFICATION more power.

[5] Placing two opposing ideas so close to one another is called ANTITHESIS The effect is to clarify and emphasize both ideas.

curtailment of income; the means of exchange are <u>frozen in the currents</u>[6] <u>of trade</u>[7]; the <u>withered leaves of industrial enterprise</u>[8] lie on every side; farmers find no markets for their produce; the savings of many years in thousands of families are gone.

3   More important, a host of unemployed citizens face the grim problem of existence, and an equally great number toil with little return. <u>Only a foolish optimist can deny</u>[9] the dark realities of the moment.

3   Yet our distress comes from <u>no failure of substance</u>.[10] We are stricken by <u>no plague of locusts</u>.[11] Compared with the perils which our forefathers conquered because <u>they believed and were not afraid</u>,[12] we have still much to be thankful for. Nature still offers her bounty and human efforts have multiplied it. Plenty is at our doorstep, but a generous use of it languishes in the very sight of the supply. Primarily this is because the rulers of the exchange of mankind's goods have failed, through their own stubbornness and their own incompetence, have admitted their failure, and abdicated. Practices of the <u>unscrupulous money changers</u>[13] stand indicted in the court of public opinion, rejected by the hearts and minds of men.

4   <u>True they have tried, but</u>[14] their efforts have been cast in the pattern of an outworn tradition. Faced by failure of credit they have proposed only the lending of more money. Stripped of the lure of profit by which to induce our people to follow their false leadership, they have resorted to exhortations, pleading tearfully for restored confidence. They know only the rules of a generation of self-seekers. They have no vision, and when there is no vision the people perish.

Sample Student Commentary

[6] While the use of frozen to mean "trapped, paralyzed, or motionless" is almost literal, to transfer that meaning to water—current—is essentially to make a PUN. While there is no humor in the pun, the point is clear: that the traditional means of working have stopped working.

[7] Currents of trade is, of course, a METAPHOR. Roosevelt wants his audience, who are not all experts in economy, to have an image they can understand.

[8] Another METAPHOR to emphasize the deadness and stagnation of the current situation.

[9] Not a strict PROCATALEPSIS, but in dismissing any possibility of a reasonable opposition, Roosevelt is more or less addressing that opposition's (lack of) argument.

[10] This kind of understatement that involves a mild negative to suggest a positive is called LITOTES. The effect is to emphasize the positive—in this case American material abundance—by downplaying the opposite—"no failure."

[11] Another LITOTES. "Plague of locusts" is also an ALLUSION to the ten plagues of Egypt that resulted in the Exodus of the Jews from Egypt in the Book of Exodus in Judeo-Christian Bible. The purpose of this reference (combined with LITOTES) is to tame the severity of the crisis that America is facing.

[12] Probably an ALLUSION to the Gospel of Mark 5:26, in which, having been told that his daughter is dead, a man is instructed by Jesus to "be not afraid, only believe." In this section, Roosevelt will employ several biblical allusions—from both the Old and the New Testaments—in order to establish the spiritual tone of his speech and to stress what he seems to believe is the almost divine nature of his mission.

[13] Another biblical ALLUSION, this one to the money changers in the Temple whom Jesus drove out saying that they had turned a "house of prayer" into a "den of thieves." (Matthew 21:12 - 17, Mark 11:15 - 19, Luke 19: 46, John 2: 13 - 16).

[14] This is a better example of PROCATALEPSIS than the earlier one. Again, though, Roosevelt briefly acknowledges the opposition's claim ("True they have tried") but he then proceeds immediately to refute it.

5   The money changers have fled from their <u>high seats in the temple of our civilization</u>.[15] We may now restore that temple to the ancient truths. The measure of the restoration lies in the extent to which we apply social values more noble than mere monetary profit.

6   Happiness <u>lies not in the mere possession of money; it lies in the joy of achievement</u>,[16] <u>in the thrill of creative effort</u>.[17] The joy and moral stimulation of work no longer must be forgotten in the mad chase of evanescent profits. These dark days will be worth all they cost us if they teach us that our true destiny is not to be ministered unto but to minister to ourselves and to our fellow men.

7   Recognition of the falsity of material wealth as the standard of success goes hand in hand with the abandonment of the false belief that public office and high political position are to be valued only by the standards of pride of place and personal profit; and there must be an end to a conduct in banking and in business which too often has given to a <u>sacred trust</u> the <u>likeness</u> of callous and selfish wrongdoing.[18] Small wonder that confidence languishes, for it thrives only on honesty, on honor, on the sacredness of obligations, on faithful protection, on unselfish performance; without them it cannot live.

8   Restoration calls, however, not for changes in ethics alone. <u>This Nation asks for action, and action now</u>.[19]

9   Our greatest primary task is to put people to work. This is <u>no unsolvable problem</u>[20] if we face it wisely and courageously. It can be accomplished in part by direct recruiting by the Government itself, treating the task as we would treat the emergency of a war, but at the same time, through this employment, accomplishing greatly needed projects to stimulate and reorganize the use of our natural resources.

10   Hand in hand with this we must frankly recognize the overbalance of population in our industrial centers and, by engaging on a national scale in a redistribution, endeavor to provide a better use <u>of the land</u> for those best fitted <u>for the land</u>.[21] The task can be

---

Sample Student Commentary

[15] Having established his connection with Judeo-Christian tradition, Roosevelt can now be confident that this METAPHOR will make sense to his audience. The American people and the American way of life are now (at least metaphorically) the chosen people of God.

[16] Another example of ANTITHESIS. The two contrasted ideals reinforce the abstract or spiritual nature of the president's message.

[17] Another example of CLIMAX. "Effort" is even more abstract than "achievement," yet it is the source of "thrill," while "achievement" brings mere "joy."

[18] It is Roosevelt's deliberate use of allusions and metaphors that now allows him to use a word like "sacred" to describe the trust the American people had once bestowed on the banking and investment industries. The simple word "likeness," in the context of the Exodus and Temple-clearing references, is most likely intended to call to mind the golden calf of Exodus 32 and to invite Roosevelt's audience to associate the ideals that led them to the Depression as false ideals and the leaders who espoused those ideals as false leaders.

[19] While the purpose of much of this speech has been to reduce anxiety and downplay the severity of the nation's crisis, here Roosevelt employs another AMPLIFICATION to intensify the need to act before the crisis does indeed grow worse.

[20] Another LITOTES. As with the others, this use reduces anxiety by diminishing the impact of "unsolvable."

[21] The repetition of the last word or phrase at the end of successive sentences is called EPISTROPHE. While there is some emphasis on the repeated words, the device's effect is often more stylistic than emotional or psychological.

helped by definite efforts to raise the values of agricultural products and with this the power to purchase the output of our cities. It can be helped by preventing realistically the tragedy of the growing loss through foreclosure of our small homes and our farms. It can be helped by insistence that the Federal, State, and local governments act forthwith on the demand that their cost be drastically reduced. It can be helped by the unifying of relief activities which today are often scattered, uneconomical, and unequal.[22] It can be helped by national planning for and supervision of all forms of transportation and of communications and other utilities which have a definitely public character. There are many ways in which it can be helped, but it can never be helped merely by talking about it. We must act and act quickly.[23]

11 Finally, in our progress toward a resumption of work we require two safeguards against a return of the evils of the old order; there must be a strict supervision of all banking and credits and investments;[24] there must be an end to speculation with other people's money, and there must be provision for an adequate but sound currency.

12 There are the lines of attack. I shall presently urge upon a new Congress in special session detailed measures for their fulfillment, and I shall seek the immediate assistance of the several States.

13 Through this program of action we address ourselves to putting our own national house in order[25] and making income balance outgo. Our international trade relations, though vastly important, are in point of time and necessity secondary to the establishment of a sound national economy. I favor as a practical policy the putting of first things first. I shall spare no effort to restore world trade by international economic readjustment, but the emergency at home cannot wait on that accomplishment.

14 The basic thought that guides these specific means of national recovery is not narrowly nationalistic. It is the insistence, as a first consideration, upon the interdependence of the various elements in all parts of the United States—a recognition of the old and permanently important manifestation of the American spirit of the pioneer.[26] It is the way to recovery. It is the immediate way. It is the[27] strongest assurance[28] that the recovery will endure.

Sample Student Commentary

[22] CLIMAX. Three problems with current relief efforts—bad, worse, even worse.

[23] Another AMPLIFICATION, almost identical to "action and action now" in paragraph 8.

[24] The POLYSYNDETON makes the list seem longer and more ponderous than it actually is.

[25] Even in Roosevelt's time, this was a common expression, almost a CLICHÉ, certainly a form of SENTENTIA, in which the writer quotes a wise-sounding statement. It is also a probable ALLUSION to the Old Testament books of Isaiah (chapter 38) and 2 Kings (chapter 20), in which Hezekiah, King of Judah, is instructed to "put [his] house in order." Hezekiah is remembered for the religious reforms that he instituted, including destroying idolatrous temples, cleansing the Jewish Temple, and returning the rightful priests to their rightful service—all of which Roosevelt has used as METAPHORS for the current situation in the United States.

[26] Another ALLUSION, this one to a popular icon of American history.

[27] Repetition of the phrase, "It is the" is ANAPHORA. Here, it is not only a stylistic device, but it adds cohesion to the paragraph and facilitates the transition to a focus on foreign policy, while establishing that domestic policy will remain the administration's primary concern.

[28] The progression from (1) way to recovery... to (2) immediate way... and finally (3) strongest assurance... is another CLIMAX. Again, as Roosevelt has tried to lessen his listeners' fear, he wants to intensify their belief that his proposals are unquestionably sound.

15   In the field of world policy I would dedicate this Nation to the policy of the good neighbor—the neighbor who resolutely respects himself and, because he does so, respects the rights of others—the neighbor who respects his obligations and respects the sanctity of his agreements in and with a world of neighbors.

16   If I read the temper of our people correctly, we now realize as we have never realized before our interdependence on each other; that we can not merely take but we must give as well; that if we are to go forward, we must move <u>as a trained and loyal army willing to sacrifice for the good of a common discipline</u>,[29] because without such discipline no progress is made, no leadership becomes effective. We are, I know, ready and willing to submit our lives and property to such discipline, because it makes possible a leadership which aims at a larger good. This I propose to offer, pledging that the larger purposes will bind upon us all as a sacred obligation with a unity of duty hitherto evoked only in time of armed strife.

17   With this pledge taken, I assume unhesitatingly the leadership of <u>this great army of our people</u>[30] dedicated to a disciplined attack upon our common problems.

18   Action in this image and to this end is feasible under the form of government which we have inherited from our ancestors. Our Constitution is so simple and practical that it is possible always to meet extraordinary needs by changes in emphasis and arrangement without loss of essential form. That is why our constitutional system has proved itself the most superbly enduring political mechanism the modern world has produced. It has met every stress of vast expansion of territory, of foreign wars, of bitter internal strife, of world relations.

19   It is to be hoped that the normal balance of executive and legislative authority may be wholly adequate to meet the unprecedented task before us. But it may be that an unprecedented demand and need for undelayed action may call for temporary departure from that normal balance of public procedure.

20   I am prepared under my constitutional duty to recommend the measures <u>that a stricken nation in the midst of a stricken world</u>[31] may require. These measures, or such other measures as the Congress may build out of its experience and wisdom, I shall seek, within my constitutional authority, to bring to speedy adoption.

21   But in the event that the Congress shall fail to take one of these two courses, and in the event that the national emergency is still critical, I shall not evade the clear course of duty that will then confront me. I shall ask the Congress for the one remaining instrument to meet the crisis—broad Executive power to <u>wage a war against the emergency</u>,[32] as great as the power that would be given to me if we were in fact invaded by a foreign foe.

Sample Student Commentary

[29] Here we have a basic SIMILE, but its impact is quite strong. Roosevelt knows he can rely on his audience's favorable association with United States soldiers. This SIMILE also marks the first instance of a military MOTIF that will be almost as developed as the biblical one was.

[30] This METAPHOR continues the military MOTIF begun in the previous paragraph.

[31] Repetition of a key word neither at the end nor the beginning of successive phrases is called CONDUPLICATIO. It is both stylistic and emphatic, stressing the "stricken" nature of the nation and world. The progression from "stricken nation" to "stricken world" is also CLIMAX.

[32] This is the final METAPHOR and the culmination of the military MOTIF. Referring to the American people as an army and the current crisis as a war is, of course, very inspirational; but Roosevelt has another reason for ending with the military METAPHOR. In the sense that he is going to ask for Congress's approval to use powers granted to the president only during times of war, Roosevelt's military references are almost literal.

22   For the trust reposed in me I will return the courage and the devotion that befit the time. I can do no less.

23   We face the arduous days that lie before us in the warm courage of the national unity; with the clear consciousness of seeking old and precious moral values; with the clean satisfaction that comes from the stern performance of duty by old and young alike. We aim at the assurance of a rounded and permanent national life.

24   We do not distrust the future of essential democracy. The people of the United States have not failed. In their need they have registered a mandate that they want direct, vigorous action. They have asked for discipline and direction under leadership. They have made me the present instrument of their wishes. In the spirit of the gift I take it.

25   In this dedication of a Nation we humbly ask the blessing of God. May He protect each and every one of us. May He guide me in the days to come.

Franklin D. Roosevelt, Inaugural Address, March 4, 1933, as published in Samuel Rosenman, ed., *The Public Papers of Franklin D. Roosevelt, Volume Two: The Year of Crisis, 1933* (New York: Random House, 1938), 11–16.

Sample Multiple-Choice Questions

1. The effect of the amplification (*the truth, the whole truth*) in the first paragraph is to

    A. emphasize Roosevelt's integrity.

    B. heighten Roosevelt's credibility.

    C. pacify the President's audience.

    D. increase the President's popularity.

    E. assuage the President's opponents.

2. Roosevelt employs a *procatalepsis* in paragraph 4 in order to

    A. dismiss the opposing position.

    B. validate his own position.

    C. clarify his point.

    D. endear himself to his audience.

    E. suggest an alternative view.

3. The mood of this speech progresses largely from ____ to _____

    A. pessimistic to optimistic.

    B. apathetic to active.

    C. apologetic to dictatorial.

    D. alarmist to confident.

    E. reflective to decisive.

4. Through the course of this speech, Roosevelt alludes to all of the following EXCEPT

A. terminology of warfare.

B. Judeo-Christian teaching.

C. American mythology.

D. classical mythology.

E. United States law.

5. The final four paragraphs of the speech serve primarily as a

A. distraction.

B. summation.

C. conclusion.

D. retraction.

E. reiteration.

Answers and Explanations:

1. The phrase that creates the amplification will probably remind most students to the oath a witness must swear in court, *to tell the truth, the whole truth, and nothing but the truth.* There is, of course, also the impact of the amplification itself, in which Roosevelt is not promising merely not to lie but to *tell the whole truth*, even that which might be difficult to tell and difficult to hear. (A) might, therefore, tempt some students, but there is more to a person's integrity than telling the truth. It is also not the best of the five choices offered. (B) is tempting since it involves Roosevelt's insisting he will tell the truth, but an insistence that one is credible does not necessarily establish that he is. (C) will tempt those students who understand the implications of the end of the speech, but there is a larger issue in this paragraph than the audience's emotional reaction. (D) is probably the least tempting response as telling the (whole) truth has never been known to increase a person's popularity. Some students might dismiss (E) as too similar to (C), but the differences are key. By the end of this speech, Roosevelt will announce an unprecedented and potentially unpopular course of action. Knowing this, he begins his speech by insisting that what he must say is *the truth and the whole truth.* Assuring his opponents of this will, hopefully, ease their opposition to what he is going to request. **Thus, (E) is the best answer.**

2. (B), of course, is the primary function of *procatalepsis*, but the way Roosevelt identifies the opposition makes this not the best answer of the five. (C) is not very tempting, as Roosevelt's point is not that difficult to begin with. Calling one's opponents "foolish" is not likely to endear (D) one to one's audience. Likewise, since Roosevelt dismisses those who may hold an opposing view as "foolish optimists," (E) is easily eliminated. The key word in the correct answer is "dismiss." Roosevelt does not merely expressing an opposing viewpoint and argue against it, he merely dismisses anyone who might hold an opposing view as "foolish optimists." **Thus, (A) is the best answer.**

3. (A) might tempt a few, since Roosevelt does acknowledge that the United States is facing problems that require bold and decisive action, but the famous sentence, "This great Nation will endure as it has endured, will revive and will prosper," cannot be read as a pessimistic statement. (B), likewise, might tempt some, but the paralysis Roosevelt alludes to is the result of loss and fear, not from disinterest. (C) is probably the least tempting, as Roosevelt starts strongly, "I am certain that my fellow Americans expect…[that]…I will address them with a candor and a decision which the present situation of our people impel," certainly not shrinking from—or apologizing for—what he is going to say in this speech. (D) is perhaps the most tempting since Roosevelt does acknowledge the severe problems facing the nation and dismissed those who assess the situation differently as "foolish optimists." Still, his opening paragraph does include the famous, "This great Nation will endure as it has endured, will revive and will prosper. So, first of all, let me assert my firm belief that the only thing we have to fear is fear itself—nameless, unreasoning, unjustified," and these cannot be read as the words of an alarmist. The opening can, however, be described as "reflective." Roosevelt reflects on the current problems facing the nation, their emotional and psychological impact on the people, and their cause. He closes his speech having decided upon the course of action he will take—asking Congress for the broad powers granted a president during wartime. **Thus, (E) is the best answer.**

4. (A) first appears in the opening paragraph when Roosevelt alludes to the fear that "paralyzes needed efforts to convert retreat into advance." Later, he asserts, "we must move as a trained and loyal army willing to sacrifice for the good of a common discipline," and still later, he refers to "this great army of our people." (B) is easily eliminated by the numerous biblical allusions, including references to "money changers…in the temple." (C) is eliminated by the reference to the "American spirit of the pioneer." (E) is eliminated by Roosevelt's opening insistence that he "speak the truth, the whole truth," which is reminiscent of the witness oath in an American court of law. He also directly references the Constitution and the ramifications of what he is going to ask of Congress. There are, however, no references to Greek or Roman myth. **Thus, (D) is the correct answer.**

5. This question may puzzle some students who do not fully comprehend Roosevelt's shocking and ultimately controversial announcement in the fifth-from-the-last paragraph: "I shall ask the Congress for the one remaining instrument to meet the crisis—broad Executive power to wage a war against the emergency, as great as the power that would be given to me if we were in fact invaded by a foreign foe." Clearly, many in the President's audience would want to pause at that point to consider what they had just heard. (B), (D), and (E) are incorrect, as the final paragraphs simply close the speech with pat statements about dedication and gratitude. (C) is tempting but too broad. **(A) is the best answer** since the President immediately follows his shocking announcement with expressions of confidence in the American people and in American democracy, and in gratitude for having been elected to serve. Clearly, Roosevelt is to some extent hoping to distract his audience from the surprise he has just laid before them.

Sample free-response item one (text-based):

Carefully read President Franklin Delano Roosevelt's First Inaugural Address, paying special attention to Roosevelt's use of language and the techniques he employs to guide his audience to hopefully accept a possibly controversial and unpopular suggestion. Then write a thoughtful and well-supported essay in which you analyze the techniques Roosevelt uses to maintain his hearers' interest and support. Do not merely summarize the passage or list the various devices used.

As Franklin D. Roosevelt stood resolutely at his podium at his first inaugural address, he faced not only cold weather and an even colder economic climate, but also an audience and a country who had already suffered frozen bank accounts and glacial employment rates[1] due to the Great Depression of the early 1930s.[2] Roosevelt needed to deliver a speech that would extinguish the country's feelings of apprehension towards the proposal he was about to make—that Congress grant him broad and essentially unregulated power to act as if he were the president of a nation at war.[3] Through the use of his language and rhetorical devices such as amplification, litotes, and climax,[4] Roosevelt created a speech designed to kindle confidence and trust in his leadership, as well as ignite a desire for action in his audience.[5]

For the first step[6] in his rhetorical speech, Roosevelt needed to inspire enough fear in the audience to persuade them to want a change, but also have enough faith in his proposal for them to choose his method of changing.[7] Roosevelt did this through amplification, which served to intensify the country's distress, and litotes, which was used to undercut the negative and to suggest a positive outcome.[8] In the first paragraph, Roosevelt begins by commending the audience's desires and expectations of his speech. He then intensifies his listeners' expectations by

---

Scorer Commentary

[1] This student is using descriptive language to emphasize the difficulties that the nation was facing at the time.

[2] This introductory sentence offers the reader a historical background of the speech. The writers of the AP exam will not assume that you know the historical significance of the prompt, but if you do, it is valuable knowledge to demonstrate to the readers.

[3] Here, the student offers an inference of the author's needs and desires. If you can back up an inference with textual evidence, as this student does, it is appropriate to make one.

[4] The student lists in her thesis statement the three rhetorical devices she is going to analyze, which is what the prompt instructs. It is prudent to refer to the prompt to make sure you are answering all parts of the question.

[5] Here, the student uses descriptive language again to demonstrate Roosevelt's purpose for his speech. These words contrast those used in her first sentence, demonstrating to the readers that she understands motifs. The contrasting language also parallels Roosevelt's needs, which she goes into in her next paragraph. This logical construction to the essay creates a strong transition.

[6] Numerical steps are an easy transition to use.

[7] In this sentence, the student introduces the readers to the two main points of her paragraph. It is important to develop a logical progression of ideas.

[8] These are two of the three rhetorical devices which were stated in the introduction.

repeating the key word "truth" when saying, "This is preeminently the time to speak the truth, the whole truth, frankly and boldly."[9] This repetition adds clarity and also emphasizes that he is speaking to the people honestly about their situation.[10] Roosevelt further amplifies the situation by alluding to the plagues of the Bible: "Yet our distress comes from no failure of substance. We are stricken by no plague of locusts." This reference serves two purposes. First, Roosevelt alludes to the Bible to recall the audience's knowledge of past hardships and to compare it with the country's present adversity. Second, he uses litotes to mute the severity of the economic state by also calling on the people's faith; the people of the biblical plagues faced their fears and conquered them, which suggests to the listeners that they can as well.[11] Roosevelt exclaimed in his opening paragraph, "...the only thing we have to fear is fear itself." In his speech, he desired to build upon the country's foundation of fear and then tame it through positive allusions and devices, inspiring the people with positivity in the hope that they would trust his political intentions.

At this point in the speech, the audience has reached its pinnacle of both fear and desire for change.[12] Just as the listeners have reached their greatest peak of interest, Roosevelt's speech has reached its linguistic peak through the use of climax.[13] He suggests that the economy "can be helped by the unifying of relief activities which today are often scattered, uneconomical, and unequal." Here, he uses climax, the increasing degree of problems with current relief efforts, to alert the members of the audience that if they do not act quickly, the economy will become even worse. In order to not dissuade his listeners from tackling their problem, however, Roosevelt then offers a sound reassurance. According to Roosevelt, action "is the way to recovery. It is the immediate way. It is the strongest assurance." Climax is used here to simultaneously increase both the strength of his argument and the strength of the country's will. He wants his audience to be alert and aware of the economic circumstances, but he also wants to inspire them to be courageous through action.[14]

Roosevelt uses the rise and fall of his language to mirror the feelings of the audience, further emphasizing their fears, hopes, and desires. Roosevelt has grabbed the country's attention through amplification and has gotten them to trust his authority through litotes; he then culminates the listeners' fears and aspirations in a climactic peak of language and rhetoric. Once Roosevelt's audience is completely

---

Scorer Commentary

[9] This student embeds her quotations in her own words. It is vital that you do not simply plop the quotations into your essay. The readers of the AP exam will be looking for skills in both displaying and analyzing the textual evidence.

[10] Here, the student analyzes the quotations by offering insight into why Roosevelt included it in his speech.

[11] Again, she embeds her quotation and then spends the next one to two sentences explaining its purpose. This is a key skill which the writers of the AP Exam are looking for.

[12] Again, the student restates the two main purposes of the speech, which she had offered in the introduction and the second paragraph.

[13] This is the final rhetorical device listed in the introduction.

[14] Again, the student restates the author's main purposes.

enthralled in their crisis and his politics, he then offers them the solution through activism. Roosevelt's speech is persuasive through topic, rhetorical devices, and delivery. By paralleling his linguistic ethos with the pathos of the audience, he creates a political life line between himself and the listeners.[15]

Scorer Commentary

[15] In her conclusion, the student reiterates her main points, which she stated in her thesis, and summarizes the main points of her essay.

Sample free-response item two (Independent):

While the use of rhetorical and figurative devices can enrich any form of communication, public speakers especially rely on these techniques to amuse, flatter, inform, and persuade their audiences. While rhetoric can help shape the *content* of a speech, it is more often used to establish the *impact* of the address—whether it be memorable, inspiring, challenging, etc. Choose an important and well-known speech of the twentieth or twenty-first century and write a thoughtful and well-organized essay in which you evaluate the speaker's use of rhetorical devices. To what extent do these devices help the speaker achieve his or her desired impact on the audience? Do not merely summarize or paraphrase a famous speech.

In his first inaugural address, delivered on March 4, 1933, President Franklin Delano Roosevelt addressed a nation and world mired in the greatest economic depression of modern times. Severe drought and poor farming techniques had produced massive crop failures, farmers had been driven from their land, factories had closed, the stock market had crashed, and banks had failed. Roosevelt knew that, more than anything, his listeners needed hope. They needed a sense that the government understood their troubles and knew how to help them. They wanted assurance. Roosevelt also know, however, that he was about to propose a plan that would put the nation on a path toward recovery but would challenge the very foundation of United States democracy—the Constitution. In order to do this, the president would have to simultaneously intensify and alleviate the audience's anxiety. This first inaugural address succeeds, in large part because of Roosevelt's masterful application of rhetoric, the skillful use of language for emotional or psychological effect beyond mere intellectual meaning.[1] Specifically, Roosevelt uses amplification and military metaphors to create a sense of urgency and litotes to reduce that urgency. He also alludes heavily to the Old and New Testaments to suggest that there is a sense of divine will in the programs he is going to propose.[2]

First and foremost, Roosevelt must simultaneously convince his audience that the current crisis is bad but not unsolvable. The solution will, however, require extreme measures. He begins by assuring his listeners that he will tell, not only "the truth" but "the whole truth."

Scorer Commentary

[1] This is a fairly long introduction for an AP essay. It won't hurt this student as long as she does devote enough attention to actually discussing Roosevelt's use of rhetorical devices—in detail with examples.

[2] Very nice thesis.

This amplification suggests that, while past administrations have not necessarily lied, they have not been 100% honest either. "The whole truth" emphasizes that there is probably bad news to follow, even worse than the people have been led to believe in the past. He immediately backtracks a step, however, and assures the people that there is nothing to fear, "but fear itself—nameless, unreasoning, unjustified terror." The effect of this amplification is ironic. On the one hand, Roosevelt assures us that there is nothing to fear and that our fear is "unreasoning [and] unjustified." On the other hand, he amplifies this "nameless" fear to the level of "terror." He has, in one sentence, both eased his audience's fear and intensified it.[3]

To further develop this sense of urgency, Roosevelt employs another example of amplification when he acknowledges later on, "This Nation asks for action, and action now." The addition of the simple word "now" highlights the severity of the crisis. The effect itself is intensified when Roosevelt later insists, "We must act and act quickly." All of these examples of amplification serve the same purpose: Roosevelt essentially assumes the reader knows that action is required, but Roosevelt raises the stakes by suggesting that it is almost too late.[4]

The president's motive for increasing his audience's alarm while claiming to alleviate it is revealed when he prepares to reveal his plan, which he calls "the measures that a stricken nation in the midst of a stricken world may require." The final amplification extends the crisis beyond the United States to the world. Now the people are probably prepared to listen to Roosevelt's unorthodox proposal.[5]

While toying with the nation's anxiety in order to set the stage for the proposal he knows is going to be met with some opposition, Roosevelt knows he must also assure the people that a remedy is possible. For this, he uses litotes, the negative statement that suggests a weak positive.[6] The Depression, Roosevelt assures his audience, is "no failure of substance." It is "no plague of locusts." The nameless and irrational terror that Roosevelt toys with in the speech is not so bad after all. The nation has what it needs to pull through. The predicament—especially the challenge of putting people to work—is "no unsolvable problem." There's reassurance, mild reassurance, but something to counter the intensification of the fear Roosevelt is also striving for.[7]

Finally, while manipulating his audience between increased fear and reassurance, Roosevelt uses biblical allusions to cast himself and his ideas in an almost holy light. Relying on the United States' long-held belief in its "Manifest Destiny," Roosevelt subtly asserts that the solution he is going to propose might somehow be part of a divine plan for the nation.[8]

Scorer Commentary

[3] This is a nice and detailed discussion of the use of a rhetorical device, but the student must be careful not to simply walk her way through the speech. There is a very clear directive not to "merely summarize or paraphrase" the speech.

[4] This paragraph does rescue the student from the summary/paraphrase trap. She is clearly taking about the effect of the device, not simply walking through the text.

[5] This is a nice statement to draw the reader to consider the impact of the speech instead of only examining what the text means.

[6] There is no harm in defining the term, but the discussion cannot stay only on the level of identification and definition.

[7] Not as detailed a discussion as the amplification, but the student is probably aware that she is running out of time. Brief as it is, however, it does address the litotes part of the thesis.

[8] The introduction and thesis mention military metaphors before biblical allusions. Whether this student has forgotten them, or is simply running out of time and wants to finish on a more powerful note, doesn't matter. A strong discussion of allusions will count in her favor more than an unfulfilled promise from the introduction will hurt.

The first allusion comes in Roosevelt's assurance that the suffering of the people is not biblical in proportion. It is "no plague of locusts," an obvious allusion to the plagues that God sent to Egypt in the Old Testament story of the Exodus. While the litotes might suggest that the Depression is not God's judgment on the United States, the allusion also suggests that Roosevelt is the nation's Moses, who will lead the troubled nation to prosperity. And just as Roosevelt is the Moses, he decries the bankers and stock brokers who were largely responsible for the collapse of the world's economy as "unscrupulous money changers." In the New Testament, one of Jesus's more controversial actions was to kick the money changers out of the Temple in Jerusalem, saying they had turned a sacred building into a den of thieves. In another allusion to the same story, Roosevelt assures the people that "The money changers have fled from their high seats in the temple of our civilization." This makes the connection even clearer. The United States is a sacred nation (Manifest Destiny),[9] and the bankers and stock brokers have defiled it. Roosevelt even calls the job of protecting the nation's finances a "sacred trust," which the bankers have corrupted. In a final allusion to a defiled Temple and the need to restore the nation to its rightful, sacred status, Roosevelt suggests that the program he is going to propose will put "our own national house in order." This is probably an allusion to an Old Testament reference in which one of the kings of Israel was instructed to "put his house in order," which meant to restore the sacredness of the Temple and the priesthood.[10] Clearly, Roosevelt is casting the United States as a sacred, divinely ordained nation, driven into difficulty by wrongdoers, and he will be the nation's savior with his plan to restore the economy. He even begins the last paragraph of his speech by referring to the "dedication of a Nation...," which is the common theme in the Old and New Testaments, that dedication always involving a cleansing of the Temple and a restoration of the nation to its divinely-ordained role.

Franklin Roosevelt's first inaugural address, then, is a unique blend of challenge and assurance. He skillfully uses language to intensify his audience's anxiety over the Depression, ease that anxiety, and assure them that God is on his side, and the country will prevail. He closes his speech by saying, "May [God] guide me in the days to come." This could simply be an empty rhetorical phrase, or it could be the final reflection of Roosevelt's idea that the United States has a sacred role to play, and he will help restore us to that role.[11]

Scorer Commentary

[9] This is the student's second reference to something not directly mentioned in the speech or the prompt. The fact that she is able to apply "outside knowledge" of history to her understanding and discussion of the speech might be helpful, but she needs to be careful that she does not stray into a tangent about something that is not the focus of this essay.

[10] While this student is not able to cite book, chapter, and verse, she is able to identify the sources of the allusions she points out, and she does explain their significance.

[11] This is not a perfect conclusion, since it focuses more on what the speech means than its impact on the audience. The student has clearly run out of time. However, she has responded to the prompt and provided sufficient examples and discussion of rhetorical devices and their intended impact. As it is the philosophy of the College Board to reward students for what they do well more than to penalize them for what they do not achieve, this essay should receive a fairly high score.

Exercise One:

Questions 1–5. Read the following passage carefully before you choose your answers.

from:

The Tragedy of Julius Caesar (Act III, scene ii) by William Shakespeare

Brutus:

Romans, countrymen, and lovers! hear me for my cause, and be silent, that you may hear: believe me for mine honor, and have respect to mine honor, that you may believe: censure me in your wisdom, and awake your senses, that you may the better judge. If there be any in this assembly, any dear friend of Caesar's, to him I say, that Brutus's love to Caesar was no less than his. If then that friend demand why Brutus rose against Caesar, this is my answer:—Not that I loved Caesar less, but that I loved Rome more. Had you rather Caesar were living and die all slaves, than that Caesar were dead, to live all free men? As Caesar loved me, I weep for him; as he was fortunate, I rejoice at it; as he was valiant, I honor him: but, as he was ambitious, I slew him. There is tears for his love; joy for his fortune; honor for his valor; and death for his ambition. Who is here so base that would be a bondman? If any, speak; for him have I offended. Who is here so rude that would not be a Roman? If any, speak; for him have I offended. Who is here so vile that will not love his country? If any, speak; for him have I offended. I pause for a reply.

. . .

Then none have I offended. I have done no more to Caesar than you shall do to Brutus. The question of his death is enrolled in the Capitol; his glory not extenuated, wherein he was worthy, nor his offences enforced, for which he suffered death.

Here comes his body, mourned by Mark Antony: who, though he had no hand in his death, shall receive the benefit of his dying, a place in the commonwealth; as which of you shall not? With this I depart,—that, as I slew my best lover for the good of Rome, I have the same dagger for myself, when it shall please my country to need my death.

Antony:

Friends, Romans, countrymen, lend me your ears;
I come to bury Caesar, not to praise him.
The evil that men do lives after them;
The good is oft interred with their bones;
So let it be with Caesar. The noble Brutus
Hath told you Caesar was ambitious:
If it were so, it was a grievous fault,
And grievously hath Caesar answer'd it.
Here, under leave of Brutus and the rest—

For Brutus is an honorable man;
So are they all, all honorable men—
Come I to speak in Caesar's funeral.
He was my friend, faithful and just to me:
But Brutus says he was ambitious;
And Brutus is an honorable man.
He hath brought many captives home to Rome
Whose ransoms did the general coffers fill:
Did this in Caesar seem ambitious?
When that the poor have cried, Caesar hath wept:
Ambition should be made of sterner stuff:
Yet Brutus says he was ambitious;
And Brutus is an honorable man.
You all did see that on the Lupercal
I thrice presented him a kingly crown,
Which he did thrice refuse: was this ambition?
Yet Brutus says he was ambitious;
And, sure, he is an honorable man.
I speak not to disprove what Brutus spoke,
But here I am to speak what I do know.
You all did love him once, not without cause:
What cause withholds you then, to mourn for him?
O judgment! thou art fled to brutish beasts,
And men have lost their reason. Bear with me;
My heart is in the coffin there with Caesar,
And I must pause till it come back to me.

. . .

But yesterday the word of Caesar might
Have stood against the world; now lies he there.
And none so poor to do him reverence.
O masters, if I were disposed to stir
Your hearts and minds to mutiny and rage,
I should do Brutus wrong, and Cassius wrong,
Who, you all know, are honorable men:
I will not do them wrong; I rather choose
To wrong the dead, to wrong myself and you,
Than I will wrong such honorable men.
But here's a parchment with the seal of Caesar;
I found it in his closet, 'tis his will:
Let but the commons hear this testament—
Which, pardon me, I do not mean to read—
And they would go and kiss dead Caesar's wounds
And dip their napkins in his sacred blood,

Yea, beg a hair of him for memory,
And, dying, mention it within their wills,
Bequeathing it as a rich legacy
Unto their issue.

. . .

Have patience, gentle friends, I must not read it;
It is not meet you know how Caesar loved you.
You are not wood, you are not stones, but men;
And, being men, bearing the will of Caesar,
It will inflame you, it will make you mad:
'Tis good you know not that you are his heirs;
For, if you should, O, what would come of it!

. . .

Will you be patient? will you stay awhile?
I have o'ershot myself to tell you of it:
I fear I wrong the honorable men
Whose daggers have stabb'd Caesar; I do fear it.

. . .

You will compel me, then, to read the will?
Then make a ring about the corpse of Caesar,
And let me show you him that made the will.
Shall I descend? and will you give me leave?

. . .

If you have tears, prepare to shed them now.
You all do know this mantle: I remember
The first time ever Caesar put it on;
'Twas on a summer's evening, in his tent,
That day he overcame the Nervii:
Look, in this place ran Cassius' dagger through:
See what a rent the envious Casca made:
Through this the well-beloved Brutus stabb'd;
And as he pluck'd his cursed steel away,
Mark how the blood of Caesar follow'd it,
As rushing out of doors, to be resolved
If Brutus so unkindly knock'd, or no;
For Brutus, as you know, was Caesar's angel:
Judge, O you gods, how dearly Caesar loved him!
This was the most unkindest cut of all;
For when the noble Caesar saw him stab,
Ingratitude, more strong than traitors' arms,
Quite vanquish'd him: then burst his mighty heart;

And, in his mantle muffling up his face,
Even at the base of Pompey's statue,
Which all the while ran blood, great Caesar fell.
O, what a fall was there, my countrymen!
Then I, and you, and all of us fell down,
Whilst bloody treason flourish'd over us.
O, now you weep; and, I perceive, you feel
The dint of pity: these are gracious drops.
Kind souls, what, weep you when you but behold
Our Caesar's vesture wounded? Look you here,
Here is himself, marr'd, as you see, with traitors.

. . .

Good friends, sweet friends, let me not stir you up
To such a sudden flood of mutiny.
They that have done this deed are honorable:
What private griefs they have, alas, I know not,
That made them do it: they are wise and honorable,
And will, no doubt, with reasons answer you.
I come not, friends, to steal away your hearts:
I am no orator, as Brutus is;
But, as you know me all, a plain blunt man,
That love my friend; and that they know full well
That gave me public leave to speak of him:
For I have neither wit, nor words, nor worth,
Action, nor utterance, nor the power of speech,
To stir men's blood: I only speak right on;
I tell you that which you yourselves do know;
Show you sweet Caesar's wounds, poor poor dumb mouths,
And bid them speak for me: but were I Brutus,
And Brutus Antony, there were an Antony
Would ruffle up your spirits and put a tongue
In every wound of Caesar that should move
The stones of Rome to rise and mutiny.

Multiple-Choice Questions

1. A deadly structural flaw in the opening to Brutus's speech is that it is

    A. self-reflective.

    B. self-contradictory.

    C. ambiguous.

    D. circuitous.

    E. condescending.

2. Brutus employs rhetorical techniques primarily to shape the ___ of his speech.

    A. structure

    B. tone

    C. content

    D. intent

    E. delivery

3. The key distinction between Antony's and Brutus's speeches is

    A. reason versus logic.

    B. emotion versus reason.

    C. poetic versus prosaic.

    D. iambic versus trochaic.

    E. decorous versus spontaneous.

4. Antony's frequent repetition of "Brutus is an honorable man" and variations on that sentence achieves all of the following EXCEPT to

    A. contrast the claim with evidence.

    B. plant distrust in the mob.

    C. recast Caesar as innocent.

    D. suggest the conspirators' motives.

    E. confirm the claim.

5. The chief effect of Shakespeare's use of *paralepsis* when Antony brings up Caesar's will is to

    A. intensify the mob's suspense.

    B. intensify the reader's suspense.

    C. transition from the conspirators to the will.

    D. influence the mob's sympathy.

    E. foreshadow Brutus's eventual downfall.

Free-response item one (Text-based):

Carefully read the excerpts from the famous funeral speeches from Act III, scene ii of William Shakespeare's *The Tragedy of Julius Caesar*. Then write a thoughtful and well-supported essay in which you evaluate which is the more effective speech and analyze the techniques the speaker uses to give that speech its power. Do not merely summarize the speeches.

Before you write your essay:

1. **Make sure you understand exactly what you're being asked to write about.**

   - List all of the verbs in the prompt.
   - Underline the verb that describes the essay.
   - Write the direct object of that verb.

2. **Make sure you have something valid to write about.**

   - Write a sentence or two that make a positive and focused statement about the topic.
   - Make sure these sentences address all of the issues and subpoints specified in the prompt.

3. **Review the selection and find your textual support.**

4. **Write your essay.**
   - Keep referring to the prompt and whatever you underlined or highlighted in the selection to make sure you're on track and addressing everything the prompt wants you to address.

Free-response item two (Independent):

Writers and speakers are taught to consider the subject, occasion, audience, and purpose of their writing. A strong knowledge of these factors will govern every aspect of the final product, including length, tone, word choice, and use of figurative and rhetorical devices. The writer's ability to anticipate the nature of his or her audience will often be the chief determining factor in whether the piece succeeds or fails. Choose two speeches, editorials, or other passages written by two different writers on the same subject. Then write a thoughtful and well-organized essay in which you argue which of the two better suggests the writer's awareness of his audience and why it is the more successful passage.

Before you write your essay:

1. **Make sure you understand exactly what you're being asked to write about.**
   - List all of the verbs in the prompt.
   - Underline the verb that describes the essay.
   - Write the direct object of that verb.

2. **Choose an appropriate selection.**
   Actually, if you're using this book, your teacher probably wants you to write your essay on whatever story, article, or poem, etc., the writing prompt follows.

3. **Make sure you have something to say about both the topic and your selected literature.**
   - Think in terms of narrative structure: organization of ideas, etc..
   - Make sure you jot down notes that pertain to the assigned topic.
   - Jot down quotations or at least close paraphrases.
   - Jot down everything you know and remember about the assigned topic.

4. **Make sure you are clear about what you are going to say.**
   - Write a sentence or two that make a positive and focused statement about the topic.
   - Make sure these sentences address all of the issues and subpoints specified in the prompt.

5. **Write your essay.**

Prestwick House Pre-AP: Readings and Exercises

Deconstructing your free-response question

MINI-CHAPTER 2.5:

BOTH THE AP ENGLISH LANGUAGE and Composition and the AP English Literature and Composition exams require the student to write two or three essays. On both exams, these are called "Free-Response Questions" ("free-response" because you are asked to create your own answer rather just pick the best one from an offering of five).

One of the Free-Response questions on the English *Language* and Composition exam is the Synthesis Question. We will deal with that in its own section. The other essay(s) on the Language and Composition exam will be fairly similar to the essays on the Literature and Composition exam—with one key difference.

As was the case with the multiple-choice questions, the Free-Response questions on the *Language* exam will focus on language and structure while the *Literature* exam questions will focus on literary knowledge, like use of conventions and devices.

There are essentially two purposes for these questions on the exam: to allow you to demonstrate your *knowledge of literature* and to allow you to demonstrate your *ability to communicate that knowledge to someone else (i.e., write a reasonable essay)*.

That begins with understanding the question—the writing prompt—to which you are responding.

The writing prompts on both the AP Language and the AP Literature exams are more similar than different, and while they are not necessarily written to a formula, they are somewhat predictable. You may not know *exactly* what you are going to be asked to write about, but you can go into the exam *expecting* to write a certain type of essay. The rest is just details.

Passage-Based Prompts

On both exams, you're likely to face a prompt like this:

> The following passage is taken from [*some introduction to the passage—title, author, maybe a brief description of the excerpt's context*]. Read the passage carefully. Then write a [*some description of the essay, like "well-organized," or "thoughtful," or "well-supported"*] essay in which you analyze how [*some reference to literary or rhetorical devices or narrative techniques, etc.*] to [*some reference to overall meaning, impact, purpose, etc.*].

or this:

> Read carefully the following poem by [name of poet], paying close attention to [*some specification about literature like diction or rhythm and meter, etc.*]. Then, in a well-written essay, analyze how the [*specifications you were told to pay attention to*] used in this poem contribute to its overall [*something about the entire poem's impact, meaning, tone, effect, etc.*].

These are templates for your *Passage-Based* prompt. You're given a passage—a poem, short story, or excerpt from a longer work—and asked to write about *some aspect of that passage*—usually something to do with how the author constructed the piece or used a writer's tools to achieve his or her purpose.

On the AP *Language* exam, this passage will almost always be nonfiction—an essay, memoir, speech, or the like. On the AP *Literature* exam, the passage might be a poem, a short story, or an excerpt from a story or novel.

There is a good chance that this passage will be something you've never seen before—it may be something you've never even heard of before. The writers of the exam don't *expect* you to have, and that's part of the point of the essay. This portion of the exam is designed to test your knowledge of literature by having you look at and talk about a completely unfamiliar passage.

And that is an important idea for you to remember. The essay you write, ultimately, should not be about the passage, but about literature.

Consider the following prompt, similar to one of the prompts on a recent AP English *Language* and Composition exam:

> Mathilda Carrey (1863-1934) was a social worker and reformer in the early twentieth century, who was instrumental in the passage of laws to protect widows and orphans and to improve conditions for workers in the nation's factories. She delivered the following speech before the assembly of the American Women's National Congress in Washington, DC, on July 4, 1919. Read the speech carefully. Then write an essay in which you *analyze the rhetorical strategies* Carrey uses to convey her message about the plight of the urban poor. Support your analysis with specific references to the text.

To write a successful essay, it doesn't matter whether you've ever heard of Mathilda Carrey or the American Women's National Congress or know anything about the early-twentieth-century labor and women's movements.

It *does* matter whether you know anything about "rhetorical strategies."

It *does* matter that you realize you've been assigned to *analyze how* the author uses these "rhetorical strategies," not just list and define the strategies you find in the speech.

This one is similar to one that appeared on a recent AP *Literature* and Composition exam:

> The following is the opening passage of Charles Dickens's novel *A Christmas Carol* (1843). Read the passage carefully. Then, in a well-organized essay, *analyze* the *literary techniques* Dickens uses to characterize Ebenezer Scrooge.

Again, you don't need to be familiar with Charles Dickens or *A Christmas Carol*, but you do need to be able to read the opening several paragraphs of a novel and recognize that the author may use time of day, the weather, and details of the physical setting to suggest qualities of the main character. You do need to be able to explain how a metaphor or a simile gives you a clearer sense of something you are just meeting.

The best start to a strong essay, then, is to sift through all the words of the prompt and focus on the verb and the direct object used in connection with your essay:

- Write ... a well-organized essay ...
- ... analyze ... the rhetorical strategies ...
- ... analyze ... the literary techniques ...

Just as in Chapter 1, all of the models and exercises in the book will contain at least one passage-based free-response question, always based on the story, poem, article, etc., that you're looking at in that chapter.

Independent Prompts

On both the Language and Literature exams, you're also likely to face a prompt like this:

> [*Statement of a historical, social, or political issue of some relevance to a high school student.*] [*Brief explanation of the various sides of the issue.*] Using evidence drawn from your reading, coursework, and experience, write an essay in which you [*choose one side and argue it, examine both sides and evaluate them, etc.*].

or this:

> One characteristic of [*name a genre of literature or a school of literary thought*] is the [*description of the characteristics*]. [*Name of author*] describes it as "[*pertinent quotation*]." Choose a [*specification of the genre*] in which [*some version of the pertinent character*] is a significant element. Then write an essay in which you [*describe or analyze, etc.*] the presence of function of [*the characteristic*].
>
> **You may select a work from the list below or another appropriate novel or play of comparable literary merit.**

The first template, the introduction of a social issue and your arguing a particular stance on that issue, is typical of the *Language* exam. Your familiarity with the issue is not important. Your stance isn't even all that important. What *is* important, however, is *how you communicate that stance* to your reader, *whether or not you provide solid and convincing evidence*, and *how you present that evidence*.

The second template is typical of the *Literature* exam. You will be given a literary idea and then asked to write about how that idea plays out in a piece of literature of your choice. The writers of the exam will almost always provide you with a list of titles from which you can choose the literature you want to write about, or you can simply choose your own.

There is no penalty for choosing your own title. This is not a test to see whether you're able to discuss something from a prescribed list of titles. Be careful, however, because when the prompt specifies "another appropriate novel or play of comparable literary merit." To a certain extent, this is a test to make sure you've developed an ability to recognize this literary merit.

We'll discuss what this phrase means in a later mini-chapter. For now, simply know that most (if not all) of the titles on your high school English reading lists have that "literary merit."

Now, as was the case with the passage-based prompts, you need to pay close attention to the verbs and direct objects:

> An epiphany is a sudden realization or insight into the truth of something. As a literary convention, a character's epiphany tends to be the climactic moment in a story and usually results in the character's disillusionment or disappointment. *Choose* a *novel or story* that you have studied and *write* a *well-organized essay* in which you *describe* a *character's epiphany* and *explain how it functions* as the climactic episode, shaping the structure and meaning of the work as a whole. Avoid mere plot summary.
>
> You may select a work from the list below or another appropriate novel or story of comparable literary merit.

- Choose ... a novel or story ...
- ... write ... a well-organized essay ...
- ... describe ... a character's epiphany ...
- ... explain ... how it functions ...

Absolutely understanding what the prompt wants you to do and then making sure that you do specifically what the prompt asks (and don't do what it doesn't ask), is an important first step to a strong—and high-scoring—essay.

Identification and Beyond II—What to Do with Narrative Devices, Conventions, and Vehicles

CHAPTER 3

JUST AS WE DID AT THE BEGINNING of Chapter 2, let's look at some typical multiple-choice questions that probably reflect your current knowledge and understanding of the content of this chapter. Then we'll look at *why* it's important to have the factual knowledge of terms and definitions, as well as why it's important to take that knowledge to the next level and actually *use* the terms when you discuss literature.

1. The first sentence of Henry James's story, "The Real Thing"—*When the porter's wife (she used to answer the house-bell), announced "A gentleman—with a lady, sir," I had, as I often had in those days, for the wish was father to the thought, an immediate vision of sitters.*—reveals that the narrative point of view is going to be
   A. third person omniscient.
   B. third person limited omniscient.
   C. second person.
   D. first person protagonist.
   E. first person observer.

2. Which of the following is the best definition of the term *plot exposition.*
   A. background information
   B. character development
   C. story line
   D. rising action
   E. sequence of events

3. A *foil* is a character who

    A. does not grow or change through the course of a story.

    B. opposes the main character.

    C. supports the main character.

    D. represents the author in the story.

    E. helps develop the main character by contrasting him or her.

4. In his story "The Real Thing," Henry James uses dialogue as a vehicle for all of the following EXCEPT

    A. plot exposition.

    B. comic effect.

    C. character development.

    D. plot advancement.

    E. thematic development.

5. Henry James's short story "The Real Thing" begins *in medias res*, which means that it begins

    A. with dialogue.

    B. with a quotation.

    C. after the action has begun.

    D. after the exposition is complete.

    E. with rising action.

These questions may have presented a few new terms to you: *in medias res*, "vehicle"; but you almost certainly already know basic terms like "exposition," "dialogue," and "narrative point of view." All of those terms are defined—with examples—in the glossary at the end of this book. To know the meaning of a term is really no great accomplishment, and to be able to identify the name of a device when you see it being used is hardly a college-level skill.

After all, if you forget the name, you can always look it up.

Of course, it's helpful not to have to look up *every term* you want to use when talking or writing about literature—and on your Advanced Placement exam, you won't be allowed to use a dictionary or glossary—but much more important, however, is your ability to use the term properly in your discussion of a piece of literature.

To be able to select the best definition of *hammer* from five choices does not mean you know how to build a house.

So, What Are Narrative Devices, Conventions, and Vehicles?

You should already be familiar with the word *device*. We've already talked about literary and rhetorical devices. *Device* is commonly defined as a "contrivance," created or used to achieve a particular effect or purpose. A list of *literary devices* will often contain many of the same terms as a list of *narrative devices*. To distinguish between the two, it might be helpful to think of a *literary device* as something that contributes a *literary quality* to a text…a contrivance of words that makes the text more artful, more a pleasure to read. To compare a sports enthusiast on a season's opening day to a "kid in a candy shop" is more fun than to say he was "really, really excited." The *simile* or *metaphor* does not necessarily change the message itself, but it does color the message and change how the message affects the reader.

A *narrative device* is part of the way the story is told. Narrative devices include the "contrivances" that allow the writer to control sequencing of events, how much information the reader will receive and when and how the reader will receive it, and even who or what is telling the story (and when).

Narrative Point of View (*first person*, *third person omniscient*, *third person limited omniscient*) is a narrative device. It is the writer's choice who will tell the story, and this choice will determine the nature of the narrative and how the reader should deal with it.

Dialogue (both *direct dialogue* and *indirect dialogue*) is a narrative device.

Flashbacks, narrative or *editorial intrusion*, and so on, are all narrative devices.

Narrative devices are the floor, walls, and ceiling of the room. *Literary devices* are the carpet, wallpaper, and paint.

A *convention* is simply the way something is commonly done. Some people like to use the word *rule* when they really mean *convention*. People who write and print books (or keyboard for Internet publication) generally agree on the *convention* of capitalizing the first letter of a sentence and ending a sentence with some form of end punctuation (. ? !). They decided that this would be a convenient *convention* by which to signal the reader that one thought is complete, and another is beginning. Indenting the first line of a new paragraph is a similar *convention*. How speakers and writers of a language spell words are conventions.

Rules rarely change, or if they do change, there are those who will insist that the former rule is the real one. *Conventions*, however, can change. A century or so ago, the use of apostrophes was not absolutely *conventional* in the creation of a contraction. The ampersand (&) was *conventionally* used much more frequently than it is today (the Latin phrase that we indicate *etc.* was written &c.). Before the invention of typewriters, there were conventions about how an author would prepare a handwritten manuscript to send to a publisher. Eventually, typewritten manuscripts became the standard, and a new set of conventions evolved about how to prepare a submission. As the computer keyboard and printer replaced the typewriter, the conventions also changed.

Also unlike rules, *conventions* can change across regions or nations. Many words that end in *or* in American English end in *our* in British English (colour, flavour, labour). Many British words that end in *ise* end in *ize* in the United

States (centralise, localise, organise). In some areas of the United States, the conventional terms are *bag* and *soda*. In other areas, they are *sack* and *pop*.

Narrative Conventions are those common uses that writers and readers agree upon that make it possible for the writer to communicate ideas and for the reader to understand them. Dividing a long book into chapters is a convention. Beginning a story *in medias res* (in the middle of the action) is a narrative convention. The convention used to be to provide most of the exposition first and then begin the story (think of the pyramid chart that very well might be hanging on your English classroom wall!). Telling a story in chronological order (with or without flashbacks) is a narrative convention, as is establishing a sense of the time and place of the story.

Just as there is considerable overlap between narrative and literary devices, many devices can rightly be called conventions and *vice versa*. The good news is that, as long as you talk about the devices and conventions intelligently in terms of how the author is using them and what they are contributing to the overall impact or meaning of the piece you're studying, no one is going to ridicule you for using the "wrong term."

Generally, however, while it is almost always interesting to analyze a writer's use of a particular *device*—the way a writer uses puns in the description of her setting to create a comic effect, or the repetition of a particular word so the sound of the text echoes the emotional mood—we rarely comment on an author's *adherence* to a convention. Rather, it tends to be most interesting when an author *violates* or *stretches* a convention—a story told in reverse-chronological order; the use of pictures, charts, and graphs in the telling of a story, etc.

A *vehicle* is a tool. It is especially the use of something for a purpose that is different from the one for which it was intended. It is the means to an end; you want your reader to laugh; the joke you tell is the vehicle by which you evoke that laughter. In *Romeo and Juliet*, Shakespeare needs Romeo and Juliet to meet and fall in love before each knows who the other is. The Capulet's masked ball is the *vehicle* he uses to achieve this end. In *The Wizard of Oz*, and Alice's adventures in both Wonderland and Looking Glass Land, dreams are the vehicles by which the authors allow their characters to enter their respective mysterious lands.

Quite literally *anything* can be a vehicle. A *foil* is a vehicle by which the writer emphasizes certain traits in the main character. A storm can be the vehicle by which the author can gather a number of different people in an enclosed space.

Remember, though, that knowing the term and its definition is not even half the battle. Granted, you cannot analyze another writer's work or discuss it meaningfully if you don't know the words to use to express your ideas, but the bottom line is, *you must use the terms to express your thoughts*, not merely define them or pick out the best definitions from a list of five.

Examine the following passages and notice their authors' use of narrative devices and their adherence to—and departure from—the narrative conventions of their time and genres. Henry James's "The Real Thing," has been annotated to reflect how a student taking an Advanced Placement exam in English might consider these issues, and the answers to the multiple-choice and free-response questions reflect how these topics might appear on an AP exam.

The second passage, Tillie Olsen's "I Stand Here Ironing," is for you to read and work out.

The Real Thing

HENRY JAMES

Henry James (1843 – 1916) was an American-born writer who is generally regarded as one of the key figures of 19th-century literary realism. He moved to England in 1876 and became a British subject in 1915. While his work has always been popular among academics and persons of letters, he never achieved the popular appeal he longed for. Even among other writers, James's work often received severe criticism.

Novelist E.M. Forster complained that James's style was "difficult and obscure." Oscar Wilde criticized him for writing fiction "as if it were a painful duty."

Argentinian writer and critic Jorge Luis Borges wrote, "Despite the scruples and delicate complexities of James his work suffers from a major defect: the absence of life."

Even Virginia Woolf once wrote, "Please tell me what you find in Henry James. ... Is there really any sense in it?"

Although James is considered (and considered himself) a literary realist, many critics find strong elements of impressionism, a recreation of life as it appears rather than as it is.

CHAPTER I.

WHEN THE PORTER'S WIFE (she used to answer the house-bell), announced "A gentleman—with a lady, sir," I[1] had, as I often had in those days, for the wish was father to the thought, an immediate vision of <u>sitters</u>. Sitters my visitors in this case proved to be; but not in the sense <u>I should have</u>[2] preferred. However, there was nothing at first to indicate that they might not have come <u>for a portrait</u>.[3] <u>The gentleman, a man of fifty,</u>[4] very high and very straight, with a moustache slightly grizzled and a dark grey walking-coat admirably fitted, both of which I noted professionally—I don't mean as a barber or

---

Sample Student Commentary

[1] first-person narration (device) in medias res (device/convention)

[2] British convention: *should* is often used where Americans would use *would*.

[3] Now we know what "sitters" are.

[4] After an in medias res beginning, the story transitions into exposition fairly early. James was not too far removed from the time when the convention was to begin with the exposition.

yet as a tailor—<u>would have struck me as a celebrity if celebrities often were striking</u>.[5] It was a truth of which I had for some time been conscious that a figure with a good deal of frontage was, as one might say, almost never a public institution. A glance at the lady helped to remind me of this <u>paradoxical</u> law: she also looked <u>too distinguished to be a "personality."</u>[6] Moreover one would scarcely come across two variations together.[7]

Neither of the pair spoke immediately—they only prolonged the preliminary gaze which suggested that each wished to give the other a chance. They were visibly shy; they stood there letting me take them in—which, as I afterwards perceived, was the most practical thing they could have done. In this way their embarrassment served their cause. I had seen people painfully reluctant to mention that they desired anything so gross as <u>to be represented on canvas</u>;[8] but <u>the scruples of my new friends appeared almost insurmountable</u>.[9] Yet the gentleman might have said "I should like a portrait of my wife," and the lady might have said "<u>I should like a portrait of my husband.</u>"[10]

Perhaps they were not husband and wife—this naturally would make the matter more delicate. Perhaps they wished to be done together—<u>in which case they ought to have brought a third person to break the news</u>.[11]

"<u>We come from Mr. Rivet</u>,"[12] <u>the lady said at last</u>, with a dim smile which had the effect of a moist sponge passed over a "sunk" piece of painting, as well as of a vague allusion to vanished beauty. She was as tall and straight, in her degree, as her companion, and with ten years less to carry. She looked <u>as sad as a woman could look whose face was not charged with expression</u>;[13] that is her tinted oval mask showed friction as an exposed surface shows it. The hand of time had played over her freely, but only to simplify. She was slim and stiff, and so well-dressed, in dark blue cloth, with lappets and pockets and buttons, that it was clear she employed the same tailor as her husband. The couple had an indefinable air of <u>prosperous thrift</u>[14]—they evidently got a good deal of luxury for their money. If I was to be one of their luxuries it would behoove me to consider my terms.

"Ah, Claude Rivet recommended me?" I inquired; and I added that it was very kind of him, though I could reflect that, as he only painted landscape, <u>this was not a sacrifice</u>.[15]

Sample Student Commentary

[5] James uses the device *chiasmus* as a vehicle to introduce some wry humor into his narrative.

[6] The narrator's description of his callers becomes the vehicle by which he introduces the device, paradox, which will become very important in this story.

[7] This second paragraph combines more exposition with a continuation of the action introduced in the first paragraph.

[8] This is our first clue that the narrator is a painter.

[9] Having offered a possible explanation for their hesitation, James then uses the extremity of their shyness as a vehicle to build some suspense. Why are they so reluctant?

[10] This is our second clue about the narrator's occupation.

[11] More sarcastic humor.

[12] Now, we return fully to the action of the story.

[13] The device is understatement. The effect is, again, a mildly mocking humor.

[14] This oxymoron is the first clue to the callers' financial situation.

[15] We have the third, more specific clue to the narrator's occupation. Landscape painter Rivet sacrificed nothing to recommend the narrator, so the narrator must be a portrait painter.

The lady looked very hard at the gentleman, and the gentleman looked round the room. Then staring at the floor a moment and stroking his moustache, he rested his pleasant eyes on me with the remark:

"He said you were the right one."

"I try to be, when people want to sit."

"Yes, we should like to," said the lady anxiously.

"Do you mean together?"

My visitors exchanged a glance. "If you could do anything with ME, I suppose it[16] would be double," the gentleman stammered.

"Oh yes, there's naturally a higher charge for two figures than for one."

"We should like to make it pay," the husband confessed.[17]

"That's very good of you," I returned, appreciating so unwonted a sympathy—for I supposed he meant pay the artist.[18]

A sense of strangeness seemed to dawn on the lady. "We mean for the illustrations— Mr. Rivet said you might put one in."

"Put one in—an illustration?" I was equally confused.

"Sketch her off, you know," said the gentleman, colouring.[19]

It was only then that I understood the service Claude Rivet had rendered me; he had told them that I worked in black and white, for magazines, for story-books, for sketches of contemporary life, and consequently had frequent employment for models. These things were true, but it was not less true (I may confess it now—whether because the aspiration was to lead to everything or to nothing I leave the reader to guess), that I couldn't get the honours, to say nothing of the emoluments, of a great painter of portraits out of my head. My "illustrations" were my pot-boilers;[20] I looked to a different branch of art (far and away the most interesting it had always seemed to me), to perpetuate my fame. There was no shame in looking to it also to make my fortune; but that fortune was by so much further from being made from the moment my visitors wished to be "done" for nothing. I was disappointed; for in the pictorial sense I had immediately SEEN them. I had seized their type—I had already settled what I would do with it. Something that wouldn't absolutely have pleased them, I afterwards reflected.

"Ah, you're—you're—a—?" I began, as soon as I had mastered my surprise. I couldn't bring out the dingy word "models"; it seemed to fit the case so little.

"We haven't had much practice," said the lady.

"We've got to DO something,[21] and we've thought that an artist in your line might perhaps make something of us," her husband threw off. He further mentioned that they

---

Sample Student Commentary

[16] The "it" is intentionally ambiguous. The narrator believes it to be the fee the callers will pay to have their portrait painted. We will soon find the gentleman means the stipend they will be paid for posing.

[17] The continued ambiguity is the vehicle by which James maintains some humor and suspense.

[18] James does not want the reader to miss the two almost-contradictory interpretations of this conversation.

[19] The use of *our* in a word that, in the United States, would end in *or* is a common British spelling convention.

[20] A potboiler is an inferior work of art—writing, painting, or film—that the artist creates purely for money. The narrator is confessing to being a book illustrator who aspires to become a renowned (and wealthy) portrait painter.

[21] Here is another clue to the callers' poverty.

didn't know many artists and that they had gone first, on the off-chance (he painted views of course, but sometimes put in figures—perhaps I remembered), to Mr. Rivet, whom they had met a few years before at a place in Norfolk where he was sketching.[22]

"We used to sketch a little ourselves," the lady hinted.

"It's very awkward, but we absolutely MUST do something," her husband went on.[23]

"Of course, we're not so VERY young," she admitted, with a wan smile.[24]

With the remark that I might as well know something more about them, the husband had handed me a card extracted from a neat new pocket-book (their appurtenances were all of the freshest) and inscribed with the words "Major Monarch."[25] Impressive as these words were they didn't carry my knowledge much further; but my visitor presently added: "I've left the army, and we've had the misfortune to lose our money. In fact our means are dreadfully small."[26]

"It's an awful bore," said Mrs. Monarch.

They evidently wished to be discreet—to take care not to swagger because they were gentlefolks. I perceived they would have been willing to recognise this as something of a drawback, at the same time that I guessed at an underlying sense—their consolation in adversity—that they HAD their points. They certainly had; but these advantages struck me as preponderantly social; such for instance as would help to make a drawing-room look well. However, a drawing-room was always, or ought to be, a picture.

In consequence of his wife's allusion to their age Major Monarch observed: "Naturally, it's more for the figure that we thought of going in. We can still hold ourselves up." On the instant I saw that the figure was indeed their strong point. His "naturally" didn't sound vain, but it lighted up the question. "SHE has got the best," he continued, nodding at his wife, with a pleasant after- dinner absence of circumlocution. I could only reply, as if we were in fact sitting over our wine, that this didn't prevent his own from being very good; which led him in turn to rejoin: "We thought that if you ever have to do people like us, we might be something like it."

"SHE, particularly—for a lady in a book, you know."

I was so amused by them that, to get more of it, I did my best to take their point of view; and though it was an embarrassment to find myself appraising physically, as if they were animals on hire or useful blacks, a pair whom I should have expected to meet only in one of the relations in which criticism is tacit, I looked at Mrs. Monarch judicially enough to be able to exclaim, after a moment, with conviction: "Oh yes, a lady in a book!" She was singularly like a bad illustration.[27]

Sample Student Commentary

[22] Indirect dialogue is a device commonly used as a vehicle for providing exposition without interrupting the flow of the narrative.

[23] The repetition really does not clarify their plight, but it does emphasize it.

[24] Interesting litotes.

[25] The use of allegorical names is a common device to help establish character. The gentleman's name emphasizes the larger-than-life quality the narrator has already described.

[26] This is no surprise, as James has dropped several clues to this fact.

[27] Notice that what was understated sarcasm is escalating into outright cruelty.

"We'll stand up, if you like," said the Major; and he raised himself before me with a really grand air.

I could take his measure at a glance—he was six feet two and a perfect gentleman. It would have paid any club in process of formation and in want of a stamp to engage him at a salary to stand in the principal window. What struck me immediately was that in coming to me they had rather missed their vocation; they could surely have been turned to better account for advertising purposes. I couldn't of course see the thing in detail, but I could see them make someone's fortune—I don't mean their own. There was something in them for a waistcoat-maker, an hotel-keeper or a soap-vendor. I could imagine "We always use it" pinned on their bosoms with the greatest effect; I had a vision of the promptitude with which they would launch a table d'hote.[1]

Mrs. Monarch sat still, not from pride but from shyness, and presently her husband said to her: "Get up my dear and show how smart you are." She obeyed, but she had no need to get up to show it. She walked to the end of the studio, and then she came back blushing, with her fluttered eyes on her husband.[28] I was reminded of an incident[29] I had accidentally had a glimpse of in Paris—being with a friend there, a dramatist about to produce a play—when an actress came to him to ask to be intrusted with a part. She went through her paces before him, walked up and down as Mrs. Monarch was doing. Mrs. Monarch did it quite as well, but I abstained from applauding. It was very odd to see such people apply for such poor pay. She looked as if she had ten thousand a year. Her husband had used the word that described her: she was, in the London current jargon, essentially and typically "smart." Her figure was, in the same order of ideas, conspicuously and irreproachably "good." For a woman of her age her waist was surprisingly small; her elbow moreover had the orthodox crook. She held her head at the conventional angle;[30] but why did she come to ME? She ought to have tried on jackets at a big shop. I feared my visitors were not only destitute, but "artistic"—which would be a great complication. When she sat down again I thanked her, observing that what a draughtsman most valued in his model was the faculty of keeping quiet.[31]

"Oh, SHE can keep quiet," said Major Monarch. Then he added, jocosely: "I've always kept her quiet."

"I'm not a nasty fidget, am I?" Mrs. Monarch appealed to her husband.

He addressed his answer to me. "Perhaps it isn't out of place to mention—because we

---

[1] Literally, a "host's table"; a restaurant term for a menu that offers multiple-course meals with limited selections, charged at a fixed total price. Also commonly called prix fixe.

Sample Student Commentary

[28] Here James is adhering to the convention of "show, don't tell." He does not explicitly tell the reader that Mrs. Monarch was "embarrassed"; he shows her actions and demeanor and allows the reader to infer the embarrassment.

[29] A very small narrative flashback (narrative device), a vehicle to clarify Mrs. Monarch's movements through a parallel situation.

[30] This is not merely description of Mrs. Monarch, but a description of her "pose" as she auditions.

[31] More indirect dialogue.

ought to be quite business-like, oughtn't we?— that when I married her she was known as the Beautiful Statue."[32]

"Oh dear!" said Mrs. Monarch, ruefully.

"Of course I should want a certain amount of expression,"[33] I rejoined.

"Of COURSE!" they both exclaimed.

"And then I suppose you know that you'll get awfully tired."

"Oh, we NEVER get tired!" they eagerly cried.

"Have you had any kind of practice?"

They hesitated—they looked at each other. "We've been photographed, IMMENSELY," said Mrs. Monarch.

"She means the fellows have asked us," added the Major.

"I see—because you're so good-looking."[34]

"I don't know what they thought, but they were always after us."

"We always got our photographs for nothing," smiled Mrs. Monarch.

"We might have brought some, my dear," her husband remarked.

"I'm not sure we have any left. We've given quantities away," she explained to me.

"With our autographs and that sort of thing," said the Major.

"Are they to be got in the shops?" I inquired, as a harmless pleasantry.

"Oh, yes; hers—they used to be."

"Not now," said Mrs. Monarch, with her eyes on the floor.

CHAPTER II.[35]

I could fancy the "sort of thing" they put on the presentation-copies of their photographs, and I was sure they wrote a beautiful hand. It was odd how quickly I was sure of everything that concerned them.[36] If they were now so poor as to have to earn shillings and pence, they never had had much of a margin. Their good looks had been their capital, and they had good-humouredly made the most of the career that this resource marked out for them. It was in their faces, the blankness, the deep intellectual repose of the twenty years of country-house visiting which had given them pleasant intonations. I could see the sunny drawing-rooms, sprinkled with periodicals she didn't read, in which Mrs. Monarch had continuously sat; I could see the wet shrubberies in which she had walked, equipped to admiration for either exercise. I could see the rich covers the Major had helped to shoot and the wonderful garments in which, late at night, he repaired to the smoking-room to talk about them. I could imagine their leggings and waterproofs, their

---

Sample Student Commentary

[32] It would be interesting here to go back and review the narrator's descriptions of Mrs. Monarch.

[33] Understatement.

[34] More embarrassment on the part of the Monarchs and sarcasm on the part of the narrator.

[35] Dividing a work into chapters is a common convention for longer works, but the break is never arbitrary. Here, James wants to shift the reader's attention from the plot to the narrator's conjecture about the Monarchs.

[36] The possibility of the first person narrator's being wrong or untruthful is a popular fiction convention. Here, the narrator is ironically contradicting himself by admitting that this exposition about the Monarchs is "fancy," yet he is "sure of everything that concerned them." What he is telling us is pure speculation.

knowing tweeds and rugs, their rolls of sticks and cases of tackle and neat umbrellas; and I could evoke the exact appearance of their servants and the compact variety of their luggage on the platforms of country stations.

They gave small tips, but they were liked; they didn't do anything themselves, but they were welcome. They looked so well everywhere; they gratified the general relish for stature, complexion and "form." They knew it without fatuity or vulgarity,[37] and they respected themselves in consequence. They were not superficial; they were thorough and kept themselves up—it had been their line. People with such a taste for activity had to have some line. I could feel how, even in a dull house, they could have been counted upon for cheerfulness. At present something had happened—it didn't matter what, their little income had grown less, it had grown least—and they had to do something for pocket-money. Their friends liked them, but didn't like to support them. There was something about them that represented credit—their clothes, their manners, their type; but if credit is a large empty pocket in which an occasional chink reverberates, the chink at least must be audible. What they wanted of me was to help to make it so. Fortunately they had no children—I soon divined that. They would also perhaps wish our relations to be kept secret: this was why it was "for the figure"—the reproduction of the face would betray them.

I liked them—they were so <u>simple</u>;[38] and I had no objection to them <u>if they would suit</u>.[39] But, somehow, with all their perfections <u>I didn't easily believe in them</u>[40]

After all they were amateurs, and the ruling passion of my life was the detestation of the amateur. Combined with this was another perversity—an <u>innate preference</u> for <u>the represented subject over the real one</u>:[41] the defect of the real one was so apt to be a lack of representation. I liked things that appeared; then one was sure. <u>Whether they WERE or not was a subordinate and almost always a profitless question</u>.[42] There were other considerations, the first of which was that I already had two or three people in use, notably a young person with big feet, in alpaca, from Kilburn, who for a couple of years had come to me regularly for my illustrations and with whom I was still—perhaps ignobly—satisfied. I frankly explained to my visitors how the case stood; but they had taken more precautions than I supposed. <u>They had reasoned out their</u>[43] <u>opportunity</u>, for Claude Rivet had told them of the projected edition de luxe of one of the writers of our

---

Sample Student Commentary

[37] They were neither foolish nor common or base.

[38] Uncomplicated.

[39] "If they would suit" sounds like a passing phrase, but we will find it actually hints at the main conflict of the story. It also suggests the main theme.

[40] Here's the paradox as introduced earlier. These are the real things, and yet he does not "believe in" them. There is some inconsistency between what is real and what is believable.

[41] Here James states the paradox more clearly. The "represented subject" is the artist's portrayal.

[42] This is both an artistic and a philosophical question. To what extent must art mirror "reality"?

[43] Given the suggested conflict of whether or not these desperately poor people will "do" as models and the suggested theme of the difference between reality and a representation of reality, we now understand why James chose an artist as his main character. The narrator's occupation is the vehicle by which James can introduce these reflections about art and reality.

day—the rarest of the novelists—who, long neglected by the multitudinous vulgar and dearly prized by the attentive (<u>need I mention Philip Vincent[1]?</u>)[44] had had the happy fortune of seeing, late in life, the dawn and then the full light of a higher criticism—an estimate in which, on the part of the public, there was something really of expiation. The edition in question, planned by a publisher of taste, <u>was practically an act of high reparation;</u>[45] the wood-cuts with which it was to be enriched were the homage of English art to one of the most independent representatives of English letters. Major and Mrs. Monarch confessed to me that they had hoped I might be able to work THEM into my share of the enterprise. They knew I was to do the first of the books, "Rutland Ramsay," but I had to make clear to them that my participation in the rest of the affair—this first book was to be a test—was to depend on the satisfaction I should give. If this should be limited my employers would drop me without a scruple. It was therefore a crisis for me, and naturally I was making special preparations, looking about for new people, if they should be necessary, and securing the best types. <u>I admitted however that I should like to settle down to two or three good models who would do for everything</u>.[46]

"Should we have often to—a—put on special clothes?" Mrs. Monarch timidly demanded.

"Dear, yes—that's half the business."[47]

"And should we be expected to supply our own costumes?"

"Oh, no; I've got a lot of things. A painter's models put on—or put off—anything he likes."

"And do you mean—a—the same?"

"The same?"

Mrs. Monarch looked at her husband again.

"Oh, she was just wondering," he explained, "if the costumes are in GENERAL use." I had to confess that they were, and I mentioned further that some of them (I had a lot of genuine, greasy last-century things), had served their time, a hundred years ago, on living, world-stained men and women. "We'll put on <u>anything that fits</u>," said the Major.[48]

---

[1] P. Vincent is an obscure British writer who published two works in 1637-38. The first was *An Account of the Mystic Massacre of the Pequot War*. A fairly popular work, it went through two. Another work by "P. Vincent," *The lamentations of Germany*, wherein, as in a glasse, we may behold her miserable condition, composed by Dr Vincent, Theo, was also published in 1638.

Sample Student Commentary

[44] Usually, the rhetorical question is used to emphasize a point on which writer and reader are going to readily agree. The obvious intended answer here is, "No." But the allusion is so obscure that James knows his audience will be able to respond with, at best, "only tentatively."

[45] James has probably chosen an utterly obscure allusion to poke fun at the many critics who disapproved of his own work, predicting that, eventually, his talent and artistry would be widely recognized and celebrated.

[46] James is still setting the groundwork, hinting at the conflict. They need work, but the narrator must have top-notch models, or he will be fired from the project.

[47] Not identifying the speaker of every quotation in dialogue is a common narrative convention. It might be unclear who is answering Mrs. Monarch's question, but the next line spoken by the narrator suggests that it is he who is speaking here.

[48] Another interesting double meaning. "Fits" means both the idea of being the correct size and being appropriate. The Monarchs might be saying they will be unwilling to dress in anything but what would suggest their real social station.

"Oh, I arrange that—they fit in the pictures."

"I'm afraid I should do better for the modern books. I would come as you like," said Mrs. Monarch.

"She has got a lot of clothes at home: they might do for contemporary life," her husband continued.

"Oh, I can fancy scenes in which you'd be quite natural." And indeed I could see the slipshod rearrangements of stale properties—the stories I tried to produce pictures for without the exasperation of reading them[49]—whose sandy tracts the good lady might help to people. But I had to return to the fact that for this sort of work—the daily mechanical grind—I was already equipped; the people I was working with were fully adequate.

"We only thought we might be more like SOME characters," said Mrs. Monarch mildly, getting up.

Her husband also rose; he stood looking at me with a dim wistfulness that was touching in so fine a man. "Wouldn't it be rather a pull sometimes to have—a—to have—?" He hung fire; he wanted me to help him by phrasing what he meant. But I couldn't—I didn't know. So he brought it out, awkwardly: "The REAL thing; a gentleman, you know, or a lady."[50] I was quite ready to give a general assent—I admitted that there was a great deal in that. This encouraged Major Monarch to say, following up his appeal with an unacted gulp: "It's awfully hard—we've tried everything." The gulp was communicative; it proved too much for his wife. Before I knew it Mrs. Monarch had dropped again upon a divan and burst into tears. Her husband sat down beside her, holding one of her hands; whereupon she quickly dried her eyes with the other, while I felt embarrassed as she looked up at me. "There isn't a confounded job I haven't applied for—waited for—prayed for. You can fancy we'd be pretty bad first. Secretaryships and that sort of thing? You might as well ask for a peerage. I'd be ANYTHING—I'm strong;[51] a messenger or a coalheaver. I'd put on a gold-laced cap and open carriage-doors in front of the haberdasher's; I'd hang about a station, to carry portmanteaus; I'd be a postman. But they won't LOOK at you;[52] there are thousands, as good as yourself, already on the ground. GENTLEMEN, poor beggars, who have drunk their wine, who have kept their hunters!"

I was as reassuring as I knew how to be, and my visitors were presently on their feet again while, for the experiment, we agreed on an hour. We were discussing it when the door opened and Miss Churm came in with a wet umbrella. Miss Churm had to take the omnibus to Maida Vale and then walk half-a-mile. She looked a trifle blowsy and slightly splashed. I scarcely ever saw her come in without thinking afresh how odd it was that, being so little in herself, she should yet be so much in others. She was a meagre little Miss Churm, but she was an ample heroine of romance. She was only a freckled cockney, but

---

Sample Student Commentary

[49] Remember that, earlier, the narrator said Mrs. Monarch looked "singularly like a bad illustration."

[50] Here we have the explanation of the story's title and a reminder of the central paradox of the story.

[51] Given their hesitance to wear costumes, their insistence that they are "best suited" to only a certain type of role, the reader has to wonder how accurate it is that the Monarchs have truly been willing to debase themselves for the sake of "any" position.

[52] Part of the issue is that they don't "look" the part. James uses the Monarchs as the vehicle by which he introduces this idea.

<u>she could represent everything, from a fine lady to a shepherdess</u>; she had the faculty, as she might have had a fine voice or long hair.[53]

She couldn't spell, and she loved beer, but she had two or three "points," and practice, and a knack, and mother-wit, and a kind of whimsical sensibility, and a love of the theatre, and seven sisters, and not an ounce of respect, especially for the H.[54] The first thing my visitors saw was that her umbrella was wet, and in their spotless perfection they visibly winced at it. The rain had come on since their arrival.

"<u>I'm all in a soak; there WAS a mess of people in the 'bus. I wish you lived near a stytion</u>,"[55] said Miss Churm. I requested her to get ready as quickly as possible, and she passed into the room in which she always changed her dress. But before going out she asked me what she was to get into this time.

"It's the Russian princess, don't you know?" I answered; "the one with the 'golden eyes,' in black velvet, for the long thing in the Cheapside."

"Golden eyes? I SAY!" cried Miss Churm, while my companions watched her with intensity as she withdrew. She always arranged herself, when she was late, before I could turn round; and I kept my visitors a little, on purpose, so that they might get an idea, from seeing her, what would be expected of themselves. I mentioned that she was quite my notion of an excellent model—she was really very clever.

"Do you think she looks like a Russian princess?" Major Monarch asked, with lurking alarm.

"<u>When I make her, yes</u>."[56]

"<u>Oh, if you have to MAKE her—!</u>"[57] he reasoned, acutely.

"That's the most you can ask. There are so many that are not makeable."

"Well now, HERE'S a lady"—and with a persuasive smile he passed his arm into his wife's—"who's already made!"

"Oh, I'm not a Russian princess," Mrs. Monarch protested, a little coldly. I could see that she had known some and didn't like them. There, immediately, was a complication of a kind that I never had to fear with Miss Churm.

This young lady came back in black velvet—the gown was rather rusty and very low on her lean shoulders—and with a Japanese fan in her red hands. I reminded her that in the scene I was doing she had to look over someone's head. "I forget whose it is; but it doesn't matter. Just look over a head."

"I'd rather look over a stove," said Miss Churm; and she took her station near the fire. She fell into position, settled herself into a tall attitude, gave a certain backward inclination to her head and a certain forward droop to her fan, and looked, at least to

---

Sample Student Commentary

[53] Bring in Miss Churm as a foil—to contrast with the Monarchs.

[54] As was (stereotypically) the case with many underclass and uneducated Londoners, Miss Churm did not pronounce the H at the beginning of words: "'is 'ighness, 'er Majesty, 'ere's a man with a big 'eart, " etc.

[55] Here is a violation of a spelling convention in order to illustrate the character's pronunciation.

[56] A reminder of the role of the artist.

[57] A reminder of the appearance versus reality paradox, and a suggestion that the Monarchs do not understand the artistic process.

my prejudiced sense, distinguished and charming, foreign and dangerous. We left her looking so, while I went down-stairs with Major and Mrs. Monarch.

"I think I could come about as near it as that," said Mrs. Monarch.[58]

"Oh, you think she's shabby, but you must allow for the alchemy of art."[59]

However, they went off with an evident increase of comfort, founded on their demonstrable advantage in being the real thing. I could fancy them shuddering over Miss Churm. She was very droll about them when I went back, for I told her what they wanted.

"Well, if SHE can sit I'll tyke to bookkeeping," said my model.

"She's very lady-like," I replied, as an innocent form of aggravation.

"So much the worse for YOU. That means she can't turn round."

"She'll do for the fashionable novels."

"Oh yes, she'll DO for them!" my model humorously declared. "Ain't they had enough without her?" I had often sociably denounced them to Miss Churm.

CHAPTER III.

It was for the elucidation of a mystery in one of these works that I first tried Mrs. Monarch. Her husband came with her, to be useful if necessary—it was sufficiently clear that as a general thing he would prefer to come with her. At first I wondered if this were for "propriety's" sake—if he were going to be jealous and meddling. The idea was too tiresome, and if it had been confirmed it would speedily have brought our acquaintance to a close. But I soon saw there was nothing in it and that if he accompanied Mrs. Monarch it was (in addition to the chance of being wanted), simply because he had nothing else to do. When she was away from him his occupation was gone—she never HAD been away from him. I judged, rightly, that in their awkward situation their close union was their main comfort and that this union had no weak spot. It was a real marriage, an encouragement to the hesitating, a nut for pessimists to crack. Their address was humble (I remember afterwards thinking it had been the only thing about them that was really professional), and I could fancy the lamentable lodgings in which the Major would have been left alone. He could bear them with his wife—he couldn't bear them without her.

He had too much tact to try and make himself agreeable when he couldn't be useful; so he simply sat and waited, when I was too absorbed in my work to talk. But I liked to make him talk—it made my work, when it didn't interrupt it, less sordid, less special. To listen to him was to combine the excitement of going out with the economy of staying at home.[60] There was only one hindrance: that I seemed not to know any of the people

---

Sample Student Commentary

[58] This is probably the moment when the conflict becomes completely clear. The aristocrats will be in competition with the servant-class Miss Churm for modeling engagements.

[59] In most literature, there will be a strong hint, or even a blatant statement, of theme. While there certainly is room for inference, the writer does not intend his work to be a guessing game for the reader.

[60] An interesting use of antithesis and a contrast of the artist's life with the aristocrat's.

he and his wife had known. I think he wondered extremely, during the term of our intercourse, whom the deuce I DID know. He hadn't a stray sixpence of an idea to fumble for; so we didn't spin it very fine—we confined ourselves to questions of leather and even of liquor (saddlers and breeches-makers and how to get good claret cheap), and matters like "good trains" and the habits of small game. His lore on these last subjects was astonishing, he managed to interweave the station-master with the ornithologist. When he couldn't talk about greater things he could talk cheerfully about smaller, and since I couldn't accompany him into reminiscences of the fashionable world he could lower the conversation without a visible effort to my level.

So earnest a desire to please was touching in a man who could so easily have knocked one down. He looked after the fire and had an opinion on the draught of the stove, without my asking him, and I could see that he thought many of my arrangements not half clever enough. I remember telling him that if I were only rich I would offer him a salary to come and teach me how to live.[61] Sometimes he gave a random sigh, of which the essence was: "Give me even such a bare old barrack as THIS, and I'd do something with it!" When I wanted to use him he came alone; which was an illustration of the superior courage of women. His wife could bear her solitary second floor, and she was in general more discreet; showing by various small reserves that she was alive to the propriety of keeping our relations markedly professional—not letting them slide into sociability. She wished it to remain clear that she and the Major were employed, not cultivated, and if she approved of me as a superior, who could be kept in his place, she never thought me quite good enough for an equal.[62]

She sat with great intensity, giving the whole of her mind to it, and was capable of remaining for an hour almost as motionless as if she were before a photographer's lens. I could see she had been photographed often, but somehow the very habit that made her good for that purpose unfitted her for mine. At first I was extremely pleased with her lady-like air, and it was a satisfaction, on coming to follow her lines, to see how good they were and how far they could lead the pencil. But after a few times I began to find her too insurmountably stiff; do what I would with it my drawing looked like a photograph or a copy of a photograph. Her figure had no variety of expression—she herself had no sense of variety. You may say that this was my business, was only a question of placing her. I placed her in every conceivable position, but she managed to obliterate their differences. She was always a lady certainly, and into the bargain was always the same lady. She was the real thing, but always the same thing. There were moments when I was oppressed by the serenity of her confidence that she WAS the real thing. All her dealings with me and all her husband's were an implication that this was lucky for ME. Meanwhile I found myself trying to invent types that approached her own, instead of making her own transform itself—in the clever way that was not impossible, for instance, to poor Miss

---

Sample Student Commentary

[61] Note the sarcasm.

[62] To further the central paradox, the narrator points out that the Monarchs can debase themselves to work for the narrator and accept wages from him, but they still consider him their social inferior and cannot (or will not) socialize with someone of a "lower class."

Churm. Arrange as I would and take the precautions I would, she always, in my pictures, came out too tall—landing me in the dilemma of having represented a fascinating woman as seven feet high, which, out of respect perhaps to my own very much scantier inches, was far from my idea of such a personage.

The case was worse with the Major—nothing I could do would keep HIM down, so that <u>he became useful only for the representation of brawny giants</u>.[63] <u>I adored variety and range, I cherished human accidents, the illustrative note; I wanted to characterise closely, and the thing in the world I most hated was the danger of being ridden by a type</u>.[64] I had quarrelled with some of my friends about it—I had parted company with them for maintaining that <u>one HAD to be</u>, and that if the type was beautiful (witness Raphael and Leonardo), the servitude was only a gain. I was neither Leonardo nor Raphael; I might only be a presumptuous young modern searcher, but I held that everything was to be sacrificed sooner than character. When they averred that the haunting type in question could easily BE character, I retorted, perhaps superficially: "Whose?" It couldn't be everybody's—it might end in being nobody's.[65]

After I had drawn Mrs. Monarch a dozen times I perceived more clearly than before that the value of such a model as Miss Churm resided precisely in the fact that she had no positive stamp, combined of course with the other fact that what she did have was a curious and inexplicable talent for imitation. Her usual appearance was like a curtain which she could draw up at request for a capital performance. This performance was simply suggestive; but it was a word to the wise—it was vivid and pretty. Sometimes, even, I thought it, though she was plain herself, too insipidly pretty; I made it a reproach to her that the figures drawn from her were monotonously (bêtement[1], as we used to say) graceful. Nothing made her more angry: it was so much her pride to feel that she could sit for characters that had nothing in common with each other. She would accuse me at such moments of taking away her "reputytion."

It suffered a certain shrinkage, this queer quantity, from the repeated visits of my new friends. Miss Churm was greatly in demand, never in want of employment, so I had no scruple in putting her off occasionally, to try them more at my ease. It was certainly amusing at first to do the real thing—it was amusing to do Major Monarch's trousers. They WERE the real thing, even if he did come out colossal. It was amusing to do his wife's back hair (it was so mathematically neat,) and the particular "smart" tension of her tight stays. She lent herself especially to positions in which the face was somewhat averted or

---

[1] French for "stupidly" or "idiotically."

Sample Student Commentary

[63] The implication is that there is a sense of exaggeration in art. The "real thing" plus the exaggeration amounts to something too big for the illusion.

[64] Considering the criticism of his work that James received in his lifetime, it clearly seems as if he is using this artist-narrator as the vehicle through which to express his own views and frustrations.

[65] The sentence structure is difficult here, and the exact referent for "one" is unclear, but the narrator is most likely saying that the friends insisted the artist should imitate greatness, while the narrator is arguing that each artist should develop his own character.

blurred; she abounded in lady-like back views and profils perdus[1]. When she stood erect she took naturally one of the attitudes in which court-painters represent queens and princesses; so that I found myself wondering whether, to draw out this accomplishment, I couldn't get the editor of the Cheapside to publish a really royal romance, "A Tale of Buckingham Palace." Sometimes, however, the real thing and the make-believe came into contact; by which I mean that Miss Churm, keeping an appointment or coming to make one on days when I had much work in hand, encountered her invidious rivals. The encounter was not on their part, for they noticed her no more than if she had been the housemaid; not from intentional loftiness, but simply because, as yet, professionally, they didn't know how to fraternise, as I could guess that they would have liked—or at least that the Major would. They couldn't talk about the omnibus—they always walked; and they didn't know what else to try—she wasn't interested in good trains or cheap claret. Besides, they must have felt—in the air—that she was amused at them, secretly derisive of their ever knowing how. She was not a person to conceal her scepticism if she had had a chance to show it. On the other hand Mrs. Monarch didn't think her tidy; for why else did she take pains to say to me (it was going out of the way, for Mrs. Monarch), that she didn't like dirty women?

One day when my young lady happened to be present with my other sitters (she even dropped in, when it was convenient, for a chat), I asked her to be so good as to lend a hand in getting tea—a service with which she was familiar and which was one of a class that, living as I did in a small way, with slender domestic resources, I often appealed to my models to render. They liked to lay hands on my property, to break the sitting, and sometimes the china[66]—I made them feel Bohemian. The next time I saw Miss Churm after this incident she surprised me greatly by making a scene about it—she accused me of having wished to humiliate her. She had not resented the outrage at the time, but had seemed obliging and amused, enjoying the comedy of asking Mrs. Monarch, who sat vague and silent, whether she would have cream and sugar, and putting an exaggerated simper into the question. She had tried intonations—as if she too wished to pass for the real thing; till I was afraid my other visitors would take offence.[67]

Oh, THEY were determined not to do this; and their touching patience was the measure of their great need. They would sit by the hour, uncomplaining, till I was ready to use them; they would come back on the chance of being wanted and would walk away cheerfully if they were not. I used to go to the door with them to see in what magnificent order they retreated. I tried to find other employment for them—I introduced them to several artists. But they didn't "take," for reasons I could appreciate, and I became conscious, rather anxiously, that after such disappointments they fell back upon me with a heavier weight. They did me the honour to think that it was I who was most

---

[1] Literally "lost profiles." Probably a side view of the model with the face turned away from the artist or photographer. Also, possibly a side view with the appearance of the model in motion.

Sample Student Commentary

[66] Here is an interesting use of the relatively rare zeugma.

[67] The phrase "the real thing" is itself ambiguous. In one sense, Miss Churm and the Monarchs are the same class—both penniless and without a practical education in order to find skilled employment.

THEIR form. They were not picturesque enough for the painters, and in those days there were not so many serious workers in black and white. Besides, they had an eye to the great job I had mentioned to them—they had secretly set their hearts on supplying the right essence for my pictorial vindication of our fine novelist. They knew that for this undertaking I should want no costume-effects, none of the frippery of past ages—that it was a case in which everything would be contemporary and satirical and, presumably, genteel. If I could work them into it their future would be assured, for the labour would of course be long and the occupation steady.[68]

One day Mrs. Monarch came without her husband—she explained his absence by his having had to go to the City. While she sat there in her usual anxious stiffness there came, at the door, a knock which I immediately recognised as the subdued appeal of a model out of work. It was followed by <u>the entrance of a young man whom I easily perceived to be a foreigner</u> and who proved in fact an Italian acquainted with no English word but my name,[69] which he uttered in a way that made it seem to include all others. I had not then visited his country, nor was I proficient in his tongue; but as he was not so meanly constituted—what Italian is?—as to depend only on that member for expression he conveyed to me, in familiar but graceful mimicry, that he was in search of exactly the employment in which the lady before me was engaged. I was not struck with him at first, and while I continued to draw I emitted rough sounds of discouragement and dismissal. He stood his ground, however, not importunately, but with a dumb, dog-like fidelity in his eyes which amounted to innocent impudence—the manner of a devoted servant (he might have been in the house for years), unjustly suspected. Suddenly I saw that this very attitude and expression made a picture, whereupon I told him to sit down and wait till I should be free. There was another picture in the way he obeyed me, and I observed as I worked that there were others still in the way he looked wonderingly, with his head thrown back, about the high studio. He might have been crossing himself in St. Peter's. Before I finished I said to myself: "The fellow's a bankrupt orange-monger, but he's a treasure."

When Mrs. Monarch withdrew he passed across the room like a flash to open the door for her, standing there with the rapt, pure gaze of the young Dante spellbound by the young Beatrice[1]. As I never insisted, in such situations, on the blankness of the British domestic, I reflected that he had the making of a servant (and I needed one, but couldn't pay him to be only that), as well as of a model; in short I made up my mind to adopt my bright adventurer if he would agree to officiate in the double capacity. He jumped at my offer, and in the event my rashness (for I had known nothing about him), was not

---

[1] Dante Alighieri, Italian Renaissance poet most famous for his *Divine Comedy*, the first book of which is *The Inferno*. The reference is to Beatrice di Folco Portinari, the young Florentine woman who was Dante's "muse." It is an idealized Beatrice who sends Dante on his journey to salvation in The Inferno and serves as his guide in The Paradiso, the third book of the Comedy.

Sample Student Commentary

[68] Summing up the action of several days or weeks in a single paragraph is a common convention.

[69] The introduction of a new character this far into a story is almost always a vehicle to achieve some end. As the conflict of the Monarchs' being needy but unusable is well established, this new arrival might introduce a new complication: another rival.

brought home to me. He proved a sympathetic though a desultory ministrant, and had in a wonderful degree the sentiment de la pose. It was uncultivated, instinctive; a part of the happy instinct which had guided him to my door and helped him to spell out my name on the card nailed to it. He had had no other introduction to me than a guess, from the shape of my high north window, seen outside, that my place was a studio and that as a studio it would contain an artist. He had wandered to England in search of fortune, like other itinerants, and had embarked, with a partner and a small green handcart, on the sale of penny ices. The ices had melted away and the partner had dissolved in their train. My young man wore tight yellow trousers with reddish stripes and his name was Oronte. He was sallow but fair, and when I put him into some old clothes of my own he looked like an Englishman. He was as good as Miss Churm, who could look, when required, like an Italian.[70]

CHAPTER IV.

I thought Mrs. Monarch's face slightly convulsed when, on her coming back with her husband, she found Oronte installed. It was strange to have to recognise in a scrap of a lazzarone[1] a competitor to her magnificent Major. It was she who scented danger first, for the Major was anecdotically unconscious. But Oronte gave us tea, with a hundred eager confusions (he had never seen such a queer process), and I think she thought better of me for having at last an "establishment."[71] They saw a couple of drawings that I had made of the establishment, and Mrs. Monarch hinted that it never would have struck her that he had sat for them. "Now the drawings you make from US, they look exactly like us," she reminded me, smiling in triumph; and I recognised that this was indeed just their defect.[72] When I drew the Monarchs I couldn't, somehow, get away from them—get into the character I wanted to represent; and I had not the least desire my model should be discoverable in my picture.[73] Miss Churm never was, and Mrs. Monarch thought I hid her, very properly, because she was vulgar; whereas if she was lost it was only as the dead who go to heaven are lost—in the gain of an angel the more.

By this time I had got a certain start with "Rutland Ramsay," the first novel in the great projected series; that is I had produced a dozen drawings, several with the help of the Major and his wife, and I had sent them in for approval. My understanding with the publishers, as I have already hinted, had been that I was to be left to do my work, in this

---

[1] A homeless beggar, originally a homeless or impoverished resident of Naples, Italy.

Sample Student Commentary

[70] Notice how James uses the introduction of this new character as a vehicle to complicate his conflict with a second rival and advance his theme about the paradox of the real versus the apparent.

[71] Note the use of quotation marks, which typically indicate a non-literal use of a word. In this case, a single servant, probably unpaid, who doubles as a model, hardly constitutes an established household of the type the Majors might be accustomed to.

[72] Several levels of irony here. What the Monarchs are most proud of is exactly what makes them least fit for their jobs.

[73] Here is another fairly blatant statement of the theme, this one from the narrator.

particular case, as I liked, with the whole book committed to me; but my connection with the rest of the series was only contingent. There were moments when, frankly, it WAS a comfort to have the real thing under one's hand; for there were characters in "Rutland Ramsay" that were very much like it. There were people presumably as straight as the Major and women of as good a fashion as Mrs. Monarch. There was a great deal of country-house life—treated, it is true, in a fine, fanciful, ironical, generalized way—and there was a considerable implication of knickerbockers and kilts. There were certain things I had to settle at the outset; such things for instance as the exact appearance of the hero, the particular bloom of the heroine. The author of course gave me a lead, but there was a margin for interpretation. I took the Monarchs into my confidence, I told them frankly what I was about, I mentioned my embarrassments and alternatives. "Oh, take HIM!" Mrs. Monarch murmured sweetly, looking at her husband; and "What could you want better than my wife?" the Major inquired, with the comfortable candour that now prevailed between us.

I was not obliged to answer these remarks—I was only obliged to place my sitters. I was not easy in mind, and I postponed, a little timidly perhaps, the solution of the question. The book was a large canvas, the other figures were numerous, and I worked off at first some of the episodes in which the hero and the heroine were not concerned. When once I had set THEM up I should have to stick to them—I couldn't make my young man seven feet high in one place and five feet nine in another. I inclined on the whole to the latter measurement, though the Major more than once reminded me that HE looked about as young as anyone. It was indeed quite possible to arrange him, for the figure, so that it would have been difficult to detect his age. After the spontaneous Oronte had been with me a month, and after I had given him to understand several different times that his native exuberance would presently constitute an insurmountable barrier to our further intercourse, I waked to a sense of his heroic capacity. He was only five feet seven, but the remaining inches were latent. I tried him almost secretly at first, for I was really rather afraid of the judgment my other models would pass on such a choice. If they regarded Miss Churm as little better than a snare, what would they think of the representation by a person so little the real thing as an Italian street-vendor of a protagonist formed by a public school?

If I went a little in fear of them it was not because they bullied me, because they had got an oppressive foothold, but because in their really <u>pathetic decorum</u> and mysteriously <u>permanent newness</u>[74] they counted on me so intensely. I was therefore very glad when <u>Jack Hawley</u> came home:[75] he was always of such good counsel. He painted badly himself, but there was no one like him for putting his finger on the place. He had been absent from England for a year; he had been somewhere—I don't remember where—to get a fresh eye. I was in a good deal of dread of any such organ, but we were old friends; he

---

Sample Student Commentary

[74] Probably to reinforce the paradox as the heart of this story, James uses quite a few oxymora to emphasize the pervasive self-contradiction of the Monarchs.

[75] Another new character. This one is probably intended to verify for the reader the narrator's evaluation of the Monarchs as models.

had been away for months and a sense of emptiness was creeping into my life. I hadn't dodged a missile for a year.[77]

He came back with a fresh eye, but with the same old black velvet blouse, and the first evening he spent in my studio we smoked cigarettes till the small hours. He had done no work himself, he had only got the eye; so the field was clear for the production of my little things. He wanted to see what I had done for the Cheapside, but he was disappointed in the exhibition. That at least seemed the meaning of two or three comprehensive groans which, as he lounged on my big divan, on a folded leg, looking at my latest drawings, issued from his lips with the smoke of the cigarette.

"What's the matter with you?" I asked.

"What's the matter with YOU?"

"Nothing save that I'm mystified."

"You are indeed. You're quite off the hinge. What's the meaning of this new fad?" And he tossed me, with visible irreverence, a drawing in which I happened to have depicted both my majestic models. I asked if he didn't think it good, and he replied that it struck him as execrable, given the sort of thing I had always represented myself to him as wishing to arrive at;[78] but I let that pass, I was so anxious to see exactly what he meant. The two figures in the picture looked colossal, but I supposed this was NOT what he meant, inasmuch as, for aught he knew to the contrary, I might have been trying for that. I maintained that I was working exactly in the same way as when he last had done me the honour to commend me. "Well, there's a big hole somewhere," he answered; "wait a bit and I'll discover it." I depended upon him to do so: where else was the fresh eye? But he produced at last nothing more luminous than "I don't know—I don't like your types." This was lame, for a critic who had never consented to discuss with me anything but the question of execution, the direction of strokes and the mystery of values.

"In the drawings you've been looking at I think my types are very handsome."

"Oh, they won't do!"

"I've had a couple of new models."

"I see you have. THEY won't do."

"Are you very sure of that?"

"Absolutely—they're stupid."

"You mean I am—for I ought to get round that."

"You CAN'T—with such people. Who are they?"

I told him, as far as was necessary, and he declared, heartlessly: "Ce sont des gens qu'il faut mettre a la porte.[1]"

---

[1] French for "These people need to have the door." That is, You need to show these people to the door.

Sample Student Commentary

[77] To "dodge a missile" might mean the same thing as the modern American "to dodge a bullet," that is, to avoid trouble. The context, however, that the narrator's friend is returning, and the narrator has been feeling lonely, suggests that "dodg[ing] a missile" might have something to do with fun or some social activity, perhaps something dangerous or madcap.

[78] Remember that earlier hints suggested that the narrator was attempting to develop some kind of "character," some uniqueness of style, and some believable depiction of reality, rather than a mere imitation of reality.

"You've never seen them; they're awfully good," I compassionately objected.

"Not seen them? Why, all this recent work of yours drops to pieces with them. It's all I want to see of them."

"No one else has said anything against it—the Cheapside people are pleased."

"Everyone else is an ass, and the Cheapside people the biggest asses of all. Come, don't pretend, at this time of day, to have pretty illusions about the public, especially about publishers and editors. It's not for SUCH animals you work—it's for those who know, coloro che sanno[1]; so keep straight for ME if you can't keep straight for yourself. There's a certain sort of thing you tried for from the first—and a very good thing it is. But this twaddle isn't IN it." When I talked with Hawley later about "Rutland Ramsay" and its possible successors he declared that I must get back into my boat again or I would go to the bottom. <u>His voice in short was the voice of warning.</u>[79]

I noted the warning, but I didn't turn my friends out of doors. They bored me a good deal; but the very fact that they bored me admonished me not to sacrifice them—if there was anything to be done with them—simply to irritation. <u>As I look back</u>[80] at this phase they seem to me to have pervaded my life not a little. <u>I have a vision</u>[81] of them as most of the time in my studio, seated, against the wall, on an old velvet bench to be out of the way, and looking like a pair of patient courtiers in a royal ante-chamber. <u>I am convinced</u>[82] that during the coldest weeks of the winter they held their ground because it saved them fire. Their newness was losing its gloss, and it was impossible not to feel that they were objects of charity. Whenever Miss Churm arrived they went away, and after I was fairly launched in "Rutland Ramsay" Miss Churm arrived pretty often. They managed to express to me tacitly that <u>they supposed</u> I wanted her for the low life of the book, <u>and I let them suppose it,</u>[83] since they had attempted to study the work—it was lying about the studio—without discovering that it dealt only with the highest circles. They had dipped into the most brilliant of our novelists without deciphering many passages. I still took an hour from them, now and again, in spite of Jack Hawley's warning: it would be time enough to dismiss them, if dismissal should be necessary, when the rigour of the season was over. Hawley had made their acquaintance—he had met them at my fireside—and thought them a ridiculous pair. Learning that he was a painter they tried to approach him, to show him too that they were the real thing; but he looked at them, across the big room, as if they were miles away: they were a compendium of everything that he most objected to in the social system of his country. Such people as that, all convention and patent-leather, with ejaculations that stopped conversation, had no business in a studio.

---

[1] Italian for "those who know."

Sample Student Commentary

[79] The introduction of the friend is a vehicle for James to introduce conflict—an opposing viewpoint—into the story.

[80] Note the use of the first person narrator. This is clearly a narrator in the "present" telling a story from his past.

[81] This is blatantly the narrator's recollection. It is his impression of the past, not necessarily a factual account. Compare this device with the problem he has faced all along with the representation of reality versus the appearance of reality.

[82] As in Chapter II, this is the narrator's conjecture. It is what he believes of them, not what he knows about them.

[83] Truth, appearance of truth, supposition, and conjecture.

A studio was a place to learn to see, and how could you see through a pair of feather beds?

The main inconvenience I suffered at their hands was that, at first, I was shy of letting them discover how my artful little servant had begun to sit to me for "Rutland Ramsay." They knew that I had been odd enough (they were prepared by this time to allow oddity to artists,) to pick a foreign vagabond out of the streets, when I might have had a person with whiskers and credentials; but it was some time before they learned how high I rated his accomplishments. They found him in an attitude more than once, but they never doubted I was doing him as an organ-grinder. There were several things they never guessed, and one of them was that for a striking scene in the novel, in which a footman briefly figured, it occurred to me to make use of Major Monarch as the menial. I kept putting this off, I didn't like to ask him to don the livery—besides the difficulty of finding a livery to fit him. At last, one day late in the winter, when I was at work on the despised Oronte (he caught one's idea in an instant), and was in the glow of feeling that I was going very straight, they came in, the Major and his wife, with their society laugh about nothing (there was less and less to laugh at), like country-callers—they always reminded me of that—who have walked across the park after church and are presently persuaded to stay to luncheon. Luncheon was over, but they could stay to tea—I knew they wanted it. The fit was on me, however, and I couldn't let my ardour cool and my work wait, with the fading daylight, while my model prepared it. So I asked Mrs. Monarch if she would mind laying it out—a request which, for an instant, brought all the blood to her face.[84] Her eyes were on her husband's for a second, and some mute telegraphy passed between them. Their folly was over the next instant; his cheerful shrewdness put an end to it. So far from pitying their wounded pride, I must add, I was moved to give it as complete a lesson as I could. They bustled about together and got out the cups and saucers and made the kettle boil. I know they felt as if they were waiting on my servant, and when the tea was prepared I said: "He'll have a cup, please—he's tired." Mrs. Monarch brought him one where he stood, and he took it from her as if he had been a gentleman at a party, squeezing a crush-hat[1] with an elbow.

Then it came over me that she had made a great effort for me—made it with a kind of nobleness—and that I owed her a compensation. Each time I saw her after this I wondered what the compensation could be. I couldn't go on doing the wrong thing to oblige them. Oh, it WAS the wrong thing, the stamp of the work for which they sat— Hawley was not the only person to say it now. I sent in a large number of the drawings I had made for "Rutland Ramsay," and I received a warning that was more to the point than Hawley's. The artistic adviser of the house for which I was working was of opinion that many of my illustrations were not what had been looked for. Most of these illustrations were the subjects in which the Monarchs had figured. Without going into the question of what HAD been looked for, I saw at this rate I shouldn't[85] get the other books to do.

---

[1] A collapsible hat designed to be flattened when not worn and carried under the arm.

Sample Student Commentary

[84] This act absolutely places her on the same level as Miss Churm and Oronte.

[85] Again, the British convention often uses "shouldn't" as we would use "wouldn't" in the United States.

I hurled myself in despair upon Miss Churm, I put her through all her paces. I not only adopted Oronte publicly as my hero, but one morning when the Major looked in to see if I didn't require him to finish a figure for the Cheapside, for which he had begun to sit the week before, I told him that I had changed my mind—I would do the drawing from my man. At this my visitor turned pale and stood looking at me. "Is HE your idea of an English gentleman?" he asked.

I was disappointed, I was nervous, I wanted to get on with my work; so I replied with irritation: "Oh, my dear Major—I can't be ruined for YOU!"

He stood another moment; then, without a word, he quitted the studio. I drew a long breath when he was gone, for I said to myself that I shouldn't see him again. I had not told him definitely that I was in danger of having my work rejected, but I was vexed at his not having felt the catastrophe in the air, read with me the moral of our fruitless collaboration, the lesson that, in the deceptive atmosphere of art, even the highest respectability may fail of being plastic.

I didn't owe my friends money, but I did see them again. They re- appeared together, three days later, and under the circumstances there was something tragic in the fact. It was a proof to me that they could find nothing else in life to do. They had threshed the matter out in a dismal conference—they had digested the bad news that they were not in for the series. If they were not useful to me even for the Cheapside their function seemed difficult to determine, and I could only judge at first that they had come, forgivingly, decorously, to take a last leave. This made me rejoice in secret that I had little leisure for a scene; for I had placed both my other models in position together and I was pegging away at a drawing from which I hoped to derive glory. It had been suggested by the passage in which Rutland Ramsay, drawing up a chair to Artemisia's piano-stool, says extraordinary things to her while she ostensibly fingers out a difficult piece of music. I had done Miss Churm at the piano before—it was an attitude in which she knew how to take on an absolutely poetic grace. I wished the two figures to "compose" together, intensely, and my little Italian had entered perfectly into my conception. The pair were vividly before me, the piano had been pulled out; it was a charming picture of blended youth and murmured love, which I had only to catch and keep. My visitors stood and looked at it, and I was friendly to them over my shoulder.

They made no response, but I was used to silent company and went on with my work, only a little disconcerted (even though exhilarated by the sense that THIS was at least the ideal thing), at not having got rid of them after all. Presently I heard Mrs. Monarch's sweet voice beside, or rather above me: "I wish her hair was a little better done." I looked up and she was staring with a strange fixedness at Miss Churm, whose back was turned to her. "Do you mind my just touching it?" she went on—a question which made me spring up for an instant, as with the instinctive fear that she might do the young lady a harm. But she quieted me with a glance I shall never forget—I confess I should like to have been able to paint THAT—and went for a moment to my model. She spoke to her softly, laying a hand upon her shoulder and bending over her; and as the girl, understanding, gratefully assented, she disposed her rough curls, with a few quick passes, in such a way as to make Miss Churm's head twice as charming. It was one of the most heroic personal services I have ever seen rendered. Then Mrs. Monarch turned away with a low sigh and, looking about her as if for something to do, stooped to the floor with a noble humility and picked up a dirty rag that had dropped out of my paint-box.

The Major meanwhile had also been looking for something to do and, wandering to the other end of the studio, saw before him my breakfast things, neglected, unremoved. "I say, can't I be useful HERE?" he called out to me with an irrepressible quaver. I assented with a laugh that I fear was awkward and for the next ten minutes, while I worked, I heard the light clatter of china and the tinkle of spoons and glass. Mrs. Monarch assisted her husband—they washed up my crockery, they put it away. They wandered off into my little scullery, and I afterwards found that they had cleaned my knives and that my slender stock of plate had an unprecedented surface. When it came over me, the latent eloquence of what they were doing, I confess that my drawing was blurred for a moment—the picture swam. They had accepted their failure, but they couldn't accept their fate. They had bowed their heads in bewilderment to the perverse and cruel law in virtue of which the real thing could be so much less precious than the unreal; but they didn't want to starve. If my servants were my models, my models might be my servants. They would reverse the parts—the others would sit for the ladies and gentlemen, and THEY would do the work. They would still be in the studio—it was an intense dumb appeal to me not to turn them out. "Take us on," they wanted to say—"we'll do ANYTHING."

When all this hung before me the afflatus[1] vanished—my pencil dropped from my hand. My sitting was spoiled and I got rid of my sitters, who were also evidently rather mystified and awestruck. Then, alone with the Major and his wife, I had a most uncomfortable moment, He put their prayer into a single sentence: "I say, you know— just let US do for you, can't you?" I couldn't—it was dreadful to see them emptying my slops; but I pretended I could, to oblige them, for about a week. Then I gave them a sum of money to go away; and I never saw them again. I obtained the remaining books, but my friend Hawley repeats that Major and Mrs. Monarch did me a permanent harm, got me into a second-rate trick. If it be true I am content to have paid the price—for the memory.

---

[1] A sudden and inexplicable inspiration.

Sample Multiple-Choice Questions

1. By the end of the story, the title, "The Real Thing," proves to be

    A. paradoxical.

    B. oxymoronic.

    C. ironic.

    D. ambiguous.

    E. sarcastic.

2. James introduces Oronte primarily as a vehicle to

    A. highlight Major Monarch's character.

    B. quicken the pace of the plot.

    C. clarify the paradoxical theme.

    D. complement Miss Churm's mother-wit.

    E. complicate the chief conflict.

3. The principal function of the scene in which Mrs. Monarch fixes Miss Churn's hair is most likely to

    A. present the climax of the plot.

    B. resolve the central conflict.

    C. reveal a dynamic character.

    D. provide the last bit of exposition.

    E. suggest the character's epiphany.

4. Throughout the story, James uses oxymora and double-meanings to achieve

    A. verbal irony.

    B. situational irony.

    C. dramatic irony.

    D. paradox.

    E. sarcasm.

5. All of the following quotations suggest that James contrived his portrait-painter first-person-protagonist narrator as a vehicle to assert his own theories and frustrations EXCEPT

    A. "I looked to a different branch of art ... to perpetuate my fame."

    B. "I remember telling him that if I were only rich I would offer him a salary to come and teach me how to live."

    C. "the ruling passion of my life was the detestation of the amateur. Combined with ... an innate preference for the represented subject over the real one."

    D. "the rarest of the novelists—who, long neglected by the multitudinous vulgar and dearly prized by the attentive ... had had the happy fortune of seeing, late in life, the dawn and then the full light of a higher criticism—an estimate in which, on the part of the public, there was something really of expiation."

    E. "I asked if he didn't think it good, and he replied that it struck him as execrable, given the sort of thing I had always represented myself to him as wishing to arrive at."

Answers and Explanations:

1. The title, of course, refers to the Monarchs, who believe themselves better suited to model for aristocratic figures because they would need no artifice to make them look like what they are. While the *story* proves to be paradoxical (A) because the servant-class models provide a better appearance of aristocracy than "the real thing," the phrase itself is not a paradox. Nor is there any self-contradiction or oxymoron in the phrase itself (B). Much of the story does indeed depend on double meanings and ambiguities (D), but this phrase does indeed mean what it says. Oronte and Miss Churm are *not* the real things; they can merely be made to *look* real. (E) is tempting, but the phrase itself has no tone without the context of the story, and even then, James is neither criticizing nor mocking the Monarchs for being what they are. **The best answer is (C)**. The Monarchs remain proud of the fact that they are, indeed, the real thing until the very end when they see the transformations that art can make. The irony is in the awareness that the real thing is not necessarily the best thing for art. Appearance is more important than the reality behind it.

2. Oronte might be considered a foil for Major Monarch (A) as Muss Churn is for Mrs. Monarch, but he is introduced into the story too late for this to be his primary function. The Major's stiffness and inappropriateness for modeling have already been established. (B) is unlikely since the play has very little of a traditional "plot," and Oronte's presence may alter the direction of the plot somewhat but not the generally slow pacing. (C) is tempting because his presence does emphasize the unsuitability of "the real thing" to portray itself in art, but this theme has not been in need of *clarification*, so this is not the best choice. (D) is considerably less tempting as, while some readers may see Oronte as a complement to Miss Churm, we never hear him speak, and we never *see* (or hear) Miss Churm's wit. **(E) is the best answer**. The chief conflict has been established as the Monarchs' need for money opposing their unsuitability for the job. This unsuitability is emphasized by the presence of the servant-class models. With Oronte present, Major Monarch has yet another obstacle to overcome in his quest for gainful employment.

3. (B) might tempt some, as it seems this gesture makes it clear how the conflict will be resolved, but the resolution has not been reached yet. (C) might also tempt some, as the gesture does, perhaps, indicate change or growth in Mrs. Monarch, but this action by itself does not fully *reveal* a new character. (D) is the least tempting of the five as this gesture reveals something new. (E) is, perhaps, the most tempting of the four incorrect choices because it is clear that the Monarchs have had some sort of epiphany, but, like (B) and (C), this is a *component* of the principal function, not the function itself. The part of the plot that points to the final resolution of the conflict, reveals the change taking place in a dynamic character, and suggests the character's epiphany is the climax of the story. **Thus, (A) is the best answer**.

4. Oxymora and double-meaning are elements of verbal irony (A), so that cannot be the intended effect. While the situation of "the real thing" not being suited to represent itself might be ironic, these language devices do not create the situational irony (B). The reader knows only what the first-person narrator tells us, and he admits that much of what he "knows" is supposition and conjecture, so (C) is unlikely. James does often make his narrator sarcastic (E), and this sarcasm is often achieved through language devices like oxymora and ambiguities, but not *all* of these devices contribute to the sarcasm. Some heighten the irony of the situation and the central paradox of the story. **Thus, (D) is the best answer**.

5. (A) could be interpreted to express not only the narrator's desire to be recognized as an "artist," but James's own longing for literary recognition. (C), likewise, might explore James's literary theory of realism versus impressionism. (D) is almost blatant, as he is decrying a novelist's lack of literary recognition, which mirrors his own. (E) could easily be interpreted to reflect James's frustration at the contrast between his actual work with his stated goals. **Thus, (B) is the best answer**.

Sample free-response item 1 (Text-based):

Read Henry James's "The Real Thing." Then write a well-organized and well-supported essay in which you analyze the literary and narrative techniques James uses to convey to the reader his narrator's attitude toward the Monarchs. Do not merely provide a description of the narrator's attitude.

> The unnamed narrator of Henry James's short story, "The Real Thing" seems at times to dislike the Monarchs, a once-aristocratic couple who have fallen on hard times, while at others, he seems to like them. He admires what he portrays as a strength of character while, at the same time pitying them. In short, the narrator is ambivalent toward this puzzling couple and their plight.[1] He conveys this ambivalence through careful scene selection and through sarcasm, verbal ironies, and double entendres that make the narrator's ambivalence apparent even on the surface of the story.[2]
>
> The first appearance of the Monarchs is an example of James's careful scene selection. The narrator, a portrait painter, misunderstands the Monarchs' reason for coming. Because they are "genteel," he assumes they are there to pay him to paint

---

Scorer Commentary

[1] While the prompt does specify not to provide merely a description of the narrator's attitude, it is not wrong to mention what that attitude is in order then to describe how it is communicated.

[2] Here is where this student promises to fulfill the requirement of the prompt—to address how the attitude is conveyed, not what the attitude is.

their portrait, when in fact they are there to be paid for posing for book illustrations.[3] There is also a good deal of verbal irony in these opening scenes as well. The ambiguities and double meanings contribute to the narrator's confusion and the reader's amused understanding of that confusion.[4] This opening scene is so important to James's establishment of the narrator's attitude that he devotes the entire first "chapter" and a significant portion of the second to it. It tells of something similar to admiration ("The gentleman, a man of fifty, very high and very straight, with a ... a dark grey walking-coat admirably fitted, ... which I noted professionally ... would have struck me as a celebrity if celebrities often were striking.") Here, the narrator is saying Major Monarch presents a striking appearance in a way that celebrities do not. He describes Mrs. Monarch similarly ("A glance at the lady helped to remind me ... she also looked too distinguished to be a 'personality.'") The ambivalence is established when the narrator's admiration turns to amusement at their plight: "I was so amused by them that, to get more of it, I did my best to take their point of view; and though it was an embarrassment to find myself appraising physically, as if they were animals on hire or useful blacks ..."[5]

After this initial scene, the pace of the story picks up and a period of weeks or months passes in only a few pages. James is very careful to portray only those scenes that help to reveal the narrator's attitude. When Miss Churm makes her first entrance, the narrator defends her skill as a model with "an innocent form of aggravation." From that moment, James carefully arranges the episodes to follow the form of action rising to a climax while also allowing the narrator to waver between respect and pity for and exasperation with the Monarchs. The introduction of new characters, Oronte and Jack Hawley, provides a basis for comparison until the narrator arrives at the conclusion, "Oh, my dear Major—I can't be ruined for YOU!"

This is not, however, a final declaration of a clear feeling. Even after this outburst, James has the narrator witness the final humiliation of the Monarchs as they demote themselves to the level of household servants while the household servants take on the guise of the lady and gentleman of the house. Even in his asking the Monarchs to leave and not return, he neither loves nor hates, respects nor pities them. He is ambivalent.

Of course the actions of the plot should illustrate a significant character's attitude, but James is more masterful than to employ this one obvious technique alone.[6] James also contrives verbal irony—often taking the form of sarcasm—that helps the reader to understand the narrator's ambivalence. The double meaning of the narrator's being

---

Scorer Commentary

[3] The thesis is a formulaic, two-point thesis that will probably lead to a variation on the five-paragraph essay. While this might not be the best organizational pattern for a top-scoring essay, at this point, it will help this student write the "well-organized" essay demanded in the prompt. NOTE that the first point of the thesis speaks of scene selection, and this first paragraph is about scene selection.

[4] Mentioning the verbal irony here does not ruin the organization of the essay, as long as the student does not digress into a full discussion of the ambiguities in the scene.

[5] This student needs to be careful because it seems as if he might be digressing into a simple description of the narrator's attitude.

[6] Not a bad transition. Remember that the thesis does promise to discuss James's language as well.

"the right one," and Major Monarch's supposing "it would be double" if they both posed, and the Major's insisting that they would "like to make it pay" reflects the narrator' confusion—he believes he is being interviewed by a couple who will pay to have their portrait done—and illustrates the beginning of his ambivalence. He admires their aristocratic bearing, their presence, perhaps because they will be able to do him good. While admiring them, however, he is amused by their inability to state their business clearly. "Perhaps they wished to be done [painted] together," he quips, "in which case they ought to have brought a third person to break the news." Once he learns that their mission is to secure positions as models, he compares them—almost cruelly—to "animals on hire or useful blacks." In the next paragraph, however, the "animal on hire" is "six feet two and a perfect gentleman." His wife, on the other hand, is "singularly like a bad illustration." The very language James uses to describe the Monarchs typifies his ambivalence without his ever having to lay it out for the reader.

The verbal ironies that James use to express his mixed feelings toward the Monarchs include a few puns that come at the Monarchs' expense. The narrator observes that he has no objection to using the couple "if they would suit," and a few sentences later, Mrs. Monarch asks whether they would have to wear costumes. The Major insists they'll wear any costume that "fits," and the reader is left to consider whether he means any right-sized article of clothing, any garment suitable to their station, or both.

Even the words James has the Monarchs themselves speak reveal the narrator's two-sided, love-hate attitude. While the fallen aristocrats are proud of being aristocrats and feel they do not have to pretend in order to represent their class in illustrations, the narrator is unable to portray them in this manner. His artistry allows him to translate a Miss Churm into a Russian princess, while Mrs. Monarch boasts, "... the drawings you make from US, they look exactly like us." For her, this is a source of triumph. For the narrator, it is "just their defect." Yet the narrator cannot merely dismiss them. He describes his inability in two oxymora, citing their "pathetic decorum" and their "permanent newness." The apparently contradictory terms with which he describes their presence in his household reflect the contradictory feelings he has about them. The climax arrives—the turning point at which the narrator's ambivalence tips toward antipathy—when the Major questions the narrator's choice of Oronte to model for the gentleman, and the narrator blurts out, "Oh, my dear Major—I can't be ruined for YOU!"

It is now clear. The ambivalence has vanished. The Monarchs are not useful to the narrator as models, and he cannot bear to employ them in any other capacity. After they too realize what the narrator's outburst means, and they begin to clear away the dishes from tea, the narrator is finally able to ask them not to return. Never once, however, does the author, Henry James, intrude his observation on the reader. Rather than telling us that the narrator both likes and despises, enjoys and pities his new acquaintances, he shows us through careful selection of incidents and use of language, especially double entendres and verbal ironies like sarcasm.[7]

Scorer Commentary

[7] For his "well-organized essay," the student returns us back to his thesis.

Sample free-response item 2 (Independent):

All art, including literary art, is sometimes self-reflective rather than outward-looking. Occasionally, the artist, like the critic, expounds on what art is, how it is created, and what purposes it is to serve. The best of these works, however, do not just teach but remain artistic in their own right. Choose such a work of literature and write an essay in which you explore the ways the author manages to weave together the instructional and artistic aspects of the work. Do not merely summarize the plot or explain the artistic theory.

It isn't surprising that a painter might write about painting, or a writer might sometimes write about writing. For a writer to find a way to fictionalize the creative process and describe to his readers what he considers to be his relationship to his work is a little like telling an inside joke. When, as a reader, you "get it," you feel as if you're on the inside with the writer.[1] Henry James, in his otherwise dull and uneventful "The Real Thing,"[2] uses the characters of a financially struggling aristocratic couple as the vehicles to explore the artist's obligation to depict, not reality, but his or her vision of reality. Is art an imitation of life, James's narrator asks, or is life on some level an imitation of art? Ultimately, James's narrator concludes, the artist's view might just be more real than "the real thing."[3] The story isn't, however, just a treatise on artistic theory and philosophy; it is a piece of literature in its own right. This is especially evident in James's language—the mocking sarcasm with which he discusses his subjects and the word play with which he tells his story.[4]

The central issue of "The Real Thing" is the difference between what James's narrator calls "the alchemy of art" and reality. Major and Mrs. Monarch are real aristocrats, and they believe—as most would—that they are uniquely qualified to represent their class in book illustrations. The fact is, however, that their being "the real thing" is exactly what renders them all but useless to this artistic purpose. The artist, according to the narrator, cannot be bothered with what is "real": the artist's concern is with representation, appearance, only. Perhaps, this story asks the reader to ponder, the artist's vision is the more real because the characters eventually become in the end what the narrator saw them to be from the beginning.[5]

Scorer Commentary

[1] To paraphrase the question is a step or two more powerful than merely restating it.

[2] You are under no obligation to like the literature you are assigned to examine, but you must be careful not to let personal taste interfere with composing an appropriate response to the question.

[3] This statement addresses the first half of the assignment. This student must be careful not to discuss only the theory.

[4] Here the student addresses the second half of the question.

[5] Notice how this student handles the issue of plot summary. Clearly he must refer to the plot, but in order to support his point, he does not need a point-by-point, beginning-to-end review of the entire story.

The fact that James views the aristocrats as the true servants and the servants as the true "upper class" from the beginning of the story when he first meets the Monarchs is not apparent in the surface meaning of the text, but is certainly clear in James's language. From the first, even when he thinks that they are paying clients and might help him establish himself as a great portrait painter, the narrator speaks of them in a mocking, sarcastic tone. Misunderstanding their reluctance to state the purpose of their visit, he says, "the scruples of my new friends appeared almost insurmountable," the "scruples" being their hesitance to admit that they "desired anything so gross as to be represented on canvas." Speculating on their reluctance to state their business, he finally concludes, "they ought to have brought a third person to break the news." From the narrator's introduction to the subjects of his story, before he knows even their names, he mocks them.

He maintains this mocking tone throughout, describing Major Monarch as "a figure with a good deal of frontage" and Mrs. Monarch as, "singularly like a bad illustration." They amuse him. He believes he knows all about them just from studying them "as if they were animals on hire or useful blacks." Despite his claims that he tries long and hard to use them, the narrator expresses not a bit of compassion for the Monarchs or their plight until the end of the story. Once they witness the transformation of the servants into the aristocrats for the narrator's series of books, they become the servants.[6] Once they assume the roles the narrator had always seen them in, he speaks of them kindly:

> ...alone with the Major and his wife, I had a most uncomfortable moment. He put their prayer into a single sentence: 'I say, you know—just let US do for you, can't you?' I couldn't—it was dreadful to see them emptying my slops; but I pretended I could, to oblige them, for about a week.

Life has imitated art. The artist's vision has proven to be more real than reality, and the aristocrats have become the servants. The transformation has been the story's plot, and it has been mirrored in James's language and tone—from mocking to compassionate—as "the real things" slowly transform into what they really are.

On the surface, then, "The Real Thing" is a relatively boring story about the decline of a once-aristocratic couple to menial servitude. It is amusing only as much as the narrator's tone is amusing—mocking and sarcastic. Beneath this surface is James's true thesis, that the artist sees reality more clearly, that he must be free to depict reality as he sees it because, in the end, his view is the more honest. Art should not imitate life, James insists, because eventually life will prove to be an imitation of art.

Scorer Commentary

[6] Again, the manner with which the student refers to the plot assumes that the reader of the essay has also read the story. He does not waste time simply retelling the story.

Exercise One:

Questions 1–5. Read the following passage carefully before you choose your answers.

I Stand Here Ironing

BY TILLIE OLSEN (1912-2007)

1   I STAND HERE IRONING, and what you asked me moves tormented back and forth with the iron.

2   "I wish you would manage the time to come in and talk with me about your daughter. I'm sure you can help me understand her. She's a youngster who needs help and whom I'm deeply interested in helping."

3   "Who needs help,"…Even if I came, what good would it do? You think because I am her mother I have a key, or that in some way you could use me as a key? She has lived for nineteen years. There is all that life that has happened outside of me, beyond me.

4   And when is there time to remember, to sift, to weigh, to estimate, to total? I will start and there will be an interruption and I will have to gather it all together again. Or I will become engulfed with all I did or did not do, with what should have been and what cannot be helped.

5   She was a beautiful baby. The first and only one of our five that was beautiful at birth. You do not guess how new and uneasy her tenancy in her now-loveliness. You did not know her all those years she was thought homely, or see her poring over her baby pictures, making me tell her over and over how beautiful she had been—and would be, I would tell her—and was now, to the seeing eye. But the seeing eyes were few or nonexistent. Including mine.

6   I nursed her. They feel that's important nowadays. I nursed all the children, but with her, with all the fierce rigidity of first motherhood, I did like the books then said. Through her cries battered me to trembling and my breasts ached with swollenness. I waited till the clock decreed.

7   Why do I put that first? I do not even know if it matters, or if it explains anything.

8   She was a beautiful baby. She blew shining bubbles of sound. She loved motion, loved light, loved color and music and textures. She would lie on the floor in her blue overalls patting the surface so hard in ecstasy her hands and feet would blur. She was a miracle to me, but when she was eight months old I had to leave her daytimes with the woman downstairs to whom she was no miracle at all, for I worked or looked for work and for Emily's father, who "could no longer endure" (he wrote in his good-bye note) "sharing want with us."

9   I was nineteen. It was the pre-relief, pre WPA world of the depression. I would start running as soon as I got off the streetcar, running up the stairs, the place smelling sour, and awake or asleep to startle awake, when she saw me she would break into a clogged weeping that could not be comforted, a weeping I can hear yet.

10   After a while I found a job hashing at night so I could be with her days, and it was better. But I came to where I had to bring her to family and leave her.

11   It took a long time to raise the money for her fare back. Then she got chicken pox and I had to wait longer. When she finally came, I hardly knew her, walking quick and nervous like her father, looking like her father, thin, and dressed a shoddy red that yellowed her skin and glared at the pockmarks. All the baby loveliness gone.

12   She was two. Old enough for nursery school they said, and I did not know then what I did now—the fatigue of the long day, and the lacerations of group life in the kinds of nurseries that are only parking places for children.

13   Except that it would have made no difference if I had known. It was the only place there was. It was the only way we could be together, the only way I could hold a job.

14   And even without knowing, I knew. I knew the teacher that was evil because all these years it has curdled into my memory, the little boy hunched in the corner, her rasp, "why aren't you outside, because Alvin hits you? that's no reason. go out. scaredy." I knew Emily hated it even if she did not clutch and implore "don't go Mommy" like the other children, mornings.

15   She always had a reason why we should stay home. Momma, you look sick. Momma, I feel sick. Momma, the teachers aren't there today, they're sick. Momma, we can't go, there was a fire there last night. Momma, it's a holiday today, no school, they told me.

16   But never a direct protest, never rebellion. I think of our others in their three-four-year-oldness—the explosions, the tempers, the denunciations, the demands—and I feel suddenly ill. I put down the iron. What in me demanded that goodness in her? And what was the cost, the cost of her such goodness?

17   The old man living in the back once said in his gentle way: "You should smile more at Emily when you look at her." What *was* in my face when I looked at her? I loved her. There were all the acts of love.

18   It was only with the others I remembered what he said, and it was the face of joy, and not of care or tightness or worry I turned to—too late for Emily. She does not smile easily, let alone almost always as her brothers and sisters do. Her face is closed and somber, but when she wants, how fluid. You must have seen it in her pantomimes, you spoke of her rare gift for comedy on the stage that rouses laughter out of the audience so dear they applaud and applaud and do not want to let her go.

19   Where does it come from, that comedy? There was none of it in her when she came back to me that second time, after I had had to send her away again. She had a new daddy now to learn to love, and I think perhaps it was a better time.

20   Except when we left her alone nights, telling ourselves she was old enough.

21   "Can't you go some other time, Mommy, like tomorrow?" she would ask, "Will it be just a little while you'll be gone? Do you promise?"

22   The time we came back, the front door open, the clock on the floor in the hall. She rigid awake. "It wasn't just a little while. I didn't cry. Three times I called you, just three times, and then I ran downstairs to open the door so you could come faster. The clock talked loud. I threw it away, it scared me what it talked."

23   She said the clock talked loud again that night I went to the hospital to have Susan. She was delirious with the fever that comes before red measles, but she was fully conscious all the week I was gone and the week after we were home when she could not come near the new baby or me.

24   She did not get well. She stayed skeleton thin, not wanting to eat, and night after night she had nightmares. She would call for me, and I would rouse from exhaustion to sleepily call back: "You're all right, darling, go to sleep, it's just a dream," and if she still called, in a sterner voice, "now go to sleep, Emily, there's nothing to hurt you." Twice, only twice, when I had to get up for Susan anyhow, I went in to sit with her.

25   Now when it is too late (as if she would let me hold and comfort her like I do the others) I get up and go to her at once at her moan or restless stirring. "Are you awake, Emily? Can I get you something?" And the answer is always the same: "No, I'm all right, go back to sleep, Mother."

26   They persuaded me at the clinic to send her away to a convalescent home in the country where "she can have the kind of food and care you can't manage for her, and you'll be free to concentrate on the new baby." They still send children to that place. I see pictures on the society page of sleek young women planning affairs to raise money for it, or dancing at the affairs, or decorating Easter eggs or filling Christmas stockings for the children.

27   They never have a picture of the children so I do not know if the girls still wear those gigantic red bows and the ravaged looks on every other Sunday when parents can come to visit "unless otherwise notified"—as we were notified the first six weeks.

28   Oh it is a handsome place, green lawns and tall trees and fluted flower beds. High up on the balconies of each cottage the children stand, the girls in their red bows and white dresses, the boys in white suits and giant red ties. The parents stand below shrieking up to be heard and the children shriek down to be heard, and between them the invisible wall: "Not to Be Contaminated by Parental Germs or Physical Affection."

29   There was a tiny girl who always stood hand in hand with Emily. Her parents never came. One visit she was gone. "They moved her to Rose Cottage," Emily shouted in explanation. "They don't like you to love anybody here."

30   She wrote once a week, the labored writing of a seven-year-old. "I am fine. How is the baby. If I write my letter nicely I will have a star. Love." There was never a star. We wrote every other day, letters she could never hold or keep but only hear read—once. "We simply do not have room for children to keep any personal possessions," they patiently explained when we pieced one Sunday's shrieking together to plead how much it would mean to Emily, who loved to keep things, to be allowed to keep her letters and cards.

31   Each visit she looked frailer. "She isn't eating," they told us.

32   (They had runny eggs for breakfast or mush with lumps, Emily said later, I'd hold it in my mouth and not swallow. Nothing ever tasted good, just when they had chicken.)

33   It took us eight months to get her released home, and the fact that she gained back so little of her seven lost pounds convinced the social worker.

34   I used to try to hold and love her after she came back, but her body would stay stiff, and after a while she'd push away. She ate little. Food sickened her, and I think much of life too. Oh she had physical lightness and brightness, twinkling by on skates, bouncing like a ball up and down up and down over the jump rope, skimming over the hill; but these were momentary.

35   She fretted about her appearance, thin and dark and foreign-looking at a time when every little girl was supposed to look or thought she should look a chubby blond replica of Shirley Temple. The doorbell sometimes rang for her, but no one seemed to come and play in the house or be a best friend. Maybe because we moved so much.

36   There was a boy she loved painfully through two school semesters. Months later she told me how she had taken pennies from my purse to buy him candy. "Licorice was his favorite and I bought him some every day, but he still liked Jennifer better'n me. Why, Mommy? The kind of question for which there is no answer.

37   School was a worry to her. She was not glib or quick in a world where glibness and quickness were easily confused with ability to learn. To her overworked and exasperated teachers she was an overconscientious "slow learner" who kept trying to catch up and was absent entirely too often.

38   I let her be absent, though sometimes the illness was imaginary. How different from my now-strictness about attendance with the others. I wasn't working. We had a new baby, I was home anyhow. Sometimes, after Susan grew old enough, I would keep her home from school, too, to have them all together.

39   Mostly Emily had asthma, and her breathing, harsh and labored, would fill the house with a curiously tranquil sound. I would bring the two old dresser mirrors and her boxes of collections to her bed. She would select beads and single earrings, bottle tops and shells, dried flowers and pebbles, old postcards and scraps, all sorts of oddments; then she and Susan would play Kingdom, setting up landscapes and furniture, peopling them with action.

40   Those were the only times of peaceful companionship between her and Susan. I have edged away from it, that poisonous feeling between them, that terrible balancing of hurts and needs I had to do between the two, and did so badly, those earlier years.

41   Oh there are conflicts between the others too, each one human, needing, demanding, hurting, taking—but only between Emily and Susan, no, Emily toward Susan that was corroding resentment. It seems so obvious on the surface, yet it was not obvious. Susan, the second child, Susan, golden and curly-haired and chubby, quick and articulate and assured, everything in appearance and manner Emily was not; Susan, not able to resist Emily's precious things, losing or sometimes clumsily breaking them; Susan telling jokes and riddles to company for applause while Emily sat silent (to say to me later: that was *my* riddle, Mother, I told it to Susan); Susan, who for all the five years' difference in age was just a year behind Emily in developing physically.

42   I am glad for that slow physical development that widened the difference between her and her contemporaries, though she suffered over it. She was too vulnerable for that terrible world of youthful competition, of preening and parading, of constant measuring of yourself against every other, of envy, "If I had that copper hair," "If I had that skin…" She tormented herself enough about not looking like the others, there was enough of the unsureness, the having to be conscious of words before you speak, the constant caring—what are they thinking of me? without having it all magnified by the merciless physical drives.

43   Ronnie is calling. He is wet and I change him. It is rare there is such a cry now. That time of motherhood is almost behind me when the ear is not one's own but must always be racked and listening for the child cry, the child call. We sit for a while and I hold him, looking out over the city spread in charcoal with its soft aisles of light. *"Shoogily,"*

he breathes and curls closer. I carry him back to bed, asleep. *Shoogily*. A funny word, a family word, inherited from Emily, invented by her to say: *comfort*.

44   In this and other ways she leaves her seal, I would say aloud. And startle at my saying it. What do I mean? What did I start to gather together, to try and make coherent? I was at the terrible, growing years. War years. I do not remember them well. I was working, there were four smaller ones now, there was not time for her. She had to help be a mother, and housekeeper, and shopper. She had to set her seal. Mornings of crisis and near hysteria trying to get lunches packed, hair combed, coats and shoes found, everyone to school or Child Care on time, the baby ready for transportation. And always the paper scribbled on by a smaller one, the book looked at by Susan then mislaid, the homework not done. Running out to that huge school where she was one, she was lost, she was a drop; suffering over the unpreparedness, stammering and unsure in her classes.

45   There was so little time left at night after the kids were bedded down. She would struggle over books, always eating (it was in those years she developed her enormous appetite that is legendary in our family) and I would be ironing, or preparing food for the next day, or writing V-mail to Bill, or tending the baby. Sometimes, to make me laugh, or out of her despair, she would imitate happenings at school.

46   I think I said once: "Why don't you do something like this in the school amateur show?" One morning she phoned me at work, hardly understandable through the weeping: "Mother, I did it. I won, I won; they gave me first prize; they clapped and clapped and wouldn't let me go."

47   Now suddenly she was Somebody, and as imprisoned in her difference as she had been in anonymity.

48   She began to be asked to perform at other high schools, even colleges, than at city and statewide affairs. The first one we went to, I only recognized her that first moment when thin, shy, she almost drowned herself into the curtains. Then: Was this Emily? The control, the command, the convulsing and deadly clowning, the spell, then the roaring, the stamping audience, unwilling to let this rare and precious laughter out of their lives.

49   Afterwards: You ought to do something about her with a gift like that—but without money or knowing how, what does one do? We have left it all to her, and the gift has often eddied inside, clogged and clotted, as been used and growing.

50   She is coming. She runs up the stairs two at a time with her light graceful step, and I know she is happy tonight. Whatever it was that occasioned your call did not happen today.

51   "Aren't you ever going to finish ironing, Mother? Whistler painted his mother in a rocker. I'd have to paint mine standing over an ironing board." This is one of her communicative nights and she tells me everything and nothing as she fixes herself a plate of food out of the icebox.

52   She is so lovely. Why did you want to come up at all? Why were you concerned? She will find her way.

53   She starts up the stairs to bed. "Don't get me up with the rest in the morning." "But I thought you were having midterms." "Oh, those," she comes back in, kisses me, and says quite lightly, "in a couple of years when we'll all be atom-dead they won't matter a bit."

54   She has said it before. She *believes* it. But because I have been dredging the past, and

all that compounds a human being is so heavy and meaningful in me, I cannot endure it tonight.

55   I will never total it all. I will never come to say: She was a child seldom smiled at. Her father left me before she was a year old. I had to work her first six years when there was work, or I sent her home and to his relatives. There were tears she had care she hated. She was dark and thin and foreign-looking in a world where the prestige went to blondness and curly hair and dimples, she was slow where glibness was prized. She was a child of anxious, not proud, love. We were poor and could not afford for her the soil of easy growth. I was a young mother, I was a distracted mother. There were other children pushing up, demanding. Her younger sister seemed all that she was not. There were years she did not want me to touch her. She kept too much in herself, her life was such she had to keep too much in herself. My wisdom came too late. She has much to her and probably little will come of it. She is a child of her age, of depression, of war, of fear.

56   Let her be. So all that is in her will not bloom—but in how many does it? There is still enough left to live by. Only help her to know—help make it so there is cause for her to know—that she is more than this dress on the ironing board, helpless before the iron.

Multiple-Choice Questions 1–5:

1. Tillie Olsen uses the device of the mother's ironing as a vehicle to suggest the
   A. futility of life.
   B. inability to overcome adversity.
   C. stress of single parenthood.
   D. willingness to give up.
   E. turmoil of adolescence.

2. The inciting incident of this monologue is most likely
   A. a visit from a school counselor.
   B. the daughter's entrance.
   C. an occurrence at Emily's school.
   D. the narrator's spontaneous recollection.
   E. a communication from Emily's school.

3. Despite surface appearances, Olsen adheres to all of the following narrative conventions EXCEPT
   A. chronological order.
   B. indirect dialogue.
   C. character development.
   D. establishment of setting.
   E. direct dialogue.

4. Structurally, the school's request for a conference is the
   A. introduction of the conflict.
   B. vehicle to motivate the flashback.
   C. climactic moment.
   D. moment of epiphany.
   E. device to clarify the central metaphor.

5. For what likely reason does Olsen mention Emily's talent for comedy?
   A. to add depth to Emily's character
   B. to introduce humor to the story
   C. to highlight the mother's indifference
   D. to introduce irony to the story
   E. to contrast the characters' circumstances

Free-response item 1 (Text-based):

Read Tillie Olsen's "I Stand Here Ironing." Then write a thoughtful and well-supported essay in which you analyze the literary and narrative techniques Olsen uses to reveal her narrator's character, attitude, and values. Do not merely provide a character study of the narrator.

Before you write your essay:

1. **Make sure you understand exactly what you're being asked to write about.**
     • List all of the verbs in the prompt.
     • Underline the verb that describes the essay.
     • Write the direct object of that verb.

2. **Make sure you have something valid to write about.**
     • Write a sentence or two that make a positive and focused statement about the topic.
     • Make sure these sentences address all of the issues and subpoints specified in the prompt.

3. **Review the selection and find your textual support.**

4. **Write your essay.**
   Keep referring to the prompt and whatever you underlined or highlighted in the selection to make sure you're on track and addressing everything the prompt wants you to address.

Free-response item 2 (Independent):

British mathematician and philosopher Alfred North Whitehead (1861–1947) wrote, "Symbolism is no mere idle fancy or corrupt degeneration; it is inherent in the very texture of human life." Choose a novel, story, or play in which a central symbol contributes significantly to the story's theme or meaning. Then write a thoughtful and well-reasoned essay in which you explain how that symbol supports or illustrates Whitehead's observation.

You may choose a work from the list below or another novel or play of comparable literary merit.

Before you write your essay:

1. **Make sure you understand exactly what you're being asked to write about.**
   - List all of the verbs in the prompt.
   - Underline the verb that describes the essay.
   - Write the direct object of that verb.

2. **Choose an appropriate selection.**
   If you're using this book, your teacher probably wants you to write your essay on whatever story, article, or poem, etc., the writing prompt follows.

3. **Make sure you have something to say about both the topic and your selected literature.**
   - Jot down key plot events.
   - Think in terms of plot structure: rising action, climax, falling action, and so on.
   - List characters.
   - Think in terms of function or role—protagonist or antagonist.
   - Think in terms of type—hero, anti-hero, foil, clown, etc.
   - Make sure you jot down notes that pertain to the assigned topic.
   - Jot down quotations or at least close paraphrases.
   - Jot down everything you know and remember about the assigned topic.

4. **Make sure you are clear about what you are going to say.**
- Write a sentence or two that make a positive and focused statement about the topic.
- Make sure these sentences address all of the issues and subpoints specified in the prompt.

5. **Write your essay.**

Prestwick House Pre-AP: Readings and Exercises

Some reminders for succeeding with multiple-choice questions

MINI-CHAPTER 3.5:

1. Remember that, while none of the questions will require outside knowledge about the passage or the author, they *will* most likely assume outside knowledge of literary themes, genres, structures, devices, and so on.

2. When the instructions ask you to identify the "best" choice, they mean it.
   - *Every* choice will be tempting for one reason or another.
   - Often the best way to identify this "best choice" is to eliminate the others.
   - The best choice will *always* be fully supportable by the text.

3. When two or more distracters are genuinely tempting, you must be able to justify every decision you make—why you are eliminating the one and selecting the other?

4. Most of the questions will be written in such manner that you should be able to answer the question before looking at the distracters. You will probably find it helpful to read the question and create your own answer. Then, simply select the choice that most closely matches the answer you created.

5. Most of the questions will focus on analysis rather than comprehension or even interpretation—*how* the text works, not only what it means.

6. There is no penalty for wrong answers, so it is in your best interest to eliminate the ones you can and guess from among the rest. There is nothing to be gained by leaving questions blank.

7. You can often speed up the elimination process by recognizing the *type* of wrong answer a distracter you're considering might be.

How to Frame an Interpretation... and Then Talk and Write About It

CHAPTER 4

YOU'RE PROBABLY FAMILIAR WITH the expression that a person "can't see the forest for the trees." You may or may not already realize that what this expression means is that paying too much attention to individual detail (the trees) can prevent someone from seeing, understanding, and appreciating the big picture (the forest).

So far in this book, we've been looking at trees—several types of trees—all of which contribute something to the total forest. We've also paid some attention to *what* these different types of trees contribute to the forest. But we haven't stepped back to look at the forest, the whole, literary big picture.

One big picture that an Advanced Placement exam might ask you to see is the passage's "meaning." AP literature and language free-response items even often ask you to write about what a specific detail contributes to "the overall meaning of the piece." *Overall* clearly suggests that, once you have looked at a few specific trees, you need to step back and consider the entire forest.

What exactly the writers of the AP exam mean each time they ask about *meaning* will be up to you to decide when you face the question. Generally, however, questions about *overall meaning* will want you to discuss theme, philosophical insight, social commentary or satire (for fiction, drama, and poetry), or perhaps the author's main idea, thesis, or argument (for nonfiction).

Except for the simplest and most obvious written communications, determining the meaning of something someone else has written is largely a matter of inference or interpretation.

It doesn't take much thought to understand what the writers of the following "passages" intended to communicate to their audience.

Dear John,
I do not want to go to the dance with you Saturday night. I am going
with Jeffrey instead.

Joanne

Sweetums,
Please pick up a loaf of bread and a gallon of low-fat milk on your way
home. Thanks.

Your Snookie

Other passages, while more complex and subtle, also reflect an author's purpose
or intent. The act of inference or interpretation is not merely a free-for-all of
guessing and baseless opinion. The point of interpretation is not to *make up the
meaning of the passage*; it is to *figure out the author's intent in writing it.*

How is that done? Well, that's why the previous four chapters dealt with
"trees" before we decided to step back and look at the "forest." Details like word
choice, use of figurative and rhetorical devices, selection of form and genre, and
faithfulness to (or departure from) conventions are the tools by which writers
communicate their meaning. They are also the only clues by which a reader can
expect to infer the writer's meaning.

Ignore or misread the clues, and you misinterpret the text. It's really as simple
as that.

In fact, for most of the Advanced Placement passages you'll encounter, your
interpretation won't matter as much as how you discuss and support it.

That's what this chapter is about.

Let's examine a few passages from the standpoint of developing an overall
interpretation and then arguing for the validity of your interpretation.

The first ten amendments to the United States Constitution, commonly called
"The Bill of Rights," has been annotated for you by our model students. AP-style
multiple-choice and free-response items have been completed to show you how
these students would respond to this piece on an Advanced Placement exam.

The second selection, George Washington's famous 1796 Farewell Address, is
long and very challenging. For this reason, it has been divided into three sections,
two exercise sections and one model section. The factors that make this such a
challenging piece are exactly those that a close reader must consider when trying
to interpret the meaning and intent of another writer's work: word meanings, and
grammar and sentence structure.

As interpretation is one of the main points of reading, challenges like these are
worth facing and overcoming.

Model One:

The Bill of Rights

The Preamble to The Bill of Rights[1]

Congress of the United States begun and held at the City of New York, on Wednesday the fourth of March, one thousand seven hundred and eighty nine.

THE <u>Conventions of a number of the States</u>, having <u>at the time of their adopting the Constitution</u>, expressed a desire,[2] in order <u>to prevent misconstruction or abuse of its powers</u>,[3] that <u>further declaratory and restrictive clauses should be added</u>:[4] And as extending the ground of public confidence in the Government, will best ensure the beneficent ends of its institution.[5]

RESOLVED <u>by the Senate and House of Representatives</u> of the United States of America, in Congress assembled, <u>two thirds of both Houses concurring</u>,[6] that the following Articles be proposed to the Legislatures of the several States, as amendments to the Constitution of the United States, all, or any of which Articles, when ratified by three fourths of the said Legislatures, to be valid to all intents and purposes, as part of the said Constitution; viz.[7]

ARTICLES <u>in addition to, and Amendment of</u> the[8] Constitution of the United States of America, proposed by Congress, and ratified by the Legislatures of the several States, <u>pursuant to the fifth Article of the original Constitution</u>.[9]

Sample Student Commentary

[1] PREamble is something that comes before. Like an introduction. The Constitution itself begins with a famous Preamble.

[2] The demand for a "Bill of Rights" came from the states when they were in the process of ratifying the Constitution.

[3] The antecedent to *its* is not yet clear, but the intent of this Bill is to prevent abuse or misunderstanding of "its" powers.

[4] "Declarative" statements would explain the powers. "Restrictive" statements would limit the powers.

[5] The earlier use of "its" probably also refers to the Government. "The beneficent ends of its institution" is a difficult phrase. Beneficent is probably synonymous with beneficial, meaning good or helpful. The ends would be the results. Beneficial ends would then be the advantages. Not institution as the noun meaning "an organization or formal arrangement (like an institution of higher learning)," but institution as the noun meaning" the process of being instituted" So, this phrase means "the advantages of instituting this government."

[6] Article V of the Constitution currently being debated by the states specifies this two-thirds majority of both houses in order for Congress to propose an amendment. The Constitution is not law yet, but the drafters of this Bill are following it as if it were.

[7] Viz. means "namely" or "as follows."

[8] Formal and essentially repetitive phrases that mean the proposed articles with be added to the Constitution, and they will change the Constitution.

[9] To establish the absolute legality of their proposal, and their way of proposing it, the drafters refer to the specific portion of the Constitution that allows for amendment and establishes the processes to do so.

Amendment I—Freedom of Speech, Press, Religion and Petition

Congress shall make no law respecting an <u>establishment</u> of religion, or <u>prohibiting</u> the <u>free exercise</u> thereof;[10] or <u>abridging</u> the <u>freedom</u> of speech, or of the press;[11] or <u>the right of the people</u> peaceably to assemble, and to petition the Government for a redress of grievances.[12]

Amendment II—Right to keep and bear arms

A <u>well-regulated militia</u>, being necessary <u>to the security of a free State</u>,[13] the <u>right of the people</u> to keep and bear arms, shall not be <u>infringed</u>.[14]

Amendment III—Conditions for quarters of soldiers

No soldier shall, <u>in time of peace</u> be quartered in any house, <u>without the consent of the owner</u>,[15] <u>nor in time of war, but in a manner to be prescribed by law</u>.[16]

Amendment IV—Right of search and seizure regulated

<u>The right of the people</u>[17] to be secure in their persons, houses, papers, and effects, against <u>unreasonable</u> searches and seizures,[18] shall not be violated, and no warrants shall issue, but upon <u>probable cause</u>,[19] supported by oath or affirmation, and <u>particularly describing the place to be searched, and the persons or things to be seized</u>.[20]

Amendment V—Provisions concerning prosecution

No person shall be held to answer for a capital, or otherwise <u>infamous</u> crime,[21] unless on a presentment or indictment of a Grand Jury, except in cases arising in the land or

---

Sample Student Commentary

[10] This is a much-debated phrase. A great deal of the debate centers on what exactly it means to establish religion or what types of restrictions actually constitute prohibition of free religious exercise.

[11] Similarly, the exact meanings of abridging and freedom make these provisions the subjects of debate.

[12] Structurally, this is all one sentence. Congress shall pass no law ... abridging ... the right of the people. It is interesting to note that this Article does not grant or establish a right; it recognizes a right that Congress cannot take away.

[13] Another hotly debated phrase. Does this limit the right only to arms that could be used in a volunteer militia?

[14] Again, this is presented as a right that already exists and that the Amendment merely protects. The right is attributed to the people, which may or may not help to clarify the "militia" phrase. Finally, how one interprets this amendment depends a lot on what one means by infringed.

[15] Two qualifications here that should not be overlooked: in time of peace and without consent. The implication is that in time of war, a citizen may be required to quarter soldiers without consent.

[16] This clarifies that previous implication. Still, the manner to be prescribed by law is not specified here, leaving room for further interpretation or legislation.

[17] So far, the writers have consistently taken the approach that the people already possess these rights, and this Constitution merely protects them.

[18] Unreasonable is another broad term subject to a range of interpretations.

[19] Another term subject to interpretation.

[20] These are probably the most specific provisions in all of these amendments.

[21] Infamous is also subject to interpretation.

naval forces, or in the militia, when in actual service <u>in time of war or public danger</u>;[22] nor shall any person be subject for the same offense to be twice <u>put in jeopardy of life or limb</u>;[23] nor shall be compelled in any criminal case <u>to be a witness against himself</u>,[24] nor be deprived of life, liberty, or property, without <u>due process of law</u>;[25] nor shall private property be taken for public use without <u>just compensation</u>.[26]

Amendment VI—Right to a speedy trial, witnesses, etc.

In all criminal prosecutions, the accused <u>shall enjoy the right</u>[27] to a speedy and public trial, by an impartial jury of the State and district wherein the crime shall have been committed, which district <u>shall have been previously ascertained by law</u>,[28] and to be informed of the nature and cause of the accusation; to be confronted with the witnesses against him; <u>to have compulsory process for obtaining witnesses in his favor</u>,[29] and <u>to have the assistance of counsel for his defense</u>.[30]

Amendment VII—Right to a trial by jury

In <u>suits at common law</u>,[31] where the value in controversy shall exceed twenty dollars, <u>the right of trial by jury shall be preserved</u>,[32] and <u>no fact tried by a jury shall be otherwise reexamined</u> in any court of the United States, <u>than according to the rules of the common law</u>.[33]

Sample Student Commentary

[22] This is another phrase that is often debated. The sentence structure seems to connect it to the "land or naval forces..." not to all citizens.

[23] Apparently, the amendment allows for the possibility of having a hand or an arm cut off as punishment for a crime. Jeopardy is taken to mean "brought up on charges and tried." This is the famous "double jeopardy" clause.

[24] This is the clause usually referred to when people mention the Fifth Amendment.

[25] Certainly subject to interpretation, but it is commonly taken to mean the full process of securing warrants for search and seizure, presenting before a Grand Jury, and a trial by jury—all of which are specified in these ten amendments.

[26] In the United States, even Eminent Domain requires that the government purchase the land. Notice that this clause does not require the property owner's consent.

[27] Is this right being granted or protected by the Constitution? This language is ambiguous.

[28] Future perfect tense. The "districts" are not being delineated now, but they will be in order for this provision to be met.

[29] Compulsory process establishes the right of the court to subpoena witnesses and to punish private citizens who do not obey subpoenas.

[30] This article is all one sentence. In all criminal prosecutions, the accused shall enjoy the right ... to have the assistance of counsel.

[31] To correctly interpret this phrase, we might need some additional legal knowledge. Does suits refer to litigation? Is common law the same as civil law? So, are these criminal cases (like the previous amendment), or does this article pertain only to civil cases—lawsuits?

[32] Here, this right is being presented as already existing, and this amendment is merely "preserving" it.

[33] To interpret this accurately would probably require some understanding of English common law, which is probably what the phrase refers to.

Amendment VIII—Excessive bail, cruel punishment

Excessive bail shall not be required, nor <u>excessive</u> fines imposed, nor <u>cruel</u> and <u>unusual</u> punishments inflicted.[34]

Amendment IX—Rule of construction of Constitution

The enumeration in the Constitution, of <u>certain rights</u>,[35] shall not be construed to deny or disparage others[36] <u>retained</u> by the people.[37]

Amendment X—Rights of the States under Constitution

The powers not delegated to the United States by the Constitution, nor prohibited by it to the States, are reserved to the States <u>respectively</u>,[38] or <u>to the people</u>.[39]

Sample Student Commentary

[34] Excessive, cruel, and unusual are all subject to interpretation.

[35] Certain here means specific.

[36] The fact that some rights are specified cannot be taken to mean that those not specified are not protected.

[37] Again, the stance is that the people already have the rights. This Bill of Rights is not the source of the rights.

[38] Respectively could mean "accordingly" or "correspondingly" or "likewise."

[39] Does this provision suggest that the States cannot deny the people a right, even if it is not specified in the Constitution?

Sample Multiple-Choice Questions:

1. All of the following factors come into play when determining what these amendments mean EXCEPT

   A. denotations of words.

   B. pronoun antecedents.

   C. sentence structure and syntax.

   D. individual experience.

   E. historical background.

2. Words like [*no law*] *prohibiting* (Amendment I), [*not*] *infringed* (Amendment II), and [*not*] *violated* (Amendment IV) clearly suggest that the rights specified in this document are

   A. granted by the document.

   B. natural and fundamental.

   C. limited in scope.

   D. privileges of citizenship.

   E. restricted to those specified.

3. Problems of interpretation that arise in this document are largely due to

   A. indefinite words.

   B. outmoded connotations.

   C. frequent negation.

   D. excess verbiage.

   E. double entendres.

4. Which of the following is probably not allowable according to this document?

   A. formation of a new interdenominational church

   B. an e-zine article criticizing the local school board

   C. a second prosecution following an acquittal

   D. a state's changing its driver's license regulations

   E. refusal to admit a police officer into one's home

5. The overall purpose of this document is most likely to

   A. delineate the rights of the people.

   B. undermine the newly ratified Constitution.

   C. define the legitimate role of government.

   D. protect the people's undeniable rights.

   E. assure ratification of the Constitution.

Answers and Explanations:

1. Understanding the strict denotations (A) of words like *declaratory* and *restrictive*, *compulsory*, and *respectively* is crucial for interpreting the articles in which these words appear. It is especially important to know whether the most common denotation has changed over time, or whether there are, perhaps, any archaic uses or denotations that have fallen out of use since the eighteenth century. As in the Preamble, to understand "government" as the antecedent (B) of *its* is essential to understanding the purpose of these amendments. In Article VI, to understand that *his defense* refers to *the accused* and not to the compulsory witness is equally important. Most of the articles are long, complex, or compound-complex sentences, so an understanding of the relationship between relative clause or introductory prepositional or participial phrase (C) is key to understanding the articles as written: *A well-regulated militia, being necessary to the security of a free State, the right of the people to keep and bear arms, shall not be infringed.* In what way(s) does the introductory phrase alter the meaning of the main clause? *Congress shall make no law respecting an establishment of... or prohibiting the free exercise thereof...; or abridging the freedom of... or of the ...; or the right of the people peaceably to assemble, and to...* This is an example of one sentence with a single subject (*Congress*), a single verb (*shall make*), a single direct object (*no law*), three participial phrases (*regarding..., prohibiting..., abridging...*), and six objects of the preposition. Clearly (C) is crucial to interpreting the amendment accurately. (E) comes into play when a reader considers such phrases as *common law*. However tempting (D) might be to a twentieth-century reader, and however certain we might be that the drafters of this document did indeed inform at least some of the provisions in it from their own experience, the individual experience of a contemporary reader is not relevant to an attempt to understand the writers' intent. **Thus, (D) is the best answer**.

2. The absence of restriction in the three cited amendments suggests that the specified rights exist prior to, and independent of, the document, thus eliminating (A). (C) might tempt some who ignore the language within the brackets, but the intent is clear that these amendments limit only the government's ability to restrict the rights. (D) is easily eliminated by the realization that the document is dealing with rights, not privileges, and that these rights are protected by this document, not extended or governed by conditions. (E) should tempt only those few who focus on the restrictive language without considering the total document, which explicitly states that even those rights not specified are protected. The pre-supposition of most of the amendments, that "the right [of the people]..." exists and "shall not be [limited or restricted]..." clearly suggests that these rights are a natural and fundamental element of the human condition. **Thus, (B) is the best answer**.

3. While the connotations of some of the words used by the 1789 writers of this document may certainly have changed over the past two-plus centuries, none of the key words in this document is unclear simply because of an archaic or outmoded use, (B). The document does use frequent negation, (C), to suggest that it is not within the power of any governmental document to grant a right and that this new government will do nothing to limit the right; this use and meaning is fairly straightforward. The document itself is actually quite concise. Words are used to specify, expand, and clarify, but there are rare occasions (if any) of unnecessary repetition, (D). Some students may confuse an abstract or indefinite word that is subject to interpretation as a double entendre, which is an intentional play on words in which second meaning might actually be risqué. None of the words, phrases, or clauses in this document, however, is meant to be taken lightly or ironically, (E). Many of the words themselves, however, are subject to interpretation. Words and phrases like *unreasonable*, *probable cause*, *excessive*, and *cruel and unusual* are probably intentionally open-ended to allow the document a degree of flexibility to meet a variety of situations. This open-endedness, however, does invite both dialogue and disagreement over specific interpretation. **Thus, (A) is the best answer**.

4. (A) is clearly allowed by the provisions of Amendment I forbidding the establishment of a state religion and forbidding the free exercise of religion. (B) is likewise protected by Amendment I's protections of free speech and a free press. (D) is suggested in Amendment X as "[a] power not delegated to the United States." (E) is less obviously wrong since it does not specify whether the police officer has a warrant, but Amendment IV possibly does allow for such refusal in the absence of "probable cause" and a warrant. (C), however, is explicitly prohibited by Amendment V: "nor shall any person be subject for the same offense to be twice put in jeopardy of life or limb." **Thus, (C) is the best answer**.

5. (A) might tempt some students, but Articles IX and X do not "delineate" the rights that are nonetheless reserved for the States and the people. (B) and (E) might tempt a few who do see this document as a weakening of the government outlined in the Constitution so that the states will ratify it, but the drafters themselves present this document merely as a clarification of the Constitution, not as a repudiation of anything in the original articles. (C), likewise, might tempt some, but even the "declaratory… clauses" are restricted only to the government's relationship to the people and their rights. Much more in the original articles is left untouched than is amended in these ten articles. **(D) is the best answer**. The wording of most of the amendments makes explicit that the people already have the rights, and the amendment is drafted merely to specify that the government cannot do anything to limit or revoke the right.

Sample Free-response item 1 (Text-based):

Carefully read The Bill of Rights and write a thoughtful and well-supported essay in which you defend, refute, or qualify the thesis that the original writers intended this document to be a series of guidelines and not a prescriptive set of ten commandments. Do not merely summarize the amendments.

Understanding that they could not possibly foresee every possible future situation, the authors of The Bill of Rights purposely used ambiguous language in order to allow future legislators flexibility in interpreting the Constitution. Rather than establishing a rigid document to be followed unswervingly, the authors intended for legislators and judges to use good judgment in applying these open guidelines in keeping with the basic principles the United States was founded upon.[1]

The authors' diction is a major clue to their intent. Throughout the document, ambiguous words are employed in places where a more definitive description might have led to absolute clarity. The language of Amendment VIII is a fine example. Amendment VIII reads, "Excessive bail shall not be required, nor excessive fines imposed, nor cruel and unusual punishments inflicted." Of course, the words "excessive," "cruel," and "unusual" are completely open to interpretation; further, the authors supply no examples of what may constitute "cruel and unusual punishments," leaving this issue for legislators to decide.[2]

The structure of the document likewise lends credence to the interpretation that The Bill of Rights is meant to be a set of guidelines. The first eight Amendments discuss specific (though not always precise)[3] limitations on the powers of the federal government. The final two Amendments, however, make clear that the rights described in the first eight Amendments are not the only rights protected from infringement. These final two Amendments do not tell Congress what rights to protect; instead, Amendments IX and X read as a warning to the government not to overstep its bounds. In order not to infringe on these unspecified but protected rights, legislators will have to use wisdom and restraint.

Finally, the conciseness[4] of many of the Amendments is another factor pointing toward the authors' intent. The longest Amendment, Amendment V, contains 108 words. Little in this Amendment is open to interpretation apart from "infamous," "public danger," and "just compensation." Still, these three ambiguous items allow

---

Scorer Commentary

[1] This student's argument is clear. He is going to support the assigned thesis.

[2] Because this is the text-based essay, the student knows he absolutely must quote directly. He provides three specific examples of unclear or ambiguous language.

[3] Notice the distinction this student makes between a specific limitation and a precise delineation of that limitation.

[4] It would probably have been better for this student to have dealt with all of the language issues before moving on to structure, but this is still an important point and makes the discussion of language more satisfyingly thorough.

for a wide range of interpretations; it is likely that the authors' conception of an "infamous crime" or a "public danger" would have been far different from our present ideas, and a constantly changing economy practically requires the vague "just compensation" (though, interestingly, Amendment VII sets twenty dollars as the minimum value that can be disputed in a lawsuit). However, Amendment V is relatively clear compared to most of the others. Compare Amendment V with Amendment II, which contains only 26 words. The right of the people "to keep and bear arms" is established, but nothing more is defined. What sorts of arms are the people allowed to keep and to bear? What is meant by "infringed"? Must those who keep and bear arms belong to a "well-regulated militia"?[5] These questions have no easy answers, and it is not surprising that Amendment II is one of the most heavily debated in *The Bill of Rights.* A smaller word count results in less explanation, and less explanation results in more freedom of interpretation for future legislators.

The authors could have chosen to explain these amendments more thoroughly in order to make their ideas absolutely clear, but they clearly envisioned a document that allowed for a wide range of interpretations. We cannot say for certain why they would have done this, but it is not unreasonable to believe that part of the reason was so that *The Bill of Rights* would not become an outdated document. Many of the rights enumerated in these first ten Amendments are constantly debated, but this is not necessarily a weakness of the document; values change over time, and an inflexible set of rules would not allow for these changes to be reflected in legislation.

Scorer Commentary

[5] What is interesting is that these are not really rhetorical questions. The author is not pressuring the reader into any one particular answer; the student is raising the questions himself.

Sample Free-response item 2 (Independent):

A common challenge encountered by historians is the attempt to understand the past *on its own terms* and not through the lenses of contemporary society's values and assumptions. The interpretation of key documents is often a particular challenge—using the writers' language to discern the writers' intent. Choose a significant document from United States history and write a thoughtful and well-structured essay in which you propose and support a reasonable and appropriate interpretation of the meaning and intent of the document. Do not merely summarize the document.

In writing The Bill of Rights, the authors intended to assuage public fears that the newly constituted government would abuse its power and become tyrannical. Given that the colonies had only recently secured their freedom from England, the public needed reassurances that the new federal government would not be given absolute power; to escape one oppressive government only to institute another would be no victory for the colonists. Thus, the authors took care to focus these Amendments on the rights of the people rather than on the rights of the federal government.[1]

No heavy interpretation is needed in order to understand the authors' intent; they declare their intent in the Preamble. They wish to extend "the ground of public confidence in the Government" in order to "best ensure the beneficient ends of its institution."[2]

They are going to do this by adding "further declaratory and restrictive clauses" to the original Constitution in order to "prevent [the government's] misconstruction or abuse of its powers." The key word here is "restrictive." The authors understand that in order to earn the public's trust they must restrict the government's powers.

Instead of simply enumerating the powers the government holds, however, the authors instead delineate the rights held by the people. The difference is subtle but important;[3] focusing the language on the people's rights instead of the government's powers allows the authors to define some of the government's powers while reassuring the people by placing limits on these powers. For example, take Amendment IV, which concerns search and seizure. Though this Amendment establishes that citizens are protected against "unreasonable" searches and seizures, it also establishes the government's right to perform searches and seizures under appropriate conditions. "Unreasonable" is a vague phrase, as is "probable cause,"

Scorer Commentary

[1] In order to address the question, this student first places his chosen document in its historical and social context.

[2] Here the student begins to do precisely what the question assigns: "us[e] the writers' language to discern the writers' intent."

[3] As we saw in his earlier essay, this student enjoys pointing out the subtle differences in word choice, but such distinctions do help him establish a strong case.

and these items are subject to interpretation by legislators and judges; they may decide to enhance the government's power by redefining these terms.

Ultimately, though Amendment IV ostensibly places limits on the government's power, the exact scope of these limits must be determined by those in the government. However, the authors do take care to mention that any warrant issued must be issued "upon probable cause, supported by oath or affirmation"; this clause, especially the words "supported by oath or affirmation," suggests that the decision to issue a warrant for search and seizure should not be made by one person only.[4] The specific language used here should reduce the potential that the powers granted in this Amendment will be abused. This pattern continues throughout The Bill of Rights; the authors suggest that certain rights belong to the people, while simultaneously establishing the government's powers regarding those rights.

This is not to say that The Bill of Rights is a document that has little meaning beyond mollifying eighteenth-century citizens and state governments. Clearly, because The Bill of Rights modifies the overarching law of the land, the Constitution, it is much more than a public service announcement to build public confidence in an untested and unproven government. One of the major strengths of the document is its flexibility; the language within these ten Amendments is nonspecific enough to allow legislators freedom to adapt the ideas to present situations and needs.[5] Provided legislators wield this power wisely and with discretion, The Bill of Rights can fulfill the promise its authors intended: protecting the people's inalienable rights.[6]

Scorer Commentary

[4] Again, whether you agree or disagree with this student's interpretation is irrelevant. He does use the writers' words in an attempt to discern their intent.

[5] It probably would have been better for this student to have spent more time on the non-specificity of the document.

[6] He does return to his thesis, that the document was intended more to protect people than define government.

Exercise One:

Questions 1–5. Read the following passage carefully before you choose your answers.

General George Washington refused to be a candidate for a third term as President of the United States. Not only did he long to return to private life and his beloved home, Mount Vernon, but he also feared setting the precedent of a popular president's allowing himself to become a despot. In May of 1796, he sent his longtime friend Alexander Hamilton a draft of his farewell address. The final document was published on September 19 and read to the House of Representatives. Washington's advice to Congress about the functioning of the government and the role of the still-new nation on the world stage continues to influence the ideals and policies of the United States.

The Address of General Washington To The People of The United States on his declining of the Presidency of the United States,

AMERICAN DAILY ADVERTISER, SEPTEMBER 19, 1796

Friends and Fellow-Citizens:

1 THE PERIOD FOR A NEW ELECTION OF A CITIZEN, to administer the Executive Government of the United States, being not far distant, and the time actually arrived, when your thoughts must be employed in designating the person, who is to be clothed with that important trust, it appears to me proper, especially as it may conduce to a more distinct expression of the public voice, that I should now apprize you of the resolution I have formed, to decline being considered among the number of those, out of whom a choice is to be made.

2 I beg you, at the same time, to do me the justice to be assured, that this resolution has not been taken, without a strict regard to all the considerations appertaining to the relation, which binds a dutiful citizen to his country—and that, in withdrawing the tender of service which silence in my situation might imply, I am influenced by no diminution of zeal for your future interest, no deficiency of grateful respect for your past kindness; but am supported by a full conviction that the step is compatible with both.

3 The acceptance of, and continuance hitherto in, the office to which your suffrages have twice called me, have been a uniform sacrifice if inclination to the opinion of duty, and to a deference for what appeared to be your desire.—I constantly hoped that it would have been much earlier in my power, consistently with motives, which I was not at liberty to disregard, to return to that retirement, from which I had been reluctantly drawn.—The strength of my inclination to do this, previous to the last election, had even led to the preparation of an address to declare it to you; but mature reflection on the then perplexed and critical posture of our affairs with foreign Nations, and the unanimous advice of persons entitled to my confidence, impelled me to abandon the idea.—

4   I rejoice, that the state of your concerns, external as well as internal, no longer renders the pursuit of inclination incompatible with the sentiment of duty, or propriety; and am persuaded, whatever partiality may be retained for my services, that, in the present circumstances of our country, you will not disapprove my determination to retire.

5   The impressions, with which I first undertook the arduous trust, were explained on the proper occasion. In the discharge of this trust, I will only say, that I have, with good intentions, contributed towards the organization and administration of the government, the best exertions of which a very fallible judgment was capable.—Not unconscious, in the outset, of the inferiority of my qualifications, experience in my own eyes, perhaps still more in the eyes of others, has strengthened the motives to diffidence of myself; and every day the increasing weight of years admonishes me more and more, that the shade of retirement is as necessary to me as it will be welcome.—Satisfied, that, if any circumstances have given peculiar value to my services, they were temporary, I have the consolation to believe, that, while choice and prudence invite me to quit the political scene, patriotism does not forbid it.

6   In looking forward to the moment, which is intended to terminate the career of my public life, my feelings do not permit me to suspend the deep acknowledgment of that debt of gratitude, which I owe to my beloved country,—for the many honors it has conferred upon me; still more for the stedfast confidence with which it has supported me; and for the opportunities I have thence enjoyed of manifesting my inviolable attachment, by services faithful and persevering, though in usefulness unequal to my zeal.—If benefits have resulted to our country from these services, let it always be remembered to your praise, and as an instructive example in our annals, that under circumstances in which the Passions, agitated in every direction, were liable to mislead, amidst appearances sometimes dubious, vicissitudes of fortune often discouraging, in situations in which not unfrequently want of success has countenanced the spirit of criticism, the constancy of your support was the essential prop of the efforts, and a guarantee of the plans by which they were effected.—Profoundly penetrated with this idea, I shall carry it with me to my grave, as a strong incitement to unceasing vows that Heaven may continue to you the choicest tokens of its beneficence—that your union and brotherly affection may be perpetual—that the free Constitution, which is the work of your hands, may be sacredly maintained—that its administration in every department may be stamped with wisdom and virtue—that, in fine, the happiness of the people of these States, under the auspices of liberty, may be made complete, by so careful a preservation and so prudent a use of this blessing, as will acquire to them the glory of recommending it to the applause, the affection, and adoption of every nation, which is yet a stranger to it.

7   Here, perhaps, I ought to stop.—But a solicitude for your welfare, which cannot end but with my life, and the apprehension of danger, natural to that solicitude, urge me on an occasion like the present, to offer to your solemn contemplation, and to recommend to your frequent review, some sentiments; which are the result of much reflection, of no inconsiderable observation and which appear to me all important to the permanency of your felicity as a People. These will be offered to you with the more freedom, as you can only see in them the disinterested warnings of a parting friend, who can possibly have no personal motive to bias his counsel.—Nor can I forget, as an encouragement to it, your indulgent reception of my sentiments on a former and not dissimilar occasion.

8   Interwoven as is the love of liberty with every ligament of your hearts, no recommendation of mine is necessary to fortify or confirm the attachment.—

9   The Unity of Government, which constitutes you one people, is also now dear to you.— It is justly so; for it is a main Pillar in the Edifice of your real independence; the support of your tranquillity at home; your peace abroad; of your safety; of your prosperity in every shape; of that very Liberty, which you so highly prize.—But as it is easy to foresee, that, from different causes, and from different quarters, much pains will be taken, many artifices employed, to weaken in your minds the conviction of this truth;—as this is the point in your political fortress against which the batteries of internal and external enemies will be most constantly and actively (though often covertly and insidiously) directed it is of infinite moment, that you should properly estimate the immense value of your national Union to your collective and individual happiness;—that you should cherish a cordial, habitual, and immovable attachment to it; accustoming yourselves to think and speak of it as of the Palladium of your political safety and prosperity; watching for its preservation with jealous anxiety; discountenancing whatever may suggest even a suspicion, that it can in any event be abandoned, and indignantly frowning upon the first dawning of every attempt to alienate any portion of our Country from the rest, or to enfeeble the sacred ties which now link together the various parts.

10   For this you have every inducement of sympathy and interest.—Citizens by birth or choice of a common country, that country has a right to concentrate your affections.— The name of AMERICAN, which belongs to you, in your national capacity, must always exalt the just pride of Patriotism, more than any appellation derived from local discriminations. With slight shades of difference, you have the same Religion, Manners, Habits, and Political Principles. You have in a common cause fought and triumphed together; the Independence and Liberty you possess are the work of joint counsels, and joint efforts—of common dangers, sufferings, and successes.—

11   But these considerations, however powerfully they address themselves to your sensibility, are greatly outweighed by those which apply more immediately to your Interest. Here every portion of our country finds the most commanding motives for carefully guarding and preserving the Union of the whole.

12   The *North*, in an unrestrained intercourse with the *South*, protected by the equal Laws of a common government, finds, in the productions of the latter, great additional resources of maritime and commercial enterprise—and precious materials of manufacturing industry.— The *South*, in the same intercourse, benefiting by the agency of the *North*, sees its agriculture grow and its commerce expand. Turning partly into its own channels the seamen of the *North*, it finds its particular navigation invigorated;—and, while it contributes, in different ways, to nourish and increase the general mass of the national navigation, it looks forward to the protection of a maritime strength to which itself is unequally adapted. The *East*, in a like intercourse with the *West*, already finds, and in the progressive improvement of interior communications, by land and water, will more and more find, a valuable vent for the commodities which it brings from abroad, or manufactures at home.—The *West* derives from the *East* supplies requisite to its growth and comfort, and—what is perhaps of still greater consequence, it must of necessity owe the *secure* enjoyment of indispensable *outlets* for its own productions to the weight, influence, and the future maritime strength of the Atlantic side of the Union, directed by an indissoluble community of interest as one *Nation.*—Any other tenure by which the *West* can hold this essential advantage, whether derived from its own separate strength, or from an apostate and unnatural connection with any foreign power, must be intrinsically precarious.

13   While then every part of our Country thus feels an immediate and particular interest in Union, all the parts combined in the united mass of means and efforts cannot fail to find greater strength, greater resource, proportionably greater security from external danger, a less frequent interruption of their Peace by foreign Nations; and, what is of inestimable value! they must derive from Union an exemption from those broils and wars between themselves, which so frequently afflict neighboring countries, not tied together by the same governments; which their own rivalships alone would be sufficient to produce; but which opposite foreign alliances, attachments, and intrigues would stimulate and embitter.—Hence likewise they will avoid the necessity of those overgrown Military establishments, which, under any form of government, are inauspicious to liberty, and which are to be regarded as particularly hostile to Republican Liberty. In this sense it is, that your Union ought to be considered as a main prop to your liberty, and that the love of the one ought to endear to you the preservation of the other.

Multiple-Choice Questions 1–5:

1. **Washington's frequent use of litotes in the opening paragraphs of this address (*not far distant, no diminution of zeal, no deficiency of grateful respect*) could be interpreted to suggest that Washington was**
   A. aloof.
   B. reticent.
   C. unexcitable.
   D. uneducated.
   E. haughty.

2. **In the third paragraph, Washington suggests that he**
   A. unwillingly served his second term.
   B. is too ill to serve a third term.
   C. is reluctant to retire.
   D. has been unanimously advised not to seek a third term.
   E. considers the presidency to be a loss of his liberty.

3. In the sixth paragraph, Washington attributes whatever benefits the United States has reaped during his administration to

A. the nation's reliance on reason over emotion.

B. the single-mindedness of the nation.

C. his perseverance and zeal.

D. the unfailing support of the people.

E. an unwillingness to criticize.

4. According to this speech, which of the following is the chief source of the nation's strength?

A. patriotism

B. liberty

C. tranquility

D. unity

E. government

5. In his elaboration on the benefits of a strong union (paragraphs 9 through 13) Washington's tone can best be described as

A. idealistic.

B. pragmatic.

C. optimistic.

D. pessimistic.

E. caustic.

Free-response item 1 (Text-based):

Carefully read "The Address of General Washington To The People of The United States on his declining of the Presidency of the United States" and write a thoughtful and well-supported essay in which you explain Washington's understanding of the term *patriotism* and its role in his defense of maintaining national unity. Do not merely summarize this portion of Washington's address.

Before you write your essay:

1. **Make sure you understand exactly what you're being asked to write about.**
   - List all of the verbs in the prompt.
   - Underline the verb that describes the essay.
   - Write the direct object of that verb.

2. **Make sure you have something valid to write about.**
   - Write a sentence or two that make a positive and focused statement about the topic.
   - Make sure these sentences address all of the issues and subpoints specified in the prompt.

3. **Review the selection and find your textual support.**

4. **Write your essay.**
   Keep referring to the prompt and whatever you underlined or highlighted in the selection to make sure you're on track and addressing everything the prompt wants you to address.

Free-response item 2 (Independent):

A common issue that arises from time to time in national, state, and local politics is the issue of term limits, the question of whether a legal cap should be set on the number of years an individual can serve in a particular office. Proponents of term limits argue that the founders of the United States intended the government to be run by private citizens—not career politicians—who postponed their private lives for the sake of public service. Opponents argue that established terms and regularly scheduled elections make such limits unnecessary. Both look to the past, the writings of the nation's founders and other historical leaders, to support their arguments. Choose a document from United

States history in which the writer addresses the nature of public service and/or the need for established term limits. Then write a thoughtful and well-organized essay in which you agree or disagree with the writer's argument. Be certain to support your claims with specific references to your selected document. Do not merely summarize the document.

Before you write your essay:

1. **Make sure you understand exactly what you're being asked to write about.**
   - List all of the verbs in the prompt.
   - Underline the verb that describes the essay.
   - Write the direct object of that verb.

2. **Choose an appropriate selection.**
   If you're using this book, your teacher probably wants you to write your essay on whatever story, article, or poem, etc., the writing prompt follows.

3. **Make sure you have something to say about both the topic and your selected literature.**
   - Jot down key plot events
   - Think in terms of plot structure: rising action, climax, falling action, and so on.
   - Make sure you jot down notes that pertain to the assigned topic.
   - Jot down quotations or at least close paraphrases.
   - Jot down everything you know and remember about the assigned topic.

4. **Make sure you are clear about what you are going to say.**
   - Write a sentence or two that make a positive and focused statement about the topic.
   - Make sure these sentences address all of the issues and subpoints specified in the prompt.

5. **Write your essay.**

Model Two:

The Address of General Washington To The People of The United States on his declining of the Presidency of the United States,

American Daily Advertiser, September 19, 1796 (part 2)

1 THESE CONSIDERATIONS[1] speak a persuasive language to every reflecting and virtuous mind,[2] and exhibit[3] the continuance of the Union as a primary object of Patriotic desire.[4] Is there a doubt, whether a common government can embrace so large a sphere?—Let experience solve it.[5] To listen to mere speculation in such a case were criminal.[6] —We are authorized to hope that a proper organization of the whole, with the auxiliary agency of governments for the respective subdivisions,[7] will afford a happy issue to the experiment. It is well worth a fair and full experiment.[8] With such powerful and obvious motives to Union, affecting all parts of our country, while experience shall not have demonstrated its impracticability,[9] there will always be reason to distrust the patriotism of those, who in any quarter may endeavor to weaken its bands.—[10]

2 In contemplating the causes which may disturb our Union, it occurs as matter of serious concern, that any ground should have been furnished for characterizing parties by *geographical* discriminations[11]—Northern and Southern, Atlantic and Western; whence designing men may endeavor to excite a belief, that there is a real difference

---

Sample Student Commentary

[1] These refers to the "considerations" Washington enumerated and described in the previous three or four paragraphs (the final paragraphs of the Exercise One selection).

[2] Such a statement, whether intentional or unintentional, does not allow for reasonable discourse. Those who disagree are neither "reflecting" nor "virtuous."

[3] Here is a grammatical—sentence structure concern. The subject of the sentence is These considerations. The two verbs are speak and exhibit. It is the "considerations" that are exhibiting.

[4] Continuance of Union is the direct object of exhibit. Here again, Washington is insisting that continuance of Union is a primary goal of patriotism. One cannot call himself a "patriot" if one does not support the union.

[5] Procatalepsis: acknowledging a potential objection and addressing it.

[6] Here again, Washington does not allow for much dialogue or debate.

[7] By respective subdivision, Washington probably means "state." Is he implying that the states should consider themselves "parts of the whole" rather than entire entities in their own right? His use of auxiliary to describe state government might suggest this.

[8] Perhaps he is simply asking the nation, the states, to try to see whether it is in their best interest to defer fully to union.

[9] These are all points that Washington has discussed previously. Notice the double negative: experience has not proven it impracticable. This is not necessarily the same thing as proving it practicable.

[10] Again asserting that those who do not favor union can be distrusted as unpatriotic.

[11] Washington first warns against regional divisions.

of local interests and views.[12] One of the expedients of Party[13] to acquire influence, within particular districts, is to misrepresent the opinions and aims of other districts.[14] —You cannot shield yourselves too much[15] against the jealousies and heart burnings, which spring from these misrepresentations;—they[16] tend to render alien to each other those, who ought to be bound together by fraternal affection.[17] —The inhabitants of our Western country have lately had a useful lesson on this head—they have seen, in the negotiation by the Executive, and in the unanimous ratification by the Senate, of the treaty with Spain, and in the universal satisfaction at that event, throughout the United States, a decisive proof how unfounded were the suspicions propagated among them of a policy in the General Government and in the Atlantic States unfriendly to their interests in regard to the Mississippi[18]—they have been witnesses to the formation of two Treaties, that with Great Britain, and that with Spain, which secure to them every thing they could desire, in respect to our Foreign Relations, towards confirming their prosperity.—Will it not be their wisdom to rely for the preservation of these advantages on the Union by which they were procured?—Will they not henceforth be deaf to those advisers, if such there are, who would sever them from their Brethren, and connect them with Aliens?—[19]

3   To the efficacy and permanency of your Union, a Government for the whole is indispensable.—No alliances, however strict between the parts can be an adequate substitute.[20]—They must inevitably experience the infractions and interruptions which all alliances in all times have experienced.[21] Sensible of this momentous truth, you have

---

Sample Student Commentary

12 Word choice is very important here. Designing means "scheming or conniving." As used here to excite can mean either "to create" or "to arouse." Thus, Washington is suggesting that these scheming men are creating a non-existent belief that the local interests of different regions are different from one another or from the national interest. His specifying real difference suggests that there might indeed appear to be differences, but these are not real except in the designs of these men who would disturb the Union.

13 Expedient is what is fast or easy, not necessarily what is right or best. Party here suggests the division of the people into separate groups.

14 Districts emphasizes that Washington is talking about regional divisions. According to Washington, some in the North can misrepresent the South in order to gain influence, just as some in the South can misrepresent the North for the same reason.

15 Modern readers might read this differently from the way Washington intended. Traditionally, this expression means no amount of…is too much. Today, we would probably say, "You cannot shield yourselves enough."

16 They refers to the jealousies and burnings.

17 The syntax is challenging here. Alien is used as an adjective meaning "foreign or different"; to render is "to cause to become." The jealousies and burnings cause those who ought to be bound together by fraternal affection to become foreign or different.

18 Historical Note: a recent treaty with Spain secured the border between the United States western frontier and Spanish colonies. This same treaty granted Americans the right to sail their trade ships on the Spanish-owned Mississippi River, greatly increasing their opportunity to trade.

19 Of course, Washington is assuming all of his readers will answer his rhetorical questions in the same way. By citing the treaties with Britain and Spain, however, he does provide concrete and factual support for his point about the benefits of American unity.

20 Washington is drawing the distinction between a government and an alliance.

21 Without citing specific examples, Washington refers to history in which probably every alliance entered into was, at one time or another, broken.

improved upon your first <u>essay</u>,[22] by the adoption of a Constitution of Government, better calculated than your former for an <u>intimate Union</u>, and for the <u>efficacious management</u> of your <u>common concerns</u>.[23] —This government, the offspring of our own choice uninfluenced and unawed, adopted upon full investigation and mature deliberation, completely free in its principles, in the distribution of its power, uniting security with energy, and containing within itself a provision for its own amendment, has a just claim to your confidence and your support.[24]—Respect for its authority, compliance with its Laws, acquiescence in its measures,[25] are duties enjoined by the fundamental maxims of true Liberty.—The basis of our political systems is the right of the <u>people</u> to make and to alter their Constitutions of Government.—But the Constitution which at any time exists, 'till changed by an explicit and authentic act of the whole <u>People</u>, is <u>sacredly obligatory upon all</u>.[26]—The very idea of the power and the right of the People to establish Government <u>presupposes</u> the duty of every individual to obey the established Government.[27]

4 All obstructions to the execution of the Laws, all combinations and associations, under whatever plausible character, with the real design to direct, control, counteract, or awe the regular deliberation and action of the constituted authorities, are destructive of <u>this fundamental principle</u>,[28] and of fatal tendency.—They serve to <u>organize faction</u>, to give it an artificial and extraordinary force—to put <u>in the place of the delegated will of the nation, the will of a party</u>[29];—often <u>a small but artful and enterprising minority of the community;</u>[30]—and, according to the alternate triumphs of different parties, to make the public administration the mirror of the <u>ill-concerted and incongruous projects of faction, rather than the organ of consistent and wholesome plans digested by common councils</u>,[31] and modified by <u>mutual interests</u>.[32]—<u>However</u> combinations or associations of the above descriptions may now and then answer <u>popular</u> ends,[33] they are likely, in

---

Sample Student Commentary

[22] Essay means "attempt." The first essay to which Washington is referring are the Articles of Confederation, which were replaced by the Constitution.

[23] More than merely "close" or "familiar," intimate means "relating to one's deepest nature." Washington continues to stress the commonness, the sense that, regardless of superficial differences like location, the people are one being.

[24] It is probably important to note that this is 1796; the Constitution was ratified into law in 1788. The issue Washington is addressing, then, is not whether or not to ratify the Constitution but whether to preserve the union it established.

[25] To acquiesce is to "submit" or "yield."

[26] Here again, Washington's word choice is very important. The Government is the People, and the people are obligated to it as they are to whatever religious creed they believe.

[27] The one idea [that the People have the right to establish their own laws] is based on the other idea [that the People are bound to obey the laws they establish].

[28] The right of the people to establish their own laws is founded upon their obligation to obey those laws.

[29] Washington has used the words discriminations, faction, and now party to describe the same type of division.

[30] Artful here is a synonym for the earlier designing. It means "scheming."

[31] Words associated with party or faction are *ill-conceived* and *incongruous*. Words associated with unity are *organ, consistent,* and *wholesome*.

[32] Mutual is not a strict synonym for *common*. It carries a connotation of sharing and reciprocity.

[33] Washington's understanding of however would have been similar to the modern *although*.

the course of time and things, to become potent engines, by which <u>cunning, ambitious, and unprincipled men</u> will be enabled to subvert the Power of the People, and to <u>usurp</u> for themselves the reins of Government;[34] destroying afterwards the very engines, which have lifted them to unjust dominion.—[35]

5 Towards the preservation of your Government, and <u>the permanency of your present happy state</u>,[36] it is requisite, not only that you steadily discountenance irregular oppositions to its acknowledged authority, but also that you resist with care the spirit of innovation upon its principles, however <u>specious</u>[37] the pretexts.—One method of assault may be to effect, <u>in the forms of the Constitution, alterations</u>[38] which will impair the energy of the system, and thus to <u>undermine</u> what cannot be directly <u>overthrown</u>.[39] —In all the changes to which you may be invited, remember that <u>time and habit</u> are at least as necessary to fix the true character of Governments, as of other human institutions— that <u>experience is the surest standard</u>, by which to test <u>the real tendency of the existing Constitution</u> of a Country—that facility in changes upon the <u>credit</u>[40] <u>of mere hypothesis and opinion</u>[41] exposes to perpetual change, from the endless variety of hypothesis and opinion:—and remember, especially, that, for the efficient management of your <u>common interests</u>, in a country so extensive as ours, a Government of as much vigor as is consistent with the perfect security of Liberty is indispensible.—<u>Liberty itself will find in such a government</u>, with powers properly distributed and adjusted, <u>its surest Guardian</u>.[42] —It is, indeed, little else than a name, where the Government is too feeble to withstand the enterprise of faction, to confine each member of the society within the limits prescribed by the laws, and to maintain all in the secure and tranquil enjoyment of the rights of person and property.

6 <u>I have already intimated to you the danger of parties in the State, with particular reference to the founding of them on Geographical discriminations.—Let me now take a more comprehensive view</u>,[43] and warn you in the most solemn manner against the <u>baneful effects</u> of the <u>Spirit of Party</u>, generally.[44]

Sample Student Commentary

[34] Very powerful language to describe the quality of individuals who could use party sentiments to prey on the short-term desires of the people in order to set themselves up in power.

[35] ...and then dismantle the Government that gave them their power but protected the rights of others as well.

[36] Washington is begging the question here, assuming that the people of the United State are happy.

[37] "Showy" or "deceptively attractive, seductive."

[38] Legal amendments.

[39] Another careful distinction between words. To undermine is to "weaken from within," to "subvert." There is a sense of secretiveness and wrongdoing in undermining. To "overthrow" is to mount a complete assault. It is obvious, open. Notice also the antithesis that unwise amendments undermine what cannot be overthrown.

[40] Credit here means "credibility."

[41] Here, as elsewhere in this address, Washington urges a reliance upon history and experience rather than speculation.

[42] Sentence structure note: the subject is Liberty; the verb is will find; the direct object is Guardian.

[43] Metabasis: a quick recap of what Washington has said and a brief introduction of what he is going to say.

[44] By Party, Washington means "political party." A bane is a "killer," a "poisoner," "one who destroys." By his choice of this word, Washington is suggesting that party politics could be the ruin of the United States.

Sample Multiple-Choice Questions:

6. Washington suggests that all of the following are indications of patriotism EXCEPT

    A. *willingness to enter public service.*

    B. subordination of state to federal government.

    C. private obedience to federal law.

    D. trust in history rather than speculation.

    E. avoidance of party affiliation.

7. In paragraph 4, Washington offers a strongly worded warning against

    A. tyrants.

    B. upstarts.

    C. despots.

    D. demagogues.

    E. anarchists.

8. Which of the following best summarizes Washington's argument against geographical divisions?

    A. The recent treaty with Spain illustrates the benefits of unity.

    B. The most important concerns of Americans everywhere are the same.

    C. Scheming men fuel local prejudices and sow distrust of other regions.

    D. Americans in different geographic regions cannot understand one another's needs.

    E. It is impossible for people to protect themselves from unfounded regional biases.

9. Based on his word choice in paragraph 6, what does Washington believe that the Spirit of Party will potentially do to the United States?

    A. divide it

    B. destroy it

    C. reform it

    D. alter it

    E. undermine it

10. Washington's view on amending the Constitution can best be described as

    A. opposing.

    B. neutral.

    C. fearful.

    D. aggressive.

    E. cautious.

Answers and Explanations:

6. Throughout this selection, Washington has equated *patriotism* with *preservation of the Union* (*These considerations ... exhibit the continuance of the Union as a primary object of Patriotic desire. and ...there will always be reason to distrust the patriotism of those, who in any quarter may endeavor to weaken [the Union's] bands.*) so the "indications of patriotism" would logically be those attitudes or behaviors that foster union. (B) is eliminated by Washington's paragraph 1 use of "subdivisions" to refer to the sovereign states, and "auxiliary agency" when referring to state government. Clearly, he hopes for the subordination of the state to the federal government. (C) is eliminated in paragraph 3 when Washington writes, "...the Constitution which at any time exists, 'till changed by an explicit and authentic act of the whole People, is sacredly obligatory upon all.—The very idea of the power and the right of the People to establish Government presupposes the duty of every individual to obey the established Government." Thus, the patriotic individual has a "sacred observation" to obey the federal law until that law is lawfully amended. In paragraph 1, he writes, "Is there a doubt, whether a common government can embrace so large a sphere?—Let experience solve it. To listen to mere speculation in such a case were criminal." He further develops this idea later in the same paragraph: "experience shall not have demonstrated its impracticability." Still later, in paragraph 5, he writes: "In all the changes to which you may be invited, remember that time and habit are at least as necessary to fix the true character of Governments, as of other human institutions—that experience is the surest standard, by which to test the real tendency of the existing Constitution of a Country." Thus (D) is eliminated. The selection ends with Washington warning against "the baneful effects of the Spirit of Party, generally," eliminating (E). Nowhere in this selection, however, does Washington speak about a citizen's obligation or right to participate in government beyond obedience to its laws and avoidance of party affiliation. **Thus, (A) is the correct answer.**

7. Toward the end of the paragraph, Washington warns, "...cunning, ambitious, and unprincipled men will be enabled to subvert the Power of the People, and to usurp for themselves the reins of Government." That these men, having usurped the reins of government might become tyrants (A) follows this warning, but these "cunning... unprincipled men" are not tyrants yet. It is not their tyranny that Washington is warning against. While "upstart" (B) may have the negative connotation of a presumptuous or ill-qualified person, primarily an upstart refers to anyone who rises quickly to power or influence from humble origins. Clearly, Washington would not be warning against such people. Despot (C) might also connote a tyrant, which has already been eliminated, but the word chiefly denotes a person with absolute power. As was the case with (A), these "cunning, ambitious, and unprincipled men" may become despots after they have gained power, but it is actually their nature before gaining power, the means by

which they gain power that Washington is warning against here. Anarchists (E) are those who would prefer no government. Washington is warning against those who would subvert the government for their own gain, not those who would abolish the government altogether, so (E) is eliminated. A demagogue (D) is a person who rises to power by arousing the passions and prejudices of the people. Washington argues that the "potent engines" that allowed these "cunning, ambitious, and unprincipled men" to "subvert the power of the people" were party affiliations, "combinations or associations ... [that] ... now and then answer popular ends." Having already discussed the ability of scheming men to fuel the people's biases and prejudices for the sake of fabricated divisions, it is clear that Washington fears the threat of demagogy. **Thus, (D) is the correct answer.**

8. (A) is true, but as it states, it is an illustration of the validity of the argument, not a summary of the argument itself. (C) is also one point, not the crux, of Washington's argument. (D) would be the claim of the "designing men" who "excite [the] belief" that people in different regions are "alien" to one another; it is almost the antithesis of what Washington is saying. (E) is based on a misreading of paragraph 2's "You cannot shield yourselves too much against the jealousies and heart burnings, which spring from these misrepresentations." Washington does not mean the modern sense of "you cannot shield yourselves enough..." but the older sense of "no amount of shielding can to excessive [too much]." However, when Washington accuses the "designing men [of] endeavor[ing] to excite a belief, that there is a real difference of local interests and views," he is clearly suggesting that there is not such a "real difference." Later, when he notes that "One of the expedients of Party ... is to misrepresent the opinions and aims of other districts," he is further explaining the false belief that there are real differences in interests and views across regions. Finally, when he claims that the misrepresentations of other regions' interests and beliefs "tend to render alien to each other those, who ought to be bound together by fraternal affection," he is clearly concluding that all people in all regions are alike, share a common interest, and should be bound to one another, not divided against each other. **Thus, (B) is the correct answer.**

9. (A) might tempt some, but Washington focuses on the aspect of division only when he is talking about parties established along geographical lines. "Divide" is also too general a word to fully satisfy. (C) might tempt those who misread the section on unnecessary amendments, in which Washington says that time and experience will reform the country more effectively than party-motivated amendments. (D), like (A), is too general to satisfy. (E) might tempt a few, but Washington mentions practitioners of party politics both undermining *and overthrowing* the government, so (E) as it stands is incomplete and not the best answer. This sections ends, however, with Washington's warning against the "baneful effects of the Spirit of Party, generally." Denotatively, *baneful* is killing or destructive. **Thus, (B) is the best answer.**

10. The most detailed mention of the Constitution's provisions for amendment are in the 3rd and 5th paragraphs. Washington first points out, "The basis of our political systems is the right of the people to make and to alter their Constitutions of Government," so he certainly cannot be said to oppose (A) appropriate amendments. He does, however, warn, "One method of assault may be to effect, in the forms of the Constitution, alterations which will impair the energy of the system, and thus to undermine what cannot be directly overthrown." Such a warning cannot be said to come from someone who is neutral (B). (C) is certainly tempting, but it is perhaps too strong a word and not the best choice. (D) is, likewise, too strong a word, as Washington neither opposes nor encourages amendments but acknowledges the importance of the right to amend, while cautioning against certain types of amendment. Throughout his treatment of constitutional amendment, however, Washington urges, "that you resist with care the spirit of innovation upon its principles, however specious the pretexts." When it comes to considering amending the Constitution, the people should "remember that time and habit are at least as necessary to fix the true character of Governments, as of other human institutions—that experience is the surest standard, by which to test the real tendency of the existing Constitution of a Country." He suggests "that facility in changes upon the credit of mere hypothesis and opinion exposes [the Constitution] to perpetual change." He urges caution, therefore, that any considered amendment be weighed and considered, the principles it covers tested to see whether amending the Constitution is necessary or will the problem to be addressed in the amendment solve itself in time. **Thus, (E) is the best answer.**

Sample Free-Response Item 1 (Text-based)

Carefully read the second selection from "The Address of General Washington To The People of The United States on his declining of the Presidency of the United States," in which Washington describes some of the potential internal dangers he thought the still-fledgling United States might face. In a well-written and well-supported essay, choose one of Washington's key points and evaluate the extent to which he succeeds in communicating the point and establishing its validity.

In declining to run for a third term as President of the United States, George Washington warns the infant nation of several potential dangers it will encounter.[1] Among these are the dangers of artificial divisions, specifically geographical divisions, the misconception that people in different regions are somehow separate from one another with their own, separate values and concerns.[2] His message, while inspiring on an idealistic level, is largely unconvincing because he defines the terms of his Address in such a way as to make debate difficult or impossible.[3] Indeed, one cannot disagree with Washington without being labeled "unvirtuous" and "unpatriotic." While lessening debate might be essential Washington's strategy, to utterly dismiss opposition like this is not the best way to win that opposition over to your cause. It might actually be said to be counter to the principles of American democracy. When Washington uses concrete examples to support his arguments, however, his speech is quite strong; his arguments are less when he speculates on potential problems and blithely dismisses any possibility of reasonable disagreement.[4]

In the previous section of this speech, Washington began to enumerate the number of factors that could threaten the United States' unity and the advantages of unity over disunity. This section begins with his insisting that the advantages he has listed "speak a persuasive language to every reflecting and virtuous mind." Whether he means it or not, Washington is saying that someone who is not persuaded by these advantages is somehow stupid and evil. This type of argument borders on propaganda. Certainly, this reasoning does not provide any substance for those who do not already agree with Washington to change their minds.[5] In this same sentence, Washington equates a desire for unity with patriotism: "These considerations … exhibit the continuance of the Union as a primary object

---

Scorer Commentary

[1] An innocent enough topic sentence, but not yet a thesis. It is important to note that, even though the student is answering a question, he begins the essay as if it were an independent piece.

[2] This sentence fulfills the requirement to "choose one of Washington's key points."

[3] This sentence begins to fulfill the evaluation requirement.

[4] This first paragraph successfully introduces the topic, states a thesis, and introduces two subpoints as elements of that thesis.

[5] So this first section does indeed look to the speech and evaluate the effectiveness of one of Washington's points.

of *Patriotic desire." Patriots, then, desire union. Those who suggest that people of one geographical region have basic differences in beliefs from people in another geographical location are fomenting discord and may be anti-Union agents, i.e., unpatriotic. Again, there is not much in this assertion to convince someone who disagrees to change his or her mind.*

Washington then offers his first concrete illustration, something that truly cannot be argued with as supporting his point. He writes, "In contemplating the causes which may disturb our Union, it occurs as matter of serious concern, that any ground should have been furnished for characterizing parties by geographical discriminations ... whence designing men may endeavor to excite a belief, that there is a real difference of local interests and views." Those who support unity are patriots; those who suggest that each region has its own unique needs are "designing men." But this time, Washington does, at least offer an example to support his claim. He reminds his audience about the recent signing of a treaty between the United States and Spain, a treaty with which the "inhabitants of our Western country" had some concerns. Washington's language is not entirely clear on this point, but it appears that an unspecified group was informing the inhabitants of the West that the government, in collusion with the Atlantic states, was making policy that would be detrimental to those living in the West. Washington claims that the aforementioned treaty was met with "universal satisfaction," and so these fears were unfounded. This historical, factual example supports Washington's argument in favor of Union and against regionalism and factionalism.[6]

This, however, is the only specific illustration Washington has to offer of the benefit of unity over faction. He speaks a good deal about the danger of party divisions, the "small but artful and enterprising minority" that may attempt to set its will above the will of the commonwealth. He warns that party factions are, in reality, the tools "by which cunning, ambitious, and unprincipled men will be enabled to subvert the Power of the People, and to usurp for themselves the reins of Government." He does not, however, provide any concrete facts or examples. Given his earlier reliance on abstract terms like "patriotic" and "virtuous" and the manner with which he barred any possible debate, these insistences are less than convincing.[7]

In Washington's opinion, the greatest danger facing the nation is factionalism, whether based on geographical region or political party. He may have been right, but the fact that he provides only one concrete example, speaks in such a way as to make it impossible to disagree without being labeled unintelligent and unpatriotic, and he relies almost solely on conjecture and speculation make this a fairly unconvincing argument.

Scorer Commentary

[6] This is a good use of a specific example.

[7] The student here does begin to work toward a conclusion that establishes the validity of his thesis: Washington warns of the potential danger of disunity, and his argument is strongest only when he has concrete examples to illustrate his point.

Sample Free-Response Item 2 (Independent)

The definition of an abstract concept like patriotism is a popular topic for political debate, with persons at both ends of the political spectrum criticizing the others' understanding and condemning their views as "unpatriotic" or "un-American." Choose a public document, either current or historical, that touches on an understanding of what it means to be a patriot. Then, in a thoughtful and well-developed essay, analyze both the strengths and weaknesses of this understanding. You need not provide a definition of your own. Do not merely summarize the view presented in the document you choose.

In his *Farewell Address* upon declining a third term as President of the United States, George Washington argues that being an American patriot means obeying the laws of the Constitution and protecting that document from unnecessary and damaging amendments. For Washington, patriotism is a spirit of unification: all Americans have similar ideals and, therefore, should not let petty, artificial divisions damage their solidarity. Washington's understanding of patriotism is highly idealistic, and this has its advantages and disadvantages.[1]

The major advantage of Washington's stance on patriotism is that it is based on the premise of mutual respect. Washington believes that all Americans share similar ideals and, therefore, should not discriminate against one another on any basis, whether geographical or political. This is, of course, a highly idealistic policy, one that requires people to step away from their personal ideals and remember that they must work together, despite differences in opinion. The people of the United States are part of something much larger than themselves, and Washington intends for them to remember that fact. He even makes the statement that avoiding geographical and political differences is the primary goal of the true patriot.[2] In today's heated, divisive political climate, a spirit of mutual respect and compromise would certainly be a welcome change; Washington's warnings about the deleterious effects of the "Spirit of Party" seem eerily prophetic when read today.[3] One wonders whether Washington would find many true patriots—according to his definition—among the politicians of either party today.

While maintaining unity, a patriot, according to Washington will also protect the Constitution from extensive and unwarranted amendment. Ideally, a patriot should be committed to maintaining the ideals of the country in which he or she lives, and Washington's ideas on American patriotism certainly reflect this fact. To Washington, a patriot is someone who obeys and defends the Constitution, the

---

Scorer Commentary

[1] This thesis does address the issue broached in the question, but it does not state what advantages or disadvantages are going to be addressed.

[2] This student cannot quote from the document, since he does not have the speech immediately before him, but this is a good, tight paraphrase.

[3] The application to the present, while not requested, will not hurt this student's score.

document that, more than any other, defines what the United States stands for. Washington is correct to take this stance. If the Constitution is the document that defines the ideals of the country, then those who wish to amend it must take great care to ensure that no amendment runs counter to these ideals. This caution, then, is somewhat related to the patriot's desire for unity because a person or faction who pushed for an amendment that would actually contradict the ideals of the nation would foster disunity and would be no patriot. Washington describes these politicians as "cunning, ambitious, and unprincipled men."[4] Such people, by betraying the ideals of their nation and fomenting disharmony among the people of the United States, would be no patriots in Washington's view.

However, one of the weaknesses of Washington's stance is that it seems to leave little room for rational dissent. Washington's stance on the Constitution is that it is an excellent document; he advises extreme caution when considering amendments to it. However, modern readers can easily see that the Constitution was an imperfect document in 1796; for example, the Thirteenth Amendment—abolishing slavery—was not part of the Constitution at this time, nor was the Nineteenth Amendment, which allowed women their proper right to vote. Clearly, however, these amendments are in keeping with the ideals of the United States, and those who advanced them were not disloyal or unpatriotic.[5] It is unlikely that Washington believed that the Constitution was perfect as constructed in 1796, but his concept of patriotism advocates near-absolute obedience to an imperfect document, and that is a flaw in retrospect.

By the same token, the division of the nation into parties was probably inevitable, not necessarily harmful. While the South's interests are not different from the North's, in many respects, the South's needs are different from the North's. The farmer and the industrialist must both be confident that they are being represented in their government. Perhaps, rather than warning against partisan divisions, Washington should have entreated his audience to find a way to maintain balance between the individual interests of party and the greater interest of the common good.[6]

Still, though Washington's concept of patriotism has minor flaws, one could make the argument that he advocated absolute non-partisanship and strict adherence to the Constitution to serve a greater purpose: maintaining the stability of a fledgling nation. Any criticism of this Farewell Address should be filtered to include this fact. Washington's view of patriotism is largely acceptable to the modern reader, as many of the values laid out in the original Constitution and The Bill of Rights are still applicable today. For those looking to examine a moderate and wise treatise on the proper place of patriotism, Washington's Farewell Address should be considered essential reading.

Scorer Commentary

[4] While quotations are not required in the Independent essay, it certainly does not hurt to quote when you can.

[5] The student's point is that the fact of these amendments contradicts Washington's assertion that true patriots must avoid tampering with the Constitution.

[6] This student does successfully manage to discuss a disadvantage of both aspects of Washington's definition.

Exercise Two:

Questions 11–15. Read the following passage carefully before you choose your answers.

General George Washington refused to be a candidate for a third term as President of the United States. Not only did he long to return to private life and his beloved home, Mount Vernon, he feared setting the precedent of a popular president's allowing himself to become a despot. In May of 1796, he sent to his longtime friend Alexander Hamilton a draft of his farewell address. The final document was published on September 19 and read to the House of Representatives. Washington's advice to Congress about the functioning of the government and the role of the still-new nation on the world stage continues to influence the ideals and policies of the United States.

The Address of General Washington To The People of The United States on his declining of the Presidency of the United States,

AMERICAN DAILY ADVERTISER, SEPTEMBER 19, 1796 (PART 3)

1 THIS SPIRIT [OF PARTY], UNFORTUNATELY, is inseparable from our nature, having its root in the strongest passions of the human mind.—It exists under different shapes in all Governments, more or less stifled, controlled, or repressed; but, in those of the popular form, it is seen in its greatest rankness, and is truly their worst enemy.—

2 The alternate domination of one faction over another, sharpened by the spirit of revenge, natural to party dissension, which in different ages and countries has perpetrated the most horrid enormities, is itself a frightful despotism.—But this leads at length to a more formal and permanent despotism.—The disorders and miseries, which result, gradually incline the minds of men to seek security and repose in the absolute power of an Individual; and sooner or later the chief of some prevailing faction, more able or more fortunate than his competitors, turns this disposition to the purposes of his own elevation, on the ruins of Public Liberty.

3 Without looking forward to an extremity of this kind, (which nevertheless ought not to be entirely out of sight), the common and continual mischiefs of the spirit of Party are sufficient to make it the interest and duty of a wise people to discourage and restrain it.—

4 It serves always to distract the Public Councils, and enfeeble the Public administration. It agitates the community with ill-founded jealousies and false alarms, kindles the animosity of one part against another, foments occasionally riot and insurrection.—It opens the door to foreign influence and corruption, which find a facilitated access to the Government itself through the channels of party passions. Thus the policy and the will of one country, are subjected to the policy and will of another.

5   There is an opinion, that parties in free countries are useful checks upon the Administration of the Government, and serve to keep alive the spirit of Liberty.—This within certain limits is probably true—and in Governments of a Monarchical cast, Patriotism may look with indulgence, if not with favor, upon the spirit of party.—But in those of the popular character, in Governments purely elective, it is a spirit not to be encouraged.—From their natural tendency, it is certain there will always be enough of that spirit for every salutary purpose,—and there being constant danger of excess, the effort ought to be, by force of public opinion, to mitigate and assuage it.—A fire not to be quenched; it demands a uniform vigilance to prevent its bursting into a flame, lest, instead of warming, it should consume.

6   It is important, likewise, that the habits of thinking in a free country should inspire caution in those entrusted with its administration, to confine themselves within their respective constitutional spheres; avoiding in the exercise of the powers of one department to encroach upon another. The spirit of encroachment tends to consolidate the powers of all the departments in one, and thus to create, whatever the form of government, a real despotism.—A just estimate of that love of power, and proneness to abuse it, which predominates in the human heart, is sufficient to satisfy us of the truth of this position.—The necessity of reciprocal checks in the exercise of political power, by dividing and distributing it into different depositories, and constituting each the Guardian of the Public Weal against invasions by the others, has been evinced by experiments ancient and modern; some of them in our country and under our own eyes.—To preserve them must be as necessary as to institute them. If, in the opinion of the People, the distribution or modification of the Constitutional powers be in any particular wrong, let it be corrected by an amendment in the way which the Constitution designates.—But let there be no change by usurpation; for though this, in one instance, may be the instrument of good, it is the customary weapon by which free governments are destroyed.—The precedent must always greatly overbalance in permanent evil any partial or transient benefit which the use can at any time yield.—

7   Of all the dispositions and habits, which lead to political prosperity, Religion, and Morality are indispensable supports.—In vain would that man claim the tribute of Patriotism, who should labor to subvert these great pillars of human happiness, these firmest props of the duties of Men and Citizens.—The mere Politician, equally with the pious man, ought to respect and to cherish them.—A volume could not trace all their connections with private and public felicity.—Let it simply be asked where is security for property, for reputation, for life, if the sense of religious obligation *desert* the oaths, which are the instruments of investigation in Courts of Justice? And let us with caution indulge the supposition, that morality can be maintained without religion.—Whatever may be conceded to the influence of refined education on minds of peculiar structure.—reason and experience both forbid us to expect, that national morality can prevail in exclusion of religious principle.—

8   'Tis substantially true, that virtue or morality is a necessary spring of popular government.—The rule indeed extends with more or less force to every species of Free Government.—Who that is a sincere friend to it can look with indifference upon attempts to shake the foundation of the fabric?—

9   Promote, then, as an object of primary importance, institutions for the general diffusion of knowledge. In proportion as the structure of a government gives force to public opinion, it is essential that public opinion should be enlightened.

10   As a very important source of strength and security, cherish public credit.—One method of preserving it is, to use it as sparingly as possible.—avoiding occasions of expense by cultivating peace, but remembering also that timely disbursements to prepare for danger frequently prevent much greater disbursements to repel it—avoiding likewise the accumulation of debt, not only by shunning occasions of expense, but by vigorous exertions in time of Peace to discharge the debts which unavoidable wars may have occasioned, not ungenerously throwing upon posterity the burthen which we ourselves ought to bear. The execution of these maxims belongs to your Representatives, but it is necessary that public opinion should cooperate.—To facilitate to them the performance of their duty, it is essential that you should practically bear in mind, that towards the payment of debts there must be Revenue—that to have Revenue there must be taxes—that no taxes can be devised, which are not more or less inconvenient and unpleasant—that the intrinsic embarrassment, inseparable from the selection of the proper objects (which is always a choice of difficulties) ought to be a decisive motive for a candid construction of the conduct of the Government in making it, and for a spirit of acquiescence in the measures for obtaining Revenue, which the public exigencies may at any time dictate.—

11   Observe good faith and justice towards all Nations. Cultivate peace and harmony with all.—Religion and Morality enjoin this conduct; and can it be, that good policy does not equally enjoin it?—It will be worthy of a free, enlightened, and, at no distant period, a great nation, to give to mankind the magnanimous and too novel example, of a People always guided by an exalted justice and benevolence.—Who can doubt that in the course of time and things, the fruits of such a plan would richly repay any temporary advantages, which might be lost by a steady adherence to it? Can it be that Providence has not connected the permanent felicity of a Nation with its virtue? The experiment, at least, is recommended by every sentiment which ennobles human nature.—Alas! is it rendered impossible by its vices?

12   In the execution of such a plan nothing is more essential than that permanent, inveterate antipathies against particular nations and passionate attachments for others, should be excluded; and that, in place of them, just and amicable feelings towards all should be cultivated.—The Nation, which indulges towards another an habitual hatred or an habitual fondness, is in some degree a slave. It is a slave to its animosity or to its affection, either of which is sufficient to lead it astray from its duty and its interest.—Antipathy in one nation against another disposes each more readily to offer insult and injury, to lay hold of slight causes of umbrage, and to be haughty and intractable, when accidental or trifling occasions of dispute occur.—Hence frequent collisions, obstinate, envenomed and bloody contests.—The Nation prompted by ill-will and resentment, sometimes impels to War the Government, contrary to the best calculations of policy.—The Government sometimes participates in the national propensity, and adopts through passion what reason would reject;—at other times, it makes the animosity of the Nation subservient to projects of hostility instigated by pride, ambition, and other sinister and pernicious motives.—The peace often, sometimes perhaps the Liberty, Nations has been the victim.—

13   So likewise a passionate attachment of one Nation for another produces a variety of evils.—Sympathy for the favorite nation, facilitating the illusion of an imaginary common interest in cases where no real common interest exists, and infusing into one the enmities of the other, betrays the former into a participation in the quarrels and wars of the latter, without adequate inducement or justification. It leads also to concessions to the favorite Nation of privileges denied to others, which is apt doubly to injure the Nation making the concessions; by unnecessarily parting with what ought to have been retained; and by exciting jealousy, ill-will, and a disposition to retaliate, in the parties from whom equal privileges are withheld; and it gives to ambitious, corrupted, or deluded citizens, (who devote themselves to the favorite Nation) facility to betray or sacrifice the interests of their own country, without odium, sometimes even with popularity:—gilding, with the appearances of a virtuous sense of obligation, a commendable deference for public opinion, or a laudable zeal for public good, and the base or foolish compliances of ambition, corruption, or infatuation.—

14   As avenues to foreign influence in innumerable ways, such attachments are particularly alarming to the truly enlightened and independent Patriot.—How many opportunities do they afford to tamper with domestic factions, to practise the arts of seduction, to mislead public opinion, to influence or awe the public councils! Such an attachment of a small or weak, towards a great and powerful nation, dooms the former to be the satellite of the latter.

15   Against the insidious wiles of foreign influence, I conjure you to believe me, fellow-citizens, the jealousy of a free people ought to be *constantly* awake; since history and experience prove that foreign influence is one of the most baneful foes of republican Government.—But that jealousy, to be useful, must be impartial; else it becomes the instrument of the very influence to be avoided, instead of a defense against it.—Excessive partiality for one foreign nation, and excessive dislike of another, cause those whom they actuate to see danger only on one side, and serve to veil and even second the arts of influence on the other. Real Patriots, who may resist the intrigues of the favorite, are liable to become suspected and odious; while its tools and dupes usurp the applause and confidence of the people, to surrender their interests.

16   The great rule of conduct for us, in regard to foreign Nations, is, in extending our commercial relations, to have with them as little *Political* connection as possible.—So far as we have already formed engagements, let them be fulfilled with perfect good faith.—Here let us stop.—

17   Europe has a set of primary interests, which to us have none, or a very remote relation.—Hence she must be engaged in frequent controversies, the causes of which are essentially foreign to our concerns.—Hence, therefore, it must be unwise in us to implicate ourselves, by artificial ties in the ordinary vicissitudes of her politics, or the ordinary combinations and collisions of her friendships, or enmities.

18   Our detached and distant situation invites and enables us to pursue a different course.—If we remain one People, under an efficient government, the period is not far off, when we may defy material injury from external annoyance; when we may take such an attitude as will cause the neutrality we may at any time resolve upon to be scrupulously respected. When belligerent nations, under the impossibility of making acquisitions upon us, will not lightly hazard the giving us provocation when we may choose peace or war, as our interest, guided by our justice, shall counsel.

19   Why forego the advantages of so peculiar a situation?—Why quit our own to stand upon foreign ground?—Why, by interweaving our destiny with that of any part of Europe, entangle our peace and prosperity in the toils of European ambition, rivalship, interest, humor, or caprice?—

20   'Tis our true policy to steer clear of permanent alliances, with any portion of the foreign world;—so far, I mean, as we are now at liberty to do it;—for let me not be understood as capable of patronizing infidelity to existing engagements. (I hold the maxim no less applicable to public than to private affairs, that honesty is always the best policy.)—I repeat it therefore let those engagements be observed in their genuine sense.—But in my opinion it is unnecessary and would be unwise to extend them.—

21   Taking care always to keep ourselves, by suitable establishments, on a respectable defensive posture, we may safely trust to temporary alliances for extraordinary emergencies.—

22   Harmony, liberal intercourse with all nations, are recommended by policy, humanity, and interest. But even our commercial policy should hold an equal and impartial hand:—neither seeking nor granting exclusive favors or preferences;—consulting the natural course of things;—diffusing and diversifying by gentle means the streams of commerce, but forcing nothing;—establishing with Powers so disposed—in order to give trade a stable course, to define the rights of our Merchants, and to enable the Government to support them—conventional rules of intercourse, the best that present circumstances and mutual opinion will permit; but temporary, and liable to be from time to time abandoned or varied, as experience and circumstances shall dictate; constantly keeping in view, that 'tis folly in one nation to look for disinterested favors from another;—that it must pay with a portion of its independence for whatever it may accept under that character—that by such acceptance, it may place itself in the condition of having given equivalents for nominal favors, and yet of being reproached with ingratitude for not giving more. There can be no greater error than to expect or calculate upon real favors from Nation to Nation. 'Tis an illusion, which experience must cure, which a just pride ought to discard.

23   In offering to you, my Countrymen, these counsels of an old and affectionate friend, I dare not hope they will make the strong and lasting impression, I could wish,—that they will control the usual current of the passions, or prevent our Nation from running the course which has hitherto marked the destiny of Nations. But if I may even flatter myself, that they may be productive of some partial benefit; some occasional good, that they may now and then recur to moderate the fury of party spirit, to warn against the mischiefs of foreign intrigue, to guard against the impostures of pretended patriotism, this hope will be a full recompense for the solicitude for your welfare, by which they have been dictated.—

24   How far in the discharge of my official duties, I have been guided by the principles which have been delineated, the public Records and other evidences of my conduct must witness to You and to the world.—To myself the assurance of my own conscience is, that I have at least believed myself to be guided by them.

25   In relation to the still subsisting War in Europe, my Proclamation of the 22nd of April 1793, is the index to my plan.—Sanctioned by your approving voice and by that of your

Representatives in both Houses of Congress, the spirit of that measure has continually governed me:—uninfluenced by any attempts to deter or divert me from it.

26   After deliberate examination with the aid of the best lights I could obtain, I was well satisfied that our country, under all the circumstances of the case, had a right to take, and was bound in duty and interest to take, a Neutral position.—Having taken it, I determined, as far as should depend upon me, to maintain it, with moderation, perseverance, and firmness.—

27   The considerations which respect the right to hold this conduct, it is not necessary on this occasion to detail. I will only observe, that, according to my understanding of the matter, that right, so far from being denied by any of the Belligerent Powers, has been virtually admitted by all.—

28   The duty of holding a neutral conduct may be inferred, without anything more, from the obligation which justice and humanity impose on every Nation, in cases in which it is free to act, to maintain inviolate the relations of Peace and Amity towards other Nations.—

29   The inducements of interest for observing that conduct will best be referred to your own reflections and experience.—With me, a predominant motive has been to endeavor to gain time to our country to settle and mature its yet recent institutions, and to progress without interruption to that degree of strength and consistency, which is necessary to give it, humanly speaking, the command of its own fortunes.

30   Though, in reviewing the incidents of my Administration, I am unconscious of intentional error—I am nevertheless too sensible of my defects not to think it probable that I may have committed many errors.—Whatever they may be, I fervently beseech the Almighty to avert or mitigate the evils to which they may tend.—I shall also carry with me the hope that my country will never cease to view them with indulgence; and that, after forty-five years of my life dedicated to its service with an upright zeal, the faults of incompetent abilities will be consigned to oblivion, as myself must soon be to the mansions of rest.

31   Relying on its kindness in this as in other things, and actuated by that fervent love towards it, which is so natural to a man, who views in it the native soil of himself and his progenitors for several generations;—I anticipate with pleasing expectation that retreat, in which I promise myself to realize, without alloy, the sweet enjoyment of partaking, in the midst of my fellow-citizens, the benign influence of good Laws under a free Government, the ever favorite object of my heart, and the happy reward as I trust, of our mutual cares, labors, and dangers.

Multiple-Choice Questions 11–15:

11. In the opening paragraph, Washington suggests that political parties are

    A. unfortunate and repressive.

    B. popular and controlled.

    C. ubiquitous and inevitable.

    D. natural and democratic.

    E. intelligent and rank.

12. Washington cites all of the following as dangers of party division EXCEPT

    A. bloody and vengeful regimes.

    B. the rise to power of a tyrant.

    C. fear and insecurity.

    D. susceptibility to foreign invasion.

    E. governmental discord.

13. As he uses the words in this selection, Washington understands *Religion and Morality* to mean

    A. belief and proper motivation.

    B. private and public felicity.

    C. prayer and pious behavior.

    D. obligatory and sacramental ritual.

    E. worship and right action.

14. Which of the following quotations best summarizes Washington's sentiments toward taxes in paragraph 10?

    A. "[I]t is necessary that public opinion should cooperate[.]"

    B. "One method of preserving it is, to use it as sparingly as possible."

    C. "… a spirit of acquiescence in the measures for obtaining Revenue…"

    D. "[T]owards the payment of debts there must be Revenue—that to have Revenue there must be taxes[.]"

    E. "[N]o taxes can be devised, which are not more or less inconvenient and unpleasant[.]"

15. Washington's apparent attitude regarding relations with other nations can best be described as

    A. antipathy.

    B. discriminatory patronage.

    C. amity.

    D. sympathetic indifference.

    E. benevolent neutrality.

Free-response item 1 (Text-based):

In this third and final section of "The Address of General Washington To The People of The United States on his declining of the Presidency of the United States," Washington delivers his historically famous statements on the role of religion and morality in government, the need for an educated citizenry, and the dangers of foreign entanglements. Read this section and choose one of the three issues discussed. Then, write a well-reasoned and well-supported essay in which you explain your understanding of Washington's view of that issue. Do not merely summarize the passage.

Before you write your essay:

1. **Make sure you understand exactly what you're being asked to write about.**
   - List all of the verbs in the prompt.
   - Underline the verb that describes the essay.
   - Write the direct object of that verb.

2. **Make sure you have something valid to write about.**
   - Write a sentence or two that make a positive and focused statement about the topic.
   - Make sure these sentences address all of the issues and subpoints specified in the prompt.

3. **Review the selection and find your textual support.**

4. **Write your essay.**
   - Keep referring to the prompt and whatever you underlined or highlighted in the selection to make sure you're on track and addressing everything the prompt wants you to address.

Free-response item 2 (Independent):

In order to maintain the attention and sympathy of their readers, writers occasionally rely on general or abstract words to communicate difficult or controversial ideas. It is then up to the reader to examine the text in which those words are used in order to infer an accurate understanding of the writer's meaning. Choose such a passage and write a thoughtful and well-organized essay in which you examine the context of a key term and offer a valid interpretation of the writer's meaning. Be certain to support your assertions with direct reference (summary, paraphrase, quotation if possible). Do not merely provide a definition of the selected term.

NOTE TO STUDENT AND TEACHER: By now you have probably explored the full text of Washington's address. You may, therefore, want to use the full address for support and examples in writing the following two essays.

Before you write your essay:

1. **Make sure you understand exactly what you're being asked to write about.**
    - List all of the verbs in the prompt.
    - Underline the verb that describes the essay.
    - Write the direct object of that verb.

2. **Choose an appropriate selection.**
    If you're using this book, your teacher probably wants you to write your essay on whatever story, article, or poem, etc., the writing prompt follows.

3. **Make sure you have something to say about both the topic and your selected literature.**
    - Think in terms of narrative structure: organization of ideas, etc..
    - Make sure you jot down notes that pertain to the assigned topic.
    - Jot down quotations or at least close paraphrases.
    - Jot down everything you know and remember about the assigned topic.

4. **Make sure you are clear about what you are going to say.**
   - Write a sentence or two that make a positive and focused statement about the topic.
   - Make sure these sentences address all of the issues and subpoints specified in the prompt.

5. **Write your essay.**

Prestwick House Pre-AP: Readings and Exercises

Some reminders for succeeding with free-response questions

MINI-CHAPTER 4.5:

1. The prompt will usually specify "write a thoughtful and well-supported essay" or words along those lines, but even if it doesn't, *you are being asked to write an essay.* It's time to apply everything you have learned about structure, organization, thesis and introduction, support, evidence, and examples, transitions, and a strong conclusion.

   A brilliant but poorly written answer might score more points than a dazzling essay that does not answer the question, but it will not receive a top score.

2. The purpose of the essay is to assess how well you can formulate original ideas and then articulate them to someone else.

3. Do not be distracted by advice like "be certain to address such elements as word choice and sentence structure." Even if the prompt specifies them as examples, you will *not* be penalized for writing brilliantly on other elements and not discussing the ones listed.

4. Similarly, do *not* feel obligated to write your essay on one of the suggested titles if you can do a better job with another piece you are more familiar with.

5. When you are told that you can choose the literature on which to base your essay, do make sure you pick a story, poem, novel, play, etc., worth writing about on an AP exam. Often the question will instruct you to choose something with "literary merit," but even if it doesn't, this requirement is assumed.

Prestwick House Pre-AP: Readings and Exercises

Introduction to Literary Analysis

CHAPTER 5

UP UNTIL NOW, MUCH of what you're read, discussed, and written about in English class has probably focused on interpretation—what the story, poem, play means. What is the theme? What idea is the author exploring?

You've probably also spent a good deal of time identifying story elements (this event introduces the conflict; this event is part of the rising action; this event is the climax …) and language and narrative devices. We've dealt with reasons for needing to be able to identify those devices in Chapters 2 and 3.

Your Advanced Placement exams, however, will almost never ask you merely to interpret a story. The writers and scorers of the exam *assume* you understand what you're reading. Primarily, both the AP Literature and Composition and the Language and Composition exams will ask you to *analyze* literature.

Essentially, analysis is the process of figuring out not what a piece means, but how it has been constructed to communicate that meaning to the reader.

Is the story funny? What makes it funny?

Is the plot so suspenseful that you couldn't put the book down? How did the writer structure the plot to keep you reading?

Was the editorial's argument so skillfully and subtly laid out that you found yourself nodding in agreement without even realizing it? How did the writer organize and present that argument?

Analysis, then, is not interested only in the meaning or impact of a piece of literature—meaning and impact are taken for granted. Analysis is the examination of *how the writer does it.*

Of course, you cannot intelligently discuss a writer's technique if you don't know the right terms, so all of those "identify and define" exercises weren't a waste of time and energy, after all. In fact, if you *aren't* conversant with terms like "parallelism," "interior monologue," "indirect dialogue," "rising action," "falling action," "climax," and so on, you need to devote some time to learning them.

Your inability to use these terms in your writing will lower your AP score as surely as your inability to read and understand a written piece without your teacher's assistance.

Analyzing (not merely interpreting) prose fiction

In the previous chapters, we've isolated individual elements of a literary analysis, but we haven't stepped back to look at the big picture—the complete analysis. The following two stories will help you to see that process. As we've done in the previous chapters, the first story, Dorothy Parker's "The Standard of Living," is annotated to show the kinds of thoughts and questions that would probably occur to a student taking an AP exam. The multiple-choice and free-response items illustrate how the AP exam looks more toward analysis than interpretation.

The second story, Marietta Holley's "An Unmarried Female," is for you to practice on.

The Standard of Living

DOROTHY PARKER (1893 – 1967)

1 ANNABEL AND MIDGE CAME OUT of the tea room with the arrogant slow gait of the leisured,[1] for their Saturday afternoon stretched ahead of them. They had lunched, as was their wont,[2] on sugar, starches, oils, and butter-fats. Usually[3] they ate sandwiches of spongy new white bread greased with butter and mayonnaise; they ate thick wedges of cake lying wet beneath ice cream and whipped cream and melted chocolate gritty with nuts.[4] As alternates, they ate patties, sweating beads of inferior oil, containing bits of bland meat bogged in pale, stiffening sauce; they ate pastries, limber under rigid icing, filled with an indeterminate yellow sweet stuff, not still solid, not yet liquid, like salve that has been left in the sun.[5] They chose no other sort of food, nor did they consider it. And their skin was like the petals of wood anemones, and their bellies were as flat and

---

Sample Student Commentary

[1] Parker's word choice creates a vivid image of the girls' walk and is the first clue to their overall characters.

[2] Parenthetical asides like this one create an informal, conversational tone. Parker is known for her sarcastic wit, so this tone may be colored by sarcasm.

[3] The story begins in medias res, with the girls leaving the tea room. This single word signals the beginning of the exposition.

[4] Parker creates a vivid image of the girls' habitual food by providing a few, but very specific, details. Note the word choice that emphasizes wetness and decadence: spongy, greased, wet, melted. Note also the simple list of foods known to be delicious but also fattening.

[5] Another vivid image created by a list of precise nouns and explicit adjectives. Note that from this and the previous list, we get not only a clear picture of the food the girls eat, but we also continue to develop a strong impression of the girls themselves.

<u>their flanks as lean as those of young Indian braves</u>.[6]

2   Annabel and Midge had been best friends almost from the day that Midge had found a job as stenographer with the firm that employed Annabel. By now, Annabel, two years longer in the stenographic department, had worked up to the wages of eighteen dollars and fifty cents a week; Midge was still at sixteen dollars. Each girl lived at home with her family and paid half her salary to its support.

3   The girls sat side by side at their desks, they lunched together every noon, together they set out for home at the end of the day's work. Many of their evenings and most of their Sundays were passed in each other's company. Often they were joined by two young men, but there was no steadiness to any such quartet; the two young men would give place, <u>unlamented</u>, to two other young men, and lament would have been inappropriate, <u>really</u>,[7] since the newcomers were scarcely distinguishable from their predecessors. Invariably the girls spent the fine idle hours of their hot-weather Saturday afternoons together. <u>Constant use had not worn ragged the fabric of their friendship</u>.[8]

4   They looked alike, though the resemblance did not lie in their features. It was in the shape of their bodies, their movements, their style, and their adornments. Annabel and Midge did, <u>and completely</u>,[9] all that young office workers are besought not to do. They painted their lips and their nails, they <u>darkened their lashes and lightened their hair</u>,[10] and scent seemed to shimmer from them. They wore thin, bright dresses, tight over their breasts and high on their legs, and tilted slippers, fancifully strapped. They looked <u>conspicuous and cheap and charming</u>.[11]

5   Now, as they walked across to Fifth Avenue with their skirts swirled by the hot wind, they received audible admiration. Young men grouped lethargically about newsstands awarded them murmurs, exclamations, <u>even—the ultimate tribute—whistles</u>.[12] Annabel and Midge passed without the condescension of hurrying their pace; they held their

---

Sample Student Commentary

[6] These similes assume the reader knows how smooth or blemish-free wood anemone petals are, but, clearly, any comparison to flower petals would evoke beauty and softness. Parker also assumes we can imagine the leanness and strength of a "young Indian brave" in order to picture the smooth leanness of the girls' bodies. It is important to note that the girls' leanness is in stark contrast to the fatty foods they consume.

[7] More parenthetical asides, these more sarcastic than the first.

[8] A common enough, easy-to-understand metaphor. Perhaps the simplicity of this metaphor helps to emphasize the girls' basic simplicity and the effortlessness of their friendship.

[9] Another parenthetical aside. Parker wants to emphasize that, not only did the girls do this, they did it to its fullest extent.

[10] Rhetorically, this is antithesis. It probably emphasizes that, in their cosmetic efforts, the girls leave nothing of their appearances unchanged. They violate the convention of standard office wear "completely."

[11] Here is a particularly effective blend of polysyndeton, alliteration, antithesis, and climax. The polysyndeton and alliteration maintain Parker's lighthearted tone. The antithesis sets the reader up for surprise: we think Parker is criticizing the girls, but she is actually delighted by them. The climax delivers the surprise.

[12] Note how the dashes emphasize the aside. The commas that separate the others more or less de-emphasize their content. Here, through the dashes, Parker wants to make it absolutely clear that that these young women enjoy the attention they receive from the young men.

heads higher and set their feet with exquisite precision, <u>as if they stepped over the necks of peasants</u>.[13]

6   Always the girls went to walk on Fifth Avenue on their free afternoons, for it was the ideal ground for their favorite game. The game could be played anywhere, and indeed, was, but the great shop windows stimulated the two players to their best form.

7   Annabel had invented the game; or rather she had evolved it from an old one. Basically, it was no more than the ancient sport of what-would-you-do-if-you-had-a-million-dollars? But Annabel had drawn a new set of rules for it, had narrowed it, pointed it, made it stricter. Like all games, it was the more absorbing for being more difficult.

8   · Annabel's version went like this: You must suppose that somebody dies and leaves you a million dollars, cool. But there is a condition to the bequest. <u>It is stated in the will that you must spend every nickel of the money on yourself</u>.[14]

9   There lay the hazard of the game. <u>If, when playing it, you forgot and listed among your expenditures the rental of a new apartment for your family, for example, you lost your turn to the other player</u>.[15] It was astonishing how many—and some of them among the experts, too—would forfeit all their innings by such slips.

10   It was essential, of course, that it be played in passionate seriousness. Each purchase must be carefully considered and, if necessary, supported by argument. There was no zest to playing it wildly. Once Annabel had introduced the game to Sylvia, another girl who worked in the office. She explained the rules to Sylvia and then offered her the gambit "What would be the first thing you'd do?" Sylvia had not shown the decency of even a second of hesitation. "Well," she said, "the first thing I'd do, I'd go out and hire somebody to shoot Mrs. Gary Cooper,1 and then..." So it is to be seen that she was no fun.

11   But Annabel and Midge were surely born to be comrades, for Midge played the game like a master from the moment she learned it. It was she who added the touches that made the whole thing cozier. According to Midge's innovations, the eccentric who died and left you the money was <u>not anybody you loved, or, for the matter of that, anybody you even knew. It was somebody who had seen you somewhere and had thought, "That girl ought to have lots of nice things. I'm going to leave her a million dollars when I die." And the death was to be neither untimely nor painful. Your benefactor, full of years and comfortably ready to depart, was to slip softly away during sleep and go right to heaven</u>.[16] These <u>embroideries</u>[17] permitted Annabel and Midge to play their game in the luxury of peaceful consciences.

---

[1] Gary Cooper was a popular movie star of the 1930s, '40s, and '50s.

Sample Student Commentary

[13] Simile. Note that Parker has not used many adjectives to describe their characters (such as "young," "self-confident," "immature"), but her vivid descriptions of their clothing, their food, and their manner of walking create an unmistakable impression of their characters.

[14] Annabel's stipulation suggests that the reader is supposed to like her. She finds it hard to be selfish, so she arranges the rules of the game so that the players must be.

[15] Further establishes that it is not in the girls' nature to be selfish, so the rules of the game must require them to be.

[16] Here it is established that Midge, too, is a nice girl, likeable, deserving of reader sympathy.

[17] Metaphor. Midge's extra "touches" do not change the nature of the game; they merely embellish it.

12   Midge played with a seriousness that was not only proper but extreme. The single strain on the girls' friendship had followed an announcement once made by Annabel that <u>the first thing she would buy with her million dollars would be a silver-fox coat. It was as if she had struck Midge across the mouth. When Midge recovered her breath, she cried that she couldn't imagine how Annabel could do such a thing—silver-fox coats were so common! Annabel defended her taste with the retort that they were not common, either. Midge then said that they were so. She added that everybody had a silver-fox coat. She went on, with perhaps a slight loss of head, to declare that she herself wouldn't be caught dead in silver fox.</u>[18]

13   For the next few days, though the girls saw each other as constantly, their conversation was careful and infrequent, and they did not once play their game. Then one morning, as soon as Annabel entered the office, she came to Midge and said she had changed her mind. She would not buy a silver-fox coat with any part of her million dollars. Immediately on receiving the legacy, she would select a coat of mink.

14   Midge smiled and her eyes shone. "I think," she said, "you're doing absolutely the right thing."[19]

15   Now, as they walked along Fifth Avenue, they played the game anew.[20] It was one of those days with which September is repeatedly cursed; hot and glaring, with slivers of dust in the wind. People drooped and shambled, but the girls carried themselves tall and walked a straight line, as befitted young heiresses on their afternoon promenade. There was no longer need for them to start the game at its formal opening. Annabel went direct to the heart of it.

16   "All right,"[21] she said. "So you've got this million dollars. So what would be the first thing you'd do?"

17   "Well, the first thing I'd do," Midge said, "I'd get a mink coat." But she said it mechanically, as if she were giving the memorized answer to an expected question.

18   "Yes," Annabel said. "I think you ought to. The terribly dark kind of mink." But she, too, spoke as if by rote. It was too hot; fur, no matter how dark and sleek and supple, was horrid to the thoughts.

19   They stepped along in silence for a while. Then Midge's eye was caught by a shop window. <u>Cool, lovely gleamings were there set off by chaste and elegant darkness</u>.[22]

20   "No," Midge said, "I take it back. I wouldn't get a mink coat the first thing. Know what I'd do? I'd get a string of pearls. Real pearls."[23]

21   Annabel's eyes turned to follow Midge's.

Sample Student Commentary

[18] While we are still in the plot exposition, Parker does not want to waste a lot of time and space on recreating the girls' conversation, so she employs indirect dialogue. This technique allows Parker to maintain her tone and provide a specific example of how the girls get along without interrupting the casual flow of the narrative.

[19] Here, however, Parker does provide a direct quotation. This is clearly a clue to something, even if we don't know what yet.

[20] We are leaving the exposition and returning to the action of the story that began in the first sentence. The direct quotation at the end of the previous paragraph was the beginning of this transition.

[21] Having returned to the "present," the actual day of the story, Parker now shows the reader the action as it happens. So, now the dialogue is presented directly.

[22] The image is heightened by the contrasts of "lovely" and chaste" and "gleamings" and "darkness."

[23] Since this is the first real departure from the way the girls have played the game, Midge's first sight of the pearls is probably the inciting incident. This small event is the beginning of the rising action.

22   "Yes," she said, slowly. "I think that's a kind of a good idea. And it would make sense, too. Because you can wear pearls with anything."

23   Together they went over to the shop window and stood pressed against it. It contained but one object—a double row of great, even pearls clasped by a deep emerald around a little pink velvet throat.[24]

24   "What do you suppose they cost?" Annabel said.

25   "Gee, I don't know," Midge said. "Plenty, I guess."

26   "Like a thousand dollars?" Annabel said.

27   "Oh, I guess like more," Midge said. "On account of the emerald."

28   "Well, like ten thousand dollars?" Annabel said.

29   "Gee, I wouldn't even know," Midge said.

30   The devil nudged Annabel in the ribs. "Dare you to go in and price them," she said.[25]

31   "Like fun!" Midge said.

32   "Dare you," Annabel said.

33   "Why, a store like this wouldn't even be open this afternoon," Midge said.

34   "Yes, it is so, too," Annabel said. "People just came out. And there's a doorman on. Dare you."

35   "Well," Midge said. "But you've got to come too."

36   They tendered thanks, icily, to the doorman for ushering them into the shop. It was cool and quiet, a broad, gracious room with paneled walls and soft carpet. But the girls wore expressions of bitter disdain, as if they stood in a sty.

37   A slim, immaculate clerk came to them and bowed. <u>His neat face showed no astonishment at their appearance</u>.[26]

38   "Good afternoon," he said. He implied that he would never forget it if they would grant him the favor of accepting his soft-spoken greeting.

39   "Good afternoon," Annabel and Midge said together, and in like freezing accents.

40   "Is there something—?" the clerk said.

41   "Oh, we're just looking," Annabel said. It was as if she flung the words down from a dais.

42   The clerk bowed.

43   "<u>My friend and myself</u>[27] merely happened to be passing," Midge said, and stopped, seeming to listen to the phrase. "My friend here and myself," she went on, "merely happened to be wondering how much are those pearls you've got in your window."

44   "Ah, yes," the clerk said. "The double rope. That is two hundred and fifty thousand dollars, Madam."

Sample Student Commentary

[24] Rising action: the game's stakes increase when there is no longer a hypothetical mink coat, but an actual string of pearls.

[25] Rising action; the situation intensifies when the girls actually enter the store.

[26] The clerk's reaction combines understatement and litotes. To appreciate the man's expression, we need to remember the earlier description of how the girls are dressed and made up. Parker used words like "conspicuous" and "cheap" to describe them.

[27] Hearing the characters' own words gives us the opportunity to arrive at our own conclusion. We probably both wince and smile at Annabel's futile attempt to put on airs.

45   "I see," Midge said.[28]

46   The clerk bowed. "An exceptionally beautiful necklace," he said. "Would you care to look at it?"

47   "No, thank you," Annabel said.

48   "<u>My friend and myself merely happened</u>[29] to be passing," Midge said.

49   They turned to go; <u>to go, from their manner, where the tumbrel</u>[1] <u>awaited them</u>.[30] The clerk sprang ahead and opened the door. He bowed as they swept by him.

50   The girls went on along the Avenue and disdain was still on their faces.

51   "Honestly!" Annabel said. "Can you imagine a thing like that?"

52   "Two hundred and fifty thousand dollars!" Midge said. "That's a quarter of a million dollars right there!"

53   "He's got his nerve!" Annabel said.

54   They walked on. Slowly the disdain went, slowly and completely as if drained from them, and with it went the regal carriage and tread. Their shoulders dropped and they dragged their feet; they bumped against each other, without notice or apology, and caromed away again. They were silent and their eyes were cloudy.[31]

55   Suddenly Midge straightened her back, flung her head high, and spoke, clear and strong.[32]

56   "Listen, Annabel," she said. "Look. Suppose there was this terribly rich person, see? You don't know this person, but this person has seen you somewhere and wants to do something for you. Well, it's a terribly old person, see? And so this person dies, just like going to sleep, and leaves you ten million dollars. Now, what would be the first thing you'd do?"[33]

"The Standard of Living," copyright 1941 by Dorothy Parker, renewed © 1969 by Lillian Hellman, from THE PORTABLE DOROTHY PARKER by Dorothy Parker, edited by Marion Meade. Used by permission of Viking Penguin, a division of Penguin (USA) Inc.

---

[1] A tumbrel was the type of cart used to transport condemned prisoners to their execution, especially to take victims of the French Revolution to the guillotine.

Sample Student Commentary

[28] Note again that Parker refuses to describe the reaction to the reader. We hear Midge's words and are left to build our own conclusion. Also note, we might be tempted to see this event as the turning point—the climax—of the story, but Midge's reaction is ambiguous, and the end of the story is still not determined.

[29] This is the third iteration of this phrase. Given what we have been led to believe about Midge and Annabel, we can guess fairly accurately how the tone of each iteration has changed.

[30] Suggests a new timidity? Are the girls defeated?

[31] Again, by describing only the girls' gait and posture, Parker leaves no doubt of what they are thinking and feeling.

[32] Here is the climax of the story, the turning point, the highest point in the rising action. This is the moment at which the outcome of the story is determined. The girls will not slink home, defeated, but the game will be resurrected. This incident also constitutes something of a reversal. Just when we believe the girls are defeated and their game ruined, Midge finds a way to rescue it, and the story has a completely different resolution from the one previously expected.

[33] The denouement, or resolution, maintains the lighthearted tone and establishes the girls as likeable, but static, characters. There has been no change or growth as a result of the events in this plot. In fact, the girls may be even more committed to their carefree, unselfish, confident optimism at the end of the story than they were at the beginning.

Sample Multiple-Choice Questions:

1. The images in the opening paragraph suggest that Midge and Annabel are

    A. wealthy.

    B. poor.

    C. attractive.

    D. carefree.

    E. careless.

2. Parker uses all of the following techniques to develop her characters EXCEPT

    A. qualitative description.

    B. indirect dialogue.

    C. quotation.

    D. action.

    E. imagery.

3. The overall tone of this story can best be described as

    A. comical.

    B. cheerful.

    C. didactic.

    D. sarcastic.

    E. dismissive.

4. The primary effect achieved by the *litotes* in the 37th paragraph is to

    A. suggest the clerk's arrogance.

    B. emphasize the girls' cheapness.

    C. understate the situation's incongruity.

    D. evoke reader sympathy for the girls.

    E. evoke reader sympathy for the clerk.

5. The author's attitude toward Annabel and Midge can best be described as

    A. critical.

    B. condescending.

    C. laudatory.

    D. empathetic.

    E. amused.

Answers and Explanations:

1. While it is not yet explained in the opening paragraph where the young women work or how much they are paid, there are also no details to suggest wealth (A). Certainly the lunches we are told they consume, described with words like "inferior" and "bland" do not suggest wealth. There is no reason, however, to conclude that they are poor (B) either. They are, after all, apparently able buy their lunches on a fairly regular basis. Certainly, while the descriptions of their skin and figures might suggest (C), this is not the best answer, as the bulk of the paragraph deals with the food they eat and the way they walk down the street. (E) might also be tempting as it is clear the young women routinely eat food commonly believed to contribute to skin and weight problems, but the fact that we are told they did not have such problems excludes (E). The way the girls walk, however, their arrogant swagger, the way they eat what they want with abandon, and the fact that we are told their entire Saturday afternoon lay before them, **all strongly suggest (D)**.

2. Virtually all of the dialogue communicated to the reader in the exposition of this story is in the form of indirect dialogue (B) in which the content of the conversation is summarized but not quoted word for word. The exposition ends, however, with a direct quotation, and all of the girls' conversation during the actual time of the story is presented as direct quotations (C). (D) is the first technique the reader encounters— the girl's arrogant gait, their lunch habits, and so on. (E) likewise, is used early in the story—the descriptions of the food, their clothing, their cosmetic habits. Dorothy Parker does not, however, impose a single qualitative adjective on the reader. She never once describes her characters as "nice," or "perky," or name any other trait except as it can be inferred from one of the above techniques. **Thus, (A) is the correct answer.**

3. The story is certainly lighthearted, and Parker seems genuinely amused by the Midge and Annabel, but there is nothing truly comical (A) in the story. (C) is clearly inappropriate as there are no lessons to be learned either by the characters or the reader, and certainly Parker does not seem to have a message to send with this story. While there may be a few elements of sarcasm (D), the story is not sarcastic overall. In fact, Parker seems to like her characters, and she seems to want her reader to be amused by them. (E) is unlikely; although she does say the girls look "conspicuous and cheap," she also says they are "charming." While obviously amused by these characters, Parker is certainly not dismissive of them. Parker's careful word choice, however, her use of asides, and the denouement she provides for her plot combine to create an overall lighthearted or cheerful tone. **Thus, (B) is the best answer.**

4. Litotes, in general, is used to suggest a weak positive or an understatement. The clerk does not act arrogantly toward the girls, nor does he ignore them or refuse to serve them; in fact, his failure to seem surprised at their entrance into the store is far from arrogance. Thus, (A) is easily eliminated. Likewise, (B) would be achieved by the clerk's showing surprise, not by his showing no surprise. (D) would be possible if the clerk were somehow rude or unkind to the girls, but he is not. (E) is mildly tempting because, clearly, we are not to dislike the clerk; his role is so minor that it is unlikely Parker wants the reader to care either way. Only (C) addresses the purpose and function of litotes. **Thus, (C) is the best answer.**

5. This question is not terribly different from question 3—and it is unlikely that there will be two so similar questions on your AP exam—but it does provide us with the opportunity to examine Parker's word choice and use of literary and rhetorical devices to support whatever inference we reach. While Parker does call the girls "conspicuous and cheap," she does conclude that they are "charming." While they may border on the silly, they are apparently kind and unselfish. Thus, (A) is clearly incorrect. Nor can Parker be said to be condescending (B) toward the young women. Again, they are "charming." They handle the calls and whistles from the men with dignity. They even handle the epiphany of the price of the necklace with dignity. And they end the story as optimistic as they ever were. Thus, (B) is eliminated. Some students might be tempted by (C), but while Parker seems to genuinely like these girls and does not criticize them or condescend to them, she does not overtly praise them or express admiration for them, either. Likewise, a feeling of amusement and a general sense of approval cannot be mistaken for empathy (D) and nothing in the story suggests that Parker feels a sense of solidarity with her two working-class characters. **(E) is the best answer.** Parker's attitude is clearly positive, but it cannot be read as reaching the point of admiration. She is amused by these girls, their friendship, and their spirit.

Sample free-response item (text-based):

Carefully read Dorothy Parker's short story "The Standard of Living" and write a thoughtful and well-organized essay in which you analyze Parker's language, especially her word choice, and the impact it has on the overall tone of the story. Do not merely summarize the plot.

Creative writers often use their language to show, not tell, the reader what happens in the story.[1] Through descriptive word choice and carefully chosen literary devices, authors can create a stylish depiction of their characters' personalities, actions, and dialogue without explicitly stating every detail. Much of the narrative is left to the reader's interpretation, guided by literary and verbal cues. In Dorothy Parker's short story "The Standard of Living," she uses her language to lead the reader to know her characters, understand them, like them, and then admire them.[2] She uses specific literary devices, such as simile, antithesis, and litotes, to portray their outward appearance and bearing, which then sheds light on their inner thoughts and attitudes. Because Parker herself seems to like these characters, her word choice and stylistic devices give her tone a sarcastic wit.[3]

In Dorothy Parker's first paragraph,[4] instead of blatantly describing her two characters, Annabel and Midge, as "nice" or "friendly" or "silly," she creates a powerful image of their personalities. The first depiction of the two girls is done in medias res,[5] following them as they leave the tea room "with the arrogant slow gait of the leisured." How the girls walk is the first clue to the reader that they might be haughty and possibly spoiled. The sentences of exposition that follow do not give the readers facts about Annabel and Midge, but about what they had just eaten: "[they] had lunched, as was their wont, on sugars, starches, oils, and butter fats." Parker's word choice of what the two ate argues to the reader that Annabel and Midge are decadent and do not eat or do what is necessarily good for them. The phrase, "as was their wont" is a parenthetical aside, which creates an informal and casual tone, suggesting to the reader that Parker is divulging a tidbit of information or possibly a secret about the girls.[6] At the end of the paragraph,

---

Scorer Commentary

[1] Here, the student uses a parenthetical aside to emphasize his point.

[2] The student introduces his argument, claiming that the author has a reason for writing the way she does, that style is not merely habit. It is important to explain not only what an author is doing, but also why she may be doing it. This creates a "thesis driven" and argumentative paper.

[3] The student presents his thesis at the end of the first paragraph, which helps to lead him into the following section of his paper. Here, he lists three literary terms he is planning on discussing.

[4] This student uses numerical ordering as a logical progression for his paper. It is important to use transitional elements when leading into and away from each paragraph.

[5] Here, the student uses a literary term to describe the action in the story. While it is not wise to use all the literary terms that you have learned just for the sake of using them in your essay, it is very important that you use them when it is appropriate to demonstrate your knowledge to the reader.

[6] This student embeds the quotation in his own words and follows with an explanatory sentence. It is important to demonstrate the ability to "close read" the text.

Parker finally offers a small hint at the physicality of the two girls, but not through direct description or explicit details. She merely suggests through simile, stating that "their bellies were as flat and their flanks as lean as those of young Indian braves." Annabel and Midge are depicted as fit, strong, and lean characters, which starkly contrasts their leisurely activities and fatty food choices. Parker does not give away anything about her characters; the reader is meant to dissect her language and infer from her word choice what the girls are like.[7]

Later in the story, Parker continues to hint[8] at the physicality and character of Annabel and Midge, not by describing them but by describing others' reactions to them: "Young men grouped lethargically about newsstands awarded them murmurs, exclamations, even—the ultimate tribute—whistles." These are attractive young women, and they know it. They attract attention, and they seem to enjoy attracting attention.

The most blatant bit of describing Parker does is still more visual and suggestive than expository: "[they] did, and completely, all that young office workers are besought not to do. They painted their lips and nails, they darkened their lashes and lightened their hair." Again, we learn through her contrast in language that the girls behave not as they should. As "young office workers," Annabel and Midge are expected to dress plainly, with little make-up.[9] Instead, as Parker describes, they are their peers' antithesis. Parker's opposing word choices of "darkening" and "lightening" complement her sarcastically contrary tone. As the girls walk by the jewelry shop, Parker uses the slow exposition of the plot to further challenge the reader to infer what she is really saying about the girls. Parker explains that the two "...stepped along in silence for a while. Then Midge's eye was caught by a shop window. Cool, lovely gleamings were there set off by chaste and elegant darkness." Here, Parker heightens the image by using contrasting language: the words "lovely" and "chaste" and "gleamings" and "darkness." Parker is provoking her audience to be active readers and to look through her descriptions to discover the true nature of the characters.

"Chaste" and "elegant" also provide a sharp contrast to the image Parker has already provided of the bleached-blonde friends. The girls are "conspicuous and cheap"; the necklace is "cool," and its setting is "chaste" and "elegant."

The understated litotes[10] of the clerk's reaction is another example of careful word choice. While not saying anything about the girl's appearance, Parker manages to announce loud and clear how inappropriate they are for their current setting.

Scorer Commentary

[7] This ending sentence goes back to the student's original argument from his introductory paragraph. You should always make sure that your paper is staying close to your original argument and that it progresses logically through the use of transitional sentences.

[8] This student uses careful word choices, such as "hint," to suggest his own casual and suggestive tone to his paper.

[9] He offers further explanation of his "close reading" by discussing the expectations of the girls' employment, which was not mentioned in the text. While the grades of the AP exam will not expect you to have any outside knowledge of the text, it is a good idea to demonstrate that knowledge if you do have it.

[10] Here, the student offers the final literary term he outlined in his introductory paragraph.

The foundation Parker has carefully laid pays off at the end of the story, when with a single smile and comment, she communicates to her reader her characters' true personalities. Midge's "my friend here and myself" sounds sophisticated to her ear, but the reader and the clerk both know she is using improper grammar. They look cheap, and they sound cheap.

For one brief moment, they might seem to be defeated. They probably even feel as if they have been "discovered" in their playacting. They leave the store as if they expected to be executed. They are disappointed. They are angry. They may feel humiliated that what had to them seemed like an unlimited amount of money could be spent so easily. That may be what they are admitting when Midge says, "That's a quarter of a million dollars right there!" and Annabel replies, "He's got his nerve!" The two girls, who at the beginning of the story were so confident—almost arrogant—are defeated. Parker does not tell the reader they are defeated, she shows them to be defeated: "the disdain went, slowly and completely as if drained from them, and with it went the regal carriage and tread. Their shoulders dropped and they dragged their feet; they bumped against each other, without notice or apology, and caromed away again. They were silent and their eyes were cloudy."[11]

The reader can't help but sympathize with these frivolous young women who eat what they want, dress as they please, enjoy the attention of young men, and are now crushed by their first real glimpse into what had been their fantasy world. Their game is ruined.

Then, however, without ever telling the reader what the girls think or feel, Parker makes it clear that the girls' spirits cannot be defeated. They are every bit as confident and pleased with themselves as they ever were. Parker tells the reader, "Suddenly Midge straightened her back, flung her head high, and spoke, clear and strong." By restating the rules of the game, and then increasing the ante to ten million dollars, Parker makes it clear that the girls are not defeated. Their confident bearing and carefree attitude were not pretense.

And Parker has been able to guide her reader to this conclusion without a single direct description asserting what the girls are or how they act. That Parker is amused by Midge and Annabel and wants her reader to be as well is evident in her style, her word choice, and use of common literary devices. She chooses words to show her reader, not to tell.

Scorer Commentary

[11] This important paragraph returns us to the opening point about authors' showing rather than telling.

Sample free-response item (independent):

Poet and essayist Ralph Waldo Emerson wrote in his journal, "In good writing, words become one with things" (July 8, 1831). Choose a story, poem, or novel in which the author's attention to word choice reflects this philosophy. Then write a thoughtful and well-supported essay in which you analyze how the "words become things" and how such attention to language contributes to "good writing." Avoid plot summary.

No short story illustrates Ralph Waldo Emerson's observation, "In good writing, words become one with things," better than Dorothy Parker's delightful "The Standard of Living." Parker's descriptions, especially of the main characters' favorite lunch foods and the pearl necklace in the jewelry shop window, are perfect examples of how words become things.

When describing the girls' lunches, Parker doesn't merely <u>name</u> the foods Annabelle and Midge eat,[1] she describes them so clearly the reader can taste them. The girls eat sugars, starch, oils, and fats. Parker describes their hamburgers as patties "sweating beads" of oil and swathed in sauce. The sandwiches are made with "spongy white bread," laden with butter and mayonnaise. Their desserts consist of wedges of cake saturated with ice cream and crusted with nuts and of pastries so plastered with icing, they are "limber."[2] The nouns Parker uses are vivid, naming the characteristics of the food (beads of oil, sugars, starch, and oil) rather than the food itself (hamburgers). The result is that the reader can picture the hamburger, glistening in fat and sauce, and almost long for a taste. The words she uses to describe the food <u>become</u> the food.

Parker uses the same technique later in the story when one of the girls notices the necklace in the jewelry shop window.[3] She never even identifies specifically what type of necklace the girls are attracted to, simply describing it in terms of its brilliance contrasting with the cool darkness of the shop window. Parker uses phrases like "lovely gleamings" and "chaste, elegant darkness"[4] to create an image far more powerful than if she were simply to identify the necklace as pearls or diamonds. It is only later, after the value and beauty have been established, that

---

Scorer Commentary

[1] Since this is the independent essay and the student does not have the story in front of her, this minor misspelling of the character's name is forgivable. To use the wrong name would be a more serious error.

[2] Again, the student does not have the story right before her, so she quotes when she is fairly certain she is using the right word, and she paraphrases when she must. The point is, however, that she does recreate to the best of her ability the details of the story; she does not simply tell her reader that the details are there.

[3] The student apparently cannot remember specifically which girl first noticed the necklace. It is better for her to be vague here than to misidentify the character.

[4] Knowing that you are going to have to write an essay not very different from this one, it might be helpful to keep a file of key words and phrases from the literature you read so you will be able to provide the occasional quotation in your essay.

Parker identifies the necklace as pearls—a double rope. Just as Parker's precise word choice teased the reader into wanting a taste of Annabelle's and Midge's hamburgers and ice cream, her ambiguous but graphic description of the necklace makes the identification of the substance redundant.

As Emerson wrote, in good writing, the words become the things. This is especially true in Dorothy Parker's "The Standard of Living," in which Parker is able to create for her reader unhealthy but delicious food and unimaginably expensive jewelry. For the reader, Parker's words truly <u>become</u> the things she is describing.[5]

Scorer Commentary

[5] This is a nice essay. It addresses the assigned topic, uses specific and detailed examples, and never strays from a discussion of the point into plot summary. The student quotes when she can but always stays close to the text of the story.

Exercise One:

Questions 1–5. Carefully read the following passage before you choose your answers.

Though largely forgotten by the time she died, Marietta Holley was a best-selling American humorist and satirist during the second half of the nineteenth century. She was so popular that she was often compared to Mark Twain, with whom she shared a close friendship. Known to be shy and retiring, Holley published her first poems in her local newspaper, the Adams Journal. *She never married.*

An Unmarried Female

MARIETTA HOLLEY (1836–1926)

1   I SUPPOSE WE ARE ABOUT AS HAPPY as the most of folks, but as I was sayin' a few days ago to Betsey Bobbet, a neighborin' female of ours—"Every station-house in life has its various skeletons. But we ort to try to be contented with that spear of life we are called on to handle." Betsey hain't married, and she don't seem to be contented. She is awful opposed to wimmin's rights—she thinks it is wimmin's only spear to marry, but as yet she can't find any man willin' to lay holt of that spear with her. But you can read in her daily life, and on her eager, willin' countenance, that she fully realizes the sweet words of the poet, "While there is life there is hope."

2   Betsey hain't handsome. Her cheek-bones are high, and she bein' not much more than skin and bone they show plainer than they would if she was in good order. Her complexion (not that I blame her for it) hain't good, and her eyes are little and sot way back in her head. Time has seen fit to deprive her of her hair and teeth, but her large nose

he has kindly suffered her to keep, but she has got the best white ivory teeth money will buy, and two long curls fastened behind each ear, besides frizzles on the top of her head; and if she wasn't naturally bald, and if the curls was the color of her hair, they would look well. She is awful sentimental; I have seen a good many that had it bad, but of all the sentimental creeters I ever did see, Betsey Bobbet is the sentimentalest; you couldn't squeeze a laugh out of her with a cheeze-press.

3   As I said, she is awful opposed to wimmin's havin' any right, only the right to get married. She holds on to that right as tight as any single woman I ever see, which makes it hard and wearyin' on the single men round here.

4   For take the men that are the most opposed to wimmin's havin' a right, and talk the most about its bein' her duty to cling to man like a vine to a tree, they don't want Betsey to cling to them; they won't let her cling to 'em. For when they would be a-goin' on about how wicked it was for wimmin to vote—and it was her only spear to marry, says I to 'em, "Which had you ruther do, let Betsey Bobbet cling to you or let her vote?" and they would every one of 'em quail before that question. They would drop their heads before my keen gray eyes—and move off the subject.

5   But Betsey don't get discouraged. Every time I see her she says in a hopeful, wishful tone, "That the deepest men of minds in the country agree with her in thinkin' that it is wimmin's duty to marry and not to vote." And then she talks a sight about the retirin' modesty and dignity of the fair sect, and how shameful and revoltin' it would be to see wimmin throwin' 'em away and boldly and unblushin'ly talkin' about law and justice.

6   Why, to hear Betsey Bobbet talk about wimmin's throwin' their modesty away, you would think if they ever went to the political pole they would have to take their dignity and modesty and throw 'em against the pole and go without any all the rest of their lives.

7   Now I don't believe in no such stuff as that. I think a woman can be bold and unwomanly in other things besides goin' with a thick veil over her face, and a brass-mounted parasol, once a year, and gently and quietly dropping a vote for a Christian President, or a religious and noble-minded pathmaster.

8   She thinks she talks dreadful polite and proper. She says "I was cameing," instead of "I was coming"; and "I have saw," instead of "I have seen"; and "papah" for paper, and "deah" for dear. I don't know much about grammer, but common sense goes a good ways. She writes the poetry for the *Jonesville Augur*, or "*Augah*," as she calls it. She used to write for the opposition paper, the *Jonesville Gimlet*, but the editor of the *Augur*, a longhaired chap, who moved into Jonesville a few months ago, lost his wife soon after he come there, and sense that she has turned Dimocrat, and writes for his paper stidy. They say that he is a dreadful big feelin' man, and I have heard—it came right straight to me—his cousin's wife's sister told it to the mother-in-law of one of my neighbors' brother's wife, that he didn't like Betsey's poetry at all, and all he printed it for was to plague the editor of the *Gimlet*, because she used to write for him. I myself wouldn't give a cent a bushel for all the poetry she can write. And it seems to me, that if I was Betsey, I wouldn't try to write so much. Howsumever, I don't know what turn I should take if I was Betsey Bobbet; that is a solemn subject, and one I don't love to think on.

9   I never shall forget the first piece of her poetry I ever see. Josiah Allen and I had both on us been married goin' on a year, and I had occasion to go to his trunk one day, where

he kept a lot of old papers, and the first thing I laid my hand on was these verses. Josiah went with her a few times after his wife died, on Fourth of July or so, and two or three camp-meetin's and the poetry seemed to be wrote about the time *we* was married. It was directed over the top of it, "Owed to Josiah," just as if she were in debt to him. This was the way it read:

OWED TO JOSIAH

Josiah, I the tale have hurn,
With rigid ear, and streaming eye,
I saw from me that you did turn,
I never knew the reason why.
Oh, Josiah,
It seemed as if I must expiah.

Why did you—oh, why did you blow
Upon my life of snowy sleet,
The fiah of love to fiercest glow,
Then turn a damphar on the heat?
Oh, Josiah,
It seemed as if I must expiah.

I saw thee coming down the street,
She by your side in bonnet bloo,
The stuns that grated 'neath thy feet,
Seemed crunching on my vitals, too.
Oh, Josiah,
It seemed as if I must expiah.

I saw thee washing sheep last night,
On the bridge I stood with marble brow.
The waters raged, thou clasped it tight,
I sighed, 'should both be drownded now'—
I thought, Josiah,
Oh, happy sheep to thus expiah.

10   I showed the poetry to Josiah that night after he came home, and told him I had read it. He looked awful ashamed to think I had seen it, and, says he, with a dreadful sheepish look: "The persecution I underwent from that female can never be told; she fairly hunted me down. I hadn't no rest for the soles of my feet. I thought one spell she would marry me in spite of all I could do, without givin' me the benefit of law or gospel." He see I looked stern, and he added, with a sick-lookin' smile, "I thought one spell, to use Betsey's language, 'I was a gonah.'"

11   I didn't smile. Oh, no, for the deep principle of my sect was reared up. I says to him in a tone cold enough to almost freeze his ears: "Josiah Allen, shet up; of all the cowardly things a man ever done, it is goin 'round braggin' about wimmin likin' 'em, and follern' 'em up. Enny man that'll do that is little enough to crawl through a knot-hole without

rubbing his clothes." Says I: "I suppose you made her think the moon rose in your head and set in your heels. I daresay you acted foolish enough round her to sicken a snipe, and if you makes fun of her now to please me, I let you know you have got holt of the wrong individual.

12 "Now," says I, "go to bed"; and I added, in still more freezing accents, "for I want to mend your pantaloons." He gathered up his shoes and stockin's and started off to bed, and we hain't never passed a word on the subject sence. I believe when you disagree with your pardner, in freein' your *mind* in the first on't, and then not to be a-twittin' about it afterward. And as for bein' jealous, I should jest as soon think of bein' jealous of a meetin'-house as I should of Josiah. He is a well-principled man. And I guess he wasn't fur out o' the way about Betsey Bobbet, though I wouldn't encourage him by lettin' him say a word on the subject, for I always make it a rule to stand up for my own sect; but when I hear her go on about the editor of the *Augur*, I can believe anything about Betsey Bobbet.

13 She came in here one day last week. It was about ten o'clock in the morning. I had got my house slick as a pin, and my dinner under way (I was goin' to have a b'iled dinner, and a cherry puddin' b'iled with sweet sass to eat on it), and I sot down to finish sewin' up the breadth of my new rag carpet. I thought I would get it done while I hadn't so much to do, for it bein' the first of March I knew sugarin' would be comin' on, and then cleanin'-house time, and I wanted it to put down jest as soon as the stove was carried out in the summer kitchen. The fire was sparklin' away, and the painted floor a-shinin' and the dinner a-b'ilin', and I sot there sewin' jest as calm as a clock, not dreamin' of no trouble, when in came Betsey Bobbet.

14 I met her with outward calm, and asked her to set down and lay off her things. She sot down but she said she couldn't lay off her things. Says she: "I was comin' down past, and I thought I would call and let you see the last numbah of the *Augah*. There is a piece in it concernin' the tariff that stirs men's souls. I like it evah so much."

15 She handed me the paper folded, so I couldn't see nothin' but a piece of poetry by Betsey Bobbet. I see what she wanted of me, and so I dropped my breadths of carpetin' and took hold of it, and began to read it.

16 "Read it audible, if you please," says she. "Especially the precious remahks ovah it; it is such a feast for me to be a-sittin' and heah it rehearsed by a musical vorce."

17 Says I, "I s'pose I can rehearse it if it will do you any good," so I began as follows:

18 "It is seldom that we present the readers of the *Augur* (the best paper for the fireside in Jonesville or the world) with a poem like the following. It may be, by the assistance of the Augur (only twelve shillings a year in advance, wood and potatoes taken in exchange), the name of Betsey Bobbet will yet be carved on the lofty pinnacle of fame's towering pillow. We think, however, that she could study such writers as Sylvanus Cobb and Tupper with profit both to herself and to them.

19 "Editor of the *Augur*."

20 Here Betsey interrupted me. "The deah editah of the *Augah* has no need to advise me to read Tuppah, for he is indeed my most favorite authar. You have devorhed him, haven't you, Josiah's Allen wife?"

21 "Devoured who?" says I, in a tone pretty near as cold as a cold icicle.

22   "Mahten, Fahqueah, Tuppah,[1] that sweet authar," says she.

23   "No, mom," says I shortly; "I hain't devoured Martin Farquhar Tupper, nor no other man. I hain't a cannibal."

24   "Oh! you understand me not; I meant, devorhed his sweet, tender lines."

25   "I hain't devoured his tenderlines, nor nothin' relatin' to him," and I made a motion to lay the paper down, but Betsey urged me to go on, and so I read:

GUSHINGS OF A TENDAH SOUL

Oh let who will,
Oh let who can,
Be tied onto
A horrid male man.

Thus said I 'ere
My tendah heart was touched,
Thus said I 'ere
My tendah feelings gushed.

But oh a change
Hath swept ore me,
As billows sweep
The 'deep blue sea.'

A voice, a noble form
One day I saw;
An arrow flew,
My heart is nearly raw.

His first pardner lies
Beneath the turf,
He is wandering now,
In sorrow's briny surf.

Two twins, the little
Deah cherub creechahs
Now wipe the teahs
From off his classic feachahs.

Oh sweet lot, worthy
Angel arisen,
To wipe teahs
From eyes like hisen.

"What think you of it?" says she, as I finished readin'.

---

[1] Martin Farquhar Tupper (1810-1889) was a British poet whose work, though once wildly popular, is remembered as second-rate, inflated verse enjoyed only by the uneducated masses. He also survives in other poets' spoofs and parodies of his trite and overly sentimental rhymes.

26   I looked right at her 'most a minute with a majestic look. In spite of her false curls and her new white ivory teeth, she is a humbly critter. I looked at her silently while she sot and twisted her long yellow bunnet-strings, and then I spoke out. "Hain't the editor of the Augur a widower with a pair of twins?"

27   "Yes," says she with a happy look.

28   Then says I, "If the man hain't a fool, he'll think you are one."

29   "Oh!" says she, and she dropped her bunnet-strings and clasped her long bony hands together in her brown cotton gloves. "Oh, we ahdent soles of genious have feelin's you cold, practical natures know nuthing of, and if they did not gush out in poetry we should expiah. You may as well try to tie up the gushing catarack of Niagarah with a piece of welting-cord as to tie up the feelin's of an ahdent sole."

30   "Ardent sole!" says I coldly. "Which makes the most noise, Betsey Bobbet, a three-inch brook or a ten-footer? which is the tearer? which is the roarer? Deep waters run stillest. I have no faith in feelin's that stalk round in public in mournin' weeds. I have no faith in such mourners," says I.

31   "Oh, Josiah's wife, cold, practical female being, you know me not; we are sundered as fah apart as if you was sitting on the North Pole and I was sitting on the South Pole. Uncongenial being, you know me not."

32   "I may not know you, Betsey Bobbet, but I do know decency, and I know that no munny would tempt me to write such stuff as that poetry and send it to a widower with twins."

33   "Oh!" says she, "what appeals to the tendah feelin' heart of a single female woman more than to see a lonely man who has lost his relict? And pity never seems so much like pity as when it is given to the deah little children of widowehs. And," says she, "I think moah than as likely as not, this soaring sole of genious did not wed his affinity, but was united to a mere woman of clay."

34   "Mere woman of clay!" says I, fixin' my spektacles upon her in a most searchin' manner. "Where will you find a woman, Betsey Bobbet, that hain't more or less clay? And affinity, that is the meanest word I ever heard; no married woman has any right to hear it. I'll excuse you, bein' a female; but if a man had said it to me I'd holler to Josiah. There is a time for everything, and the time to hunt affinity is before you are married; married folks hain't no right to hunt it," says I sternly.

35   "We kindred soles soah above such petty feelin's—we soah far above them."

36   "I hain't much of a soarer," says I, "and I don't pretend to be; and to tell you the truth," says I, "I am glad I ain't."

37   "The editah of the *Augah*" says she, and she grasped the paper offen the stand, and folded it up, and presented it at me like a spear, "the editah of this paper is a kindred sole: he appreciates me, he undahstands me, and will not our names in the pages of this very papah go down to posterety togathah?"

38   "Then," says I, drove out of all patience with her, "I wish you was there now, both of you. I wish," says I, lookin' fixedly on her, "I wish you was both of you in posterity now."

"An Unmarried Female," from My Opinions and Betsey Bobbet's: Designed as a Beacon Light, To guide Women to Life Liberty and the Pursuit of Happiness, But which May Be read by Members of the Sterner Sect, Without Injury to Themselves or This Book. Josiah Allen's Wife. Hartford, Conn. : American Publishing Company, 1873.

Multiple-Choice Questions 1–5:

1. One of the chief sources of humor in the first paragraph is the
 A. use of alliterative character names.
 B. misuse of the word "spear."
 C. narrator's obvious lack of education.
 D. narrator's homespun philosophy.
 E. characters' apparent dislike of one another.

2. All of the following provide clues to the setting of this passage EXCEPT
 A. the dialect.
 B. details of daily life.
 C. attitudes toward women's rights.
 D. the published poems.
 E. references to clothing.

3. The tone of the second paragraph can best be described as
 A. understated.
 B. sarcastic.
 C. haughty.
 D. sincere.
 E. sympathetic.

4. As they are used in this passage, the words *pole* (paragraph 6), *pathmaster* (paragraph 7), *owed* (paragraph 9), and *tenderlines* (paragraph 24) are all examples of
 A. wordplay.
 B. dialect.
 C. idioms.
 D. puns.
 E. malapropisms.

5. The tone of this passage devolves from
 A. guarded to bitter.
 B. saccharine to sarcastic.
 C. benign to impetuous.
 D. conciliatory to confrontational.
 E. jocular to tart.

Free-Response Item (text-based):

Carefully read Marietta Holley's "An Unmarried Female." Then write a thoughtful, well-developed essay in which you analyze the techniques Holley uses to communicate to the reader her attitude toward her subject(s). Do not merely summarize the plot.

Before you write your essay:

1. **Make sure you understand exactly what you're being asked to write about.**
    - List all of the verbs in the prompt.
    - Underline the verb that describes the essay.
    - Write the direct object of that verb.

2. **Choose an appropriate selection.**
    If you're using this book, your teacher probably wants you to write your essay on whatever story, article, or poem, etc., the writing prompt follows.

3. **Make sure you have something to say about both the topic and your selected literature.**
    - Jot down key plot events.
    - Think in terms of plot structure: rising action, climax, falling action, and so on.
    - List characters.
    - Think in terms of function or role—protagonist or antagonist.
    - Think in terms of type—hero, anti-hero, foil, clown, etc.
    - Make sure you jot down notes that pertain to the assigned topic.
    - Jot down quotations or at least close paraphrases.
    - Jot down everything you know and remember about the assigned topic.

4. **Make sure you are clear about what you are going to say.**
    Write a sentence or two that make a positive and focused statement about the topic.
    Make sure these sentences address all of the issues and subpoints specified in the prompt.

5. **Write your essay.**

Free-Response Item (independent):

First person narratives often reveal as much—or more—about the narrator as they do about the supposed subject of the narrative. Choose such a literary selection and write a well-organized and supported essay in which you analyze the techniques the author uses to identify and create a vivid sense of the character study's true focus.

Before you write your essay:

1. **Make sure you understand exactly what you're being asked to write about.**
   - List all of the verbs in the prompt.
   - Underline the verb that describes the essay.
   - Write the direct object of that verb.

2. **Make sure you have something valid to write about.**
   - Write a sentence or two that make a positive and focused statement about the topic.
   - Make sure these sentences address all of the issues and subpoints specified in the prompt.

3. **Review the selection and find your textual support.**

4. **Write your essay.**
   Keep referring to the prompt and whatever you underlined or highlighted in the selection to make sure you're on track and addressing everything the prompt wants you to address.

Analyzing (not merely interpreting or explicating) a poem

Poetry is different from prose. At this point, it would not serve our purposes to try to define exactly *what* poetry is or *why* poets choose this form to express themselves. It is sufficient to know that poetry is different. Students, teachers, critics, and so on tend to read poetry in three ways. Often they confuse the methods and think they are reading one way, when they are actually reading another.

Interpretation is probably the most common type of reading and may very well be the only type you've ever performed. It is the process of figuring out what the poem means, especially on a deeper level than comprehending the surface text. In an interpretation essay, you usually provide quotations from the poem to support your claims about what it means. You may even have to discuss the meanings of individual words or the syntax of individual phrases, clauses, and sentences to support your interpretation.

Many people confuse this examination of such small parts of the poem as analysis, but it is not.

Explication is a line-by-line retelling of the poem. It is a useful activity in the processes of surface understanding and theme interpretation.

Because this process examines the poem line by line, many people believe this is analysis, but it is not.

Analysis is an examination of how the poem works—not *what it means*, but *how it means* what it means. Analysis does not ask you only to identify the tone or mood, but it asks you to figure out how the poet conveyed the tone or mood. You know that Dr. Seuss is fun to read. Analysis is the process by which you examine how Seuss's rhythm and rhyme schemes contribute to that fun. You know that limericks are humorous. Analysis is the process by which you figure out how structure, and, again, rhythm and rhyme add to the humor. Analysis does not ask you merely to identify the rhythm or rhyme scheme or point out the use of devices like onomatopoeia, alliteration, metaphor, and so on; analysis asks you to show what those conventions or devices are doing, how they are working, what their role is in the poem's overall effect.

Remember that your Advanced Placement exam will hardly ever ask you merely to interpret a piece of literature. It will almost never ask you to explicate a poem. *It will, however, ask you to perform analysis, in both the multiple-choice questions and the free-responses.*

Emily Dickinson wrote nearly eighteen hundred poems, though fewer than a dozen were published during her lifetime. Dickinson's friends and relatives astonished to discover the full extent of her work. The body of work did not adhere to the common poetic conventions of Dickinson's day, and as a result, it was widely criticized when it was finally published after her death.

The last night that she lived

EMILY DICKINSON (1830–1886)

The last night that she lived,
It was a common night,
Except the dying; this to us
Made nature different.

We noticed smallest things,—
Things overlooked before,
By this great light upon our minds
Italicized, as 'twere.

That others could exist
While she must finish quite,
A jealousy for her arose
So nearly infinite.

We waited while she passed;
It was a narrow time,
Too jostled were our souls to speak,
At length the notice came.

She mentioned, and forgot;
Then lightly as a reed
Bent to the water, shivered scarce,
Consented, and was dead.

And we, we placed the hair,
And drew the head erect;
And then an awful leisure was,
Our faith to regulate.

Sample Multiple-Choice Questions:

1. Dickinson uses the word *italicized* (stanza 2) to mean
   A. clarified.
   B. made visible.
   C. discerned.
   D. emphasized.
   E. set apart.

2. What effect does the repetition of *we* in the final stanza achieve?
   A. distance the speaker from her grief
   B. transition from the dead to the living
   C. emphasize the role of the speaker
   D. draw the reader into the scene
   E. deemphasize the uniqueness of the event

3. What about the metrical pattern of this poem alters the rhythm of the last two lines of each stanza?
   A. the uniformity of all lines
   B. the end punctuation of each line
   C. the shorter fourth line
   D. the change of metric feet
   E. the longer third line

4. A significant contrast explored by this poem is that between
   A. the ordinary and profound.
   B. faith and unbelief.
   C. companionship and aloneness.
   D. living and dying.
   E. acceptance and grief.

5. The wording of the first line of the poem is an example of
   A. tragic irony.
   B. situational irony.
   C. verbal irony.
   D. dramatic irony.
   E. poetic justice.

Answers and Explanations:

1. Stanza 2 begins, "We noticed smallest things—Things overlooked before." Therefore, (A) can be easily eliminated, as what is being described is a new awareness, not a new understanding. (B) is possibly more tempting, but the "things" are not things that were formerly invisible, only unnoticed. (C) might tempt some, but as with (A), the contrast is noticing what had been overlooked, not distinguishing between two or more objects. (E) is perhaps more tempting, but it raises the question of what is being set apart from what—the situation is the same "things" changing status from overlooked to noticed. (D), however, suggests that the "things" were indeed always there and always visible, but in the context of the death, these "things" are better noticed. **Thus, (D) is the best answer.**

2. Throughout the poem, there are several references to the speaker of the poem and the other persons present at the death. (A) is unlikely as the use of first person certainly does not create a distance between the narrator and anything or anyone else; nor does the plural. (C) might be tempting if it were singular, but the nonspecific plural does not clarify exactly who performed what. (D) is also tempting, but this has most likely occurred at the first use of the first person in Stanza 2. (E) contradicts one of the central issues of the poem—the contrast of the unique event in the midst of ordinary life. The penultimate stanza, however, has been about the dying woman and her actions at the moment of death, and the final stanza describes the futile activities of the still living. **Thus, (B) is the best answer.**

3. A quick scan of the poem reveals that each four-line stanza begins with two iambic-trimeter lines followed by a line of iambic tetrameter, then ending with iambic trimeter. Thus, (A) is immediately eliminated. (B) might tempt some students, but punctuation ultimately has nothing to do with rhythm. (C) is untrue. The third line is longer; the fourth line is the same as the others. (D) is likewise incorrect, as the meter is iambic throughout the poem. Once the ear and tongue have grown accustomed to the brevity and the sudden stops of the three-foot lines, the four-foot line seems naturally to flow directly into the final line, creating the effect of a single iambic-heptameter line. **Thus, (E) is the correct answer.**

4. (B) is mildly suggested by the final stanza, but there is nothing to suggest the unbelief. (C) is suggested by the use of first person plural, but the aloneness of the dying woman is more inferred by the reader than suggested by the poem. (D) is suggested in the first stanza, but is not really an idea explored by the poem. Likewise, (E) is vaguely suggested by the final two stanzas, but is not a significant theme. From its first mention in the first stanza, however, (A) is both mentioned and illustrated in the living's awareness of previously unnoticed things, their "jealousy" that the dying woman was "finished quite," the simplicity of the death itself, and the living's futile actions arranging the body. **Thus, (A) is the best answer.**

5. The poem is about the death of a woman and the effects this death has on the living. The first line, however, reads, "The last night that she lived," not "The night she died..." Thus, some form of irony is operating in the poet's naming the opposite of her real subject. (A) can be eliminated because the irony involved in the line does not concern anyone's misunderstanding of the situation. (B) is tempting since the line does suggest a reversal of what is happening, but it is not the case that desired or expected results are not coming to pass. (D), like (A), is eliminated by the fact that no one is misapprehending the situation. There is nothing in the poem that that dying woman "deserves" to die, thus eliminating (E). The verbal irony (C) occurs in the poet's identifying the woman's death in its opposite terms, the end of her life. **Thus, (C) is the best answer.**

Sample Free-Response Item 1 (text-based):

Carefully read Emily Dickinson's "The last night that she lived." Then write a well-organized and supported essay in which you analyze the contributions of rhythm and structure to the tone and meaning of the overall poem.

Emily Dickinson is not generally known for her creative or experimental use of poetic conventions like rhythm and rhyme. In fact, anyone who's read more than a few of Dickinson's poems quickly realizes that she tends to follow the typical 4 – 3 – 4 – 3 rhythm and A – B – C – B rhyme scheme of the traditional (and clichéd) ballad.[1] It is difficult, then, to try to offer a definitive argument about the connection between form and meaning in Dickinson's poetry. In "The Last Night that She Lived," however, there is enough evidence of intentional rhythm and rhyme scheme to suggest that Dickinson was trying to create a particular effect. If this

Scorer Commentary

[1] None of these free-response questions will require prior knowledge of the author or piece, so this statement will not hurt this student's score, but it won't necessarily help her either. However, an understanding of Dickinson's typical patterns would certainly be helpful in drafting a thesis for this essay.

were true, it might be argued that Dickinson's sense that the woman's death was an incomprehensible disruption of routine is mirrored in her inability to settle into a consistent rhyme scheme and her own disruption of her default metric pattern.[2]

The death of the woman occurs on a "common night, / Except the dying." Awaiting news of the death, the speaker and those she is with begin to see everything differently. Even commonplace things seem more important, as if they were "italicized." After the death, the speaker and the others perform insignificant acts, "plac[ing] the hair, / And [drawing] the head erect." The speaker acknowledges that they face "an awful leisure." The death, then, has been an interruption of the speaker's routine and has resulted in an alteration of her frame of mind.[3]

This disruption of routine and altered mental state are conveyed not only in Dickinson's words but in her rhythm pattern and rhyme schemes as well. The disruption to the routine, expressed at the beginning of the poem, "The last night that she lived, / It was a common night, / Except the dying," is echoed in the way Dickinson disrupts her own rhythmic pattern. The first two lines of the poem are iambic trimeter: "The last … night that … she lived / It was … a com … mon night …" The third line, however, is iambic tetrameter: "Except … the dy … ing; this … to us …" The last line returns to iambic trimeter.[4]

This pattern is interesting for a couple of reasons. First, within this poem itself there is an established pattern—iambic tetrameter—and then a disruption to that pattern, in a line that says the dying made a common night uncommon.[5] Every stanza follows this same pattern of iambic trimeter broken with iambic tetrameter—which, ironically, becomes a pattern itself—and in three of the five stanzas, the long-line variant speaks to the uncommonness of the experience of death: "By this great light upon our minds … A jealousy for her arose … Too jostled were our souls to speak …" So there is an interesting correspondence between the words telling us that the woman's dying changed things while the established rhythm of the poem also changes.[6]

This pattern is also interesting because it's almost the exact opposite of the rhythm Dickinson usually uses in her poems. Almost all of Dickinson's poems follow a pattern of alternating iambic tetrameter and iambic trimeter. This poem, about the disruption a death of a loved one can cause to one's routine and point of view, turns that rhythmic pattern upside down.[7]

Scorer Commentary

[2] Here's the student's thesis.

[3] It is usually a good idea to establish the validity of your interpretation of the poem. Remember, though, that you do not want your essay to deteriorate into mere summary.

[4] Good start, but we need to make sure we go deeper than merely identifying the metric pattern.

[5] This is good. The student is connecting her identification of the rhythm with the meaning of the poem.

[6] This student knows that she must show her reader the connection, not merely hint at it.

[7] Again, this student's prior knowledge is not required to answer this free-response question, but this is a valid and fairly well discussed argument.

The rhyme scheme of this poem is interesting in that the poem really doesn't have one. The attempt at a rhyme scheme, however, or the scheme of close rhymes, could be said to mirror the disrupting effects of the woman's death on the speaker. Of the words that should constitute the poem's rhyme scheme: "...lived ... night ... us ...different ...; ... things ... before ... minds ... 'twere ... exist ... quite ... arose ... infinite ...; ... passed ... time ... speak ... came ... forgot ... reed ... scarce ... dead ... hair ... erect ... was ... regulate ..." there are only three pairs that even come close to rhyming. For a poem with such a notable and consistent rhythm pattern, the absence of a rhyme scheme is unexpected. As the vast majority of Dickinson's poems follow an A-B-A-B rhyme scheme, this absence of rhyme is even more surprising.[8]

It could be, however, that Dickinson's departure from her own norm reflects the way the woman's death caused a departure from the norm of the speaker in the poem. The night was a common night except for the dying, and that made nature seem different to them. This strangeness caused by the death is expressed not only in the poem's words but mirrored in the poems, rhythmic pattern and rhyme scheme as well.[9]

Scorer Commentary

[8] This is not the student's strongest point, but she does make a strong effort not to ignore the instruction in the question to discuss rhythm and rhyme.

[9] The essay ends rather abruptly, but it does return to its thesis, and it has discussed the full issue of the question. It has also provided textual support to back up nearly all of its claims.

Sample Free-Response Item 2 (independent):

A common definition of poetry is "the measured language of emotion." Indeed, poetry is often considered to be the best medium for the exploration of profound and inexplicable truths. Choose a poem that exemplifies the "measured language of emotion" and write a thoughtful, well-organized essay in which you analyze the ways in which the poet "measures" language in order to communicate or recreate profound emotion. Do not merely explain the emotion communicated or offer a simple line-by-line explication of the poem.

All of Emily Dickinson's poems might be said to illustrate the idea of "the measured language of emotion," but none so well as her poem that begins with the line, "The last night that she lived."[1] This poem uses very careful word choice as well as an unexpected rhythm and almost non-existent rhyme scheme to illustrate the incomprehensible nature of the death of a loved one.[2] Some thoughts or feelings are too deep and complex to be expressed in language, and this poem is a perfect example of this principle.

The first way Dickinson "measures" language is through her very careful word choice.[3] The poem begins with the line, "The last night that she lived..." instead of "the night she died." Both mean the same thing, but by describing the night as the "last night that she lived," Dickinson is expressing her emotions in words she and the reader can understand. We know what it is to live, but we don't know what it is to die. As difficult as it might be for the reader to understand the idea that this is the "last night that she lived," this wording is still more comprehensible to us than "the night she died." We don't know, really, what that means.[4]

The rest of the poem continues to describe the experience of the woman's death from the viewpoint of the people still living. The words reflect Dickinson's difficulty finding profound words to describe a profound event. The night was "common" except for the death, and that made "nature different." The idea that someone's death would make an ordinary night "different" from other nights is an understatement. The fact that the death made them reexamine things they once took for granted can only be described by Dickinson saying it was as if the common things were now "italicized."[5] The nervousness or grief or guilt the people feel waiting to receive the news that the woman has died, Dickinson describes as their souls' being "jostled." Again, the commonness of the word in terms of the

---

Scorer Commentary

[1] Simply restating the question and making it a little more specific works well for this student to begin her essay.

[2] This second sentence effectively makes the focus of this essay even sharper.

[3] The organizational pattern this student has apparently chosen is fairly obvious, but it should still give her a nicely organized essay.

[4] Keeping in mind that this is the independent free-response essay, close direct quotations are not expected, but the student should be able to at least cite and quote the first line that doubles as the title of this poem.

[5] This student is making excellent use of individual words and phrases she is able to remember from the poem. This illustrates that it is an excellent idea to keep a running log of key words and phrases from the literature you study.

profoundness of the emotion is an understatement. On the one hand, it might seem as if the speaker was young and uneducated with a limited vocabulary, but it is just as likely that Dickinson is simply trying to express the inexpressible in terms both she and her reader can understand—"measuring language" to express emotion.[6]

Dickinson's rhythm and rhyme scheme—especially her lack of a rhyme scheme—can also be considered examples of her "measuring language" in order to express emotion. The rhythm is not unique or experimental, but it does play with the typical rhythm of a ballad stanza, or hymn stanza, which was the staple of Dickinson's poetry. Instead of the 4 – 3 – 4 – 3 alternating iambic tetrameter and iambic trimeter of the typical ballad or nineteenth-century hymn,[7] Dickinson surprises the reader with a 3 – 3 – 4 – 3 stanza (iambic trimeter interrupted by a line of iambic tetrameter). The shorter lines invite the reader to pause and reflect on the idea expressed in the line ("The last night that she lived" ... "At length the notice came"), while the longer lines seem to reflect an overflow of feeling, an inability to contain the emotions ("Too jostled were our souls to speak").[8]

Similarly, Dickinson uses an unexpected rhyme scheme—actually, no real rhyme scheme at all—to illustrate this "measured language of emotion." Typically, one expects a four-line stanza, especially one based on a ballad or hymn structure, to have an A - B - C - B or A - B - A - B rhyme scheme. This poem has neither. In fact, for the most part, there is no rhyme with the possible exception of a few close rhymes that appear at random and do not seem to be intentional on Dickinson's part. Since Dickinson does know how to rhyme, it is entirely possible that she intended this lack of rhyme with only a few, random near-rhymes to suggest a break in the pattern, the interruption of the ordinary. Just as the woman's death caused a break in the people's understanding of normalcy, so, too, does the actual structure of the poem show a break.[9]

Emily Dickinson's "The Last Night that she Lived," then, is a perfect example of the definition of poetry as "the measured language of emotion." From word choice, to rhythm, to rhyme scheme, Dickinson plans and measures her use of language to create the break in thought and the disruption of normality that are the result of the death of a loved one.[10]

Scorer Commentary

[6] The argument is not bad. It is fairly well supported with brief quotations and direct references to the text, and the student brings this part of her discussion nicely back to the thesis.

[7] Because the student—in the independent free-response essay—has chosen to write about this poet and this poem, a little prior knowledge like this is expected. It is the intention of questions like this to test the student's knowledge of literary elements like typical forms and structures.

[8] It is apparent the student has studied this poem very closely in class. For the independent free-response question, you will also want to make sure you pick a piece of literature you know extremely well.

[9] The student has demonstrated a knowledge of the poem and of Emily Dickinson's work in general. She has also shown that she has some knowledge of poem forms and structures, so her not quoting the rhyming words does not hurt her here.

[10] This last paragraph is a very nice return to the thesis and the points brought up in the introduction.

Exercise Two:

Questions 6 – 10. The poem form **rondeau** originated in France as a fifteen-line poem written on two rhymes. The English **rondeau** is typically fifteen lines and makes use of refrains, repeated according to a prescribed pattern—thirteen lines of eight syllables, plus two refrains, each with four syllables. The English rondeau is written on three rhymes. The typical fifteen lines are divided into three irregular stanzas. The rhyme scheme of the poem can be plotted: A A B B A; A A B C (refrain); and A A B B A C (refrain). The refrain is identical to the beginning of the first line of the poem.

The **rondeau redoublé** is a related form consisting of six four-line stanzas. It has the overall rhyme scheme: A B A B; B A B A; A B A B; B A B A; A B A B; A B A B C. The last line of stanzas two through five repeats one of the four lines from stanza one, and the final line of the poem repeats the beginning of the first line.

Paul Laurence Dunbar's "Beyond the Years," while neither a rondeau nor rondeau redoublé, follows an intricate pattern reminiscent of these established forms. Study the poem closely and then choose the best answers to the multiple-choice questions.

Beyond the Years

PAUL LAURENCE DUNBAR

I

Beyond the years the answer lies,
Beyond where brood the grieving skies
And Night drops tears.
Where Faith rod-chastened smiles to rise
And doff its fears,
And carping Sorrow pines and dies—
Beyond the years.

II

Beyond the years the prayer for rest
Shall beat no more within the breast;
The darkness clears,
And Morn perched on the mountain's crest
Her form uprears—
The day that is to come is best,
Beyond the years.

III

Beyond the years the soul shall find
That endless peace for which it pined,
For light appears,
And to the eyes that still were blind
With blood and tears,
Their sight shall come all unconfined
Beyond the years.

"*Beyond the Years*" *from* The Complete Poems of Paul Laurence Dunbar: Lyrics of Lowly
Life (*New York: Dodd, Mead, and Company, 1922*)

Multiple-Choice Questions 6–10:

6. All of the following are true of "Beyond the Years" EXCEPT

    A. iambic tetrameter.

    B. an ending couplet.

    C. regular stanzas.

    D. a single refrain.

    E. intricate rhyme.

7. The overall effect of the short half-lines is to

    A. increase the pace of the poem.

    B. divert the reader's attention.

    C. contrast opposing emotions.

    D. interrupt the rhythmic flow.

    E. allow the reader to reflect.

8. Laurence Dunbar achieves a shift in tone in the second stanza by

    A. beginning and ending the stanza with the refrain.

    B. reversing the rhythmic pattern.

    C. personifying abstract concepts.

    D. juxtaposing contrasting images.

    E. altering the rhyme scheme.

9. Which of the following is most true of the refrain, "Beyond the years"?

    A. Its meaning evolves with each repetition.

    B. It provides unity to the poem.

    C. It establishes a tone of expectation or longing.

    D. It emphasizes the poem's theological theme.

    E. Its tone reflects the overall tone of the poem.

10. By ending this poem as he does, Dunbar achieves

    A. emphasis.

    B. irony.

    C. clarity.

    D. catharsis.

    E. repudiation.

Free-Response Item 1 (text-based):

Carefully read Paul Laurence Dunbar's "Beyond the Years." Then write an organized, well-supported essay in which you analyze the techniques Dunbar uses to convey to the reader both an intellectual understanding and emotional appreciation of the subject of the poem. Do not merely summarize the plot or provide a line-by-line explication.

Before you write your essay:

1. **Make sure you understand exactly what you're being asked to write about.**
   - List all of the verbs in the prompt.
   - Underline the verb that describes the essay.
   - Write the direct object of that verb.

2. **Make sure you have something valid to write about.**
   - Write a sentence or two that make a positive and focused statement about the topic.
   - Make sure these sentences address all of the issues and subpoints specified in the prompt.

3. **Review the selection and find your textual support.**

4. **Write your essay.**
   Keep referring to the prompt and whatever you underlined or highlighted in the selection to make sure you're on track and addressing everything the prompt wants you to address.

Free-Response Item 2 (independent):

While modern and post-modern writers often condemn the structured and formal, many poets still write powerfully and meaningfully within the confines of formal rhythm and intricate rhyme. Choose a twentieth- or twenty-first-century poem that follows formal conventions of rhythm and rhyme and write a thoughtful and well-reasoned essay in which you analyze the contribution these conventions make to other literary elements like tone and meaning. Do not merely identify the conventions or demonstrate how they are applied in the poem.

Before you write your essay:

1. **Make sure you understand exactly what you're being asked to write about.**
   - List all of the verbs in the prompt.
   - Underline the verb that describes the essay.
   - Write the direct object of that verb.

2. **Choose an appropriate selection.**

   If you're using this book, your teacher probably wants you to write your essay on whatever story, article, poem, etc., the writing prompt follows.

3. **Make sure you have something to say about both the topic and your selected literature.**
   - Think in terms of narrative structure: organization of ideas, etc.
   - Make sure you jot down notes that pertain to the assigned topic.
   - Jot down quotations or at least close paraphrases.
   - Jot down everything you know and remember about the assigned topic.

4. **Make sure you are clear about what you are going to say.**

   Write a sentence or two that make a positive and focused statement about the topic.

   Make sure these sentences address all of the issues and subpoints specified in the prompt.

5. **Write your essay.**

Assessing "Literary Merit"

MINI-CHAPTER 5.5:

THERE IS A SCENE IN THE 1989 MOVIE *Dead Poet's Society* in which the students are reading page 23 of the introduction to their literature text *Understanding Poetry*, by Dr. J. Evans Pritchard, Ph.D. The text describes two criteria—after one is "fluent with [the work's] meter, rhyme, and figures of speech"—by which a work's literary merit may be assessed: the work's *perfection* (How artfully has the objective of the poem been rendered?) and its *importance* (How important is that objective?). According to the fictional Dr. Pritchard, one can construct a graph with a work's perfection indicated on the horizontal and its importance on the vertical. The work's overall "greatness" is the area created by plotting the horizontal and the vertical.

The boys' teacher, played by Robin Williams, has them tear these pages out of their texts and throw them away.

Sadly, the determination of a work's "greatness" (a synonym for "literary merit") is not as easy as a mathematical formula. What do we mean by artful? Are Ernest Hemingway's short, simple sentences more or less "artful" than Henry James's long, complicated ones? Is Hawthorne's use of adjectives and adverbs more "artful" than Poe's?

Similarly, what do we mean by "important"? Is James's exploration of an artist's perception in "The Real Thing" important? How about the girls' disillusionment in "The Standard of Living"? Yet both of these stories are still in print, anthologized, and might possibly appear on a test like an AP exam several decades after the authors' deaths.

Shakespeare's been dead for centuries. Chaucer died nearly a millennium ago (give or take a couple hundred years). But other writers whose works have appeared on recent AP exams are still alive and writing. So it cannot be simply a matter of age and whether the author is alive or dead.

While the issue might not be as simple as plotting two coordinates on a graph, there are some criteria by which we can assess whether something might be appropriate to write about on an AP exam when you are told to "choose a title of comparable literary merit."

Plot driven vs. Character driven: A nineteenth-century French writer by the name of Georges Polti hypothesized that, in all the world's literature, there are only thirty-six basic plots. Everything else is details. Therefore, many critics argue that a work's "literary merit" does not stem from the plot but from the characters who operate within the plot.

When reduced to a basic plot level, even the most unquestionably literary works sound trivial, maybe even silly.

- An old fisherman catches a big fish, but it gets eaten by sharks before he can bring it home.
- A man whose wife has committed adultery wreaks vengeance on his wife's lover, the father of her illegitimate child.
- Two teenagers meet, fall in love, impulsively marry and then commit suicide when they think they won't be allowed to be together.
- A young lawyer rescues his fiancée from the clutches of a centuries-old vampire.

Literary merit, these critics argue, lies in the *characters*.

- Santiago is a fiercely independent man, once the best fisherman in his village, beloved by his townspeople, especially by young Manolin, who loves him like a grandfather.
- Roger Chillingworth does not love his wife, but he resents that his "marital rights" have been violated, and his one wish is to destroy the man who does not have the strength of character to reveal his identity. Hester is strong-willed and independent. While recognizing the unlawful nature of her adulterous affair, she does not believe that she has sinned since she never loved her husband, and she did love the father of her child. [*Spoiler alert!*] Arthur Dimmesdale is plagued with guilt over his violation of human law, but his knowledge of his own sin gives him an ironic charisma as the town's minister. The one man he grows to trust as a friend is the man whose chief goal is to destroy him.
- Romeo is fickle and impulsive, fawning and swooning for every beautiful girl he meets. Juliet is strong-willed and independent, but unable to stand up to her father, who is about to force her into marrying against her will.
- Jonathan Harker is a young idealist, and his fiancée Mina, while devoted to him, is unable to resist the overwhelming charisma and supernatural power of Count Dracula.

No matter how trivial or clichéd the plot may be—after all, there are only thirty-six—if the reader can care about the characters, then the work has one element of "literary merit."

Still, there are many books, plays, films, television shows, and so on, whose characters we love or hate, empathize with, or understand, but we would not choose to write about them on our AP exam.

Broad appeal: This is not the same thing as "popular," though you might be surprised how many works that are now considered "literary classics" were wildly popular when they were originally published. Broad appeal in this instance, however, means that something in the work touches people across age, gender, nationality. Different people may not "like" the same thing in the same work, but there is something about "good" literature that appeals to a broad base of readers.

This is one reason that you see so few "genre" books on AP-style reading lists. If the book is clearly "young adult" or "chick lit" or "sci-fi/fantasy" and does not have that quality that makes it appeal also to readers who are *not* fans of that particular category, it is probably not destined for "literary greatness."

This does not mean, however, that *no* genre books can qualify. Aldous Huxley's *Brave New World* is often considered a science fiction novel. Ray Bradbury's *Fahrenheit 451* is unquestionably science fiction. The "breadth" of these titles' appeal comes in their exploration of "big ideas" like *Do humans need "more" than just creature comforts in order to be happy? Is Western culture becoming "rich in things" but "poor in soul?"* and so on.

Whatever the source of that *broad appeal*, however—well-drawn and fascinating characters, exploration of big ideas—the fact that a wide variety of readers finds something of value in a book, story, or play suggests that it has "literary merit."

Lasting appeal: There is a reason so many of the works on the AP exam and on AP-style reading lists are "old." Something may be "all the rage" this week and even appeal to readers of every age, race, and nationality imaginable, but within a few years, it's out of print, and no one remembers having read it. Or it might have been your "favorite book of all time," and when you read it again a few years later, you wonder what you saw in it in the first place.

Works that continue to be read, that are constantly reprinted, that keep appearing in collections or anthologies have this lasting appeal that other works lack. Works that you can read over and over again, sometimes over periods of years, and still love also have a quality we can call "lasting appeal."

Sometimes, of course, worthwhile books, authors, etc., are forgotten and then rediscovered later. The fact that readers find something of value in a book years after was originally published (or in a play produced decades or centuries after being written) suggests that it has lasting appeal and probably some "literary merit."

Artistry: Finally, even though it's an indefinable, abstract term, at some point we do have to talk about the artistry of a work with literary merit. After all, there's a very good chance that what you're going to be asked to write about will fall into the category of "artistry"—literary or rhetorical devices, diction, organization, structure, and so on. This does not mean that "literary" works must be oppressively ornamented with dozens of dazzling but distracting devices, or that the structures of the sentences must be such as can be understood only by persons to whom advanced degrees in linguistics or morphology have been awarded; it means only that the author is in control. Like any good craftsperson, the writer understands his or her tools and knows how to use them.

We don't count metaphors to assess a work's artistry, but we *might* evaluate the appropriateness of the metaphor. Does it fit the context of the story, or does it stand out? Does the metaphor seem so natural that you weren't even aware it was a metaphor, or is it so obvious that you can *feel* it arrive? Is it original or clichéd?

Let's look at two passages and see whether we can judge the "artistry" of either one.

> *Then after long search into the minister's dim interior, and turning over many precious materials, in the shape of high aspirations for the welfare of his race, warm love of souls, pure sentiments, natural piety, strengthened by thought and study, and illuminated by revelation—all of which invaluable gold was perhaps no better than rubbish to the seeker—he would turn back, discouraged, and begin his quest towards another point. He groped along as stealthily, with as cautious a tread, and as wary an outlook, as a thief entering a chamber where a man lies only half asleep—or, it may be, broad awake—with purpose to steal the very treasure which this man guards as the apple of his eye. In spite of his premeditated carefulness, the floor would now and then creak; his garments would rustle; the shadow of his presence, in a forbidden proximity, would be thrown across his victim. In other words, Mr. Dimmesdale, whose sensibility of nerve often produced the effect of spiritual intuition, would become vaguely aware that something inimical to his peace had thrust itself into relation with him. But Old Roger Chillingworth, too, had perceptions that were almost intuitive; and when the minister threw his startled eyes towards him, there the physician sat; his kind, watchful, sympathising, but never intrusive friend.*

In this example, we're using metaphor as our measure of "artistry," but it could be any tool at the writer's disposal: diction, figurative language, sentence structure, and so on. In fact, your evaluation of a piece's "artistry" will probably involve your examination of all of these in some combination. Still, since we're looking at metaphors, let's notice how subtly Hawthorne takes us from a conversation— Chillingworth is asking questions and listening to Dimmesdale speak in order to (literally) "search into the minister's dim interior." At some point, however, this psychological examination becomes a physical journey, one from which Chillingworth can "turn back." The journey quickly becomes something dark and treacherous, so that Chillingworth must "grope … stealthily." As Chillingworth "creeps" in Dimmesdale's soul, "the floor would now and then creak; his garments would rustle; the shadow of his presence, in a forbidden proximity, would be thrown across his victim."

This is *not* Chillingworth's physically creeping into Dimmesdale's bedroom; it is all a metaphoric stealth into Dimmesdale's mind, heart, and conscience. But Hawthorne's control is so complete, and the entry into the metaphor is so subtle that the reader follows along, somehow resolving the double meaning of a literal villain trying to probe another man's deepest secret and a figurative thief creeping into a dark bedroom.

That subtlety, that control, that sense that the metaphor *needs to be there* or the paragraph would be less good ... that is artistry.

Now look at the following, an excerpt from an unpublished short story

> *Her mind filled with smoke before her lungs did. Her panic drove her blindly to smash out the window, even though you could see the flames through the glass. Now the room was getting hotter—a pizza kitchen in August, the brick oven itself—and every breath was a hot knife stabbing her heart.*
>
> *"Help!" she tried to scream, but there was not enough air. Her lungs struggled like birthday balloons after the party is over.*
>
> *Exhausted and only semi-conscious, she collapsed to the floor, where the air was still breathable, and she started to revive. The sound of a cannon shot, or a clap of thunder, and she heard voices.*
>
> *Angels' voices. No, men's voices.*
>
> *Kevlar arms scooped her up, and she gazed gratefully into her own face reflected in the visor of her savior's helmet.*
>
> *She was being rescued.*

Hopefully you can see the difference between this passage and the one from *The Scarlet Letter*. There is no apparent connection between the intensifying heat in the room and a pizza kitchen or oven. The difference in tone between a woman's suffocating in a smoke-filled room and the partially deflated balloons after a birthday party is almost laughable. The noise—is it an explosion? the sound of the door being kicked in?—besides being described in clichés (cannon cracks and thunder claps) is also unclear.

If we were to count the kinds of devices that one would expect to go into "artistry," we might actually find that the second passage has more. But clearly, the author is not in control. The devices are there for the sake of being there, not for the sake of clarity or impact.

This is not artistry.

Ultimately, the assessment of one piece as "artistic" and another as "trite" or "overwritten" is largely a matter of taste. but beyond that wide range lie uses that no serious readers would consider artistic. By and large, works in those extremes would not be considered to have "literary merit."

"Literary merit" is, then, largely a matter of personal taste and largely not. It cannot be calculated by a mathematical formula or plotted on a graph. It cannot *really* be defined except to suggest in broad terms that it involves a text's being largely character driven, having broad and lasting appeal, and a sense of artistry or control.

A good exercise would be to make two lists: works that do possess literary merit and works that do not. Then, for each work on each list, write a paragraph or two (or at least list) the reasons. And make sure the reasons amount to more than just *I liked it* or *I thought it was boring*.

Synthesizing Information from Multiple Sources

CHAPTER 6

What Is Synthesis?

Here's a good word-attack exercise. The word *synthesis* is pretty obviously formed by a combination of *thesis* and the prefix *syn-*.

You should already be familiar with *thesis*: your essays are supposed to be *thesis-based*; two ideas that contradict one another are said to be *antithetical*. The rhetorical device that places two opposing or contradictory ideas close together is called *antithesis*. You can probably guess that *thesis* has to do with *idea*, *thought*, or *argument*.

You probably also have some experience with the prefix *syn-*: synonym, synergy, synecdoche … You may even already be familiar with the idea of *synthetic* materials or processes like photo*synthesis*. In all of these, the prefix *syn-* carries with it a sense of parts or elements, especially if those parts are assembled to create a whole.

Synergy is a process by which two or more cooperating forces produce a result that could not be produced by any of them independently.

Synecdoche is the use of a part of something to represent the whole (Many hands make light work.)

Photosynthesis is the process by which a plant uses light (*photo*) and carbon dioxide to create (*synthesize*) sugar.

Synthetic materials are those that are created by combining two or more "ingredients."

Synthesis, then, is the process by which a number of elements are combined (*syn*) to create something new (*thesis*).

For the purposes of the Advanced Placement in English Language and Composition exam, the elements are sources of information—both print and graphic (words as well as charts and pictures)—and the new creation is *your original argument*.

Another, almost oversimplified, explanation of this process was developed by a German philosopher by the name of G. W. F. Hegel:

The *thesis* is an intellectual proposition.

The *antithesis* is the negation of the thesis, an opposing reaction to the proposition.

The *synthesis* resolves the conflict between the thesis and antithesis, drawing whatever is useful from each, and creating a new proposition.

There are two key elements to this explanation of *synthesis* that are absolutely essential to your synthesis essay:

1. **The "new idea" *must* be drawn or derived from other sources.** It cannot be pure, original thought, your own "light bulb" experience. You must be able to cite every source from which you gleaned any information or ideas—even ideas that disagree with the source—and you should be able to discuss how each source shaped your thinking.

2. **The idea must be "new."** It is, after all, a *thesis*. Most likely, the instructions on the AP exam will tell you explicitly not to simply summarize or paraphrase your sources, but even if they don't, *you know that the purpose of this essay is to support your thesis.*

 Consider this: Every sample essay you've read in this book and every essay you've written while using this book has been based on a passage you read and then responded to. The synthesis essay is not terribly different. It simply requires you to consult and cite more sources.

Anatomy of a Synthesis Essay Question

Just as knowing what your multiple-choice and free-response questions will look and sound like will save you precious time and brainpower on the day you take your exam, being prepared for the basic format and function of the synthesis essay question can only help.

First, it's important to note that there is no distinct section of the exam called the "Synthesis Essay." It is simply one of the three free-response questions on your exam—usually the first. While the fact that this particular free-response requires you to synthesize your response from a number of sources is pretty hard to miss, it's still important to note that this is your synthesis essay, even if it is not labeled so.

The first page of the question will contain the introduction of your topic, your instructions, and a list of the sources provided for you. In 2011, the format of these instructions changed, but the College Board stresses that the nature of the synthesis exam is the same as it has been since it was first instituted.

The **first page** of your synthesis question will look something like this:

Neo-Luddism[1] is a personal stance that opposes any modern technology that displaces workers and increases unemployment. Its name is based on the British Luddite movement of the early nineteenth century, which was a reaction to the displacement of both laborers and craftsmen during the Industrial Revolution. This anti-technological view also warns of the effects technology can have on individuals and communities.

Carefully read the following [usually six or seven] sources,[2] including the introductory information for each source. Then synthesize information from at least three of the sources and incorporate it into a coherent, well-developed essay[3] that evaluates both the logic and the folly of their reasoning and develops an argument that ultimately supports or repudiates the Neo-Luddite view.[4]

Make sure that your argument is central; use the sources to illustrate and support your reasoning. Avoid merely summarizing the sources.[5] Indicate clearly which sources you are drawing from,[6] whether through direct quotation, paraphrase, or summary. You may cite the sources as Source A, Source B, etc., or by using the descriptions in parentheses.

Source A (McMahon)
Source B (Pearl)
Source C (Spencer and Reed)
Source D (chart)
Source E (Gilmore)
Source F (painting)

---

[1] The first paragraph introduces a topic or an issue. It won't matter whether or not you know anything about this topic because you will be given sources from which to draw information to support a thesis.

[2] The instructions to read the sources and write the essay might not always be in a separate paragraph.

[3] This language is fairly standard for all questions.

[4] Do not get lulled into carelessness by the fact that much of the language is standard. Pay close attention to the specific verbs that define the nature of the essay you are to write.

[5] This paragraph is quoted verbatim from the 2011 exams forms A and B. It is identical to the previous years' instructions.

[6] This is crucial. Your essay is to be thesis-based. You are to mention the sources only in terms of explaining where you got the information you are using to support your thesis.

The key elements of these instructions are

> the introduction of the **topic** itself,
> the **specific verbs** that define the essay,
> the directive to **support an argument**, *not* survey the sources.

In this question, the **topic** of Neo-Luddism is introduced. Whether you've ever heard of it—whether you've ever heard of the nineteenth-century Luddites—is irrelevant. This introduction basically tells you everything you need to know—Neo-Luddism is a stance that opposes especially the replacement of workers with machines, thus resulting in higher unemployment; the Luddite Movement was a nineteenth-century reaction to the Industrial Revolution.

Your essay is to *evaluate … the logic and the folly of [neo-Luddites'] reasoning.* You are to tell your reader where and how the points of Neo-Luddism make sense, where they are questionable, and where they are actually wrong, misguided, or crazy.

Further, your essay is to *develop an argument that ultimately supports or repudiates the neo-Luddite view.* That means you get to agree or disagree with the neo-Luddites. But your agreement or disagreement must be reasonable and based on and supported by information gleaned from the sources.

Once you're absolutely clear on what you're supposed to do in your essay (including *not* merely summarize, paraphrase, or survey the sources), you're ready to look at the sources themselves.

The **pages that follow the instructions page** will contain the source material. There will generally one source per page. Some of the text passages may be more than one page long, but there will rarely, if ever, be two or more sources on a single page.

> ### Source A
> excerpted from: McMahon, Matthew. "Declaration of a Neo Luddite." In *Encyclopedia of Media Studies: Views and Voices,* vol. 1, ed. Leslie Bayard. New York: Underground Press, 2009.

Most apologists of twenty-first-century Western civilization dismiss the Luddites of 19th-century England as a sort of radical fringe, extremists who smashed machines and tried to halt the wheels of progress. This is, however, an oversimplified and largely inaccurate understanding of an important social movement rooted in a clash between two worldviews.

The Luddites simply protested the spread of technology like mechanized looms to do work that was formerly done by people. They held marches, destroyed factories, and engaged in other types of activism in an attempt to stem the tide of technological encroachment. The worldview embraced by the Luddites was centered on the village or town and recognized the near-sacred trinity of work, community, and family. Their "corporation" was the trade guild, and their "social network" was the arrangement of farm, shop, and marketplace in which each produced what the other needed, and the whole achieved a harmonic balance.

The encroaching worldview they challenged was that of laissez-faire capitalism, with its increasing consolidation of power and wealth in the hands of a few at the expense of the many.

We neo-Luddites believe that the use of technology has serious ethical, moral, and social consequences. We are, therefore, wary of technology and urge caution in the development and use of any new device or process. We are not opposed to technology; we merely urge a more serious discussion of the role technology plays in the lives of human beings and its impact on the natural environment.

We believe that the sheer ubiquity of personal electronics has cut us off from our communities and isolated us in private universes of our own creation, while the invasion of communications technology and social networking media render us incapable of ever being truly alone with our thoughts.

We are citizens of the twenty-first century who challenge the dominant worldview that equates unchecked technology with progress.

We have the courage to tell the truth: The technologies created by modern Western civilization threaten to compromise every aspect of life on Earth.

Like our nineteenth-century brothers and sisters, we seek only to protect our livelihoods, communities, and families.

We assert the following as the principal tenets of Neo-Luddism:

1. We do not oppose technology. We oppose only those kinds of technology that, by their very nature, destroy human lives and communities.

2. We oppose technologies spawned by a worldview that sees reason as the most important human attribute, material gain as the chief means of human fulfillment, and technological advancement as the primary means by which the hungry are fed, the sick are healed, and the enslaved are freed.

3. Technology is not neutral. Every technological innovation is consciously structured to serve a specific end in a specific situation—that end being primarily to perpetuate and spread the society and structure that created it.

4. Technological innovation is governed by no ideal other than the short-term benefits of convenience and profit.

   For example,
   - the Internet does not merely deliver entertainment and information to households worldwide, it provides corporations global means of hawking their goods or services, expanding their markets, and controlling social and political thought.
   - personal entertainment technologies undermine family communication and narrow people's experience of life.
   - advancements in the field of pharmacology do not only cure or lessen disease, they create tremendous profits for pharmaceutical corporations and their investors. They also create untold harm and destroy the quality of life for thousands of human souls subjected to improperly tested or prematurely approved medications whose side effects are often worse than the conditions the drugs are designed to treat.

5. Each person's view of his or her own use of technology is dangerously narrow. One's dependence on the "latest thing" is formed without consideration of the consequences of the mass production, widespread use, and eventual discarding of that device.

   Those who create, manufacture, and market technological innovations (and therefore profit from them) publicly announce only glorified or idealized benefits of the advancement, often keeping the public utterly unaware of any dangers, personal or environmental, associated with the product. Consumers are, thus, unable to make truly informed and conscientious decisions regarding their use of technology.

6. Any thorough and just evaluation of technology requires a full examination of its social and cultural context, economic consequences, and political significance. Creators, manufacturers, and consumers must consider not only what is to be gained—but what is to be lost as well—and by whom. A just evaluation of any new or potential technology must involve an examination of its impact on other living beings and the environment.

Source B

Pearl, Albert. "I'm No Neo-Luddite." found at *Pearls of Wisdom.*
http://www.pearlsofwisdomblogspot.com

This is my formal protest of a recent characterization of Yours Truly as a neo-Luddite:

>>Link disabled<<

First of all, I am a blogger, so any accusations that I am anti-technology are completely unfounded and unjust. And, while it is true that, up to this point, I have been hesitant to dip my toe into the water of social media technology, to characterize me as a Linked-In, Facebook Neo-Luddite is extreme. I prefer to think of myself as "cautious." I want to test the waters, acclimate myself to the idea. I want to know the pros and cons, the whys and the wherefores. I don't want to jump in blindly.

But, given what I learned as a technology conference just this weekend, I will almost certainly jump in.

I can't afford not to.

The term neo-Luddite has its origins in the term Luddite, which has *its* origins in Ned Ludd. Poor old Ned had a problem in England back in 1811. In the midst of the Industrial Revolution, which was really a technology revolution, mill owners were installing the new mechanized looms that allowed unskilled labor to produce fabric at a faster rate and a fraction of the cost than skilled craftsmen like Ludd. Lower labor costs plus increased production led to increased profits—for the mill owners. The laborers were still paid only pennies, and the skilled craftsmen found themselves out of work.

The story goes that Ludd himself lost his job as a weaver and then, unemployed, was fined for "idleness" for hanging around in his village square in the middle of a work day.

He was so mad that he grabbed an ax and smashed all the mechanized looms in his village. This started a movement, and other artisans began to destroy other mechanized looms. The smashing continued until 1812, when the British Army was called in to restore law and order.

This is not a digression. There is a point to it.

Old Ned did spark a movement, and his name does appear in the history books (and this blog), but seriously, did you ever hear of him before you read this?

I never had until last week when I was called a social media neo-Luddite.

Ned might have been right—the machines *were* destroying his livelihood— but he didn't have a strong enough network. He had an ax, and society rarely sympathizes with the guy who smashes things. People surely heard more about the smashed looms than they heard about the starving weavers. But if Ned and the Luddites had been able to Link-In or form a Facebook group, they might actually have swayed public opinion in their favor. They might have been able to meet the mill owners halfway and create a new working model that protected both the skilled craftsmen and the owners' profits.

At this conference last week, I saw a couple of presentations by this guy who's written a few books and made a few videos with the catchy title, "Socionometrics." The slogan is "Spread the good world." (There's a pun there, did you get it?) Here's what I learned: It took 38 years for radio to reach fifty million listeners. It took Facebook *only nine months* to reach 100 million viewers.

When you consider the role these social media sites have played in recent events in Japan and Egypt—and even those two girls who were trapped in a storm drain and used Facebook to call for help—what's there to be afraid of? I'm a businessman. I'm a writer. Just as Ned Ludd's livelihood depended on his operating a loom, mine depends on reaching a lot of people.

Sorry, Ned, I'm going with the social media. I'll Tweet you how it's going.

Source C

from Spencer, Daniel and Derek Reed. *Cynical Thoughts on the Twentieth Century.* Delaware: Prestwick House, Inc., 2002.

Henry Ford should have thought that whole assembly-line thing all the way through.

Photo property of the Farm Security Administration—Office of War Information Photograph Collection in the Library of Congress. Photograph by John Collier, who was acting as an agent of the United States Government. The image is therefore in the public domain.

Caption © Prestwick House Inc., 2011.

This should give you an idea of how the sources will be presented in your exam packet. Among the five, or six, or seven sources provided will be print as well as graphic and pictorial sources. Some will be slanted in one direction or the other, and some will make sincere attempts at complete neutrality. Ultimately, it won't matter.

It won't matter whether you agree or disagree with any of the sources. It won't really matter what your thesis is.

What does matter is how you support that thesis with information gleaned from the sources—and how you cite the sources in your essay.

Remember that you are specifically warned against summarizing, paraphrasing, or surveying your sources. You do not want to spend any time at all arguing with Matt McMahon or Al Pearl. But the information about *Socionometrics* might be helpful. The fact that, assuming the role of spokesperson for the neo-Luddite movement, Matt McMahon seems to advocate more stringent testing of new drugs might support one of your points.

Building An Argument and Crafting a Thesis

After you look at the sources (typically you are advised to spend 15 minutes reading and 40 minutes writing), make sure you go back and understand the specific language of the question. This one has told you to write a well-developed essay that (1) **evaluates both the** (1. a.) **logic and the** (1. b.) **folly** of their reasoning and (2) **develops an argument** that ultimately supports or repudiates the neo-Luddite view.

The next step, then, is to build that argument. To address this question and support either thesis, you need to answer three questions:

1. Which neo-Luddite claims are logical? (This will address part 1. a. of your question.)

2. Which claims are not logical? (This will address 1. b.)

3. How and why does one type outweigh the other? (This will address part 2.)

You are also instructed to *synthesize information from at least three of the sources.* So, now is when you go back simply gather what you need to meet the demands of your prompt. On an actual exam, you will be allowed to write on the test sheet, so this step can be as simple as underlining, asterisking, or otherwise highlighting the material you want.

Here are the bits of information one student chose when preparing her essay in response to this question. There's also some commentary to reflect the student's thoughts as she began to lay out her argument.

Logic:

(A) *"We oppose only those kinds of technology that, by their very nature, destroy human lives and communities."* Sounds reasonable, but what are those technologies? Are we talking about only weapons?

(A) *"Every technological innovation is consciously structured to serve a specific end in a specific situation..."* True enough.

(A) *"Technological innovation is governed by no ideal other than the short-term benefits of convenience and profit."* In a capitalist society, this is probably true.

(B) is a blogger but admits to having been *"hesitant to dip [his] toe into the water of social media technology"* because he wants to *"test the waters, acclimate [him]self to the idea. [He] want[s] to know the pros and cons, the whys and the wherefores ... [not] jump in blindly."*

(C) illustrates an unintended consequence of a new technology that seems completely beneficial

* (B) supports anti-Luddites: *"the role these social media sites have played in recent events in Japan and Egypt—and even those two girls who were trapped in a storm drain and used Facebook to call for help—what's there to be afraid of?"*

Folly:

(A) *"The technologies created by modern Western civilization threaten to compromise every aspect of life on Earth."* Overemotional. Clearly an exaggeration.

(A) *"Technology is not neutral. Every technological innovation is consciously structured to serve a specific end in a specific situation"* True, but *"—that end being primarily to perpetuate and spread the society and structure that created it."* Made to sound more ominous than it necessarily is?

(A) *"advancements in the field of pharmacology ... create tremendous profits for pharmaceutical corporations and their investors."* True, but is this bad if the investors have originally funded the research and development?

(A) *"advancements in the field of pharmacology ... also create untold harm and destroy the quality of life for thousands of human souls subjected to improperly tested or prematurely approved medications whose side effects are often worse than the conditions the drugs are designed to treat."* Gross exaggeration: Not all new pharmaceuticals are dangerous; one's physician (an educated professional) plays a role in deciding whether or not a certin drug is appropriate; pharmaceutical companies are required by law to list all the known side effects in all advertising or literature about the new drug.

(B) *"People surely heard more about the smashed looms than they heard about the starving weavers."* "Starving weavers" seems a little exaggerated, overemotional.

(B) *"But if Ned and the Luddites had been able to Link-In or form a Facebook group, they might actually have swayed public opinion in their favor. They might have been able to meet the mill owners halfway and create a new working model that protected both the skilled craftsmen and the owners' profits."* Silly speculation.

Argument:

The neo-Luddites have a point. Some of the arguments they make are sensationalized exaggerations or slightly misleading. But, all-in-all, they're more right than crazy.

Another student, examining the same evidence, framed this argument:

The anti-technology stance adopted by neo-Luddites is more an emotional reaction to factors ultimately unrelated to the technology itself. Some of the points they raise are valid, but their arguments are too emotional and exaggerated to be convincing.

Once you've laid out your argument and know the evidence you have to support it, crafting your thesis is relatively easy. Remember the terms and specifications of question you were assigned, and make sure you address them. Your thesis for this essay is going to have both a judgment (this makes sense, this is silly), and a stance (they're right, they're wrong.)

One workable thesis might read:

While many of the neo-Luddites' claims are more emotional appeals than valid arguments (1. a.), they raise enough compelling questions (1. b.) to warrant being listened to (2).

The reverse thesis would also work:

Although some of the arguments raised by neo-Luddites are worth consideration (1. a.), so many of their claims are mere emotional appeals (1. b.) that to consider them as serious participants in a discussion of ethics and technology would only waylay an important and valid discussion.

Both of these theses address all three parts of the topic and, if followed, will lead to an essay that fulfills the specifications of the question.

How To Use Your Sources

This is, after all, your synthesis essay, not an opinion piece, and your instructions specify that you are to *synthesize information from at least three of the sources and incorporate it* into your essay. You've already begun the synthesize part by formulating your argument and crafting your thesis. It's important, however, to know how to *incorporate* the information without *merely summarizing the sources.*

You have, of course, already started on the right track by focusing on the question and making sure your gleaned information addresses each and every specification of the question. Notice how our model students' notes follow the logic, folly, and argument demanded by the question with information from more than one source for each part.

The thesis also addresses each specification.

If you follow through and discuss the logic (with information from all or most of your sources), the folly (with information from all or most of your sources), and then make your argument, you'll have a top-scoring essay.

If you can glean information from only one source for a section of your essay, you must be careful to make it clear that you are discussing the point and not the source. It might actually help you to find one bit of information from a fourth source to avoid the trap of making the essay about the sources.

How To Cite Your Sources

Just as you would with any other essay or paper, you must, of course, credit your sources. In other words, any time you use another person's words or ideas, you must give that other person credit.

Your question instructs you to

> *Indicate clearly which sources you are drawing from, whether through direct quotation, paraphrase, or summary. You may cite the sources as Source A, Source B, etc., or by using the descriptions in parentheses.*

Handling your references to your sources will certainly contribute to a favorable impression and might make the difference of a "nudge up" in a scorer's mind if your information and presentation places your essay on the line between, say a 6 and a 7.

In **direct quotation**, you actually use the words verbatim from the source. You *must* place the sources within quotation marks (" "), and you *should* orient your reader to the fact that you are going to be quoting a source.

EXAMPLES: According to Source A, neo-Luddites "oppose only those kinds of technology that ... destroy human lives and communities."

Pearl concludes, "When you consider the role these social media sites have played in recent events in Japan and Egypt—and even those two girls who were trapped in a storm drain and used Facebook to call for help—what's there to be afraid of?"

For a piece the length of your synthesis essay, you should keep all direct quotations short (no more than a sentence), and you should reserve quotation only for instances in which the source's language is so specific or technical that you cannot paraphrase or summarize it accurately.

Sprinkling your "own" writing with individual words in quotation marks, even if those "words" are "borrowed" from your source is usually "very distracting to your reader." Save direct quotation for important occasions.

A **paraphrase** is a retelling of the source's content—keeping the source's order, tone, cutting out no details, etc., *but stating it in your words rather than the source's.*

EXAMPLE: Pearl concludes that the use of social networks to spread information during recent political unrest in the Middle East, along with the fact that young adolescents resort first to social networking rather than traditional emergency communications, makes a strong case for the benefits of participating in these media.

Paraphrase comes in handy when you need to present a larger bit of information than you can reasonably quote, but you still want to establish that you have not altered—abbreviated, evaluated, interpreted—the source's content in any way.

Summary is the use of your own words to provide your reader with brief overview of the source's key points or point. Summary is most effective if you simply want to offer an entire essay's main point as support, or if time and space limitations will not allow you to provide a more detailed discussion of the source.

EXAMPLES: Source A posits three key tenets of neo-Ludditism: caution in embracing new technology, broadening one's view of the impact of personal technology use, and full examination of the global repercussions of technological innovation.

Source B makes a strong case for caution even if one considers oneself a technophile.

We cannot stress enough, however, that even though you *must* take information from your sources to support your thesis, and you *must* cite the sources you use, your essay is about your thesis, *not* the sources. Make sure you keep your focus clear, or you will be very disappointed in the score your essay receives.

Synthesis Sample 1:

English Language and Composition
Reading Time: 15 minutes
Suggested Writing Time: 40 minutes

Manifest Destiny is a phrase coined in 1845 by journalist and publisher John L. O'Sullivan. The phrase not only became the motto of the American attitude toward westward expansion since the end of the Revolutionary War, it aptly described the United States' policy toward Native Americans.

Carefully read the following seven sources, including the introductory information for each source. Then synthesize information from at least three of the sources and incorporate it into a coherent, well-developed essay that either defends or repudiates the eighteenth- and nineteenth-century view that the United States had a "Manifest Destiny" to expand until it filled the entire North American continent.

Make sure that your argument is central; use the sources to illustrate and support your reasoning. Avoid merely summarizing the sources. Indicate clearly which sources you are drawing from, whether through direct quotation, paraphrase, or summary. You may cite the sources as Source A, Source B, etc., or by using the descriptions in parentheses.[1]

Source A (O'Sullivan)
Source B (Thoreau)
Source C (Map: Westward Expansion)
Source D (Jefferson 1)
Source E (Jefferson 2)
Source F (painting: Gast; text: Croffut)
Source G (Indian Removal Act of 1830)

Continued on next page ▶

Sample Student Commentary

[1] Nothing new or surprising in this prompt.

Synthesis Sample 1:

> **Source A**
>
> O'Sullivan, John L. "The Great Nation of Futurity," *The United States Magazine and Democratic Review*, 1839.

John L. O'Sullivan founded The United States Magazine and Democratic Review *in 1837.* Its motto, "The best government is that which governs least,"[2] *was made famous by transcendentalist Henry David Thoreau in his essay "On the Duty of Civil Disobedience."*

O'Sullivan himself is probably most famous for a later editorial in this magazine in which he coined the phrase "Manifest Destiny." This essay, written some five years earlier, already begins to discuss the territorial expansion of the United States in terms of its "destiny."

The American people having derived their origin from many other nations, and the Declaration of National Independence being entirely based on the great principle of human equality, these facts demonstrate at once our disconnected position as regards any other nation; that <u>we have</u>, in reality, <u>but little connection with the past history of any of them, and</u> still <u>less with all antiquity</u>, its glories, or its crimes.[3] On the contrary, our national birth was the beginning of a new history, the formation and progress of an untried political system, <u>which separates us from the past and connects us with the future only</u>;[4] and so far as regards the entire development of the natural rights of man, in moral, political, and national life, we may <u>confidently assume</u> that <u>our country is destined to be the great nation of futurity</u>.[5]

It is so destined, because <u>the principle upon which a nation is organized fixes its destiny</u>,[6] and that of equality is perfect, is universal. It presides in all the operations of the physical world, and it is also the conscious law of the soul— the self-evident[7] <u>dictates</u> of morality, which accurately defines the duty of man

Continued on next page ▶

Sample Student Commentary

[2] This is an interesting fact. Since one of the sources is "Civil Disobedience," there might be a way to use this.

[3] According to O'Sullivan, we are completely independent of other nations and their histories.

[4] Not just a reiteration of the previous idea but an implication about our connection to the future.

[5] This conclusion almost begs the question. In order to embrace this concept of national destiny, we must agree with the earlier points about our disconnection to the past, which remain arguable.

[6] Also more a thesis than a statement of truth.

[7] The "Self-Evident Proposition" is another logical fallacy. By claiming something to be self-evident, we are precluding all search for evidence either to support or refute it.

Synthesis Sample 1:

to man, and consequently man's rights as man. Besides, <u>the truthful annals of any nation furnish abundant evidence, that its happiness, its greatness, its duration, were always proportionate to the democratic equality in its system of government.</u>[8]

. . .

<u>What friend of human liberty, civilization, and refinement, can cast his view over the past history of the monarchies and aristocracies of antiquity, and not deplore that they ever existed?</u>[9] What philanthropist can contemplate the oppressions, the cruelties, and injustice inflicted by them on the <u>masses of mankind, and not turn with moral horror</u> from the retrospect?[10] America is destined for better deeds. It is our unparalleled glory that <u>we have no reminiscences of battle fields, but in defence of humanity, of the oppressed of all nations,</u>[11] describe no scenes of horrid carnage, where men were led on by hundreds of thousands to slay one another, dupes and victims to emperors, kings, nobles, demons in the human form called heroes. We have had patriots to defend our homes, our liberties, but no aspirants to crowns or thrones; <u>nor have the American people ever suffered themselves to be led on by wicked ambition to depopulate the land,</u>[12] to spread desolation far and wide, that a human being might be placed on a seat of supremacy.

We have no interest in the scenes of antiquity, only as lessons of avoidance of nearly all their examples. The expansive future is our arena, and for our history. We are entering on its untrodden space, with the truths of God in our minds, beneficent objects in our hearts, and with a clear conscience unsullied by the past. We are the nation of human progress, and <u>who will, what can, set limits</u>[13] to our onward march? <u>Providence is with us, and no earthly power can.</u>[14] We point to the everlasting truth on the first page of our national

Continued on next page ▶

Sample Student Commentary

[8] One or two factual examples would be helpful.

[9] This is a rhetorical question. O' Sullivan is not inviting inquiry or discussion.

[10] O' Sullivan is employing strong language, but staying on the level of the arguable thesis. He is assuming his reader's agreement with the terms he uses and their meaning.

[11] To judge O' Sullivan fairly, we must remember that he is approaching United States history from a different perspective from today's predominant view.

[12] Interesting. This is the issue of the essay—support or repudiation of the concept of Manifest Destiny.

[13] Challenging syntax and sentence structure. He's saying, "Who can limit ... and what can limit ... our march into the future?"

[14] To raise an apparently rhetorical question and then answer it is a device called hypophora. It is useful here because O' Sullivan has relied for so long on his reader's already agreeing with his points that he takes this opportunity to reorient those of us who might be in strong agreement with him.

Synthesis Sample 1:

declaration, and we proclaim to the millions of other lands, that "the gates of hell"—the powers of aristocracy and monarchy --"shall not prevail against it."

The far-reaching, the boundless future will be the era of American greatness. In its magnificent domain of space and time, the nation of many nations is destined to manifest[15] to mankind the excellence of divine principles; to establish on earth the noblest temple ever dedicated to the worship of the Most High—the Sacred and the True. Its floor shall be a hemisphere—its roof the firmament of the star-studded heavens, and its congregation an Union of many Republics, comprising hundreds of happy millions, calling, owning no man master, but governed by God's natural and moral law of equality, the law of brotherhood—of "peace and good will amongst men."

. . .

Yes, we are the nation of progress, of individual freedom, of universal enfranchisement.[16] Equality of rights is the cynosure of our union of States, the grand exemplar of the correlative equality of individuals; and while truth sheds its effulgence, we cannot retrograde, without dissolving the one and subverting the other. We must onward to the fulfilment of our mission—to the entire development of the principle of our organization—freedom of conscience, freedom of person, freedom of trade and business pursuits, universality of freedom and equality. This is our high destiny, and in nature's eternal, inevitable decree of cause and effect we must accomplish it. All this will be our future history, to establish on earth the moral dignity and salvation of man—the immutable truth and beneficence of God. For this blessed mission to the nations of the world, which are shut out from the life-giving light of truth, has America been chosen; and her high example shall smite unto death the tyranny of kings, hierarchs, and oligarchs, and carry the glad tidings of peace and good will where myriads now endure an existence scarcely more enviable than that of beasts of the field. Who, then, can doubt that our country is destined to be *the great nation of futurity*?[17]

Continued on next page ▶

Sample Student Commentary

[15] Already we see O' Sullivan experimenting with the concept and the terms that will evolve into the notion of "Manifest Destiny."

[16] Just as a historical note, it might be important to remember that in 1839, when O'Sullivan wrote this essay, blacks were residents but not citizens, and women were citizens but could not vote.

[17] All in all, a very optimistic look forward. One must be careful, however, to examine all the claims and assumptions about the past on which O' Sullivan bases his conclusions.

Synthesis Sample 1:

> **Source B**
> excerpted from: Thoreau, Henry David.
> "On the Duty of Civil Disobedience," 1849.

In 1848, Thoreau presented a series of lectures titled "The Rights and Duties of the Individual in Relation to Government." These lectures became the basis for this essay, first published in 1849 under the title "Resistance to Civil Government." While the primary issue in the lectures and essay was the escalating problem of slavery, Thoreau also condemned what he considered American Imperialism, having currently expressed itself in the Mexican-American War.

The Mexican War was an armed conflict between the United States and Mexico from 1846 to 1848. In the aftermath of the United States' annexation of Texas, United States forces invaded New Mexico, the California Republic, and parts of what is currently northern Mexico. The United States Navy conducted a blockade along the Pacific coast.

Although American territorial expansion to the Pacific coast had always been the goal of President James K. Polk, the leader of the Democratic Party, the war was highly controversial and opposed by the Whig Party and abolitionists. The cost of the War was high in terms of both human casualties and financial cost. The major consequence was Mexico's cession of territories·in California and New Mexico. The Rio Grande was established as the United States-Mexico border.

I heartily accept the motto,—"Underline: That government is best which governs least";[18] and I should like to see it acted up to more rapidly and systematically. Carried out, it finally amounts to this, which also I believe,—"That government is best which governs not at all"; and when men are prepared for it,[19] that will be the kind of government which they will have.

***

Continued on next page ▶

Sample Student Commentary

[18] Paraphrased from the motto of John L. O' Sullivan's The United States Magazine and Democratic Review (1837 – 1859).

[19] An important provision many readers of this essay ignore.

Synthesis Sample 1:

This American government ... never of itself furthered any enterprise, but by the alacrity with which it got out of its way.[20] It does not keep the country free.[21] It does not settle the West.[22] It does not educate. The character inherent in the American people has done all that has been accomplished;[23] and it would have done somewhat more, if the government had not sometimes got in its way.

***

...a government in which the majority rule in all cases cannot be based on justice, even as far as men understand it. Can there not be a government in which majorities do not virtually decide right and wrong, but conscience?[24]— in which majorities decide only those questions to which the rule of expediency is applicable? Must the citizen ever for a moment, or in the least degree, resign his conscience to the legislator? Why has every man a conscience, then? I think that we should be men first, and subjects afterward.[25] It is not desirable to cultivate a respect for the law, so much as for the right.[26] The only obligation which I have a right to assume is to do at any time what I think right. It is truly enough said that a corporation has no conscience; but a corporation of conscientious men is a corporation *with* a conscience. Law never made men a whit more just; and, by means of their respect for it, even the well-disposed are daily made the agents of injustice.[27]

***

How does it become a man to behave toward this American government to-day? I answer, that he cannot without disgrace be associated with it. I cannot for an instant recognize that political organization as *my* government which is the *slave's* government also.

Continued on next page ▶

Sample Student Commentary

[20] The only way the United States government has furthered any enterprise is to get out of its way.

[21] "It" refers to the United States government.

[22] Thoreau lists this as a worthy endeavor, one that the government does not really assist.

[23] Considering maintaining freedom, settling the west, and educating the people to be "accomplishments," Thoreau claims that these are accomplishments of the American people, not the government.

[24] This is a common theme in transcendentalist writing: One should follow the dictates of one's own conscience, not bend to the wills of the majority or the most powerful.

[25] What seems like a series of rhetorical questions is really hypophora. Thoreau is not assuming his readers will answer these questions the way he intends.

[26] As is typical of Thoreau, he restates the same idea several times before moving on to the next.

[27] Thoreau begs the question of whether there are times when one is compelled to follow the law in violation of his or her conscience.

Synthesis Sample 1:

***

Paley[1], a common authority with many on moral questions, in his chapter on the "Duty of Submission to Civil Government," resolves all civil obligation into expediency; and he proceeds to say that "so long as the interest of the whole society requires it, that is, so long as the established government cannot be resisted or changed without public inconveniency, it is the will of God that the established government be obeyed, and no longer" ... But Paley appears never to have contemplated those cases to which the rule of expediency does not apply, in which a people, as well as an individual, must do justice, cost what it may. If I have unjustly wrested a plank from a drowning man, I must restore it to him though I drown myself. This, according to Paley, would be inconvenient. But he that would save his life, in such a case, shall lose it. <u>This people must cease to hold slaves, and to make war on Mexico, though it cost them their existence as a people.</u>[28]

Practically speaking, the opponents to a reform in Massachusetts are not a hundred thousand politicians at the South, but a hundred thousand merchants and farmers here, who are more interested in commerce and agriculture than they are in humanity, and are not prepared to do justice to the slave and to Mexico, *cost what it may*. <u>I quarrel not with far-off foes, but with those who, near at home, co-operate with, and do the bidding of those far away, and without whom the latter would be harmless.</u>[29] ... There are thousands who are *in opinion* opposed to slavery and to the war, who yet in effect do nothing to put an end to them; who, esteeming themselves children of Washington and Franklin, sit down with their hands in their pockets, and say that they know not what to do, and do nothing; who even postpone the question of freedom to the question of free-trade, and quietly read the prices-current along with the latest advices from Mexico, after dinner, and, it may be, fall asleep over them both. <u>What is the price-current of an honest man and patriot to-day?</u>[30] They hesitate, and they regret, and sometimes they petition;

---

[1] William Paley (July 1743–25 May 1805), a British theologian, philosopher, and utilitarian. As a theologian during the Enlightenment, he was a strong proponent of the "absent watchmaker" view of the creator.

Continued on next page ▶

Sample Student Commentary

[28] Interesting leap from the drowning man to the war in Mexico. But Thoreau does not elaborate on the similarities.

[29] Challenging syntax and sentence structure. Thoreau seems to be saying that the enemy is not some far-off entity, but those at home who simply accept the status quo, who willingly sacrifice justice toward others for the sake of their own convenience and profit.

[30] Thoreau here begs the question, assuming that his reader will agree with him on what constitutes an "honest man" and a "patriot."

Synthesis Sample 1:

but they do nothing in earnest and with effect. <u>They will wait, well disposed, for others to remedy the evil, that they may no longer have it to regret.</u>[31] At most, they give only a cheap vote, and a feeble countenance and Godspeed, to the right, as it goes by them. ... Even voting *for the right* is *doing* nothing for it. It is only expressing to men feebly your desire that it should prevail. A wise man will not leave the right to the mercy of chance, nor wish it to prevail through the power of the majority. There is but little virtue in the action of masses of men. When the majority shall at length vote for the abolition of slavery, it will be because they are indifferent to slavery, or because there is but little slavery left to be abolished by their vote. *They* will then be the only slaves. Only *his* vote can hasten the abolition of slavery who asserts his own freedom by his vote.

***

It is not a man's duty, as a matter of course, to devote himself to the eradication of any, even the most enormous wrong; he may still properly have other concerns to engage him; but <u>it is his duty, at least, to wash his hands of it, and, if he gives it no thought longer, not to give it practically his support.</u>[32] If I devote myself to other pursuits and contemplations, I must first see, at least, that I do not pursue them sitting upon another man's shoulders. I must get off him first, that he may pursue his contemplations too. See what gross inconsistency is tolerated. I have heard some of my townsmen say, "<u>I should like to have them order me out to help put down an insurrection of the slaves, or to march to Mexico;—see if I would go</u>";[33] and yet these very men have each, directly by their allegiance, and so indirectly, at least, by their money, furnished a substitute. <u>The soldier is applauded who refuses to serve in an unjust war by those who do not refuse to sustain the unjust government which makes the war;</u>[34] is applauded by those whose own act and authority he disregards and sets at naught; as if the state were penitent to that degree that it hired one to scourge it while it sinned, but not to that degree that it left off sinning for a moment. Thus, under the name of Order and Civil Government, we are all made at last to pay homage to and support our own meanness. After the first blush of sin comes its indifference; and from immoral it becomes, as it were, unmoral, and not quite unnecessary to that life which we have made.

Continued on next page ▶

Sample Student Commentary

[31] Illustrating a point by describing a type is a common convention in this kind of editorializing. Still, it relies on the reader's willingness to concede that such a type exists.

[32] Thoreau is saying that it is not necessary to end injustice, just not support it.

[33] Thoreau is recreating sarcasm. The townspeople to whom he is referring are saying they would refuse to obey an order to put down an insurrection of slaves or march to Mexico.

[34] Thoreau is pointing out the inconsistency of protesting an injustice while still paying the taxes that fund the injustice.

Synthesis Sample 1:

***

Unjust laws exist; shall we be content to obey them, or shall we endeavor to amend them, and obey them until we have succeeded, or shall we transgress them at once? Men generally, under such a government as this, think that they ought to wait until they have persuaded the majority to alter them. They think that, if they should resist, the remedy would be worse than the evil. But it is the fault of the government itself that the remedy is worse than the evil. It makes it worse. Why is it not more apt to anticipate and provide for reform? Why does it not cherish its wise minority? Why does it cry and resist before it is hurt? Why does it not encourage its citizens to be on the alert to point out its faults, and do better than it would have them? Why does it always crucify Christ, and excommunicate Copernicus and Luther, and pronounce Washington and Franklin rebels?

***

If the injustice is part of the necessary friction of the machine of government, let it go, let it go; perchance it will wear smooth—certainly the machine will wear out. If the injustice has a spring, or a pulley, or a rope, or a crank, exclusively for itself, then perhaps you may consider whether the remedy will not be worse than the evil; but if it is of such a nature that it requires you to be the agent of injustice to another, then, I say, break the law. Let your life be a counter friction to stop the machine. What I have to do is to see, at any rate, that <u>I do not lend myself to the wrong which I condemn.</u>[35]

As for adopting the ways which the State has provided for remedying the evil, I know not of such ways. They take too much time, and a man's life will be gone. I have other affairs to attend to. I came into this world, not chiefly to make this a good place to live in, but to live in it, be it good or bad. A man has not everything to do, but something; and because he cannot do everything, it is not necessary that he should do something wrong. It is not my business to be petitioning the Governor or the Legislature any more than it is theirs to petition me; and if they should not hear my petition, what should I do then? But in this case the State has provided no way; its very Constitution is the evil. This may seem to be harsh and stubborn and unconciliatory; but it is to treat with the utmost kindness and consideration the only spirit that can appreciate or deserves it. So is an change for the better, like birth and death which convulse the body.

Continued on next page ▶

Sample Student Commentary

[35] Again Thoreau says we are not responsible for ending injustice, but we must not support or contribute to it.

Synthesis Sample 1:

Source C
Map: Westward Expansion.

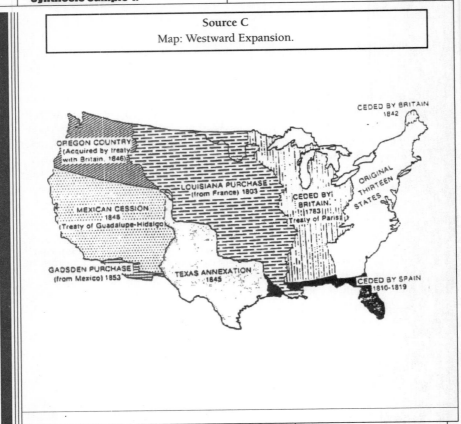

Continued on next page ▶

Synthesis Sample 1:

Source D
Thomas Jefferson's Letter to William Henry Harrison, 1803

As President of the United States, Thomas Jefferson pursued a policy toward Native American nations that had two primary goals. The first was to ensure the security of the United States allying Indian nations with the United States through treaties. Granted, these treaties were written to facilitate the United States' acquisition of land and increase trade, but they were also drafted to prevent Native American nations from allying themselves with European powers, namely England in Canada and Spain in the regions of Florida, the Gulf Coast, and lands west of the Mississippi River. Jefferson's second goal was to further the program— begun under President Washington and then Secretary of War Henry Knox—of gradual assimilation of Native Americans (Jefferson and his colleagues called it "civilizing the Indians"). Through treaties and trade, Jefferson hoped to continue to urge American Indians to adopt European agricultural practices, shift from a nomadic to a sedentary way of life, and thus open hunting grounds for further white settlement.

President Thomas Jefferson to William Henry Harrison, Governor of the Indiana Territory, 1803

You will receive from the Secretary of War ... from time to time information and instructions as to our Indian affairs. These communications being for the public records, are restrained always to particular objects and occasions; but this letter being unofficial and private,[36] I may with safety give you a more extensive view of our policy respecting the Indians, that you may the better comprehend the parts dealt out to you in detail through the official channel, and observing the system of which they make a part, conduct yourself in unison with it in cases where you are obliged to act without instruction. Our system is to live in perpetual peace with the Indians, to cultivate an affectionate attachment from them, by everything just and liberal which we can do for them within the bounds of reason, and by giving them effectual protection against wrongs from our own people.[37] The decrease of game rendering their subsistence by hunting insufficient, we wish to draw them to agriculture, to spinning and weaving. The latter branches they take up with

Continued on next page ▶

Sample Student Commentary

[36] Interesting. As early as the administration of the third president, government policies were enacted in secret.

[37] These sound like worthy goals.

Synthesis Sample 1:

great readiness, because they fall to the women, who gain by quitting the labors of the field for, those which are exercised within doors.[38] When they withdraw themselves to the culture of a small piece of land, they will perceive how useless to them are their extensive forests, and will be willing to pare them off from time to time in exchange for necessaries for their farms and families. To promote this disposition to exchange lands, which they have to spare and we want, <u>for necessaries, which we have to spare and they want, we shall push our trading uses,</u>[39] and be glad to see the good and influential individuals among them run in debt, because we observe that <u>when these debts get beyond what the individuals can</u> pay, they become willing to lop them off <u>by a cession of lands.</u>[40] At our trading houses, too, we mean to sell so low as merely to repay us cost and charges, so as neither to lessen or enlarge our capital. This is what private traders cannot do, for they must gain; they will consequently retire from the competition, and <u>we shall thus get clear of this pest</u> without giving offence or umbrage to the Indians.[41] In this way our settlements will gradually <u>circumscribe</u>[42] and approach the Indians, and they will in time either incorporate with us a citizens or the United States, or remove beyond the Mississippi. The former is certainly <u>the termination of their history</u>[43] most happy for themselves; but, in the whole course of this, it is essential to cultivate their love. As to their fear, we presume that our strength and their weakness is now so visible that they must see we have only to shut our hand to crush them, and that all our liberalities to them proceed from motives of pure humanity only.[44] Should any tribe be foolhardy enough to take up the hatchet at any time, the seizing the whole country of that tribe, and driving them across the Mississippi, as the only condition of peace, would be an example to others, and a furtherance of our final consolidation.

Continued on next page ▶

Sample Student Commentary

[38] This is a description of the "civilizing" program mentioned in the introductory notes.

[39] Still sounds ethical and just.

[40] This seems perhaps a little unethical.

[41] Is the "pest" Jefferson is referring to the Native American presence or simply Native American ownership of land that the United States wants?

[42] *Circumscribe* means to limit or confine.

[43] An ominous phrase. By some modern standards, this kind of forced assimilation would be considered a form of genocide.

[44] Behind the nation's official policy lies this thinly veiled threat of annihilation.

Synthesis Sample 1:

> **Source E**
> Thomas Jefferson's Indian Addresses: To the Brothers of
> the Choctaw Nation, December 17, 1803

The notion of "civilizing" the indigenous Americans originated with George Washington and was thoroughly in keeping with Jefferson's Enlightenment principles, especially the theory of "environmentalism," which held that environment, especially climate and geography, shaped human appearance, culture, and political organization. Environmentalism was the theory Europeans used to judge that the plants, animals—and the native peoples—of America were inferior to those of Europe. While Jefferson embraced environmentalism, he disagreed that Native Americans were inherently inferior to Europeans. It was the Indians' semi-nomadic way of life that led Jefferson and others to consider Indians "savages." If they were to adopt European-style agriculture and live in European-style towns and villages, then they would rise from "savagery" to "civilization" and eventually become the white man's equal.

In a letter to William Henry Harrison, then governor of the Indiana Territory (see Source D), Jefferson suggested that if Native Americans could be encouraged to purchase goods on credit, they would fall into debt, which they could relieve through the sale of lands to the government. The "civilization program" thus profited the Indians by "raising" them to equality with whites. At the same time, it furthered the United States' territorial interests.

BROTHERS OF THE CHOCTAW NATION:

We have long heard of your nation as a numerous, peaceable, and friendly people; but this is the first visit we have had from its great men at the seat of our government. I welcome you here; am glad to take you by the hand, and to assure you, for your nation, that we are their friends. Born in the same land, we ought to live as brothers, doing to each other all the good we can, and not listening to wicked men, who may endeavor to make us enemies. By living in peace, we can help and prosper one another; by waging war, we can kill and destroy many on both sides; but those who survive will not be the happier for that. Then, brothers, let it forever be peace and good neighborhood between us.

Continued on next page ▶

Synthesis Sample 1:

Our seventeen States compose a great and growing nation. Their children are as the leaves of the trees, which the winds are spreading over the forest. But we are just also. We take from no nation what belongs to it. Our growing numbers make us always willing to buy lands from our red brethren, when they are willing to sell. But be assured <u>we never mean to disturb them in their possessions</u>.[45] On the contrary, the lines established between us by mutual consent, shall be sacredly preserved, and <u>will protect your lands from all encroachments</u> by our own people or any others.[46] We will give you a copy of the law, made by our great Council, for punishing our people, who may encroach on your lands, or injure you otherwise. Carry it with you to your homes, and preserve it, as the shield which we spread over you, to protect your land, your property and persons.

It is at the request which you sent me in September, signed by Puckshanublee and other chiefs, and which you now repeat, that I listen to your proposition to sell us lands. You say you owe a great debt to your merchants, that you have nothing to pay it with but lands, and <u>you pray us to take lands, and pay your debt</u>.[47] The sum you have occasion for, brothers, is a very great one. We have never yet paid as much to any of our red brethren for the purchase of lands. You propose to us some on the Tombigbee, and some on the Mississippi. Those on the Mississippi suit us well. We wish to have establishments on that river, as resting places for our boats, to furnish them provisions, and to receive our people who fall sick on the way to or from New Orleans, which is now ours. <u>In that quarter, therefore, we are willing to purchase as much as you will spare</u>.[48] But as to the manner in which the line[49] shall be run, we are not judges of it here, nor qualified to make any bargain. But we will appoint persons hereafter to treat with you on the spot, who, knowing the country and quality of the lands, will be better able to agree with you on a line which will give us a just equivalent for the sum of money you want paid.

Continued on next page ▶

Sample Student Commentary

[45] This was the United States' official policy, to buy land when available but never to coerce.

[46] Jefferson is saying that it is a sacred trust that Europeans will respect the land-ownership rights of the Native Americans.

[47] This is precisely the plan Jefferson described to Harrison in Source D. Apparently it was working.

[48] Apparently after the Indians are driven into debt and offer to sell their land, there is still no guarantee that the offered lands will be bought or bought at a price to allow the Indians to pay their debts.

[49] By "line," Jefferson most likely means the lines defining the lands to be bought.

Synthesis Sample 1:

You have spoken, brothers, of the lands which your fathers formerly sold and marked off to the English, and which they ceded to us with the rest of the country they held here; and you say that, though you do not know whether your fathers were paid for them, you have marked the line over again for us, and do not ask repayment. It has always been the custom, brothers, when lands were bought of the red men, to pay for them immediately, and none of us have ever seen an example of such a debt remaining unpaid. It is to satisfy their immediate wants that the red men have usually sold lands; and in such a case, they would not let the debt be unpaid. The presumption from custom then is strong; so it is also from the great length of time since your fathers sold these lands. But we have, moreover, been informed by persons now living, and who assisted the English in making the purchase, that the price was paid at the time. Were it otherwise, as it was their contract, it would be their debt, not ours.[50]

I rejoice, brothers, to hear you propose to become cultivators of the earth for the maintenance of your families.[51] Be assured you will support them better and with less labor, by raising stock and bread, and by spinning and weaving clothes, than by hunting. A little land cultivated, and a little labor, will procure more provisions than the most successful hunt; and a woman will clothe more by spinning and weaving, than a man by hunting. Compared with you, we are but as of yesterday in this land. Yet see how much more we have multiplied by industry, and the exercise of that reason which you possess in common with us. Follow then our example, brethren, and we will aid you with great pleasure.

The clothes and other necessaries which we sent you the last year, were, as you supposed, a present from us. We never meant to ask land or any other payment for them; and the store which we sent on, was at your request also; and to accommodate you with necessaries at a reasonable price, you wished of course to have it on your land; but the land would continue yours, not ours.[52]

Continued on next page ▶

Sample Student Commentary

[50] But Jefferson says the Choctaws were not asking for payment for those lands, so this does not seem like a major issue.

[51] That is the goal of the "civilization program" begun under Washington.

[52] Is Jefferson referring to a store that was placed on Indian land to sell goods to the Indians? Is this perhaps how they were seduced into debt?

Synthesis Sample 1:

As to the removal of the store,[53] the interpreter, and the agent, and any other matters you may wish to speak about, the Secretary at War will enter into explanations with you, and whatever he says, you may consider as said by myself, and what he promises you will be faithfully performed.

I am glad, brothers, you are willing to go and visit some other parts of our country. Carriages shall be ready to convey you, and you shall be taken care of on your journey; and when you shall have returned here and rested yourselves to your own mind, you shall be sent home by land. We had provided for your coming by land, and were sorry for the mistake which carried you to Savannah instead of Augusta, and exposed you to the risks of a voyage by sea. Had any accident happened to you, though we could not help it, it would have been a cause of great mourning to us. But we thank the Great Spirit who took care of you on the ocean, and brought you safe and in good health to the seat of our great Council; and we hope His care will accompany and protect you, on your journey and return home; and that He will preserve and prosper your nation in all its just pursuits.

Continued on next page ▶

Sample Student Commentary

[53] It is not completely clear, but it seems as if the Choctaw may have requested the removal of the store to prevent their incurring further debt.

Synthesis Sample 1:

Source F
painting: *American Progress* (1872), John Gast
text: Croffut, George A. "Subject,
The United States of America,"1873.

This painting by John Gast is called American Progress. *The figure of* Columbia, *a popular personification of the United States, leads civilization westward. Native Americans and animals flee as American settlers journey west by covered wagon, coach, and rail.*

Continued on next page ▶

Sample Student Commentary

Why is Columbia a woman? Why is she so scantily dressed? He left breast is nearly exposed. Is there symbolism? The heart is generally believed to be behind the left breast.

Notice the sun shining to the east and the darkness and clouds to the west.

In her right hand is a book and a coil of telegraph wire. Behind her trails a line of telegraph poles as if she is laying the wire herself as she travel westward.

One of the "Indians" looks as if he is shaking his fist at her.

Synthesis Sample 1:

George A. Croffut, a publisher of travel literature encouraging Americans to travel west, published Gast's iconic image in his magazine, Crofutt's Western World. He wrote the following to accompany the image. The image and commentary quickly became popular color lithographs that people purchased to display in their homes.

Subject, The United States of America

This rich and wonderful country—the progress of which at the present time, is the wonder of the old world—was until recently, inhabited exclusively by the lurking savage and wild beasts of prey.[54] If the rapid progress of the "Great West" has surprised our people, what will those of other countries think of the "Far West," which was destined at an early day, to be the vast granary,[55] as it is now the treasure chamber of our country?...

In the foreground, the central and principal figure, a beautiful and charming Female, is floating westward through the air bearing on her forehead the "Star of Empire..."[56] On the right of the picture is a city, steamships, manufactories, schools and churches over which beams of light are streaming and filling the air—indicative of civilization. The general tone of the picture on the left declares darkness, waste and confusion.[57] From the city proceed the three great continental lines of railway... Next to these are the transportation wagons, overland stage, hunters, gold seekers, pony express, pioneer emigrant and the warrior dance of the "noble red man." Fleeing from "Progress"...are Indians, buffaloes, wild horses, bears, and other game, moving Westward, ever Westward, the Indians with their squaws, papooses, and "pony lodges," turn their despairing faces towards, as they flee the wondrous vision.[58] The "Star" is *too much for them.*

...What home, from the miner's humble cabin to the stately marble mansion of the capitalist, should be without this Great National Picture,[59] which illustrates in the most artistic manner all the gigantic results of the American Brains and Hands! Who would not have such a beautiful token to remind them of the country's grandeur and enterprise which have cause the mighty wilderness to blossom like the rose!!!

Continued on next page ▶

Sample Student Commentary

[54] Very different word choice from Jefferson's brotherly language (Source E).

[55] A now-familiar metaphor: the nation's "bread basket."

[56] Empire...?

[57] City, manufacturing = civilization. This is in keeping with—but a vast extension of—Jefferson's encouragement of the Choctaws to support themselves by "industry."

[58] Again, this sentiment is very different from Jefferson's attitude. Remember that in his address to the Choctaws, he wrote of "that reason which you possess in common with us."

[59] So, ultimately, this explanation of the painting is an advertisement.

Synthesis Sample 1:

Source G
The Indian Removal Act of 1830

The Indian Removal Act of 1830

The Indian Removal Act was signed into law by President Andrew Jackson on May 28, 1830. It was a controversial and divisive bill from the start, passing the Senate on a margin of only 9 senators (28 to 19) and the House by an even smaller margin of 5 (102 to 97). The bill originated on December 8, 1829, when, in his first State of the Union address, President Jackson established as his administration's priority to impose the sovereignty of the states over the sovereignty of Indian nations and to recommend removal of all eastern Indian nations to lands west of the Mississippi River. In his December 8 speech, President Jackson asked "whether something can be done, consistently with the rights of the States, to preserve this much-injured race." He then asked the combined houses to consider "the propriety of setting apart an ample district west of the Mississippi, and without the limit of any State or Territory now formed, to be guaranteed to the Indian tribes as long as they shall occupy it." This act was Congress's response to Jackson's proposition. Despite Jackson's stated desire to "preserve this much-injured race," the resultant removal of tribes has come to be known as the "Trail of Tears."

CHAP. CXLVIII.—An Act to provide for an exchange of lands with the Indians residing in any of the states or territories, and for their removal west of the river Mississippi.

Be it enacted by the Senate and House of Representatives of the United States of America, in Congress assembled, That it shall and may be lawful for the President of the United States to cause so much of <u>any territory belonging to the United States, west of the river Mississippi, not included in any state or organized territory, and to which the Indian title has been extinguished,</u>[60] as he may judge necessary, to be divided into a suitable number of districts, for the reception of such tribes or nations of <u>Indians as may choose to exchange the lands where they now reside,</u>[61] <u>and remove there;</u> and to cause each of said districts to be so described by natural or artificial marks, as to be easily distinguished from every other.

Continued on next page ▶

Sample Student Commentary

[60] Sounds like a return of Indian land to the Indians, as long as the land is not a part of a state or territory.

[61] Does this act extend to Native Americans the right to choose whether or not to relocate?

Synthesis Sample 1:

SEC. 2. *And be it further enacted*, That it shall and may be lawful for the President to exchange any or all of such districts, so to be laid off and described, with any tribe or nation within the limits of any of the states or territories, and with which <u>the United States have</u>[62] existing treaties, for the whole or any part or portion of the territory claimed and occupied by such tribe or nation, within the bounds of any one or more of the states or territories, where the land claimed and occupied by the Indians, is owned by the United States, or the United States are bound to the state within which it lies to <u>extinguish the Indian claim thereto.</u>[63]

SEC. 3. *And be it further enacted*, That in the making of any such exchange or exchanges, it shall and may be lawful for the President solemnly to assure the tribe or nation with which the exchange is made, that the United States will <u>forever secure and guaranty to them, and their heirs or successors</u>, the country so exchanged with them;[64] and if they prefer it, that the United States will cause a patent or grant to be made and executed to them for the same: Provided always, That such lands shall revert to the United States, <u>if the Indians become extinct, or abandon the same.</u>[65]

SEC. 4. *And be it further enacted*, That if, upon any of the lands now occupied by the Indians, and to be exchanged for, there should be such improvements as add value to the land claimed by any individual or individuals of such tribes or nations, it shall and may be lawful for the President to cause such value to be ascertained by appraisement or otherwise, and to cause such ascertained value to be <u>paid to the person or persons rightfully claiming such improvements.</u>[66] And upon the payment of such valuation, the improvements so valued and paid for, shall pass to the United States, and possession shall not afterwards be permitted to any of the same tribe.

Continued on next page ▶

Sample Student Commentary

[62] Notice the use of the plural. Not the United States has, but the United States have. In 1830, the U.S. still perceives itself as a collective of individuals rather than a unified entity.

[63] This act seems to require the United States to "extinguish" any Native American claim to land within a state or territory.

[64] The land given the Native American nations west of the Mississippi is to be guaranteed "forever" to the Indians and their heirs.

[65] Perhaps an ominous provision.

[66] Individual Native Americans are to be compensated for any improvements they have made to the land they are relinquishing.

Synthesis Sample 1:

SEC. 5. *And be it further enacted*, That upon the making of any such exchange as is contemplated by this act, it shall and may be lawful for the President to cause such aid and <u>assistance</u> to be furnished to the <u>emigrants</u>[67] as may be necessary and proper to enable them to remove to, and settle in, the country for which they may have exchanged;[68] and also, to give them such aid and assistance as may be necessary for their support and subsistence for the first year after their removal.

SEC. 6. *And be it further enacted*, That it shall and may be lawful for the President to cause such tribe or nation to be protected, at their new residence, against all interruption or disturbance <u>from any other tribe or nation of Indians, or from any other person or persons whatever.</u>[69]

SEC. 7. *And be it further enacted*, That it shall and may be lawful for the President to have the same superintendence and care over any tribe or nation in the country to which they may remove, as contemplated by this act, that he is now authorized to have over them at their present places of residence: *Provided*, <u>That nothing in this act contained shall be construed as authorizing or directing the violation of any existing treaty between the United State and any of the Indian tribes.</u>[70]

SEC. 8. *And be it further enacted*, That for the purposes of giving effect to the provisions of this act, the sum of five hundred thousand dollars is hereby appropriated, to be paid out of any money in the treasury, not otherwise appropriated.

Sample Student Commentary

[67] Emigrants are people who leave a place.

[68] The president may authorize "help" in the Native Americans' leaving the old land and moving to the new.

[69] Protection of one nation from another.

[70] This act is not intended to violate any existing treaty.

Your AP test booklet will not provide anything beyond the initial assignment and the sources. Before you write your essay, however, you should make sure you have an answer to the following questions:

1. **What will the central argument of your essay be? Write a one- or two-sentence statement on what you are going to say in your essay.**

   I am going to repudiate the notion of Manifest Destiny. If the United States had really been destined by God to expand over the entire continent, the fulfillment of that destiny would not have required the U.S. to break faith, violate treaties, or participate in what could actually be considered a type of genocide.

2. **Which three or four sources resonate most strongly with you? Why?**

   Source D, Jefferson's letter to William Henry Harrison—Jefferson admits in a private letter that there is a "hidden agenda" behind the official assimilation (civilization) program, and he explains how it is going to be implemented.

   Source E, Jefferson's address to the Choctaw Nation—This shows that the plan revealed in the letter to Harrison is, in fact, working. It also illustrates the two-faced nature of the government's policy toward Native Americans—they are our brothers, but we will trick them into giving us their land.

   Source G, the Indian Removal Act—This shows the "hidden agenda" coming to its completion. It is sort of the next step for those Native Americans who did not fall into the "civilizing" trap.

3. **What specific facts or insights does each of your chosen sources provide for you?**

   First source:

   Source D, Jefferson's letter to William Henry Harrison:

   - *this is a private note: "this letter being unofficial and private, I may with safety give you a more extensive view of our policy respecting the Indians."*

 Whether you are allowed to underline in your text or you will have to copy quotations like this, the fact is that quoting key portions of the text is necessary for a top-scoring essay.

   - *the plan is to entice the Native Americans into debt: "we shall push our trading uses, and be glad to see ... them run in debt..."*

   - *to pay off these debts, they will sell their land: "when these debts get beyond what the individuals can pay, they become willing to lop them off by a cession of lands."*

   - *he's also going to fix prices to drive out private competition and force the Native Americans to shop at government-sponsored stores: ""we mean to sell* so low as merely to repay us cost ... This is what private traders cannot do ... [and] ... they will consequently retire from the competition..."

- The enticement into debt and the price-fixing just seems unethical if not downright illegal.

- There seem to be threats of war, annihilation—genocide? "[Assimilation] is certainly the termination of their history most happy for themselves: ... we presume that our strength and their weakness is now so visible that they must see we have only to shut our hand to crush them ... Should any tribe be foolhardy enough to take up the hatchet at any time, the seizing the whole country of that tribe, and driving them across the Mississippi ... would be an example to others, and a furtherance of our final consolidation.

- What does Jefferson mean by the "final consolidation"?

 At this point, it is fine for this student to ask questions. This is still his idea-gathering and note-taking stage.

Second source:

Source E, Jefferson's address to the Choctaw Nation:

- Jefferson states plainly that alliances between the U.S. and Native American nations are sacred and inviolable: "Our growing numbers make us always willing to buy lands from our red brethren, when they are willing to sell. But be assured we never mean to disturb them in their possessions. On the contrary, the lines established between us by mutual consent, shall be sacredly preserved, and will protect your lands from all encroachments by our own people or any others."

- The plan outlined by Jefferson in his letter to Harrison is working. Representatives of the Choctaws have offered to sell some of their land in order to pay off debt: "It is at the request which you sent me in September ...that I listen to your proposition to sell us lands. You say you owe a great debt to your merchants, that you have nothing to pay it with but lands, and you pray us to take lands, and pay your debt."

- But even though the debt was encouraged by U.S. traders, the government is still going to negotiate price and maybe not even buy the offered land: "The sum you have occasion for, brothers, is a very great one. We have never yet paid as much to any of our red brethren for the purchase of lands. You propose to us some on the Tombigbee, and some on the Mississippi. Those on the Mississippi suit us well ... In that quarter, therefore, we are willing to purchase as much as you will spare."

- The Choctaws' debt seems to be so severe that they may actually have asked to have the store removed. (Of course, it is a government store because Jefferson said they were going to undersell private stores and drive out the competition.): "As to the removal of the store, the interpreter, and the agent, and any other matters you may wish to speak about, the Secretary at War will enter into explanations with you, and whatever he says, you may consider as said by myself, and what he promises you will be faithfully performed."

 Note that this student is not only repeating ideas from the sources, but he is actually beginning to articulate his own ideas and clarify his own arguments.

Third source:

Source G, the Indian Removal Act

- This seems to be the "final consolidation" Jefferson wrote about in his letter to Harrison.
- Section 1 says that lands west of the Mississippi will be given to Native Americans in exchange for the lands they own east of the Mississippi.
- Section 3 sounds ominous. The U.S. gets the land back if the Native American populations ever fall into extinction: "such lands shall revert to the United States, if the Indians become extinct, or abandon the same."
- Section 5 seems to set up the event we call the "Trail of Tears": "it shall and may be lawful for the President to cause such aid and assistance to be furnished to the emigrants as may be necessary and proper to enable them to remove to, and settle in, the country for which they may have exchanged."

 Remember that you have been instructed to read all of the introductory material as well. That is where this insight comes from.

4. **What will be the main parts of your argument? In other words, what are the subpoints you are going to discuss in order to establish your main argument?**

   1. Procuring Native American land was a U.S. government policy long before it was considered the nation's "destiny."

   2. From the very beginning, the means by which these lands would be procured were deceptive and unethical.

   3. From the beginning, the true intent was not to assimilate Native Americans into a European-style life but to either remove them from society or annihilate them.

5. **What facts or insights from your sources are you going to provide to support each of your subpoints?**

 This question might seem to repeat Question 3, but it is important to organize your ideas according to your subpoints and not according to your sources.

Subpoint one: Procuring Native American land was a U.S. government policy long before it was considered the nation's "destiny."
- *Jefferson's mention of a "final consolidation" in his letter to Harrison.*
- *In address to Choctaws Jefferson says U.S. is "always willing" to buy land.*
- *Indian Removal Act seems to be the culmination of Jefferson's "final consolidation," consolidating all the Native Americans west of the Mississippi.*

Subpoint two: From the very beginning, the means by which these lands would be procured were deceptive and unethical.
- *Jefferson's letter to Harrison is private. The scheme that he can't reveal officially he calls "a more extensive view of our policy."*
- *The "voluntary" sale of Native American land is encouraged by enticing Native Americans into debt.*
- *This involves both extending unwarranted credit to the Native Americans and underselling private merchants to eliminate their competition.*
- *This is unethical to both Native Americans and American merchants.*
- *Address to Choctaws shows debt scheme to be working.*
- *Even after debt is built up, the government will "negotiate" the price—not allowing Native Americans to set their own price.*
- *Indian Removal Act has a provision for land reverting back to U.S. if Native Americans become extinct.*

Subpoint three: From the beginning, the true intent was not to assimilate Native Americans into a European-style life but to either remove them from society or annihilate them.
- *Point out again Jefferson's mysterious reference to a "final consolidation."*
- *In his letter to Harrison, Jefferson hints that assimilation should drive the Native Americans into extinction.*
- *Any failure of the Native Americans to assimilate peacefully could result in annihilation.*
- *Indian Removal Act is clearly the end result of this—Jefferson's "final consolidation."*

 Notice that, for each of the subpoints, this student has support from at least two different sources. This ensures that his essay will be organized around his points as specified in the instructions.

Once you have considered all of the above, you are ready to write your essay.

John L. O'Sullivan's phrase "Manifest Destiny" may have been adopted as the motto of the American attitude toward westward expansion, and it may have justified much of the United States' policy with Native Americans in the eighteenth and nineteenth centuries, but the notion that the United States had such a "manifest destiny" to expand over the entire North American continent was a sham.[1] It provided a convenient justification for deception, fraud, and violent cruelty that would never have been the result of a true divine mandate. The fraud is apparent when one considers that procuring Native American land was a U.S. government policy long before it was considered the nation's "destiny." From the very beginning, the means by which these lands would be procured were deceptive and unethical. It is also possible that the true intent of Native American policy from the very beginning had not been to assimilate Native Americans into a European-style life but to either remove them from society or annihilate them. "Manifest Destiny" was merely the idea that gave us an excuse for what we'd been doing all along.[2]

Procuring Native American land was a U.S. government policy long before it was considered the nation's "destiny."[3] In his letter to William Henry Harrison, Governor of the Indiana Territory (Source D), President Thomas Jefferson outlines a plan that he admits he cannot officially express. This plan involves essentially seducing the Native Americans into selling their land. Jefferson concludes the letter that the United States' policy of buying Native American land and "civilizing" them is part of an overall plan that will result in "a furtherance of our final consolidation." One can only guess, at this point, what Jefferson meant by this. Similarly, in his Address to the Choctaw Nation (Source E), Jefferson declares that the United States is "always willing to buy lands from our red brethren, when they are willing to sell." He assures them, however, that "we [the United States] never mean to disturb them in their possessions." Yet this contradicts the plan he reveals to Harrison in Source D. Here, he explains that government-run stores will entice Native Americans to mount up debt that they would not be able to pay without selling the government some of their land. So, the President of the United States is admitting to a Native American nation that the U.S. is "always willing" to purchase Native American land, while he is also explaining to one of his territorial governors how those same Native Americans can be enticed to sell. Clearly, the nation intends to expand, but it does not necessarily intend to expand morally. This desire for expansion versus rightful acquisition of land reaches its culmination in the Indian Removal Act (Source G). Here, the land acquisition includes a removal of the Native Americans from their land to established "districts" west of the Mississippi River. "Manifest Destiny" seems more like "opportune growth."[4]

Not only was American expansion the intention for almost a century before the phrase "Manifest Destiny" was coined, the intention was clearly to acquire the lands by any means necessary—unethically, if necessary. In Source D, Jefferson writes to Harrison, "this letter being unofficial and private, I may with safety give

---

Scorer Commentary

[1] There is no harm in "borrowing" words and phrases directly from the instructions. Notice that this student cleverly ends his recap of the question with his thesis, his repudiation of the attitude.

[2] With its introduction to the issue, statement of thesis, and specification of its subpoints, this is a good introduction. Notice that the sources are not mentioned in the intro. The essay is about the student's argument, not about the sources.

[3] This student is apparently going to follow the typical five-paragraph-essay format, which can be very helpful for an essay assignment like this.

[4] This first body paragraph stays fairly focused on the first subpoint.

you a more extensive view of our policy respecting the Indians." This policy is to lure the Native Americans into excessive debt so that they will be willing to sell their land to repay the debt. In Source E, we find that this scheme actually worked. Jefferson says to the leaders of the Choctaw nation, "You say you owe a great debt to your merchants, that you have nothing to pay it with but lands, and you pray us to take lands, and pay your debt." But not only were the Native Americans being lured into debt, government policy made certain that that debt would be to the government and not to private merchants. In Source D, he writes to Harrison, "we mean to sell so low as merely to repay us cost … This is what private traders cannot do … [and] … they will consequently retire from the competition …" To assert on the one hand that it is America's "Manifest Destiny" to cover the continent, and to fulfill that "destiny" by deceiving and cheating both Native Americans and United States merchants is contradictory at best.[5] It is also an apparent contradiction that, while Jefferson advocates the Native Americans' assimilation, any threat of violence from the Native Americans would result in "the seizing the whole country of that tribe, and driving them across the Mississippi … would be an example to others, and a furtherance of our final consolidation." This is an eerie foreshadowing of some of the exact terms of the Indian Removal Act (Source G). That act, then, did not reflect any change in United States policy but was the goal from the very beginning. It also makes the Removal Act's provision in Section 3: "such lands [west of the Mississippi, granted to the Native Americans] shall revert to the United States, if the Indians become extinct, or abandon the same" more frightening.[6]

Jefferson's speculating that assimilation would be "the termination of their history most happy for themselves" (Source D), coupled with his insistence that "we have only to shut our hand to crush them," and his insistence that "Should any tribe be foolhardy enough to take up the hatchet at any time, the seizing the whole country of that tribe, and driving them across the Mississippi … would be an example to others" almost suggest that the terms of the Indian Removal Act were already being considered.

This, then, leads to the final point.[7] Despite the official program of "civilizing the Indians" put in place by George Washington, at least as early as the third president's administration, it is clear that the true intent was not to assimilate Native Americans into a European-style life but to either remove them from society or annihilate them. Sources D and E make it clear that the United States was not going to simply wait until the Native Americans were ready to sell their land. The letter to Harrison also opens the possibility of a mass removal of Native Americans who do not cooperate with United States policies. By the time we arrive at the Indian Removal Act (Source G), any notion that the United States' "destiny" to cover the entire continent has been ordained by God is almost laughable.

Scorer Commentary

[5] This student has been very careful not to lose sight of the assignment, which has to do with the concept of "Manifest Destiny."

[6] Again, the student has used more than one source to elaborate on his subpoint.

[7] Not a bad transition.

John L. O'Sullivan's phrase, "Manifest Destiny," may have captured the imaginations of a nation that had always had an aggressive policy of expansion, but the idea that God had ordained the United States to expand and cover all of North America is absurd. The expansionist intention of the nation, and the nation's disinterest in how to fulfill that intention clearly do not support the notion that it was God's will for the U.S. to defraud the Native Americans of their land and prepare for their eventual extinction. The notion was a convenient justification and nothing more.

Exercise One:

English Language and Composition
Reading Time: 15 minutes
Suggested Writing Time: 40 minutes

Freedom of Expression or **Free Speech** is a hotly debated topic, not only in the United States, but in many free nations of the Western world. Passions on both sides of the ideological aisle run high; up for debate is whether one's right to freedom of expression includes *all* expression of *all* ideas. Arguments include whether free speech laws protect the use of language considered by some to be "offensive," as well as non-verbal expressions of protest like destroying important and valued national, religious, or cultural symbols.

Is a student's right *not* to recite the Pledge of Allegiance protected by the First Amendment? A female student's right to wear a tuxedo for her senior photo? What constitutes protected expression, and how does one discern between what is protected and what is not?

Carefully read the following six sources, including whatever introductory information is provided for each. Synthesize information from at least three of the sources to formulate an argument on the scope or limits of the First Amendment's protection of free expression. Then incorporate that information into a coherent, well-developed essay that supports your argument.

Make sure that your argument is central; use the sources to illustrate and support your reasoning. Avoid merely summarizing the sources. Indicate clearly which sources you are drawing from, whether through direct quotation, paraphrase, or summary. You may cite the sources as Source A, Source B, etc., or by using the descriptions in parentheses.

Source A (First Amendment)
Source B (Barnette)
Source C (photograph)
Source D (Hazlewood)
Source E (Tinker)
Source F (cartoon)

Source A
The First Amendment to the Constitution of the
United States of America, ratified December 15, 1791.

While the proposed Constitution of the United States, signed in Philadelphia on September 17, 1787, faced many challenges on its nine-month path to ratification, one of the most severe was the call for a specific "Bill of Rights," a document that bore the weight of law and laid out explicitly the rights of citizens, rights that could not and would not be denied by the government.

This "Bill of Rights" took the form of the first ten amendments to the Constitution and was drafted and adopted almost immediately after the ratification of the Constitution.

The First Amendment is arguably the most important of these. It protects five of the most basic liberties: religion, speech, press, assembly, and the right to petition the government. These rights were the most fundamental demanded by those who initially opposed the Constitution.

Congress shall make no law respecting an establishment of religion, or prohibiting the free exercise thereof; or abridging the freedom of speech, or of the press; or the right of the people peaceably to assemble, and to petition the Government for a redress of grievances.

Source B
from:
WEST VIRGINIA STATE BOARD OF EDUCATION et al. v. BARNETTE et al.
Argued March 11, 1943.
Decided June 14, 1943.

On January 9, 1942, the West Virginia Board of Education adopted a series of resolutions that included a mandate for all students in West Virginia Public Schools to salute the United States flag and recite the Pledge of Allegiance as "a regular part of the program of activities in the public schools." All teachers and students were required to "participate in the salute honoring the Nation represented by the Flag," and that "refusal to salute the Flag [would] be regarded as an Act of insubordination, and shall be dealt with accordingly."

The right of a state school board to mandate the salute and recitation had been challenged in 1940 in Minersville School District v. Gobitis, *in which a Jehovah's Witness argued that the requirement violated his First Amendment rights to freedom of religion. In this case, the Supreme Court found in favor of the Minersville School District.*

In 1943, the Barnettes, a Jehovah's Witness family in West Virginia, challenged the West Virginia regulation. The United States District Court found in favor of the Burnettes. The West Virginia State School Board appealed directly to the Supreme Court.

Lastly, and this is the very heart of the Gobitis[1] opinion, it reasons that "National unity is the basis of national security," that the authorities have "the right to select appropriate means for its attainment," and hence reaches the conclusion that such compulsory measures toward "national unity" are constitutional.

Upon the verity of this assumption depends our answer in this case.

National unity as an end which officials may foster by persuasion and example is not in question. The problem is whether under our Constitution compulsion as here employed is a permissible means for its achievement.

Struggles to coerce uniformity of sentiment in support of some end thought essential to their time and country have been waged by many good as well as by evil men. Nationalism is a relatively recent phenomenon but at other times and places the ends have been racial or territorial security, support of a dynasty or regime, and particular plans for saving souls. As first and moderate methods to attain unity have failed, those bent on its accomplishment must resort to an ever-increasing severity. As governmental pressure toward unity becomes greater, so strife becomes more bitter as to whose unity it shall be. Probably no deeper division of our people could proceed from any provocation than from finding it necessary to choose what doctrine and whose program public

---

[1] *Minersville School District v. Gobitis* was a 1940 Supreme Court case in which the court found that the school district could indeed require Jehovah's Witnesses to salute the flag and recite the pledge. The suit had been pressed on the grounds that the requirement violated the Jehovah's Witnesses' religious freedoms.

educational officials shall compel youth to unite in embracing. Ultimate futility of such attempts to compel coherence is the lesson of every such effort from the Roman drive to stamp out Christianity as a disturber of its pagan unity, the Inquisition, as a means to religious and dynastic unity, the Siberian exiles as a means to Russian unity, down to the fast failing efforts of our present totalitarian enemies. Those who begin coercive elimination of dissent soon find themselves exterminating dissenters. Compulsory unification of opinion achieves only the unanimity of the graveyard.

It seems trite but necessary to say that the First Amendment to our Constitution was designed to avoid these ends by avoiding these beginnings. There is no mysticism in the American concept of the State or of the nature or origin of its authority. We set up government by consent of the governed, and the Bill of Rights denies those in power any legal opportunity to coerce that consent. Authority here is to be controlled by public opinion, not public opinion by authority.

The case is made difficult not because the principles of its decision are obscure but because the flag involved is our own. Nevertheless, we apply the limitations of the Constitution with no fear that freedom to be intellectually and spiritually diverse or even contrary will disintegrate the social organization. To believe that patriotism will not flourish if patriotic ceremonies are voluntary and spontaneous instead of a compulsory routine is to make an unflattering estimate of the appeal of our institutions to free minds. We can have intellectual individualism and the rich cultural diversities that we owe to exceptional minds only at the price of occasional eccentricity and abnormal attitudes. When they are so harmless to others or to the State as those we deal with here, the price is not too great. But freedom to differ is not limited to things that do not matter much. That would be a mere shadow of freedom. The test of its substance is the right to differ as to things that touch the heart of the existing order.

If there is any fixed star in our constitutional constellation, it is that no official, high or petty, can prescribe what shall be orthodox in politics, nationalism, religion, or other matters of opinion or force citizens to confess by word or act their faith therein. If there are any circumstances which permit an exception, they do not now occur to us.

We think the action of the local authorities in compelling the flag salute and pledge transcends constitutional limitations on their power and invades the sphere of intellect and spirit which it is the purpose of the First Amendment to our Constitution to reserve from all official control.

The decision of this Court in *Minersville School District v. Gobitis* and the holdings of those few *per curiam* decisions[2] which preceded and foreshadowed it are overruled, and the judgment enjoining enforcement[3] of the West Virginia Regulation is affirmed.

---

[2] A *per curiam* decision is a ruling issued by an appellate court of multiple judges in which the decision rendered is made by the court as a whole. Typically, a decision is rendered and signed by individual judges with other justices in the court having the opportunity to state and sign their dissent.

[3] This case was originally filed in U.S. District Court for the Southern District of West Virginia by the Barnettes representing themselves and others of their persuasion against the West Virginia State Board of Education. The court decided to restrain enforcement of the Board of Education's resolution. The Board of Education subsequently brought the case directly to the Supreme Court.

Source C
Photograph:

> ## Source D
> from:
> ## HAZLEWOOD SCHOOL DISTRICT v. KUHLMEIER
> Argued: October 13, 1987.
> Decided: January 13, 1988.

The Hazlewood case is a landmark Supreme Court case involving the extent to which school and district officials are entitled to censor school-sponsored newspapers that exist as a part of the school's curriculum. On May 10, 1983, Howard Emerson, the journalism teacher and faculty sponsor of the Hazlewood East High School Spectrum, *gave a proof copy of the* Spectrum's *final issue for the year, scheduled for distribution on May 13, to Hazlewood East principal Robert Eugene Reynolds. This principal review was standard practice in Hazlewood East.*

Principal Reynolds objected to two articles in the proof. His objections were based on concerns that the articles, if published, might violate certain students' right to privacy and breach professional journalists' rules of fairness. Due to the closeness of the publication date, as well as Reynolds' desire for the publication to be distributed on time and before the close of the school year, Reynolds, rather than requesting the two articles be rewritten, removed the two pages that included the articles from the paper.

Three Hazlewood graduates, former Spectrum *staff members, sued the Hazlewood School District, Principal Reynolds, and Howard Emerson on the grounds that by removing the two pages in question, Reynolds had violated the then-students' First Amendment right to freedom of speech.*

The United States District Court for the Eastern District of Missouri found in favor of the Hazlewood School District; the students' First Amendment rights had not been violated.

On appeal, the Court of Appeals for the Eighth Circuit reversed the District Court's decision, claiming the students' First Amendment rights had indeed been violated.

Justice Byron White wrote the majority decision of the United States Supreme Court.

Petitioners are the Hazlewood School District in St. Louis County, Missouri; various school officials; Robert Eugene Reynolds, the principal of Hazlewood East High School; and Howard Emerson, a teacher in the school district.

Respondents are three former Hazlewood East students who were staff members of Spectrum, the school newspaper. They contend that school officials violated their First Amendment rights by deleting two pages of articles from the May 13, 1983, issue of Spectrum.

Spectrum was written and edited by the Journalism II class at Hazlewood East. The newspaper was published every three weeks or so during the 1982-1983 school year.

More than 4,500 copies of the newspaper were distributed during that year to students, school personnel, and members of the community.

The Board of Education allocated funds from its annual budget for the printing of *Spectrum*. These funds were supplemented by proceeds from sales of the newspaper. The printing expenses during the 1982-1983 school year totaled $4,668.50; revenue from sales was $1,166.84. The other costs associated with the newspaper—such as supplies, textbooks, and a portion of the journalism teacher's salary—were borne entirely by the Board.

The Journalism II course was taught by Robert Stergos for most of the 1982-1983 academic year. Stergos left Hazelwood East to take a job in private industry on April 29, 1983, when the May 13 edition of *Spectrum* was nearing completion, and petitioner Emerson took his place as newspaper adviser for the remaining weeks of the term.

The practice at Hazelwood East during the spring 1983 semester was for the journalism teacher to submit page proofs of each *Spectrum* issue to Principal Reynolds for his review prior to publication. On May 10, Emerson delivered the proofs of the May 13 edition to Reynolds, who objected to two of the articles scheduled to appear in that edition. One of the stories described three Hazelwood East students' experiences with pregnancy; the other discussed the impact of divorce on students at the school.

Reynolds was concerned that, although the pregnancy story used false names "to keep the identity of these girls a secret," the pregnant students still might be identifiable from the text. He also believed that the article's references to sexual activity and birth control were inappropriate for some of the younger students at the school. In addition, Reynolds was concerned that a student identified by name in the divorce story had complained that her father "wasn't spending enough time with my mom, my sister and I" prior to the divorce, "was always out of town on business or out late playing cards with the guys," and "always argued about everything" with her mother. Reynolds believed that the student's parents should have been given an opportunity to respond to these remarks, or to consent to their publication. He was unaware that Emerson had deleted the student's name from the final version of the article.

Reynolds believed that there was no time to make the necessary changes in the stories before the scheduled press run, and that the newspaper would not appear before the end of the school year if printing were delayed to any significant extent. He concluded that his only options under the circumstances were to publish a four-page newspaper instead of the planned six-page newspaper, eliminating the two pages on which the offending stories appeared, or to publish no newspaper at all. Accordingly, he directed Emerson to withhold from publication the two pages containing the stories on pregnancy and divorce. He informed his superiors of the decision, and they concurred.

Respondents subsequently commenced this action in the United States District Court for the Eastern District of Missouri, seeking a declaration that their First Amendment rights had been violated, injunctive relief, and monetary damages. After a bench trial, the District Court denied an injunction, holding that no First Amendment violation had occurred.

The District Court concluded that school officials may impose restraints on students' speech in activities that are "an integral part of the school's educational function"—including the publication of a school-sponsored newspaper by a journalism class—so long as their decision has "a substantial and reasonable basis." The court found that Principal Reynolds' concern that the pregnant students' anonymity would be lost and their privacy invaded was "legitimate and reasonable," given "the small number of pregnant students at Hazelwood East and several identifying characteristics that were disclosed in the article." The court held that Reynolds' action was also justified "to avoid the impression that [the school] endorses the sexual norms of the subjects" and to shield younger students from exposure to unsuitable material. The deletion of the article on divorce was seen by the court as a reasonable response to the invasion of privacy concerns raised by the named student's remarks. Because the article did not indicate that the student's parents had been offered an opportunity to respond to her allegations, said the court, there was cause for serious doubt that the article complied with the rules of fairness which are standard in the field of journalism and which were covered in the textbook used in the Journalism II class. Furthermore, the court concluded that Reynolds was justified in deleting two full pages of the newspaper, instead of deleting only the pregnancy and divorce stories or requiring that those stories be modified to address his concerns, based on his reasonable belief that he had to make an immediate decision and that there was no time to make modifications to the articles in question.

The Court of Appeals for the Eighth Circuit reversed [the District Court's decision]. The court held at the outset that *Spectrum* was not only "a part of the school adopted curriculum," but also a public forum, because the newspaper was "intended to be and operated as a conduit for student viewpoint." The court then concluded that *Spectrum's* status as a public forum precluded school officials from censoring its contents except when "necessary to avoid material and substantial interference with school work or discipline ... or the rights of others."

The Court of Appeals found no evidence in the record that the principal could have reasonably forecast that the censored articles or any materials in the censored articles would have materially disrupted classwork or given rise to substantial disorder in the school. School officials were entitled to censor the articles on the ground that they invaded the rights of others, according to the court, only if publication of the articles could have resulted in tort liability to the school. The court concluded that no tort action for libel or invasion of privacy could have been maintained against the school by the subjects of the two articles or by their families. Accordingly, the court held that school officials had violated respondents' First Amendment rights by deleting the two pages of the newspaper.

We granted certiorari[1], and we now reverse.

* * *

The judgment of the Court of Appeals for the Eighth Circuit is therefore Reversed.

1. The two pages deleted from the newspaper also contained articles on teenage marriage, runaways, and juvenile delinquents, as well as a general article on teenage

---

[1] the term for an appeals court's agreeing to review a lower court's decision.

pregnancy. Reynolds testified that he had no objection to these articles, and that they were deleted only because they appeared on the same pages as the two objectionable articles.

2. The Statement also cited Tinker v. Des Moines Independent Community School Dist. (1969), for the proposition that

[o]nly speech that "materially and substantially interferes with the requirements of appropriate discipline" can be found unacceptable and therefore be prohibited. This portion of the Statement does not, of course, even accurately reflect our holding in Tinker. Furthermore, the Statement nowhere expressly extended the Tinker standard to the news and feature articles contained in a school-sponsored newspaper. The dissent apparently finds as a fact that the Statement was published annually in *Spectrum*; however, the District Court was unable to conclude that the Statement appeared on more than one occasion. In any event, even if the Statement says what the dissent believes that it says, the evidence that school officials never intended to designate *Spectrum* as a public forum remains overwhelming.

3. The distinction that we draw between speech that is sponsored by the school and speech that is not is fully consistent with Papish v. University of Missouri Board of Curators, (1973), which involved an off-campus "underground" newspaper that school officials merely had allowed to be sold on a state university campus.

4. The dissent perceives no difference between the First Amendment analysis applied in Tinker and that applied in Fraser. We disagree. The decision in Fraser rested on the "vulgar," "lewd," and "plainly offensive" character of a speech delivered at an official school assembly, rather than on any propensity of the speech to "materially disrup[t] classwork or involv[e] substantial disorder or invasion of the rights of others." Indeed, the Fraser Court cited as "especially relevant" a portion of Justice Black's dissenting opinion in Tinker "disclaim[ing] any purpose . . . to hold that the Federal Constitution compels the teachers, parents, and elected school officials to surrender control of the American public school system to public school students." Of course, Justice Black's observations are equally relevant to the instant case.

5. We therefore need not decide whether the Court of Appeals correctly construed Tinker as precluding school officials from censoring student speech to avoid "invasion of the rights of others," except where that speech could result in tort liability to the school.

6. We reject respondents' suggestion that school officials be permitted to exercise prepublication control over school-sponsored publications only pursuant to specific written regulations. To require such regulations in the context of a curricular activity could unduly constrain the ability of educators to educate. We need not now decide whether such regulations are required before school officials may censor publications not sponsored by the school that students seek to distribute on school grounds.

7. A number of lower federal courts have similarly recognized that educators' decisions with regard to the content of school-sponsored newspapers, dramatic productions,

and other expressive activities are entitled to substantial deference. We need not now decide whether the same degree of deference is appropriate with respect to school-sponsored expressive activities at the college and university level.

8. The reasonableness of Principal Reynolds' concerns about the two articles was further substantiated by the trial testimony of Martin Duggan, a former editorial page editor of the *St. Louis Globe Democrat* and a former college journalism instructor and newspaper adviser. Duggan testified that the divorce story did not meet journalistic standards of fairness and balance because the father was not given an opportunity to respond, and that the pregnancy story was not appropriate for publication in a high school newspaper because it was unduly intrusive into the privacy of the girls, their parents, and their boyfriends. The District Court found Duggan to be "an objective and independent witness" whose testimony was entitled to significant weight.

9. It is likely that the approach urged by the dissent would, as a practical matter, have far more deleterious consequences for the student press than does the approach that we adopt today. The dissent correctly acknowledges "[t]he State's prerogative to dissolve the student newspaper entirely." It is likely that many public schools would do just that rather than open their newspapers to all student expression that does not threaten "materia[l] disrup[tion of] classwork" or violation of "rights that are protected by law," regardless of how sexually explicit, racially intemperate, or personally insulting that expression otherwise might be.

Source E
from:
TINKER v. DES MOINES INDEPENDENT COMMUNITY SCHOOL DISTRICT
Argued: November 12, 1968.
Decided: February 24, 1969

In December 1965, a group of adults and students in Des Moines, Iowa, held a meeting at the home of sixteen-year-old Christopher Eckhardt. The group decided to wear black armbands during the holiday season as a means of publicly protesting the United States' growing involvement in the Vietnam conflict.

Learning of the planned protest, the principals of Des Moines schools met on December 14 and adopted a policy forbidding the wearing of such armbands. A student wearing an armband would be asked to remove it. If he refused, he would be suspended from school until he agreed to comply.

Christopher Eckhardt and his thirteen-year-old sister Mary Beth wore black armbands to their schools on December 16. Fifteen-year-old John Tinker wore his the next day. They were all suspended from school until they agreed to return without their armbands. They remained on suspension until after the holiday vacation, after the period during which they had planned to wear the armbands had ended.

A complaint filed in the United States District Court by the Tinker and Eckhardt families asked the court to enjoin school and district authorities from disciplining the suspended students and seeking nominal damages.

The District Court dismissed the complaint, claiming they found no violation of the students' rights.

On appeal, the Court of Appeals for the Eighth Circuit was divided, and the District Court's decision was upheld by default.

The Supreme Court agreed to review the case and the lower courts' decisions.

From the Supreme Court majority decision, written by Justice Abe Fortas:

The District Court recognized that the wearing of an armband for the purpose of expressing certain views is the type of symbolic act that is within the Free Speech Clause of the First Amendment. As we shall discuss, the wearing of armbands in the circumstances of this case was entirely divorced from actually or potentially disruptive conduct by those participating in it. It was closely akin to "pure speech" which, we have repeatedly held, is entitled to comprehensive protection under the First Amendment.

First Amendment rights, applied in light of the special characteristics of the school environment, are available to teachers and students. It can hardly be argued that either students or teachers shed their constitutional rights to freedom of speech or expression at the schoolhouse gate.

* * *

In West Virginia v. Barnette, supra, this Court held that, under the First Amendment, the student in public school may not be compelled to salute the flag. Speaking through Mr. Justice Jackson, the Court said:

The Fourteenth Amendment, as now applied to the States, protects the citizen against the State itself and all of its creatures—Boards of Education not excepted. These have, of course, important, delicate, and highly discretionary functions, but none that they may not perform within the limits of the Bill of Rights. That they are educating the young for citizenship is reason for scrupulous protection of Constitutional freedoms of the individual, if we are not to strangle the free mind at its source and teach youth to discount important principles of our government as mere platitudes.

On the other hand, the Court has repeatedly emphasized the need for affirming the comprehensive authority of the States and of school officials, consistent with fundamental constitutional safeguards, to prescribe and control conduct in the schools.

II

The problem posed by the present case does not relate to regulation of the length of skirts or the type of clothing, to hair style, or deportment. It does not concern aggressive, disruptive action or even group demonstrations. Our problem involves direct, primary First Amendment rights akin to "pure speech."

The school officials banned and sought to punish petitioners for a silent, passive expression of opinion, unaccompanied by any disorder or disturbance on the part of petitioners. There is here no evidence whatever of petitioners' interference, actual or nascent, with the schools' work or of collision with the rights of other students to be secure and to be let alone. Accordingly, this case does not concern speech or action that intrudes upon the work of the schools or the rights of other students.

Only a few of the 18,000 students in the school system wore the black armbands. Only five students were suspended for wearing them. There is no indication that the work of the schools or any class was disrupted. Outside the classrooms, a few students made hostile remarks to the children wearing armbands, but there were no threats or acts of violence on school premises.

* * *

In order for the State in the person of school officials to justify prohibition of a particular expression of opinion, it must be able to show that its action was caused by something more than a mere desire to avoid the discomfort and unpleasantness that always accompany an unpopular viewpoint. Certainly where there is no finding and no showing that engaging in the forbidden conduct would "materially and substantially interfere with the requirements of appropriate discipline in the operation of the school," the prohibition cannot be sustained [*Burnside v. Byars*, (1966)].

In the present case, the District Court made no such finding, and our independent examination of the record fails to yield evidence that the school authorities had reason to anticipate that the wearing of the armbands would substantially interfere with the work of the school or impinge upon the rights of other students. Even an official memorandum prepared after the suspension that listed the reasons for the ban on wearing the armbands made no reference to the anticipation of such disruption.

On the contrary, the action of the school authorities appears to have been based upon an urgent wish to avoid the controversy which might result from the expression, even by the silent symbol of armbands, of opposition to this Nation's part in the conflagration in Vietnam. It is revealing, in this respect, that the meeting at which the school principals decided to issue the contested regulation was called in response to a student's statement to the journalism teacher in one of the schools that he wanted to write an article on Vietnam and have it published in the school paper. (The student was dissuaded.)

It is also relevant that the school authorities did not purport to prohibit the wearing of all symbols of political or controversial significance. The record shows that students in some of the schools wore buttons relating to national political campaigns, and some even wore the Iron Cross, traditionally a symbol of Nazism. The order prohibiting the wearing of armbands did not extend to these. Instead, a particular symbol—black armbands worn to exhibit opposition to this Nation's involvement in Vietnam—was singled out for prohibition. Clearly, the prohibition of expression of one particular opinion, at least without evidence that it is necessary to avoid material and substantial interference with schoolwork or discipline, is not constitutionally permissible.

In our system, state-operated schools may not be enclaves of totalitarianism. School officials do not possess absolute authority over their students. Students in school, as well as out of school, are "persons" under our Constitution. They are possessed of fundamental rights which the State must respect, just as they themselves must respect their obligations to the State. In our system, students may not be regarded as closed-circuit recipients of only that which the State chooses to communicate. They may not be confined to the expression of those sentiments that are officially approved. In the absence of a specific showing of constitutionally valid reasons to regulate their speech, students are entitled to freedom of expression of their views. As Judge Gewin, speaking for the Fifth Circuit, said, school officials cannot suppress "expressions of feelings with which they do not wish to contend." *Burnside v. Byars* (1966).

* * *

The principle of these cases is not confined to the supervised and ordained discussion which takes place in the classroom. The principal use to which the schools are dedicated is to accommodate students during prescribed hours for the purpose of certain types of activities. Among those activities is personal intercommunication among the students. This is not only an inevitable part of the process of attending school; it is also an important part of the educational process. A student's rights, therefore, do not embrace merely the classroom hours. When he is in the cafeteria, or on the playing field, or on the campus during the authorized hours, he may express his opinions, even on controversial subjects like the conflict in Vietnam, if he does so without "materially and substantially interfer[ing] with the requirements of appropriate discipline in the operation of the school" and without colliding with the rights of others (*Burnside v. Byars*). But conduct by the student, in class or out of it, which for any reason—whether it stems from time, place, or type of behavior—materially disrupts classwork or involves substantial disorder or invasion of the rights of others is, of course, not immunized by the constitutional guarantee of freedom of speech. Cf. *Blackwell v. Issaquena County Board of Education* (1966).

Under our Constitution, free speech is not a right that is given only to be so circumscribed that it exists in principle, but not in fact. Freedom of expression would not truly exist if the right could be exercised only in an area that a benevolent government has provided as a safe haven for crackpots. The Constitution says that Congress (and the States) may not abridge the right to free speech. This provision means what it says.

* * *

If a regulation were adopted by school officials forbidding discussion of the Vietnam conflict, or the expression by any student of opposition to it anywhere on school property except as part of a prescribed classroom exercise, it would be obvious that the regulation would violate the constitutional rights of students, at least if it could not be justified by showing that the students' activities would materially and substantially disrupt the work and discipline of the school. In the circumstances of the present case, the prohibition of the silent, passive "witness of the armbands," as one of the children called it, is no less offensive to the Constitution's guarantees.

As we have discussed, the record does not demonstrate any facts which might reasonably have led school authorities to forecast substantial disruption of or material interference with school activities, and no disturbances or disorders on the school premises in fact occurred. These petitioners merely went about their ordained rounds in school. Their deviation consisted only in wearing on their sleeve a band of black cloth, not more than two inches wide. They wore it to exhibit their disapproval of the Vietnam hostilities and their advocacy of a truce, to make their views known, and, by their example, to influence others to adopt them. They neither interrupted school activities nor sought to intrude in the school affairs or the lives of others. They caused discussion outside of the classrooms, but no interference with work and no disorder. In the circumstances, our Constitution does not permit officials of the State to deny their form of expression.

We express no opinion as to the form of relief which should be granted, this being a matter for the lower courts to determine. We reverse and remand for further proceedings consistent with this opinion.

Reversed and remanded.

1. In *Burnside* [*Burnside v. Byars*], the Fifth Circuit ordered that high school authorities be enjoined[1] from enforcing a regulation forbidding students to wear "freedom buttons." It is instructive that, in *Blackwell v. Issaquena County Board of Education* (1966), the same panel on the same day reached the opposite result on different facts. It declined to enjoin enforcement of such a regulation in another high school where the students wearing freedom buttons harassed students who did not wear them, and created much disturbance.

2. *Hamilton v. Regents of Univ. of Cal.* (1934) is sometimes cited for the broad proposition that the State may attach conditions to attendance at a state university that require individuals to violate their religious convictions. The case involved dismissal of members of a religious denomination from a land-grant college for refusal to participate in military training. Narrowly viewed, the case turns upon the Court's conclusion that merely requiring a student to participate in school training in military "science" could not conflict with his constitutionally protected freedom of conscience. The decision cannot be taken as establishing that the State may impose and enforce any conditions that it chooses upon attendance at public institutions of learning, however violative they may be of fundamental constitutional guarantees. See, e.g., West Virginia v. Barnette (1943).

3. The only suggestions of fear of disorder in the report are these:

   A former student of one of our high schools was killed in Vietnam. Some of his friends are still in school, and it was felt that if any kind of a demonstration existed, it might evolve into something which would be difficult to control.

   Students at one of the high schools were heard to say they would wear armbands of other colors if the black bands prevailed.

   Moreover, the testimony of school authorities at trial indicates that it was not fear of disruption that motivated the regulation prohibiting the armbands; the regulation was directed against "the principle of the demonstration" itself. School authorities simply felt that "the schools are no place for demonstrations," and if the students didn't like the way our elected officials were handling things, it should be handled with the ballot box, and not in the halls of our public schools.

4. The District Court found that the school authorities, in prohibiting black armbands, were influenced by the fact that [t]he Vietnam War and the involvement of the United States therein has been the subject of a major controversy for some time. When the armband regulation involved herein was promulgated, debate over the Vietnam War had become vehement in many localities. A protest march against the war had been recently held in Washington, D.C. A wave of draft-card burning incidents protesting the war had swept the country. At that time, two highly publicized draft-card burning cases were pending in this Court. Both individuals supporting the war and those opposing it were quite vocal in expressing their views.

---

[1] In law, to be enjoined from doing something is to be legally forbidden to do it; to be enjoined to do something is to be legally required to do it.

5. After the principals' meeting, the director of secondary education and the principal of the high school informed the student that the principals were opposed to publication of his article. They reported that we felt that it was a very friendly conversation, although we did not feel that we had convinced the student that our decision was a just one.

6. In *Hammond v. South Carolina State College* (1967), District Judge Hemphill had before him a case involving a meeting on campus of 300 students to express their views on school practices. He pointed out that a school is not like a hospital or a jail enclosure. It is a public place, and its dedication to specific uses does not imply that the constitutional rights of persons entitled to be there are to be gauged as if the premises were purely private property.

Source F
cartoon: *Flag Burners* (2005), John Trevor

Before you write your essay, make sure you have an answer to the following questions:

1. **What will the central argument of your essay be? Write a one- or two-sentence statement on what you are going to say in your essay.**

2. **Which three or four sources resonate most strongly with you? Why?**

3. **What specific facts or insights does each of your chosen sources provide for you?**

   First source:

   Second source:

   Third source:

   Fourth source:

   Additional sources:

4. **What will be the main parts of your argument? In other words, what are the subpoints you are going to discuss in order to establish your main argument?**

5. **What facts or insights from your sources are you going to provide to support each of your subpoints?**

   Subpoint one:

   Subpoint two:

   Subpoint three:

   Additional subpoints:

Once you have considered all of the above, you are ready to write your essay.

APPENDICES

APPENDIX 1: Answer Keys

Chapter 1, Exercise One

1. While it is clear in the story that the season is early autumn (A), such a use of season would not be capitalized. (C) might be the most tempting choice for students who understand this idiomatic use of the word, and it is probably not completely wrong, but there is no mention of social activities in the story other than attending Sunday afternoon concerts in the park, and there are several allusions to the age and apparent loneliness of the majority of attendees at these concerts. (D) might tempt a few, but references to a seasonal change are few and mild. (E) is easily eliminated by the fact that the text states the band plays "every Sunday," including the prior Sunday, before the Season "had begun." The comparison of the number of people at this week's concert compared to last week's and the observation that the band seems to be playing better now that there were strangers present, clearly suggests that strangers—tourists—have arrived, and the Season has begun. **Thus, (B) is the best answer.**

2. (A), (B), and (C) are all materials out of which fashionable clothing is made, and it is clear through the entire story that Miss Brill judges others by their clothing (even as she misjudges the quality and presentability of her own). (D) and (E) are both objects associated with the people she observes. The cupboards (E) are the people's presumed homes and emphasizes her judgment of the people as lonely and isolated. There is, however, no judgment of the woman based on the type of hat she is wearing, only its age and condition. **Thus, (D) is the best answer.**

3. While both (A) and (E) are tempting, and to some degree correct, neither is the best of the five choices. Likewise, (B) is too general. (D) is probably the least tempting answer as, while color may be effectively associated with character, it is not generally considered a character technique. (C), however, is demonstrated by Mansfield's frequent contrast of the grey [sic] people and clothing, the colors of the younger attendees, the green of the bandstand with the yellow of the leaves. The vibrant blues and golds of the sky and ocean beyond the bandstand stand in stark contrast to the colorless suits and dingy hats of the elder patrons of the park. **Thus, (C) is the best answer.**

4. (B) might tempt some by the description of the way the "staggerers" come "suddenly" out into the open, stop, and stare, as if they realize they are late to the concert, but this interpretation is not supported by the rest of the description. The reference to "French Dolls" in the previous sentence is simply a metaphor for the cute little girls who are playing in the park with the "little boys with big white silk bows under their chins." There is nothing to suggest that either the girls or boys are playing with wind-up toys (C).

Certainly, there are musicians in this story, but nothing suggests that they or anyone else is inebriated. Thus, (D) is easily eliminated. Likewise, while Miss Brill notes that many of the park's patrons are old, none seems particularly "unsteady" (E), and the "staggerer" in the story is rescued by his mother. The sentences immediately before the one containing the "staggerer," however, are about the children playing: the boys with their silk bows, and the girls who look like pretty French dolls. The "staggerer," then comes out into the open, stops, stares, and then sits down "flop" on the ground. The mother, then, runs out to rescue him. Clearly, the image of a small child, just learning to walk, *staggering* out into the open and plopping onto the ground. **Thus, (A) is the best answer**.

5. While the story is told by a third-person narrator, there is virtually no narrative intrusion (A). Every detail the reader receives is filtered through Miss Brill's frame of reference. (B) is tempting because there is a good deal of indirect dialogue, and these summative/speculative passages do contribute significantly to the mood, but they alone do not account for the mood. (C) is factually incorrect. "Miss Brill" has a third-person narrator. (E) might tempt some who cannot distinguish between stream-of-consciousness, interior monologue, and indirect dialogue. While told strictly from Miss Brill's viewpoint and colored by her impressions and reactions, the story follows a logical order, the narrative is not interrupted by random or disconnected thoughts, and neither the protagonist's nor the narrator's frame of mind plays a significant role; thus, this is simply not a stream-of-consciousness story. The entire story is shaped by Miss Brill's impressions and reactions, *including her own misperception of herself*; thus, the poignancy at the end of the story is the result of her gaining new information—how other people actually see her. **Thus, (D) is the best answer.**

Chapter 1, Exercise Two

6. (A) might tempt some students, as there is considerable conversation about what's uncivil and rude, but the "madness" is not so much the result of the Hatter's and Hare's behavior as it is the result of the words they use and what those words mean. (B) is probably the least tempting choice as there is no suggestion of linguistic difficulties between Alice and anyone she encounters in Wonderland. (C) might also tempt some students, as both hatters and March hares were stereotypically associated with madness, but the passage does not rely only on readers' associations; it illustrates the characters' "madness." (E) might tempt a few, but a close examination of the characters' dialogue reveals the exact opposite. **The correct answer is (D)**. The chiasmus built on meaning what one says versus saying what one means and the issue of whether one can have more or less than none are the two clearest examples. The reader is most likely to understand the commonly accepted meanings of these phrases, while the Hare and Hatter are using them in their most literal sense. Thus, their meaning seems "mad" to the reader.

7. It is important for students to note that this question asks about the *language* of the passage and not the content. The student must, therefore, examine word choice, syntax, use of idioms, and so on. Those elements that apply to structure or meaning are probably eliminated simply by the fact that they do not necessarily apply to language. (A) is therefore eliminated because it points more to thesis and support than to language. (B) and (C) point more to meaning or theme than to the impact of language. (D) does suggest the impact of language on the reader and may actually tempt some students, but, while the wordplay and flawed logic are puzzling, the puzzlement is the means to an end, not the end itself. **Well beyond the comic situation and madcap characters, however, the essence of this passage is the wordplay, the puns, plays on sound and meaning, and so on. Thus, the best answer is clearly (E).**

8. Civility and incivility are issues in this passage, but most of the accusations of rudeness stem not from actual rudeness, but from the characters' inability to understand one another. Thus, (A) is eliminated. (C) might tempt some, but while Alice may be the first, she is certainly not the only character to act rudely. (D) might also tempt some, but it is impossible to state absolutely whether the Hatter and March Hare are caricatures or mere representations of ideas in folklore. Nor is the portrayal of these characters—caricature or not—the sole or primary point of the passage (E). (D) is fairly easily eliminated by the fact that none of the characters exhibit more than superficial humor, rudeness, or anything else that might be interpreted as an emotion. **Language, ambiguity, wordplay, the tension between literal and connotative meanings motivate the conflict and drive the plot of this passage. Thus, (B) is the best answer.**

9. This question is, of course, a strictly linguistic question that relies on the students' knowledge of parts of speech, speech patterns, and the idiosyncrasies of written and spoken language that the writers of an Advanced Placement exam will assume have been studied. It is an example of the only type of question that requires outside language likely to appear on an exam. Still, it illustrates the need to devote some time in an English language arts class to language arts. (B) is tempting, and might be a defensible choice, as homophones are pronounced the same, have different meanings, and may or may not be spelled the same; but it is not the *best* answer, given that homonym (A) is more strictly correct. (C) is eliminated by the fact that homographs are spelled the same but are pronounced differently, which is not the case with the two uses of *draw* in this passage. Synonyms (D) are different words with similar meanings, which is, of course, not the case with *draw*. Antonyms (E) are likewise different words, related by their antithetical meanings. **The correct answer is (A). Homonyms are two words that are spelled and pronounced identically but have different (but not necessarily antithetical) meanings.**

10. While (A) is not the chief source of comedy, it is apparent that Carroll chose a Mad Hatter and a March Hare for his characters in this scene specifically because of their associations with madness. (B) is eliminated by the many instances of Alice's not

understanding—and actually questioning—the conventions on which the tea party is based, as well as the instances in which the Wonderland characters are unable to understand Alice's point of view. (D) is easily eliminated because much of the comedy springs from the illogical sequence of topics in the conversation. Similarly, (E) is eliminated by the number of puns and absolute literal applications of many of the words and phrases. **The correct answer is (C). The humor in this scene is intellectual, not physical, and even what little physical humor there is—the dormouse's sleepiness and the arrangement of the table—are based on logic and stereotype; they are not broad or exaggerated enough to be considered slapstick.**

Chapter 1, Exercise Three

11. The phrase "little minds" occurs in the paragraph almost immediately after "little friends." Since "little" in the first phrase is literal, referring to the size and age of the friends, (A) and (C) are both tempting. The next sentence, however, says "All minds... whether they be men's or children's are little," thus eliminating these two choices. (B) is eliminated by the fact that, whether literal or somehow figurative, "little" is used in the sense of small, narrow, etc. "Little mind" is usually used as an insult, which would indicate (D), but the proximity of "little friends" and "little minds" makes this choice not completely satisfactory. Because there is the close association of "little minds" with "little friends," and a literal interpretation cannot be completely ruled out, yet there is the equally close association of "little minds" with "all minds...are little" and the judgmental interpretation cannot be completely ruled out, **(E) is the best answer.**

12. This is a relatively easy question for students who know that that fantasy (D) is an out-of-fashion denotation for the word. Others should be able to recognize that all of the words in the list (*faith, poetry, love, romance*) are nouns, so (A) and (B), which are adjectives, can be easily eliminated. Three of the terms (*faith, love, romance*) are abstract ideals, so (E) is unlikely. (C) can be either a noun or a verb, but even as a noun, it does not fit contextually with the ideals of faith and love or the concrete noun *poetry*. Fantasy (D), however, fits with the rest of the sentence as an abstract ideal that has the power to lift the veil to reveal the "supernal beauty and glory" of the "unseen world." It is also, as mentioned earlier, an outmoded denotation of the word. **Thus, (D) is the best answer.**

13. "Truth" is an abstract ideal, subject to a variety of understandings and uses. Also, the figure of Santa Claus is literally a fiction. (B) is eliminated by the fictional nature of Santa Claus. There is no context in the passage to support (C). In Church's letter, Santa Claus exists in the world of Virginia in the same sense that love and beauty exist in her world. (D) is tempting, but as with (C), in this letter, Santa Claus is not a metaphor, symbol, analogy, or any other device in which one thing represents or clarifies another.

(E) is unlikely as, whatever Santa Claus is in the context of this letter remains constant, along with the other ideals of love, fantasy, romance, and so on. **Church's frequent use of *romance*, however, gives evidence of (A)'s being the best answer.** Romance, in the sense of idealism, is the theme of Church's letter. Skeptics do not allow for ideals like love, imagination, poetry, and so one, to enrich their lives. These are the ones who deny the existence of Santa Claus. Thus, the truth of Santa Claus is an idealistic notion, and **(A) is the best answer.**

14. Clearly the writer of an editorial that asserts the existence of Santa Claus and criticizes his fellow human beings as little minded and skeptical is quite likely an idealist (A). Church's claim that Virginia's friends have been tainted by "the skepticism of a skeptical age" suggests both (B) and (D). The fact of the letter itself and that Church did not simply destroy the child's illusions supports (E). Even though Church accuses his fellow humans of being skeptical and little minded, the strong evidence of his idealism and his empathy for childhood do not support an interpretation that he was a misanthrope. **Thus, (C) is the best answer.**

15. In paragraph 4, Church asserts, "Nobody sees Santa Claus." He likewise reminds Virginia that no one has ever seen fairies dancing on the lawn. Silly as they may seem, these are facts; they are not unproven hypotheses (B) or untrue premises (D). As these statements (no one sees Santa, and Virginia has never seen fairies dance) are undeniable facts, any conclusion that follows, however faulty, is not begging the question (C). The mention of the baby's rattle is not an analogy; there is no comparison between the rattle and the unseen world because the "workings" of the rattle *can* be seen. **(A) is the best answer**. While Church does not explicitly claim that the existence of Santa and fairies must be true because they cannot be disproved, his reasoning is that no one's ever seeing them means nothing. In the absence of positive proof, he allows an absence of disproof to suffice.

Chapter 2, Exercise One

1. (A) is easily eliminated because the lines simply do not draw the listeners' attention either to themselves or to Brutus. (B) might tempt several students who misdiagnose the illogic of the sentences, but there are no contradictory sentiments or directives expressed in these sentences. (C) might tempt a few, but Brutus's intent is clear. He is essentially inviting the audience to shut up and take his word about what he is going to say. (E) is actually not incorrect, but condescension is an emotional flaw or a flaw in tone, not a structural flaw. Brutus's sentence structure and word choice, however, are circuitous (D). "Hear me for my cause…" could connote "listen to me" or "consider what I am saying," but he follows it with the command to be quiet so they can literally hear. The second phrase is even more convoluted. He asserts his status as evidence of the truth of what he is going to say, and then appeals to their belief in his honor as the

means by which they can accept what he has to say as truth. In both cases, cause and effect, claim and evidence become confused and unclear. **Thus, (D) is the best answer.**

2. The speech is certainly condescending, but this tone (B) is more evident in the word choice than in the specific devices Brutus employs. The content (C) is established by the fact of Caesar's death and funeral. The rhetoric of the speech might have an impact on how the hearers receive the content, but not on the content itself. Likewise, the intent (D) is independent of the specific devices used. The devices might help Brutus achieve his intent, but they do not form that intent for him. (E) is probably the least tempting choice as the language and language devices must have a much greater impact on the reception of the speech than on the delivery. Two speakers could deliver the same speech with the same rhetorical devices in two vastly different ways. Brutus primarily uses parallelism (…I loved Caesar less, but that I loved Rome more; As Caesar … I, as he… I, as he … I: but, as he … I); anaphora (Who is here so…); and symploce (If any, speak; for him have I offended), all of which have strong implications for ordering of ideas, transitions between ideas, and all of which contribute to the overall structure of a speech. **Thus, (A) is the best answer.**

3. (A) does not identify a real "distinction," unless one considers "logic" as a more formal manner of reasoning. Still, it is not the best choice of the five. (C) might tempt some who recognize that Antony's speech is in verse while Brutus's is in prose, but even Brutus's prose is rich with rhetoric and cannot really be described as "banal" or "humdrum." (D) is easily excluded by the understanding that Brutus's speech is in prose and, therefore, not in any formal metrical pattern. (E) likewise can be excluded by the understanding that, again while Brutus's speech is in prose, its richness of rhetoric clearly indicates careful planning. Brutus's speech is founded on his attempts to reason with the mob, to explain that killing Caesar was the rational choice, given the threat to their freedoms and liberties as Roman citizens. Antony appeals to the mob's emotions—appealing to Caesar supposed love of the mob, his heartbreak at having been betrayed by his friend Brutus, etc. **Thus, (B) is the best answer.**

4. (A) is actually Antony's purpose, and through the entire speech, he provides examples of Caesar's magnanimity, humility, and generosity, counters it with Brutus's assertion that Caesar was ambitious, and concludes [but] *Brutus is an honorable man.* The contrast of Brutus's "honor" with the concrete examples of his misrepresentation of the truth about Caesar eliminate (A). With the success of (A), (B) is eliminated. The mob will begin to distrust the "honorable man" who killed their strongest friend. (C) is less likely but is still achieved by the line in its context. The blame lies, not with Caesar, but with Brutus, who is an honorable mean." (D) is not unlike (A) and (B). By casting doubt on Brutus's honor, the supposedly honorable motives of all the conspirators comes into question. Variations of the "honorable man" line include at least two reference to "honorable men," thus involving all of the conspirators. Ironically, however, the repetition—especially in the context of the positive qualities Antony attributes to Caesar—serves more to weaken the

claim that Brutus is an honorable man than confirm it (like Gertrude's famous line in Act III, scene ii of *Hamlet*, "the Lady doth protest too much.") **Thus, (E) is the best answer.**

5. It is important that the student pay close attention to the wording of this question. It asks about *Shakespeare's* use of *paralepsis*, not Antony's. Therefore, the question is about the playwright's craft and how the play is constructed, not what is happening within the world of the play. This understanding quite easily excludes (A) and (D), which might be possible reasons for *Antony's* using the device in his speech. (C) and (E) do address Shakespeare's craft, but (C) is untrue because, even after the first mention of the will, Antony describes every gash in Caesar's cloak and names the conspirator who made it. So, he has not yet stopped talking about the conspirators. (E) is tempting, but it is the *entire speech* and Antony's ability to manipulate the mob that foreshadows Brutus's downfall, not this one device. By having Antony mention the will and then claim he will not read it, however, Shakespeare most certainly knows he will pique his audience's curiosity and listen more closely to the rest of the speech. **Thus, (B) is the best answer.**

Chapter 3, Exercise One

1. While both the narrator's and Emily's lives have been difficult and disappointing, the only mention of futility comes from Emily when she claims, "in a couple of years when we'll all be atom-dead they won't matter a bit." This futility is not connected with the ironing, so (A) can be eliminated. (C) is tempting, but the ironing is connected at the beginning of the story with the question asked by the counselor and at the end of the story with Emily herself. On the surface, (D) might tempt some, but it is actually the antithesis of what the narrator means at the end of the story. (E) is also tempting, since the mother is ironing, but the iron and the dress are more connected to Emily, but the difficulties of Emily's life including her infancy and childhood, not just her adolescence. The metaphoric significance of the iron, the dress, and the act of ironing is a little ambiguous. The narrator first suggests that the ironing represents the difficulty she has answering the counselor's question, perhaps her own guilt and sense of inadequacy: "what you asked me moves tormented back and forth with the iron." The story ends with the narrator's asking the counselor to reassure Emily that Emily is "more than this dress on the ironing board, helpless before the iron," suggesting that the iron represents those circumstances that determine the shape and character of a person and her life. The narrator wants Emily to know that Emily is *not* helpless like the dress. **Thus, (B) is the best answer.**

2. From the beginning of the story, it is clear that there is a second person either physically present or in the narrator's mind: "...what you asked me moves tormented back and forth..." Many students might be tempted by (A), but there are a few clues that the person to whom the mother is speaking is not physically present. First, whatever the means of the counselor's contact with the narrator, he/she asks the

mother "to come in and talk." This clearly eliminates (A). (B) is less tempting since Emily is cheerful when she arrives home, and this arrival occurs more than halfway through the story. (C) is tempting, since even the mother wonders what motivated the communication from the school, but with Emily's entrance, she notes, "Whatever it was that occasioned your call did not happen today." (D) is easily eliminated by the narrator's quoting the invitation to come in and talk. (E) is the only fully plausible choice. The counselor is not present. This is clearly established by the invitation for the mother to "come in and talk," and the narrator's mentioning, "Ronnie is calling. He is wet and I change him," which she would not have to tell a person in the room. Still, some sort of communication has arrived, either a note, as would seem likely by what the mother quotes in the beginning of the story: "I wish you would manage the time to come in and talk with me…" or a phone call as suggested by the mother's observing, "Whatever it was that occasioned your call did not happen today." Whatever the case, whether note or telephone call, **(E) is the best answer.**

3. Although the story is a reminiscence, almost an extended flashback, the information presented by the narrator about Emily begins with Emily's infancy and works through her childhood, adolescence, school years, and so on. The reminiscence ends at the "present," with Emily arriving home and the youngest baby needing to be changed and fed. (A) is therefore eliminated. The direct dialogue, "You're all right, darling, go to sleep, it's just a dream," and indirect dialogue, "Months later she told me how she had taken pennies from my purse to buy him candy," eliminate (B) and (E). (C) is clearly incorrect, as the characters of both the mother and Emily come out strong in this narrative. There are hints of a setting (D), though, and the time period of Emily's birth and growing up (the Great Depression and World War II—" It was the pre-relief, pre WPA world of the depression"; "…writing V-mail to Bill…"). But there is no clear sense, no clear signs, of *location*: urban, rural, lower-class, middle-class. When Emily returns home, she "runs up the stairs two at a time with her light graceful step," which suggests an apartment building, but then she "starts up the stairs to bed," which suggests a house. Since time is suggested but location is left completely unclear, **(D) is the best answer.**

4. (A) might tempt some who confuse an introduction with a motivating incident. Even with the narrator's response to the invitation, we do not know whether the story will involve an internal or external conflict, whether it will be between the narrator and the school, the narrator and Emily, etc. Thus, (A) is eliminated. (C) is fairly easily eliminated simply by virtue of the fact that the invitation *begins* the story. (D) might also tempt some, but the resulting story is clearly a recollection and not a new realization. (E), like (A), hinges on understanding that, while the invitation might motivate the introduction of the metaphor, there is nothing in being invited to a parent conference to explain the significance of the mother's ironing a dress. The story is a reminiscence, however, a sort of flashback. Rather than simply have a mother ironing and thinking about her troubled daughter, Olsen wants there to be a *reason* for the thinking. The reason becomes the invitation. **Thus, (B) is the best answer.**

5. There really is nothing that can be considered humorous in this sad little story, and the mere mention of comedy does not add that element, so (B) is easily eliminated. It is a matter of interpretation whether the mother can be called indifferent, but she certainly does not respond to Emily's comedy or her talent show victory with indifference, thus eliminating (C). (D) is a little tempting, but the irony of Emily's comic talent is a relatively small element in the entire story, so this is not the best choice. Similarly, (E) can be eliminated by the fact that the comedy is a small element in the story. **(A) is clearly the best choice.** Throughout the story, Emily is described as dark, melancholy, sickly. She becomes almost a clichéd victim of circumstance. The fact that she can perform comedy well adds a bit of depth to her character.

Chapter 4, Exercise One

1. Litotes might indeed contribute to a formal tone that might sound aloof (A) or haughty (E) to some readers, but this is not the conventional use or application of the device. By the same token, the content of the paragraphs, despite the devices used to express it, does not support these negative interpretation of Washington's character or delivery. (B) is ironic because litotes usually involve more words than might otherwise be necessary. Thus, the use of litotes might actually be the opposite of reticence. (D) can certainly be eliminated because the intentional use of *any* device suggests, if not a formal education, at least attention to the speaking and writing of educated people. As the primary function of litotes is to create a mild positive, an understatement, it is reasonable to infer that a man given to speaking in understatements is calm, composed, and unexcitable. **Thus, (C) is the best answer.**

2. (B) might tempt a few students who either misread or read too much into Washington's brief mention of "motives, which I was not at liberty to disregard." While it is impossible to exclude the possibility of illness from Washington's motives, there is nothing in this paragraph or the rest of this address to determine that illness is the motive. (C) is also the result of a misread. Washington states that he "had been reluctantly drawn... *from* [his] retirement, not that he was reluctant to retire. (D) is likewise the result of a misread. The "idea" that "the unanimous advice of persons entitled to [his] confidence, impelled [him] to abandon" was the idea to retire after his first term: (*The strength of my inclination to do this [return to that retirement, from which I had been reluctantly drawn], previous to the last election, had even led to the preparation of an address to declare it to you.*) (E) is yet another misread of this challenging sentence structure. His only mention of "liberty" is in the sense that he was not at liberty to ignore whatever factors motivated him to retire at the end of his first term. The entire paragraph states, however, that he desired to retire at the end of his first term, that he could not "disregard" the motives he had to retire, that he had been "reluctantly drawn" from his retirement to serve his first term, and that he was so strong in his desire to retire that he had actually prepared "an address to declare it to you." It was only upon some

reflection and "the unanimous advice of persons entitled to my confidence" that he was "*impelled*" to "*abandon*" his intent to retire. The content and the language all strongly suggest that Washington was essentially unwilling to serve his second term as president. **Thus, (A) is the best answer.**

3. This sixth paragraph contains several enormously bulky and difficult sentences, which make a strict examination of grammar and syntax essential.

   Rather than claim that, during his eight years as President, the United States has always been governed by reason (A), Washington writes that there were "circumstances in which the Passions, agitated in every direction, were liable to mislead…" Times, in other words, when people of all opinions and mindsets allowed themselves to be governed by their passions. Similarly, Washington acknowledges that these passions "agitated in *every direction.*" Clearly there were multiple views and each was governed by passion instead of reason. He does admit to having persevered, but he mentions his zeal (C) only as a comparison. Whatever positive service he may have rendered was inevitably less than his desire—his zeal—to serve. (E) is eliminated by the realization that, according to Washington, the "Passions" that "agitated in every direction," often in the face of failure ("want of success"), allowed for or actually encouraged criticism ("countenanced the spirit of criticism"). Despite the passions, however, despite the differences of opinion and the spirit of criticism, Washington writes, "let it always be remembered to [the people's] praise…that… the constancy of your support was the essential prop of the efforts, and a guarantee of the plans…" **Thus, (D) is the best answer.**

4. Most of the choices, while specifically mentioned in the address, are listed as the results or benefits of the one chief source. Patriotism (A) is attending to one's *national* identity over one's local or regional identity. ("The name of AMERICAN, which belongs to you, in your national capacity, must always exalt the just pride of Patriotism, more than any appellation derived from local discriminations.") Early in paragraph 9, Washington writes, "it [this chief source] is … the support … of that very Liberty which you so highly prize." (B), then, is not the support but the thing supported. Likewise, (C) is supported by the same "main Pillar in the Edifice." (E) might tempt some students because "Unity of Government" is the "main Pillar" that supports all of the other values, but grammatically, the subject noun (simple subject) of the entire sentence is "unity," not "government. This "unity" is also emphasized as the source of [national] patriotism as "Americans" rather than identifying first with one's region or state. **Thus, (D) is the best answer.**

5. Some students might be quickly drawn to (A) or (C) because this section does deal with benefits and positive results of union; fairly early in the section he admits that he is addressing what is in *each section's best and immediate interest*. This eliminates (A). Furthermore, he addresses these benefits as more or less dependent on national unity, with no expression of his belief that this unity *can* be maintained, so (C) is also eliminated. There is no more reason to expect that the nation will fail (D) than that it will succeed.

While Washington is, perhaps, being more direct here than elsewhere in his address, there is nothing biting, sarcastic, or caustic (E) in this address. Opening the section by stating that considerations that "apply more immediately to [the people's] Interest" "greatly outweigh" the abstract benefits he has just been describing, clearly suggests a pragmatic (B) tone. The next several paragraphs, likewise, enumerate practical benefits in terms of trade, goods, and mutual protection. **Thus, (B) is the best answer.**

Chapter 4, Exercise Two

11. (A) is eliminated by examining the structure of the opening sentence. The fact that the Spirit of Party is inseparable from human nature is unfortunate, not the spirit itself. Later, Washington says that party spirit is "more or less ...repressed," not that party is repressive. (B) might be more tempting because Washington does indeed address the popular nature of some parties, but he is making an observation about those "of the popular form." This is not to suggest that all parties are popular. (D) is tempting because, in writing that party spirit is "inseparable from our nature," he is suggesting the tendency to split into parties is natural, but there is no suggestion that such a tendency is democratic. Rather, this tendency is unfortunate and "exists under different shapes in all Governments." (E) is fairly easily eliminated. Washington does say that party spirit has "root in the strongest passions of the human mind." This is an emotional (passionate) function, not an intellectual one. In this opening paragraph, Washington writes that the Spirit of Party "exists under different shapes in all Governments [ubiquitous]." He also asserts that party spirit is "inseparable from our nature [inevitable], having its root in the strongest passions of the human mind." **Thus, (C) is the best answer.**

12. The second paragraph begins "The alternate domination of one faction over another... which in different ages and countries has perpetrated the most horrid enormities...," thus eliminating (A). (B) is eliminated in the second half of the paragraph: "sooner or later the chief of some prevailing faction, more able or more fortunate than his competitors, turns this disposition to the purposes of his own elevation." (C) is eliminated when Washington writes, "The disorders and miseries, which result, gradually incline the minds of men to seek security and repose." Likewise, (E) is eliminated by the opening of the paragraph when Washington acknowledges the "spirit of revenge, natural to party dissension." In the third paragraph, Washington does warn that party spirit can "open the door to foreign influence and corruption," but it is clear in this paragraph that he is not talking about outright invasion. **Thus, (D) is the correct answer.**

13. Washington uses the words *Religion* and *Morality* three times in this section. The first is his assertion that *Religion and Morality are indispensable supports of political prosperity*. In this sentence, he includes *religion* and *morality* among *all the dispositions and habits*. Parallel structure would suggest that *religion* is a

disposition—a tendency of the mind or spirit—while *morality* is a *habit*, which connotes behavior. Washington's second use of these words is in the same paragraph when he notes that it is *religious obligation* that assures the solemnity of an oath and safeguards the United States' judicial process. He follows that *morality* is impossible without *religion*. Apparently, it is the tendency of the mind that keeps the behavior (of honoring an oath) in check. His final use of the words comes several paragraphs later, when he asserts that *Religion and Morality* demand the nation's observation of *good faith and justice towards all Nations*. While Washington clearly understands there to be a private and public aspect to religion and morality, (B) is eliminated by the fact that *felicity* is one of the benefits or products of this *disposition* and this *habit*. (C) might tempt some because Washington does group the *pious man* with the *mere politician*, but nowhere in this section does Washington refer to church attendance, prayer, the singing of hymns, or any other behavior associated with "worship." In fact, his first use of the words "religion and morality" seems to connect morality with the behavior, not religion. Thus, (C) and (E) can both be eliminated. (E) might tempt some because to honor an oath and to "observe good faith and justice towards all nations" can certainly be considered "right action"; but there is still no sense of *worship* in Washington's use of *religion*. (D) can be eliminated for the same reason. The honoring of an oath is the result of a *sense of religious obligation*, but this does not suggest that religion itself is obligatory, and nothing in this section suggests prescribed actions like sacrament and ritual. Washington's association of *Religion and Morality* with *dispositions and habits*, in the absence of any further elaboration on those *dispositions and habits* (except for the honoring of oaths and observing good will and justice to all nations), suggests a broad, relatively undefined understanding of the beliefs and the motivations that inform right action. **Thus, (A) is the best answer.**

14. The cooperation of public opinion (A) is a factor in the issue of taxation, but at this point in the paragraph, Washington is talking about the avoidance of public debt, not the raising of revenue. In (B) as well, *it* refers to "public credit," not taxation. (C) does, of course, refer to taxation, but "spirit of acquiescence" refers to the point Washington has asserted; it does not really summarize it. (E) is true and tempting, but this statement follows Washington's declaration about taxes and leads to a continuation of his point about revenues and taxation. When speaking of public debt, however, Washington broaches the difficult issue of taxes by saying that debt cannot be paid without revenue, and revenue requires taxes, however unpleasant those taxes may be. **Thus, (D) is the best answer.**

15. (A) is fairly easily eliminated by Washington's injunction to "Cultivate peace and harmony with all [nations]." (B), likewise, is almost the antithesis of Washington's advice *not* to discriminate and favor one nation over another. (C) is tempting, but is perhaps too strong a word. *Good faith and justice*, and *peace and harmony*, are not necessarily the same as "friendly." (D) is a contradiction within itself. *Good faith, justice, peace,* and *harmony* can hardly be interpreted as "indifference." By exhorting

the United States to remain on just and peaceable terms with *all nations*, he is clearly advocating neutrality. That this neutrality is expressed in *peace and harmony* clearly suggests a benevolent stance. **Thus, (E) is the best answer.**

Chapter 5, Exercise One

1. (A) is fairly easily eliminated as Betsey Bobbett is the only alliterative name in the paragraph. Thus, although it may contribute to the humor of the vignette, it cannot be considered a *chief* source of humor. (C) is tempting, as the use of dialect and the malapropisms do make it apparent this narrator is not educated, but this in and of itself is not a source of humor. The narrator's philosophy (D) that people should be satisfied in whatever sphere fate has placed them is not—without the style of narration, the narrator's observations, and the language—humorous. (E) becomes apparent later but is not clear in this first paragraph. (B) is clearly the best answer. When the narrator says one should be content with her "spear," and that a woman's "spear" is to be married, she means "sphere." However, the malapropism becomes ironically laughable when she says that no man ever wanted to take up Betsey Bobbett's "spear," here clearly meaning the weapon, emphasizing Betsey's undesirability as a marriage partner. **Thus, (B) is the best answer.**

2. (A) is probably the strongest clue that this passage is set in the past and in a rural, possibly New England, setting. (B) is also a strong clue that the setting is rural America of the late nineteenth or early twentieth century: the manners of cooking food, the sewing of a rag rug, the approach of sugaring time (again, probably New England), carrying the stove to the summer kitchen, etc. (C) is likewise very strong because women clearly do not yet have to vote, and a woman's place is still largely believed to be in the home. Some students might be tempted to eliminate (E), but there are references to the narrator's "bonnet bloo" and Betsey's "bunnet-strings" and "brown cotton gloves." The two poems, however, bad as they are, do not help to identify any specific time or place. **Thus, (D) is the best answer.**

3. (A) is not incorrect, because every critical statement is tempered with some mild qualifier, but given the other choices, it is not the best answer. (B) is likewise tempting, but the verbal irony, the qualifiers, and the understatements tend to make the tone milder than what could be considered truly sarcastic. (D) and (E) might tempt students who accept the understatement and qualifiers at face value. The narrator's attitude toward Betsey in the rest of the passage, however, does not support either reading. The narrator's transparent attempts not to criticize openly—especially in the context of her attitude as revealed in the rest of the passage—strongly suggest an underlying sense of disapproval or superiority. **Thus, (C) is the best answer.**

4. (A) is not incorrect, but is certainly not the *best* of the choices as it implies a deliberate device by the author. Dialect (B) and (C) might tempt some who recognize the "unconventional" uses of the words, but these uses cannot all be attributed to dialect or idiom. (D) is also a strong choice, but the pun relies on the punned words' being used correctly, and the words in this question are not. **The best answer is (E).** The effect of the use of *pole* for *poll*, *pathmaster* for *postmaster*, *owed* for *ode*, and *tenderlines* for *tenderloins* is not humor based on the words' similar meanings or pronunciations; it is based on the character's mistaking the word she uses for the word she means. This is a **malapropism**.

5. For a question like this, it is important that the student remember that if one part of the answer can be eliminated, then the entire answer can be eliminated. (B), therefore, can be eliminated by the fact that the tone of the opening paragraph, while guarded, is not so kind as to be interpreted as "saccharine." (C) might tempt some, but the anger or indignation at the end of the passage, given that this is the narrator's response to the second poem, cannot be regarded as "impetuous." The beginning paragraphs are, at best, cautious or neutral, not at all conciliatory (D), and, while the narrator's observations and descriptions might be humorous to the reader, the narrator's tone cannot be described as jocular (E). **Therefore, (A) is the best answer.**

Chapter 5, Exercise Two

6. (A) might tempt some students since the poem is not *strictly* iambic tetrameter, but this metrical pattern is, nonetheless, true of the poem. Each of the three stanzas contains seven lines, thus eliminating (C). A few students might be drawn to (D) since the refrain is repeated five times (after the initial iteration), but there is, nonetheless, just the one refrain, "Beyond the years." (E) is eliminated fairly simply by plotting the AABABAB rhyme of each stanza, further complicated by the fact that the B rhyme remains consistent all across stanzas. The poem, however, does not end in a couplet. **Thus, (B) is the best answer.**

7. In nearly every instance, the half-line either completes the sentence begun in the line before it or begins a sentence that continues to the next. A reader's natural tendency is to speed up when the sense of one line continues to the next. So, (A) might tempt some students, but the opposite is actually the case. The reader is lulled into the iambic tetrameter by the two lines at the beginning of each stanza. The sudden change of rhythm causes an abrupt pause, even if the thought is being continued. The syntax and the tendency of concatenating one line to the next eliminates (B). There is a slight emotional shift in stanza two, but this is not the result of the metric pattern, thus eliminating (C). (D) is true, but certainly not the clearest, most specific, or best of the five choices. The interruption of the metrical patter, however, is more a cause than an

effect. The result is that there are frequent, brief breaks in the flow of the poem (which are related to the refrain by their rhyme scheme), during which the reader is invited to reflect on what the poet is saying, especially the significance of the refrain. **Thus, (E) is the best answer.**

8. (A) is fairly easily eliminated by the fact that every stanza ends with the refrain, so Stanza II is not unique in this respect. Likewise, while the rhythm does vary in each stanza between iambic tetrameter to iambic dimeter, this pattern does not denote a shift in a tone and is not unique to stanza II, thus eliminating (B). Personification of abstract concepts (C) is also not unique to stanza II, and the rhyme scheme does not alter throughout (E) Midway through stanza II, however, the images of dark and night, associated with longing, evolve into the image of Morn "uprear[ing]" her head, and the longing is fulfilled. **Thus, (D) is the best answer.**

9. The progress of the poem more emphasizes the meaning of the refrain than alters it. Thus, (A) is eliminated. (B) is certainly true, but is not the best answer, as it is not the only element of unity in the poem. (D) is eliminated because the metaphoric significance of "years" certainly contributes to the theme, but the repetition of the line has more to do with effect than theme. (E) might be tempting to students who recognize the longing and expectation conveyed by the refrain; the poem itself shifts in tone from the initial longing to a sense of fulfillment by the third stanza. (C), however, is more specific than (E) and addresses only the refrain, not the entire poem. **Thus, (C) is the best answer.**

10. While the last iteration of the refrain ("Beyond the years") might be more hopeful, looking more toward fulfillment than focusing on the emptiness to be left behind, there is nothing unexpected or surprising in this closing (B). In fact, to end a final stanza with the same line that has begun and ended every stanza is almost the opposite of irony. Nor is the sentiment expressed an ironic departure from what one might expect at the end of such a poem. (C) might tempt some, but the repetition of the refrain in and of itself cannot be said to clarify that refrain or its context. (D) might tempt those who recognize the shift in tone that occurs in stanza II, but the shift from longing to fulfillment is not dramatic enough to be considered cathartic. This final repetition is also affirming the sentiment first expressed in the first stanza, so (E) is easily eliminated. The repetition of the refrain, especially ending the poem on the repeated line, clearly establishes emphasis of the words and sentiment. **Thus, (A) is the best answer.**

APPENDIX 2: Glossary of Literary Terms

ambiguous / ambiguity: to have more than one meaning, especially if more than one meaning can apply at the same time; to be open to interpretation.

Examples:

I drank the tea in the kitchen could mean the tea that I drank was in the kitchen or that I was in the kitchen when I drank the tea.

[Name of Defendant] sentenced to nine months in jewel case. Must the defendant spend nine months in a jewelry box, or did the investigative and court case have to do with jewelry?

Red tape holds up new bridge. The humorous ambiguity in this sentence comes from two common non-literal phrases (known as *idioms*): "Red tape" is an expression used to communicate complex bureaucratic procedures, guidelines, etc., that makes it difficult to achieve a goal. To "hold [something] up" is to delay it. Thus, while most people would understand this sentence to mean that bureaucratic procedures have delayed the bridge's construction, some might take it literally to mean that the new bridge is constructed of and supported by strips of red adhesive.

anaphora: the repetition of the beginning word or words of one sentence at or near the beginning of subsequent sentences.

Examples:

I do not like you, Sam I am

I do not like green eggs and ham

I do not like them in a box

I do not like them with a fox ...

To raise a happy, healthy, and hopeful child, it takes a family; *it takes* teachers; *it takes* clergy; *it takes* business people; *it takes* community leaders; *it takes* those who protect our health and safety. It takes all of us.—Hillary Rodham Clinton, 1996 Democratic National Convention Address

antagonist: in fiction, the character who opposes the *protagonist* and, thus sets the *plot* in motion.

Examples:

In "Little Red Riding Hood," the big bad wolf, who wants to prevent the young girl from reaching her grandmother's house and wants to destroy both the young girl and her mother, is the *antagonist*.

In Disney's *The Lion King*, the king's brother, Scar, in wanting his brother destroyed and his nephew exiled, is the *antagonist*.

anthropomorphism / personification: the giving of human attributes to non-human things; the treatment of non-living things as if they were living.

Examples:

Most of Aesop's fables, including "The Tortoise and the Hare," "The Fox and the Grapes," and "The Ant and the Grasshopper" *anthropomorphize* animals in order to illustrate their morals.

To refer to the ocean as "she" or to talk about "Mother Nature" as "kind and nurturing" are both examples of *personification*.

antithesis: the placement of opposite ideas or concepts near one another in a sentence or paragraph for emphasis.

Examples:

This is not a time to rest on our laurels, but to double our efforts and push ever farther.

Many are called, few are chosen.

Fall down seven times, stand up eight.

archaic: common in the past but no longer used (or used rarely).

Examples:

"Thou" and "ye" are *archaic* forms of direct address or second person.

Not even poets use *archaic* words like "forsooth" and "methinks" in their writing anymore.

aside / parenthetical aside: An aside is a dramatic convention in which a character on stage speaks either to himself/herself, one other character, or to the audience—the audience accepts that it can hear what the character says, but the other characters onstage do not (*aside*); a parenthetical aside is a literary convention in which the narrator of a novel or story interrupts the flow in order to address the reader or simply insert a reflection or opinion.

Examples: In the famous balcony scene of Shakespeare's *Romeo and Juliet* (Act II, scene ii), when Romeo overhears Juliet on her balcony, he asks either himself or the audience, "Shall I hear more, or shall I speak at this?"

In Act II, scene ii of Shakespeare's *Julius Caesar*, several of the men who intend to assassinate Caesar have come to his house to accompany him to the Senate. Caesar asks one of them, Trebonius, to stay close to him. Trebonius remarks— so that the audience can hear (but apparently no one on stage can)—"and so near will I be,/That your best friends shall wish I had been further."

So I bought this table—it was a cheap piece of junk from a discount catalogue— and the ad had said "some assembly required." So, of course, I expected to have to screw on the legs—you know, something basic like that—but when I opened the box, I was faced with—and I kid you not—2,000 nuts and bolts and not one piece of wood touching another. It'll be the last time I buy anything from that catalogue.

authorial intrusion (editorial intrusion, narrative intrusion): any instance of the author's, editor's, or narrator's interrupting the narrative flow to insert an opinion or observation.

Examples:
In the opening paragraphs of Charles Dickens's *A Christmas Carol*:

> Marley was dead: to begin with. There is no doubt whatever about that. The register of his burial was signed by the clergyman, the clerk, the undertaker, and the chief mourner. Scrooge signed it: and Scrooge's name was good upon 'Change, for anything he chose to put his hand to. Old Marley was as dead as a door-nail.

> *Mind! I don't mean to say that I know, of my own knowledge, what there is particularly dead about a door-nail. I might have been inclined, myself, to regard a coffin-nail as the deadest piece of ironmongery in the trade. But the wisdom of our ancestors is in the simile; and my unhallowed hands shall not disturb it, or the Country's done for. You will therefore permit me to repeat, emphatically, that Marley was as dead as a door-nail.*

> Scrooge knew he was dead? Of course he did.

The second paragraph (italicized in the preceding exerpt) is an example of narrative intrusion.

In nonfiction and academic writing, the editor often indicates his or her intrusion by placing it within brackets or separating it from the main flow by dashes. Brackets are especially important when inserting an observation or comment into a direct quotation.

> While the Governor faced some of the most severe challenges in this state's history—let us never forget the horrible floods of last winter or the severe drought of the summer before—she has been level-headed, efficient, and compassionate in all of her affairs, both private and public.

> In his scandalous memoir, Boyer notes "if he [Lord Marmaduke St. John] hadn't spoilt the evening with his foul humour, this murder might never have occurred."

begging the question: a logical fallacy in which the desired conclusion assumes agreement between the parties on a question that is not yet settled. It is often used intentionally as a technique of propaganda.

Examples:

Since the Second Amendment applies only to state militias, personal handguns should simply be outlawed. (The meaning of the opening phrase of the second amendment is still under debate, and is at the heart of the gun rights versus gun control issue in the United States.)

The Internet is such a cesspool of ill-informed opinions, misinformation, and other garbage, access should be banned from public school classrooms and libraries. (While some people might certainly hold that opinion of the Internet—and be able to find evidence to support it—others would strongly disagree, and find evidence to support their argument as well.)

chiasmus: a form of *parallelism* in which the word order or grammatical structure of the parallel phrases is reversed.

Examples:

Jack and Jill went up the hill. Then, down the hill they fell.

Do not give what is holy to dogs, and do not throw your pearls before swine, lest the pigs trample them under their feet, and the dogs turn and tear you to pieces. (Matthew 7:6)

Ask not what your country can do for you; ask what you can do for your country. (President John F. Kennedy, 20 January 1961)

climax: the highest point in the rising action of a plot; the point at which the outcome of the plot is determined (even if the outcome is not yet revealed).

Examples:

In *Cinderella*, the action continues to rise through the chiming of the clock, the loss of the glass slipper and the step-sisters' trying the slipper on. At the moment Cinderella comes out of hiding and the prince demands that she try on the slipper, the outcome—that the slipper will fit and she will marry the prince—is determined.

The *climax* of Charles Dickens's *A Christmas Carol* occurs when Ebenezer Scrooge, softening but still not fully repentant, drops to his knees before the Ghost of Christmas Yet to Come and promises to change.

Also, rhetorical device in which details, ideas, or reasons are presented in order of increasing magnitude: from smallest or least important to largest or most important.

Examples:

... in Order to form a more perfect Union, establish Justice, insure domestic Tranquility, provide for the common defense, promote the general Welfare, and secure the Blessings of Liberty to ourselves and our Posterity ...

... Life, Liberty, and the Pursuit of Happiness ...

caesura: a complete stop within a line of poetry.

Examples:

To err is human; to forgive, divine. (Alexander Pope)

How do I love thee? Let me count the ways. (Elizabeth Barrett Browning)

complication: any event or incident in the rising action that intensifies the conflict and makes the protagonist's fulfilling his or her need less likely.

Examples:

An important *complication* in Shakespeare's *Romeo and Juliet* is the delay of Friar Laurence's message to Romeo. Not knowing of the Friar and Juliet's scheme, Romeo believes Juliet is really dead.

An important *complication* in Jack London's "To Build a Fire" is the smell of sulfur from the matches, which causes the man to cough and extinguish his tiny flame.

A *complication* is not the same as the *conflict*. The *conflict* is the overall tension that propels the entire plot; a *complication* intensifies the *conflict*.

conflict: the tension or struggle that triggers the plot and makes the rising action and climax possible.

Examples:

While the general tension between the Greasers and the Socs is introduced in the beginning of S.E. Hinton's *The Outsiders*, the novel's primary *conflict*— Greaser Ponyboy's attraction to Soc Cherry, and his inability to date her—is established in the second chapter.

While no one person stands in opposition to *The Red Badge of Courage's* Henry Fleming, the plot of the novel advances as Henry resolves his *conflict* with his own fear and the shame of having run from battle.

connotation: the "unofficial" but generally accepted meaning of a word; often the emotion or value associated with the word.

Examples:

"Inexpensive" and "cheap" are synonyms, but "cheap" has a *connotation* of low quality as well as low price.

Being "satisfied" has a *connotation* of having had just enough to eat, while being "full" has a *connotation* of having eaten too much.

[narrative] convention: the way something is traditionally done; a commonly-accepted practice or use. A **narrative convention** is a practice involved in the crafting or telling of a story.

Examples:

To begin a story *in medias res* (in the middle of the action) and then pause after an interest-grabbing opening scene to provide some exposition is a common *narrative convention*.

Narrative conventions include such author's decisions as who the narrator will be, whether the story will be told in chronological order, whether the action will be divided into chapters, and so on.

deductive reasoning: the thought process that begins with a general principle and applies it to a specific case; in its most formal sense, it takes the form of a syllogism: if A is true, and B is true, then C will be true.

Examples:

I always sleep late on Saturdays (A). Tomorrow is Saturday (B). I will sleep late tomorrow (C).

Elizabeth always bakes the best desserts (A). Elizabeth baked these brownies (B). These brownies will be delicious (C).

Paul criticizes everything Betsy does (A). Betsy just turned in her assignment to Paul (B). He will criticize it (C).

Occasionally the second *premise* (B is true) is omitted.

Examples:

Since Rufus likes dogs (A), he should like his sister's new poodle (C). *It is assumed that the sister's poodle is a dog (B).*

All exercise is beneficial (A), so walking to work should be good for you (C). *It is assumed that walking to work constitutes exercise (B).*

denotation: the formal definition of a word as found in a standard dictionary.

Examples:

The word "myth" is often used to mean any fiction or made-up story or false belief, but the *denotation* of the term has to do with culturally significant legends of a people's origins, heroes, and gods.

denouement: the end or outcome of a plot; the final resolution of all of the plot's complexities.

Examples:

Nineteenth-century novels, like those written by Charles Dickens, are famous for their *denouements* in which the good triumph, the evil fail, and unknown relationships are revealed.

The *denouement* of the movie *The Wizard of Oz* includes the revelation of the "man behind the curtain," his distribution of tokens to the Scarecrow, Tin Man, and Lion, and Dorothy's magical journey home.

dialogue: in literature, this is the convention by which the writer communicates to the reader the exact words that characters have spoken to one another. The characters' exact words are usually indicated by the use of quotation marks (" ").

Example:

"I am here," said Josh.

Dan replied, "So am I."

epistrophe: the stylistic repetition of a word or phrase at the end of successive clauses or sentences.

Examples:

… and that government of <u>the people</u>, by <u>the people</u>, for <u>the people</u>, shall not perish from the earth.

> —Abraham Lincoln
> The Gettysburg Address

Unless we in America work to preserve the <u>peace, there will be no</u> <u>peace</u>.

Unless we in America work to preserve <u>freedom, there will be no</u> <u>freedom</u>.

> —Inaugural Address of President Richard M. Nixon, January 20, 1973

exposition: information about the characters or setting of a piece of fiction; *exposition* is often depicted as coming before the introduction of the conflict and the rising action, but the fact is that *exposition* can be provided at any point during the plot.

Examples:

The original L. Frank Baum novel *The Wonderful Wizard of Oz* provided *exposition* about how the Tin Man and Scarecrow came into existence; this is never explained in the movie.

In Susan Glaspell's "A Jury of her Peers," Mrs. Hale provides some important *exposition* about the young girl Minnie Foster was before her marriage to John Wright.

falling action: in traditional plot structure, all of the action that occurs after the climax and leads to the conclusion or *denouement*.

> **Example:**
>
> The *falling action* in *The Wizard of Oz* is restricted to the final few minutes after Dorothy's return to Kansas when she describes her dream to the others and learns that "There's no place like home."

figurative: In language, any non-literal use, especially an intentional non-literal use in literature, can be considered figurative.

> **Examples:**
>
> A metaphor (e.g., "Some say love … it is a razor that leaves your soul to bleed."[1]) is a *figurative* comparison between two unlike objects.
>
> Synesthesia (e.g., In his anger, he saw red, smelled red, tasted red, and felt red pulsing through his veins.) is a *figurative* use of some of the five senses.

first person: the grammatical device that allows a speaker or writer to refer to himself or herself (i.e., I, we, me, us, my, mine, our, ours).

Also the *narrative mode* in which the narrator is involved in the story and describes the events and other characters from his or her viewpoint.

> **Examples:**
>
> Tillie Olsen's "I Stand Here Ironing" has a first-person narrator.

foreshadowing: an event or reference in a work of literature that suggests a future development.

> **Examples:**
>
> Dorothy's desire to find a place where she and Toto can avoid trouble *foreshadows* her journey to Oz.
>
> In the Disney cartoon, the Prince's discovery of Cinderella is *foreshadowed* by the woman's losing her shoe every time she is in a hurry.

---

[1] from "The Rose" by Amanda McBroom, 1979.

homograph: two or more words that are spelled identically but pronounced differently and have different meanings. Sometimes explained as a single word with two or more different meanings.

Examples:

address: Lincoln delivered his famous Gettysburg *Address* in November 1863. Did you *address* the envelope?
Before you can shop on that site, you have to give them your e-mail *address*.

close: The bus driver refused to stop until we were *close* to the ball field.
I can't believe you forgot to *close* the door.

desert: Some interesting plant and animal life live in the *desert*.
It is disheartening to realize that you could *desert* this cause so easily.

homonym: two or more words that are spelled and pronounced identically but have different meanings.

Examples:

bow: The violinist put rosin on his *bow*.
I like to wrap presents, but I cannot make a good *bow*.
It requires a good deal of skill to hunt with a *bow* and arrow.

board: The houseguest repaired the front steps with a *board*.
One of the biggest expenses of college is room and *board*.
The *board* of directors voted to keep her as CEO.
The attendant announced that it was time to *board* the plane.

homophone: two or more words with identical pronunciations but different spellings.

Examples:

all/awl: The selfish student wanted *all* of the credit for herself.
The leatherworker punched a hole in the leather with an *awl*.

bow/bough: The performer took a *bow* when the audience began to applaud.
The weakened *bough* broke off the tree in last night's windstorm.

see/sea: Marion turned on the light so she could *see* the book she was reading.
I'm not sure what the difference is between an ocean and a *sea*.

capital/capitol: The *capital* is the city where the government meets.
The *capitol* is the building in which the legislature sits.

principle/principal: Always to tell the truth is a fine *principle*.
The highest authority in a school is the headmaster, headmistress, or *principal*.

hyperbole: extreme and obvious exaggeration, often used to create a humorous or sarcastic effect.

Examples:

The Worst of All Days began when Dora awoke to the utter calamity of burnt toast and weak tea.

So complete was Maurice's joy at receiving his college acceptance that he shouted as no human had ever shouted before or ever would shout again.

… we loved with a love that was more than love—
I and my Annabel Lee,
With a love that the wingèd seraphs of heaven
Coveted her and me.
    —"Annabelle Lee"
    Edgar Allen Poe

inciting incident: the event, usually even earlier than the introduction of the conflict, that sets a plot in motion. Often the *inciting incident* is the arrival of a stranger, the return of a long-absent person, the arrival of news, or a sudden change, like a death.

Examples:

The *inciting incident* in *The Outsiders* is the attack on Ponyboy as he is walking home from the movies in Chapter 1.

The long-delayed *inciting incident* in the first novel of the Harry Potter series is the Chapter 3 arrival of Hagrid with the news of Harry's heritage and destiny.

indirect dialogue: the technique of presenting the contents of a conversation without directly quoting the persons involved.

Examples:

Father observed that it was easy to criticize someone else's work, and Mother countered that he frequently did the same to her cooking. A heated argument followed, in which Father and Mother accused each other of everything from cruelty to manslaughter.

At his inauguration, the President delivered a stirring speech in which he invited Americans of all races, religions, genders, and heritages to unite into a new and powerful United Stated dedicated to rising out of the ashes of previous disillusionment and finally achieving our nation's great potential.

inductive reasoning: the thought process by which a general principle is formed from the examination of several individual cases.

Examples:

Poe's control of his rhythm pattern and rhyme scheme is masterful in "The Raven." His control of rhythm and use of sound devices is what makes "The Bells" such a delight to read. In "Annabelle Lee," Poe's ironic choice of meter and his sing-song A-B-C-B rhyme scheme make the ending of the poem a morbid surprise for the first-time reader. As a poet, Poe really was a master craftsman.

Prince Hamlet dies at the end of the Shakespearean tragedy titled *Hamlet, Prince of Denmark*. Macbeth dies at the end of the Shakespearean tragedy titled *Macbeth*, and Romeo and Juliet both die in the play that bears their names. If William Shakespeare offers to base a play on your life and name it after you, respectfully decline! (The general principle, of course, is that Shakespeare's title characters all seem to get killed in their plays.)

in medias res (in the middle of things): the technique of beginning a story, novel, or play after the actual action of the plot has already begun. Despite the persistent use of Freytag's Pyramid to illustrate plot structure, most twentieth-century literature begins, not with *exposition* as the pyramid suggests, but *in medias res*.

Examples:

Both Katherine Mansfield's "Miss Brill" and Dorothy Parker's "The Standard of Living" begin *in medias res*. Miss Brill is already in the park, enjoying the day, before the author provides the background of her fur and her affection for it. "The Standard of Living" begins on the afternoon the story takes place, as the girls are just leaving the tea room, before the author pauses to provide the exposition about their friendship and their customary lunches.

interior monologue: the literary technique by which the author communicates to the reader what is going on within the mind of the character. This monologue may be long and detailed or quite brief. It may also either summarize or directly quote the character's thoughts.

Examples:

John Updike's "A & P" and Charlotte Perkins Gilman's "The Yellow Wallpaper" are both *interior monologues*.

J. D. Salinger's *Catcher in the Rye* is essentially Holden Caulfield's *interior monologue*.

literal: adhering exactly to the *denotation* with no inference, interpretation, or *connotation*.

Examples:

A fairy tale is *literally* a folk story in which the main character overcomes some kind of adversity, usually with the help of magical or supernatural beings. The expression "fairy tale" is often used, however, to refer to *any* obviously made-up story, especially an unbelievable excuse for an error or a failure.

Translated *literally*, the nursery song "Frere Jacques" would not say, "Are you sleeping ... Brother John ...?" but "Brother John ... are you sleeping?"

modernism: a school of literature that rose to prominence in the early twentieth century. Thematically, it focused on individuality. Structurally, *modernism* was marked by challenges to traditional literary conventions. Stream-of-consciousness, disjointed timelines, and multiple narrative points of view are *modernist* techniques.

Examples:

The long, uninterrupted monologue in Tillie Olsen's "I Stand Here Ironing," in which the mother is speaking to an unidentified guest exhibits many *modernist* techniques. The story told exclusively in dialogue or monologue, the distrust of institutions (in this case, the daughter's school), and the theme of individualism (the fact that the mother cannot fully know her daughter since the daughter is an individual with her own consciousness) are traits of *modernism*.

The interior monologue, indirect dialogue, and the theme of the individual's coming to know herself are all strong tendencies of *modernism* exhibited in Katherine Mansfield's "Miss Brill."

mood: the overall emotional and psychological effect of the language, including all literary and rhetorical devices, on the reader.

Examples:

The *mood* of Edgar Allen Poe's "The Fall of the House of Usher" is obvious from the opening sentence:

During the whole of a <u>dull</u>, <u>dark</u>, and <u>soundless</u> day in the <u>autumn</u> of the year, when the <u>clouds</u> hung <u>oppressively low</u> in the heavens, I had been passing <u>alone</u>, on horseback, through a <u>singularly dreary</u> tract of country, and at length found myself, as the <u>shades of evening</u> drew on, within view of the <u>melancholy</u> House of Usher.

In the opening sentence of "Miss Brill," Katherine Mansfield starts to set a festive *mood* that will prove ironic by the end of the story:

Although it was so <u>brilliantly fine</u>—the blue <u>sky powdered with gold</u> and <u>great spots of light</u> <u>like white wine splashed</u> over the *Jardins Publiques*—Miss Brill was <u>glad</u> that she had decided on her fur.

motif: any recurring element (e.g., an image, a name, a phrase of music, or line of poetry) in a narrative that, by the fact of its repetition and the context of each occurrence, takes on some deeper significance—symbolic, psychological, spiritual.

Examples:

The motif of individual incompleteness or of the individual's lacking some essential component (Scarecrow's brains, Tin Man's heart, Lion's courage) is resolved when the Wizard reveals to them that they already possess what they believed they lacked—they needed only to trust in themselves.

In Tillie Olsen's "I Stand Here Ironing," the iron and the dress being ironed become symbols of the narrator's daughter and the difficulties of her life.

narrative point of view / narrative mode: the perspective from which the story is told; in a sense, the *narrative point of view* illustrates the relationship of the narrator to the other characters and the story. A *first person* narrator is present and involved with the characters and action and is narrating events that he or she witness or participated in (e.g., <u>I</u> had been passing alone, on horseback, through a singularly dreary tract of country, and at length found <u>myself</u> ...")

A *third person* narrator is removed from the story and characters (e.g., <u>Miss Brill</u> was glad that <u>she</u> had decided on <u>her</u> fur.)

Narrative point of view also includes the narrator's level of knowledge or understanding. *First person* narrators are usually limited in their knowledge or understanding, just as an actual person would be. *Third person* narrators may be "omniscient" (having complete knowledge of everything) or "limited omniscient" (their knowledge limited to complete knowledge of a single character).

It is the author's choice of narrator that will determine the *narrative voice* of the story.

narrative structure: includes several issues in the organizing and telling of a story: the division of the plot into chapters, acts and scenes, etc.; the arrangement of plot events into a recognizable pattern; and the pacing of rising action and exposition are all elements of *narrative structure.*

Examples: ·

Freytag's Pyramid, which places plot exposition before the introduction of the conflict and the climax relatively in the middle of the plot, is a satisfactory graphic depiction of the *narrative structure* of much nineteenth-century literature, but it does not take into account twentieth-century techniques of beginning a story *in medias res*, using flashbacks or flash-forwards, or presenting the reader with a disjointed timeline.

narrative voice (voice): closely related to *tone, mood,* and *point of view; narrative voice* is the *persona*, distinct from the author, who is telling the story to the reader. Some critics mistakenly equate *narrative voice* with *narrative point of view*, but within any particular point of view, there are still numerous voices that the author can assume.

Examples:

In both *The Adventures of Tom Sawyer* and *Adventures of Huckleberry Finn*, the author, Mark Twain, assumes the *narrative voices* of young boys on the American frontier of middle of the nineteenth century.

In Harper Lee's *To Kill a Mockingbird*, the author adopts a *narrative voice* that blends the innocence of six-year-old Scout Finch with the same character as an adult remembering the events in the novel.

naturalism: a school of literature that emerged in the late nineteenth century and early twentieth centuries, largely as a reaction to *realism; naturalists* kept their focus on the commonplace, but added an understanding that human lives are often shaped by natural, scientific forces beyond human choice or control.

Example:

Given the way the author pays so much attention to the scientific and natural ¡nciples that determine the unnamed character's fate, Jack London's "To d a Fire" is an excellent example of *naturalism.*

non sequitur: a logical fallacy in which the conclusion does not necessarily follow from the premises. Latin for "it does not follow," the *non sequitur* is often used as a comic device.

Examples:

Alice's encounter with the Mad Hatter, Dormouse, and March Hare is full of *non sequiturs* including the attempt to fix the Hatter's watch with butter, offering Alice wine when there isn't any, and offering her more tea when she hasn't had any yet. Barely one point of the party's conversation follows logically from the preceding point.

parallelism: a rhetorical device *and* a structural element in which consecutive phrases, clauses, sentences, even sometimes full paragraphs follow with similar word order and grammatical patterns.

Examples:

Visitors to the United States' many national parks enjoy camping, hiking, viewing natural wonders, and watching animals in their natural habitats. (Notice the *parallel* use of gerunds and gerund phrases in the compound direct object.)

Visitors to the United States' many national parks come from all across the country to camp, hike, view natural wonders, and watch animals in their natural habitats. (Here the *parallelism* is achieved by a series of infinitives and infinitive phrases.)

Some [men] are born great; some achieve greatness; and some have greatness thrust upon them. (William Shakespeare, *Twelfth Night*, II, v.)

parenthetical aside / aside: a dramatic convention in which character on stage speaks either to himself/herself, one other character, or to the audience— the audience accepts that it can hear what the character says, but the other characters onstage do not (*aside*); or a literary convention in which the narrator of a novel or story interrupts the flow in order to address the reader or simply insert a reflection or opinion.

Examples:

In the famous balcony scene of Shakespeare's *Romeo and Juliet* (Act II, scene ii), when Romeo overhears Juliet on her balcony, he asks either himself or the audience, "Shall I hear more, or shall I speak at this?"

In Act II, scene 2 of Shakespeare's *Julius Caesar*, several of the men who intend to assassinate Caesar have come to his house to accompany him to the Senate. Caesar asks one of them, Trebonius, to stay close to him. Trebonius remarks—so that the audience can hear (but apparently no one on stage can)—"and so near will I be,/That your best friends shall wish I had been further."

So I bought this table—it was a cheap piece of junk from a discount catalogue—and the ad had said "some assembly required." So, of course, I expected to have to screw on the legs—you know, something basic like that—but when I opened the box, I was faced with—and I kid you not—2,000 nuts and bolts and not one piece of wood touching another. It'll be the last time I buy anything from that catalogue.

personification / anthropomorphism: the giving of human attributes to non-human things; the treatment of non-living things as if they were living.

Examples:

Most of Aesop's fables, including "The Tortoise and the Hare," "The Fox and the Grapes," and "The Ant and the Grasshopper" *anthropomorphize* animals in order to illustrate their morals.

To refer to the ocean as "she," or to talk about "Mother Nature" as "kind and nurturing," are both examples of *personification*.

procatalepsis: the rhetorical device in which a writer or speaker raises an objection to his or her own argument and then answers it.

Examples:

You may be tempted to say that recovery has been expensive and slow, but I would remind you that stinginess and carelessness are what brought the devastation upon us in the first place.

Students, of course, will balk at this proposal, especially the elimination of weekends and vacations, but those who can see beyond today's inconvenience anticipate the pride these students will experience with the inevitable increase in their test scores.

protagonist: in fiction, the principle character. It is the need of the protagonist, faced with the opposition of the antagonist, that establishes the conflict and propels the plot.

Examples:

Tom Sawyer, Huckleberry Finn, and David Copperfield are the *protagonists* of the novels named for them.

quantum leap: an informal term for a type of *non sequitur*; the cause of a *quantum leap* is often the elimination of one or more minor premises between the first and the conclusion. Is also related to the *slippery slope*.

Examples:

To compromise on the removal of this cartoon from our publication would be to open the door to an administrative police state in which students' rights are but a dim memory.

Allowing students to wear jeans to school on Friday is only the first step in the complete descent of society into slovenliness.

realism: a school of literature that emerged in the late nineteenth century and claimed to present a view of life "as it was"; the focus of *realism* was on the commonplace and the everyday, with no attempt to idealize or glamorize life and people's struggles.

Examples:

Mark Twain (*Tom Sawyer, Huck Finn*) and Stephen Crane (*The Red Badge of Courage,* "The Veteran") were both popular American *realist* authors, focusing on the daily lives and very human emotions of their characters.

reversal: any event, usually unexpected, that challenges the reader's expectation of the protagonist's success and makes failure again seem possible.

Examples:

In *The Wizard of Oz,* once the characters finally arrive at the Emerald City and gain admittance to the Wizard's chamber, for him to send them away to battle the Wicked Witch of the West is a huge *reversal.*

In "Cinderella," a major *reversal* occurs when, just as the Prince is falling in love with Cinderella, the clock chimes midnight and the Fairy Godmother's magic wears off.

rhetorical question: the rhetorical device in which a writer or speaker asks a question without expecting the reader/audience to answer; usually, the writer assumes that there is only one appropriate answer that the reader/audience can provide.

Examples:

from the student essay on Jefferson's reply to the Danbury Baptists Association in the state of Connecticut: Does anyone really believe that compulsory prayer would be an effective punishment for "the man who works ill to his neighbors"?

from Washington's Farewell Address: Will it not be their wisdom to rely for the preservation of these advantages on the Union by which they were procured?—Will they not henceforth be deaf to those advisers, if such there are, who would sever them from their Brethren, and connect them with Aliens?

rising action: after the introduction of the conflict, every event that escalates the tension and intensifies the conflict is a part of the *rising action*; in order for the action to rise to a climax, each new action must be larger in significance or scope than the action that precedes it. Otherwise, the plot would simply be a series of events.

Examples:

In *The Wizard of Oz,* each of Dorothy's encounters with the Wicked Witch of the West is more intense than the previous one: first, there is a simple verbal exchange; then, the Witch bewitches the apple trees to deny Dorothy food. Next, the Witch almost foils the journey to the Emerald City by putting Dorothy and the Lion to sleep. Finally, she threatens to kill Dorothy for the ruby slippers and actually sets the Scarecrow on fire.

The conflict between the Capulets and Montagues in *Romeo and Juliet* rises to a tragic conflict. The play opens with a brawl among the servants of the two families. Then, there is a near fight when Romeo is discovered at the Capulets' party. Finally, Romeo, Mercutio, and Tybalt engage in a sword battle in which Mercutio and Tybalt are both killed, necessitating Romeo's flight from the city.

rondeau: a poem form typically consisting of fifteen lines—thirteen lines of eight syllables with a half-length refrain, which is identical to the beginning of the opening line of the poem and is repeated twice. The rhyme scheme of a **rondeau** is typically A A B B A; A A B C (refrain); and A A B B A C (refrain). The **rondeau redoublé** is a related form consisting of six four-line stanzas.

The poem has the overall rhyme scheme: A B A B; B A B A; A B A B; B A B A; A B A B; A B A B C. The last line of stanzas two through five repeats one of the four lines from stanza one, and the final line of the poem repeats the beginning of the first line.

second person: the grammatical device that allows speakers or writers to address their audience directly (you, your)

While there are examples of stories narrated from the *second person point of view*, because the *second person* is generally regarded to be the reader or listener, this *narrative mode* is not as common as the *first-* or *second-person* points of view.

slippery slope: a logical fallacy in which a catastrophe is the inevitable result of a current insignificant or innocent event; related to the *non sequitur* and *quantum leap*.

Examples:

First they came for the communists,
and I didn't speak out because I wasn't a communist.

Then they came for the trade unionists,
and I didn't speak out because I wasn't a trade unionist.

Then they came for the Jews,
and I didn't speak out because I wasn't a Jew.

Then they came for me
and there was no one left to speak out for me.

—pastor Martin Niemöller (1892–1984)

If today you can take a thing like evolution and make it a crime to teach it in the public school, tomorrow you can make it a crime to teach it in the private schools, and the next year you can make it a crime to teach it to the hustings or in the church. At the next session you may ban books and the newspapers. Soon you may set Catholic against Protestant and Protestant against Protestant, and try to foist your own religion upon the minds of men. If you can do one you can do the other. Ignorance and fanaticism is ever busy and needs feeding. Always it is feeding and gloating for more. Today it is the public school teachers, tomorrow the private. The next day the preachers and the lectures, the magazines, the books, the newspapers. After while, your honor, it is the setting of man against man and creed against creed until with flying banners and beating drums we are marching backward to the glorious ages of the sixteenth century when bigots lighted fagots to burn the men who dared to bring any intelligence and enlightenment and culture to the human mind. *Clarence Darrow, Tennessee v John Scopes: "The Monkey Trial," Day 2: July 13, 1925.*

Opponents of gun-control legislation often argue that a ban on fully automatic weapons would eventually lead to a ban on all weapons. Once the citizenry grew accustomed to having this Constitutional right abridged, "for the common good," legislatures would feel free to curtail other rights until we will find ourselves languishing in a totalitarian state.

syntax: word order and phrase construction in writing; a writer's *syntax* is a matter of convention and art as many rhetorical and stylistic devices involve varying from the expected *syntax* of a sentence.

Examples:

The *syntax* of a standard English sentence describes a subject followed by the verbs, then followed by any objects, predicate modifiers, and/or prepositional phrases

third person: the grammatical device that allows the speaker or writer (first person) to talk to the audience (second person) about people who are neither the speaker nor the audience and are presumably not present (i.e., he, she, it, they, his, her, hers, its, him, her, it).

Also the *narrative point of view* in which the narrator is detached from the story.

Examples:

Dorothy Parker's "The Standard of Living" and the folk tale "Little Red Riding Hood" are narrated from the *third-person* point of view; an unnamed and detached narrator is telling the story of Midge and Annabel.

tone: the author's attitude toward his or her subject and audience

Examples:

Dorothy Parker ("The Standard of Living") was famous for her sarcasm, a *tone* she adopted in her stories to gently mock both her characters and, to some extent, her readers.

In *A Christmas Carol*, Dickens describes the Cratchitts' Christmas celebration in a sympathetic, almost affectionate *tone*; but when he is describing Ebenezer Scrooge, his *tone* is clearly scornful.

understatement: the opposite of hyperbole; an ironic statement that emphasizes something's size, importance, or severity by appearing to downplay it.

Examples:

In *The Wizard of Oz*, the Wicked Witch of the West did not like water.

The thousand-dollar spa treatments for Rosemary's puppies are, perhaps, a bit excessive.

[literary or narrative] vehicle: a *vehicle* is a tool, a means by which an end is achieved. A *literary* or *narrative vehicle* is the tool used by the storyteller to fulfill his or her intentions.

Example:

The arrival of a letter or mysterious telephone call is often the *vehicle* by which the writer allows the protagonist to receive important information while building the reader's suspense.

villanelle: a poem form consisting of nineteen lines: five three-line stanzas (tercets) followed by a single four-line stanza (quatrain). The first and third lines of the opening tercet become refrains that alternately end each of the subsequent tercets. Both refrains end the quatrain. Most contemporary *villanelles* are written in iambic pentameter, but there is no prescribed meter for the form.

Example:

Edward Arlington Robinson, "The House on the Hill (1894)

They are all gone away,
The House is shut and still,
There is nothing more to say.

Through broken walls and gray
The winds blow bleak and shrill.
They are all gone away.

Nor is there one to-day
To speak them good or ill:
There is nothing more to say.

Why is it then we stray
Around the sunken sill?
<u>They are all gone away,</u>

And our poor fancy-play
For them is wasted skill:
There is nothing more to say.

There is ruin and decay
In the House on the Hill:
<u>They are all gone away,</u>
There is nothing more to say.

zeugma: an unexpected joining of words, phrases, or parts of a sentence for emphasis or effect.

Examples:

On his long and difficult trip home, Josiah ran out of patience and gas.

The surgeon was well-known for his skill and patients.

House guests and raw fish begin to smell after three days.